Media, Knowledge and Power

This reader is one part of an Open University integrated teaching system and the selection is therefore related to other material available to students. It is designed to evoke the critical understanding of students. Opinions expressed in it are not necessarily those of the course team or of the university.

Media, Knowledge and Power

A reader edited by OLIVER BOYD-BARRETT and PETER BRAHAM
at the Open University

ROUTLEDGE
London and New York
in association with
the Open University

First published 1987 by
Croom Helm Ltd

Reprinted 1990 by
Routledge
11 New Fetter Lane, London EC4P 4EE
29 West 35th Street, New York, NY 10001

British Library Cataloguing in Publication Data

Media, knowledge and power : a reader.
  1. Mass media in education
  I. Boyd-Barrett, Oliver II. Braham, Peter
  III. Open University
  371.3'3   LB1043

  ISBN 0-415-05874-0

Library of Congress Cataloging-in-Publication Data

Media, knowledge and power.

  Includes index.

  1. Mass media—Study and teaching. 2. Mass media—
Social aspects. 3. Mass media in education.
I. Boyd-Barrett, Oliver. II. Braham, Peter.
P91.3.M387 1987   001-51'07'15   86-19828
ISBN 0-415-05874-0

Typeset in Times Roman by Leaper & Gard Ltd, Bristol, England
Printed by Chong Moh Offset Printing Pte. Ltd.

CONTENTS

Foreword
Notes on Contributors
Editors' Introduction

Foreword

Two volumes of readings have been prepared for the Open University course, *Communication and Education* (EH207). The companion volume is *Learning to Communicate*.

The readers form components of the course which also includes correspondence texts, radio and television programmes and personal tuition. Further details about the course may be obtained from Associate Student Central Office, Open University, PO Box 76, Milton Keynes MK7 6AN.

The editors wish to acknowledge the help of the course team and its consultants in the compilation of these readers. We are particularly grateful for the secretarial support of Debbie Dickson and Yvonne Holmes. Opinions expressed in the readers are not necessarily those of the university.

Notes on Contributors

John Arnott teaches at Inverkeithing High School, Fife.

Anthony Bates is Reader in Media Research at the Institute of Educational Technology, Open University.

Arthur Asa Berger is Professor at the Department of Broadcast Communication, San Francisco State University.

Jerome Bruner is Professor of Psychology at the New School for Social Research, New York.

Richard Collins is Lecturer in Communications at the Polytechnic of Central London.

James Curran heads the Department of Communication at Goldsmiths College, London.

Harold Fishbein is Professor of Psychology at the University of Cincinnati.

Margeret Gallagher was formerly Research Officer at the Institute of Education, Open University.

Michael Gurevitch is Professor at the Department of Journalism, University of Maryland.

Andy Hargreaves lectures in English at the Department of Educational Studies, Oxford University.

Martin Harrison is Professor of Politics at the University of Keele.

John Hewitson teaches biology at Oundle School, Oundle, Peterborough.

Dai Hounsell is Director, Centre for Learning, Teaching and Assessment, University of Edinburgh.

Aletha Huston is Professor of Human Development and Psychology at the University of Kansas.

Len Masterman is Lecturer in Education, Nottingham University.

Sean McBride was President of the International Commission for the Study of Communication Problems, UNESCO.

Denis McQuail is Professor of Mass Communication, University of Amsterdam.

Herbert Menzel is Professor of Sociology at New York University.

David Olsen is Professor of Applied Psychology, Ontario Institute for Studies in Education, Toronto.

Mabel Rice is a psychologist at the Center for Research on the

Influence of Television on Children, University of Kansas.

Brent Robinson teaches at Westgate School, Winchester.

Gavriel Salomon is an Associate Professor of Educational Psychology and Communication at the Hebrew University of Jerusalem.

Herbert I. Schiller is Professor of Sociology at the University of California at San Diego.

Michael Twyman is Professor of Typography, University of Reading.

Raymond Williams is a Fellow of Jesus College, Cambridge.

Tom Wilson is Professor of Information Studies, University of Sheffield.

Janet Woollacott was formerly Lecturer in Sociology at the Open University.

John Wright is Professor of Human Development and Psychology at the University of Kansas.

EDITORS

Oliver Boyd Barrett is Lecturer in the School of Education at the Open University.

Peter Braham is Lecturer in Sociology, Faculty of Social Sciences at the Open University.

Editors' Introduction

Media, Knowledge and Power is one of two readers published in association with the Open University course *Communication and Education* (course code: EH207). *Communication and Education* sets out to explore the nature, diversity and means of human communication with particular reference to education. Within this broad field the course specifically addresses three dimensions of communication: the nature and use of language, the 'mediation' of communication by technologies such as print, television and computers, and the social organization of communication with special reference to patterns of communication among professional groups. The concept 'education' is interpreted broadly to refer to aspects of learning both inside and outside formal educational institutions. The companion reader to this present volume relates primarily to those parts of the course which have to do with the nature and acquisition of language skills. This volume is about communications media and professional communication with relevance to education.

The sections of *Communication and Education* which relate most closely to this volume have four broad objectives: to survey the role of the communications media in society with special reference to educational interests; to examine the issues raised by the use of communications media for teaching and learning; to consider the role of the state in developing policy for educational media; to look at patterns of communication among professional groups, and at the communication issues which are raised by planned innovation in organizations.

The first of these four objectives merits further elaboration in this introduction, providing as it does the *raison d'être* for the volume as a whole, and showing why the editors and their colleagues on the EH207 course team should want to investigate the various 'interfaces' between the worlds of communications media and education. Interfacing is evident in four major ways. The production and content of general audience media such as newspapers, radio and television is relevant, first of all, because it says something about the nature of the culture into which children are born, acquire language and learn to adapt to their environment. There is widespread interest in and concern about the possible effects which such communications media may have upon children's values, behaviour and cognition.

Whether such effects can be substantiated is itself an important concern of the course and of this volume. It is not only the general effects that are relevant, but also effects which may influence how children respond to education and educational media. Of course the media also pervade formal education, either as educational media specifically designed to assist teaching, or in the form of general audience programming that has been adopted for use by teachers in the context of given courses. Educational institutions increasingly are being asked to adapt to new communications technologies: for example, the dissemination of microprocessors throughout education has been spectacular in recent years. Then again, the communications media are important means of self-expression and social representation, and many schools consider it is important to provide some training in, and appreciation of what is involved in media production, and to cultivate children's ability to think critically about what the media offer them. Finally, the communications media figure prominently in formal and informal networks and channels which teachers employ to communicate with one another.

In short, the worlds of communication and education come together because, firstly, communications media may influence what children are like, and this is of interest to their teachers; secondly, because the media are important educational tools; thirdly, because it is considered important to teach about the media; and, finally, because teachers use media to communicate with each other.

Each of these four interfaces between communication and education is represented in this volume. And because they have rather different origins in terms of the research traditions on which they draw, the volume also brings together areas of research which do not usually appear within the same binding. The first of these might be described as the 'media studies' tradition, and is represented in many contributions to sections 1 and 2. This tradition is primarily sociological and characteristically is fired by an ambition to generate insight into the symbiotic relationship between communications media and the wider social structure. A second tradition, which informs several contributions to sections 3 and 4, is the application to communications media of educational psychology with specific reference to the individual learner and the implications of communications media for the learning process. Two other traditions appear in section 5: information studies, which is often regarded as a discipline in its own right; and the tradition of innovation research, which has for long enjoyed a prominent place in education studies. These different research traditions meet on common ground in so far as they each have something to offer to the understanding of how education and the communications media interrelate. This does not mean that the different traditions have yet been integrated, although particular articles may indicate the desirability of greater integration. The ways in which educational psychologists have formulated their interest in media 'forms', for instance, opens up quite a new world of potential effects which most sociologists have yet to incorporate within their own thinking about media.

The principal aim of this book, however, is to improve understanding of the role of the communications media in the production and social distribution of knowledge and in the processes whereby individuals learn from the media. In this aim the editors have of course been guided by the articles suggested by unit authors of the EH207 course team, but at the same time they have endeavoured to produce a volume which stands on its own, coherent in purpose and structure.

SECTION 1
COMMUNICATIONS ACROSS THE WORLD

INTRODUCTION

The term 'mass media' is common enough in everyday conversation, but scholars researching the media are more cautious. They hesitate over 'mass', with its connotations of a dreary, undifferentiated audience, and its implied presumptions about the distinctiveness and possibly the superiority of interpersonal, face-to-face communication. Scholars may argue that cultural products delivered to our homes and living rooms in press and television are manufactured to a considerable extent on the basis of very traditional face-to-face or interpersonal communications. And for all the apparent uniformity of the content, it is certain that the meanings which different individuals derive from these communications are extremely diverse. These same products form a part of daily discourse, fuelling conversation, lubricating the interleaving motions of human relationship in pairs and groups, creating and sustaining areas of shared experience, symbolism, knowledge and understanding. It is not just that the same content can deliver many different messages to many different people, but the content itself is becoming more diverse. Familiar communications media such as press, radio and television are becoming more regionalized and localized. It is true that patterns of ownership continue to reveal a high degree of concentration, and the control of a relatively small number of giant organizations is increasingly diversified across many different spheres of economic activity. But both older and newer communications technologies appear increasingly to allow for greater market specialization and interactivity between 'publishers' and consumers and among consumers themselves. Indeed, the term 'user' so common in relation to computers could appropriately be substituted across all media for the older and considerably more passive term 'consumer'. Such a change would carry implications for ways of thinking about how people relate to media, acquire information and more generally for how they learn: that is, not as empty vessels to be filled, but as lively and often enquiring beings who bring to the media their own experience and views of life, their developed personalities, expectations, values and prejudices, needs and demands.

In their appreciation of the continuities between traditional interpersonal and so-called 'mass' communication, the two articles which introduce this reader share a great deal of common ground, all the more significant given the different traditions of media study which they represent. The McBride Commission report represents the opening deliberations of an international group of eminent media professionals and scholars in an international policy-oriented and politically sensitive publication. It is empirically-grounded, politically cautious, basically optimistic in its view of the potential of communications technologies for the development of a better world, with particular reference to the Third World. The *quantity* of communications facilities and opportunities and the uneven dispersal of these around the globe is a major concern for McBride. By contrast, the doyen of English academic media research, Raymond Williams, is more abstract, speculative and sceptical. An issue of particular concern for him is the role of commerce in influencing how the media select from and interpret the world.

Both articles recognize, however, the importance of locating the study of communications media within the full range of different modes of human communication. The McBride Commission report does so in an empirical worldwide survey of the range and pervasiveness of different communication modes and stresses their interdependence. Williams's perspective is more historical, ident-ifying continuities as well as discontinuities between today's media and previous forms of social communication. He points to the study of sign systems (semiotics) as a possibly integrative influence in the development of understanding about communication, offer-ing as it does tools of analysis which are applicable to all forms of human expression and interpretation. But he also believes there is a need for a new kind of enquiry which transcends different tradi-tions and disciplines, and which embraces without prejudice the. different facets of human communication.

Both McBride and Williams, therefore, are concerned with change: intended and unintended changes that result from the pace of development of communications technologies, and broader changes in political, economic and cultural structures to which communications media can offer a positive contribution. Both sources are clearly doubtful whether existing patterns of study in this field are adequate for the task, and are looking for radically new ways of studying communication.

1.1 Many Voices, One World

McBRIDE COMMISSION*

The spectrum of communication in contemporary society almost defies description because of the immense variety and range of its components. It includes: human capacities; simple communication tools and media serving individuals, groups and masses; complex infrastructures and systems; advanced technologies, materials and machines which collect, produce, carry, receive, store and retrieve messages; innumerable individual and institutional partners and participants in the communication world.[1]

The symbols which make up messages and the means that carry them are simply two facets of one reality. Symbols, gestures, numbers, words, pictures, all are in themselves a means of communication, and the medium, be it a hand-printed page, radio or television, not only carries the message but is simultaneously another symbol of communication. Hence communication is an all-encompassing 'global' phenomenon, which in essence cannot be reduced to or described in terms of isolated, independent parts, each element being an integral part of the whole. But all these elements are present — obviously in different proportions and with different significance and impact — in every part of the world.

1. SIGNS AND WORDS

Since time immemorial, the human race has used primitive, simple forms of communication, which have been enhanced, extended, refined, and are still in use today in all societies despite the continuous invention of new technologies and the increasing sophistication and complexity of interaction between people. To be able to

---

*Source: The International Commission for the Study of Communication Problems, *Many Voices, One World: towards a new, more just and more efficient world information and communication order*, chapter 1 (Unesco, Paris, Kogan Page, London, 1980), pp.49-67.

externalize their feelings and needs, individuals first used their bodies to communicate. 'Body language' and other non verbal languages[2] while being used for millenia in traditional societies for a variety of purposes, have lost none of their validity and importance today, despite their obvious limitations. Hence, messages and ideas are also transmitted in many countries by means of itinerant dance and mime groups, puppet shows and other folk media which serve not only to entertain but to influence attitudes and behaviour.

Images often preceded and precede words. But language marks an immense step forward in human communication, especially in the ability to memorize and pass on knowledge and in the expression of relatively complex conceptions. It is not, indeed, the only tool in interpersonal communication, but it is indispensable; speech still has powers which cannot be replaced either by technology or by the mass media. It is the lifeblood of innumerable networks of contact.

In communities where isolation or smallness of scale, or indeed persistent illiteracy, have encouraged the survival of tradition, speech, performance and example remain the most common, if not the only, means of transmitting information. While in industrialized countries, traditional channels for direct communication have virtually disappeared as sources of information, except in the most isolated areas, the same cannot be said for other interpersonal communication networks which include provision or exchange of information in the family or extended family, in the neighbourhood, in communities and ethnic groups, in various clubs and professional associations, and in conferences and meetings which are convened by governments, by organizations of all kinds, or by commercial enterprises.[3] All these and many others provide occasions to exchange information, elucidate issues, ventilate grievances, resolve conflicts or assist in opinion-forming and decision-making on matters of common interest to individuals, groups or society as a whole. These forms of interpersonal communication are sometimes overlooked by professional observers and investigators, whose focus is narrowed predominantly to the mass media, as the purveyors of news, facts, ideas, and indeed of all vital information.

While interpersonal communication is not a primary or even major concern of this review, some of the issues it raises should not be overlooked for a number of important reasons. First, traditional

forms of communication, and particularly interpersonal communi-
cation, maintain a vital importance in all parts of the world, both
developing and developed, and are even expanding. Second, the
majority of people in the world, particularly the rural inhabitants of
developing countries, comprising as much as 60 to 70 per cent of
the world's population, continues to impart, receive and, what is
more, accept messages through these channels of communication.
Third, it is impossible to comprehend completely the advantages
and limitations of modern media if they are treated as factors separ-
ate from the interpersonal communication, for clearly communica-
tion networks grow cumulatively, with each new form adding to but
not eclipsing the older systems. On the contrary, interpersonal
communication takes on a whole new significance in the face of the
depersonalizing effects of modern technology and it remains an
essential feature in the furtherance of democracy within societies.

2. LANGUAGES

The number of languages used in verbal communication is high,
with some 3,500 identified throughout the world. However, while
speech is common to all societies and writing is not, the number of
written languages is much lower, with one estimate indicating not
more than 500.[4]

Over the centuries, the course of history has led to steady
expansion in the use of some languages. Some of these languages
have a predominant place in the circulation of information, programmes and materials.[5] It is estimated that there are at least 16
languages which are spoken by more than 50 million people: the
family of Chinese languages, English, Russian, Spanish, Hindi,
Portuguese, Bengali, German, Japanese, Arabic, Urdu, French,
Malay-Bahasa, Italian, Teluga, Tamil.

About 1,250 languages are spoken on the African continent:
some of these, such as Swahili, Wolof and Hausa, cover large areas
and indeed different nations. In Europe, there are 28 official
national languages. The people of south Asia use 23 principal
languages. Although the Arab region is, in a certain sense, mono-
lingual, vernacular languages there vary to some extent from classical Arabic, and Berber tongues which are distinct from Arabic
are spoken in some countries of north Africa. Latin America uses
two principal languages, Spanish and Portuguese, but there are

hundreds of Indian languages and dialects; some of them, like Quechua in Peru and Guarani in Paraguay, being spoken by large local populations. In addition, English, French and Dutch continue to predominate in ex-colonies of the region and in the Caribbean. Many countries have a surprising number of languages: in the USSR there are 89; India recognizes 15 for official and educational use alone, with a total number of languages and dialects exceeding 1,650; for Ghana the total is 56 and Mexican Indians have more than 200. Many of these tongues have now been transcribed, but the majority have not.

The proliferation of a great number of languages and dialects had numerous historical, ethnological, religious and social reasons. But in the course of time, the creation of new nation states, coupled with hegemonistic pressures and imperialist domination over large parts of the world led frequently to linguistic modifications in many countries and the gradual disappearance of some dialects and local patois. Conversely, colonialism ensured that a few European languages were spread right across the globe. Assimilating tendencies over small and weak cultures are still continuing.

The multiplicity of languages, each the incarnation of long traditions, is an expression of the world's cultural richness and diversity. The disappearance of a language is always a loss, and its preservation is the consequence of the struggle for a basic human right. Moreover, in the modern mass media as well as in traditional communication, the use of a variety of languages is an advantage, bringing a whole population on to equal terms of comprehension. This does not mean that there are no problems arising from multiplicity. The choice of a national 'link language', or the relationship between one language and another, has been a source of difficulty and conflict (in India, in Canada, in Belgium, to take only three examples). The multiplicity of languages presents obvious barriers to communication, gives rise to cultural problems, and can hamper scientific and technical development. The worldwide use of a small number of languages leads to a certain discrimination against other languages and the creation of a linguistic hierarchy; thus, most of the world's population lacks the linguistic means to take full advantage of much of modern research and technology.[6]

This concentration of key languages might encourage the view that the problem of 'language barriers' is overrated, but the fact is that, beyond the native speakers of such languages and the relatively small number of bi or multilingual people, who belong mainly to narrow local elites, millions of people all over the world do indeed face an incomprehensible barrier. They are discriminated against, since currently the spread of information tends to take place in the terms, and the idiom, of the linguistically powerful.

Looking to the future, there are several possible avenues of development. Many national languages could become more widely used, particularly in print and electronic media, which at present often confine themselves to the language of the local elite. Or alternatively the rapid spread of technology could concentrate and decrease the number of languages, at least for some specific purposes. Plurilingualism is an attractive solution, probably the only realistic one in most countries, yet the diffusion of one simple, universal tongue, comprehensible and accessible to all, might also strengthen national cohesion and quickly demolish the barriers to communication between different peoples. Again, improved teaching of foreign languages and extensions of learning opportunities, particularly through use of radio and recordings, offers broad potential. All these possibilities are meaningful only if one basic principle is respected: that all languages are regarded as equal in dignity and as instruments of communication. In formulating its linguistic policy, each country has an option between various alternatives, and its decision cannot be postponed or circumvented for long without harm.

The use of many languages in modern communication has also been hampered until now because not all languages have been adapted to modern means of printing, processing and transmitting messages and information. Priority has been given to languages using latin or cyrillic script. However, recent advances in standardization, codification and printing technologies now make it possible to adapt such languages as Japanese, Chinese and Arabic to all modern means of communication. A Shanghai language research institute, using the 26-letter Roman alphabet, has developed a 4-letter code for each of some 2,000 ideograms, called 'on-site encoding' for use in computer processing.[7] For Arabic, a system called ASV CODAR has been developed which standardizes codes and reduces the number of letter forms to permit easy use of the Arabic script for typewriting, printing, data processing and telecommunications. The same may and indeed should be done for many other languages.

We are thus concerned about language problems for these partic-ular reasons: (a) the development of truly national communication systems covering the entire population cannot be achieved unless more languages are used for information and cultural activities; (b) language policy should be an intrinsic part of communication policies, since the choice and promotion of languages opens up or eliminates possibilities for wider and equal communication; (c) additional efforts are needed to achieve transcription of various national and local languages, as well as adaptation of various language groups to communication machines (typewriters, lino-types, teleprinters, computers, etc.); (d) the use of a few so-called world languages is essential in international communications, yet this poses sensitive questions concerning the individuality and even the political and cultural development of some countries.

3. READING AND WRITING

If language, both spoken and written, is the primary code of human communication, illiteracy is the major obstacle to the development of communication. The lack of reading and writing skills drastically limits the expansion of a person's overall capaci-ties and abilities.[8]

There are several reasons for illiteracy: millions speak non-transcribed languages; many live in environments and particular conditions where written communication is not yet necessary or available; many more have not had, in their childhood or adult-hood, the chance to learn to read and write; some acquired that skill but reverted, for various reasons, to illiteracy during their life-time; restricted resources hamper the establishment of widespread literacy programmes; there is often a lack of political will, at decision making levels, to step up efforts to eradicate illiteracy.

Illiteracy exists to a greater or lesser extent in almost all coun-tries, although it is difficult to define precisely or to determine its worldwide dimensions. The concept of a literate person varies from country to country, ranging from the ability to decipher a simple test to the completion of full primary schooling, or to the ability of using literacy skills for 'functional' purposes in working, civic and social life. However, indicative estimates are available to provide generally acceptable national, regional and global pictures of illiteracy around the world.

The latest available figures and estimates show a continuing reduction in the illiteracy rates among the world's population aged 15 years and over, which dropped from 40 per cent in 1950 to 36 per cent around 1960, and which should fall from 32.4 per cent in 1970 to 28.9 per cent in 1980 and to 25.7 per cent in 1990. This is essentially the result of a gradual expansion of schooling, and partly of adult literacy programmes in a number of countries, as well as instruction by mass media, carried out by the press and broadcasting systems, with or without international assistance, which significantly helped campaigns against illiteracy in various parts of Asia and Africa. While percentage-wise illiteracy is decreasing in absolute terms, projections indicate that the number of illiterates will continue to increase, rising from 742 million in 1970 to 814 million in 1980 and 884 million in 1990. This discouraging development is, nevertheless, partly counterbalanced by the fact that the absolute number of literates will increase by 456 million between 1970 and 1980 and by 556 million in the next decade.

The following graph regarding the proportion of literates and illiterates aged 15 and over, from 1970 to 1990, shows that while the number of literate persons will grow by 1,000 million, the number of illiterates will increase by almost 150 million as well:[9]

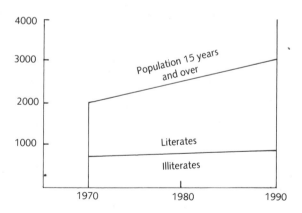

Thus, despite reductions in the rate of illiteracy, the absolute number of illiterates continues to grow. It now stands at the shocking figure of 800 million, or almost one third of the world's adult population. This is enough to demonstrate the enormous size of the problem.

The fact is that the advance of literacy does not keep pace, on a world scale, with the high rate of population growth. Equally disquieting is that, at present, nearly one young person in four enters employment without having received minimum education.

In many countries there is a marked disparity between the proportions of male and of female literates. Tradition often dictates that women should confine their interests to the domestic sphere, should not compete with men for work except at an unskilled manual level, and therefore should have no need to read and write. Girls sometimes receive a briefer and inferior education, compared to boys, and are expected to prepare themselves only for marriage. Among people who acquire a basic literacy in youth and then lose it because they find no opportunity to make use of it, the majority are probably women. When governments initiate adult literacy campaigns women are sometimes deterred from participation by their husbands, or discouraged by prevailing customs and social norms. On a world scale, it is estimated that 60% of all illiterates are women, and their numbers are increasing faster than those of male illiterates. The elimination of this disparity is a complex task, requiring a deep-rooted change in social and psychological attitudes, and involves all the issues of full human liberation.

It has been suggested that illiteracy is not so great a social and cultural evil, since new media can bring even illiterate people into the orbit of communication by the use of spoken word and image. But it is evident — without denying the power of audio-visual means of communication — that language, in both its spoken and written forms, is an irreplaceable way of communication. At the same time, literacy is not just a reading habit. We share the view that literacy means much more 'reading the world, rather than reading the word'.[10] Thus, illiteracy means that eight hundred million human beings remain second-class citizens, excluded from truly full participation in their societies and in the world.

Denial of vital communication tools to many hundreds of millions of men and women makes a mockery of the right to inform or be informed. It is therefore necessary to assemble all possible means, educational, cultural and social, along with various communication technologies and mass media, whose powerful potential may lead to the eradication of this blot on the landscape of all countries in the world. And, at the same time, since the number of illiterate people will unfortunately grow for decades, adequate communication channels, particularly audio-visual vehicles, have to be developed to bring those who cannot be reached by the printed word into the mainstream of social and economic life.

4. POST AND TELEPHONE

Interpersonal communication remains an indispensable segment of the communication network in both developed and developing countries. As already mentioned, there are innumerable ways and channels of interpersonal communication in all societies, using symbols, languages and other modes of human expression. In the contemporary world, interpersonal communication is supported or made easier by modern media and various services offered by tele-communications.

The largest organized system for delivery of point-to-point messages is the postal system. Postal services had their beginnings thousands of years ago. Today they represent a vital network in each society. The table below indicating the volume of postal operations and its growth from 1968 to 1976 shows a general trend towards expansion.

While postal services are well-established in developed countries, they continue to be inadequate in most developing countries, partly because of the remoteness of millions of villages and the poor quality of road and rail networks. There are still many centres of population which have no post office.[11] Progress in this field could be a factor for social cohesion, and contribute to the infrastructure of commerce and industry. Post offices can also

MAIL TRAFFIC (millions)

	1968	1976
Africa	3,029	4,293
North America	85,522	96,630
South America	2,236	3,350
Asia	23,488	26,117
Europe	60,073	70,420
USSR	6,954	7,923
Oceania	3,169	2,980
WORLD	184,471	211,713

Source: Based on figures in the *Statistical Yearbook* 1977, United Nations. (The figures for South America include only nine countries; the figures for the USSR are official figures communicated directly to the statistical office of the United Nations.)

serve a useful purpose as government information centres, and as focal points for activity in the fields of development and public health.

A surprising trend in recent decades has been the deterioration of postal services in certain developed countries. One reason is that the excellent services of the past depended on lavish use of manpower. Another reason is that communication authorities now prefer to invest in improvement of the telephone system, which is profitable, rather than on maintenance of the postal system, which is not; hence, the deterioration of postal services between persons, nations and continents. ...

The second largest organized interpersonal communication network is the world-wide telephone system. It has been rightly said that the telephone is a sophisticated extension and amplifier of traditional oral communication. No other media can match the telephone for direct, spontaneous dialogue.[12]

There are at present some 400 million telephones in the world, an increase of about 1,000 per cent since 1945. Virtually all nations are linked together, many by direct dialling systems, in the international web, the largest integrated machine ever built. Eighty per cent of the world's telephones are in only ten countries of North America and Europe, for a total population of about 750 million; approximately half of all telephones are in the United States alone, where several cities have more phones than people. The socialist world has 7% of the world's telephones for a population of 1,300 million, and the developing world has 7% for a population of 2,000 million.[13]

The growth of telephone communications has been equally rapid. According to ITU figures about 440 billion telephone calls are made per year (some 50% in the United States). Particularly revealing is the number of international calls; for example, in 1950 overseas messages to and from the United States totalled 773,000, but in 1977 the number was more than 50 million outgoing calls alone. Since the first transatlantic underwater cable was laid in 1956 with the capacity to carry 50 telephone calls at one time, five more have been brought into use, the last capable of handling 4,000 calls simultaneously. In all, there are 30 international submarine cables, with a total capacity of 17,074 telephone circuits. Meanwhile, in the past decade, the capacity of international satellite communications has jumped from 150 to more than 10,000 circuits; the latest generation of satellite used for transmitting telephone messages can handle 6,000 calls simultaneously.

Such increased traffic has been caused by social and economic needs for direct contacts between persons, firms and public authorities as well as by technological improvements in facilities. Another influence has been the rate reduction which has defied the usual inflationary spiral and actually reduced the cost of telephone use. It is these rapid advances in facilities, continuously decreasing costs and higher quality service which lie behind the upsurge in the use of the telephone and no limit to its utility can be seen.

It appears to us that the slow development in many countries of postal and telecommunication facilities and services is a real obstacle both to persons and societies. It is not sufficiently recognised that these facilities and services are not only the outcome of economic growth, but also a precondition of overall development and even of democratic life. The unevenness in telecommunications expansion becomes an increasing obstacle to communication between developed and developing countries. Similarly, the rates of several services which have not yet fallen commensurately to costs, hamper their use by poorer consumers. Here is an area of communication which needs to be reconsidered in many countries, particularly in view of its social, economic and cultural significance.

5. GROUP AND LOCAL MEDIA

A next step in the organization of social communication is at the level of groups or local communities. To achieve group cohesion, to mobilize local resources, and to solve problems affecting smaller or larger groups, communication is necessary, and various means are utilized. Communication at this level is increasing in both developing and developed countries. Frequently, local communication is assisted by the mass media, which have used the flexibility of modern technology to give small or remote communities new facilities, such as radio stations which are financed by a central organization and managed locally. But communities and individuals have also taken the initiative in creating their own means of communication. These means cover a wide range of media from local and wall newspapers, mimeographed leaflets, photos, posters and dazibaos, local radios and itinerant loudspeakers, to pamphlets, slides, tape recorders, exhibitions, experimentations, local fairs, film and music festivals, puppet shows, itinerant information vans, street theatre and an endless list of similar devices and means. They are often used for social purposes, as a support to local development schemes for hygienic and health campaigns, for religious and political actions, as well as in relation to all initiatives where conscious involvement of local populations is felt necessary. Among promoters of such types of information means and group media are public authorities, development officers, professionals such as agronomists and barefoot doctors, teachers and local political activists, priests and artisans.

More emphasis should be placed on these media and local activities for four main reasons: one, because they may be overshadowed and pushed into the background by the big media; two, because mass media have been expected to accomplish tasks and goals for which they are not fitted; three, because in many countries the neglect of a certain balance between big and small led to unnecessary wastage of scarce resources, by using inappropriate means for diverse audiences; four, because by establishing links between them broader horizontal communication could be developed.

Signs of such a shift of emphasis can be related to the changes taking place in overall development strategies, which are turning away from the top-down models of recent decades and concentrating on greater participation of communities in expressing their very existence and their own particular needs and formulating plans and organizing action to meet them. This change has a broad impact on the use of media to support development action, not the least of which is establishing or expanding the use of local media. Thus communication, in quite different ways, becomes an indispensable component of development efforts and of social life in every locality. In this sense, developmental media activities are not, in any way, a 'threat' to freer information flows, but on the contrary, one of the conditions of democracy, since a more active participation in development choices and activities is part of a democratic way of life. At the same time, this does not mean that the role of large-audience media is going to decline, or that countries and communities have to choose between them. For different purposes, different means — thus a combination of group media and mass media is probably the appropriate answer[14] ...

Very often local groups use modern communication means (radio or television, new printing techniques, even microprocessors and video-tapes) adapting them to the needs of their environments and to the variety of local conditions.

In developed countries, too, there is an increasing awareness of the need for media of this kind, especially by minorities, special interest groups and community or political activities. People in industrialized countries find themselves grappling with environmental problems, pollution, ecological issues, energy crises, unemployment, adaptation to technical change and similar issues. They feel a need to express themselves without delay and with such means as are at their disposal.

Group media, sometimes called little media, have a place in the whole arsenal of communication means, vehicles and techniques. They cannot and should not be confused either with point-to-point or with mass communication. Group media have their proper place — and it is with that in mind that they should be planned, financed and used.

6. THE MASS MEDIA

Since the invention of the printing-press and in more recent times of a multitude of communication forms including telegraph, telephone, telex, camera and film, phonograph, radio and television, the world has been truly transformed. Messages of all kinds are continuously transmitted to a vast number of recipients. The advent of the mass media and their presence in our daily life has been one of the major features of the contemporary world.

Quantitatively, the expansion of communication in recent decades has been steady and uninterrupted, in keeping with demographic, educational, social and political trends. It is certainly difficult to estimate the outcome of this rapid growth in information and entertainment, coupled with the efforts of an ever growing audience to assimilate it. The following figures may indicate the scale of the expansion:

Increase 1950-1975	Percentage
Press (number of copies, daily newspapers)	+ 77
Radio (number of receivers)	+ 417
TV (number of receivers)	+3235
Books (number of titles per year)	+ 111

Unesco Statistical Yearbook, 1977

Most striking of all is the size of the audience that the media now reach around the world. The number of people untouched by the mass media has dramatically decreased in only 25 years. At the present rate of progress, almost everyone everywhere will be in the audience in a matter of decades.

Media audience increase 1960-1975   Percentage

Total world population	+ 33
Daily newspapers (circulation per thousand inhabitants)	+ 5
Radio receivers (number per thousand inhabitants)	+ 95
Television receivers (number per thousand inhabitants)	+185
Book titles (published annually per million inhabitants)	+ 30

Unesco Statistical Yearbook, 1977

The geographical extension is even more significant in that it means the mass media are no longer an exclusive prerogative of urban populations. Their expansion in practically all countries and to wide rural areas brings within their reach not only regional centres and national capitals, but remote corners of the world as well. This wider coverage has produced another major change in the nature of the messages transmitted, particularly in radio and the press. Rural newspapers and, more importantly because of their wider dissemination, radio programmes are produced in local languages. Where geographical isolation once cut off hundreds of millions from most distant events, they are now fast becoming members of the national — even global — community. This, plus the astonishingly rapid spread of television in developed countries, and its steadily growing influence in the Third World, has brought with it diverse social — in the broadest sense of the term — changes which have yet to be fully explored and assessed.

The expansion of various sectors of communication, and more particularly of mass media, increases the importance and stimulates the expansion of agencies which supply and circulate news to newspapers and broadcasters, and to other specialised consumers, the public in general getting news in an indirect way. Press agencies are the major and sometimes only source of information to these media, especially for news of foreign countries. More than 100 countries now have their own national news agency, a considerable increase over the past 10 years.

Among the news agencies there are five — Agence France-

DISTRIBUTION OF NATIONAL NEWS AGENCIES

Africa	Arab World	Asia	Europe	Latin America	North America	Oceania
26	18	19	28	11	3	2

Presse (France), Associated Press (USA), Reuters (UK), Tass (USSR) and United Press International (USA) — which have a particularly wide international role due to the size and technological strength of their systems of collecting news and distributing it in many languages all over the world. Each has offices in more than a hundred countries, and employs thousands of full-time staff and part-time correspondents. They collect hundreds of thousands of words a day and, domestic distribution included, transmit millions of words. Each issues news twenty-four hours a day to thousands of national agencies, subscribing newspapers, radio and television organizations in over a hundred countries. All have regular services, usually daily, in Arabic, English, French, German, Portuguese, Russian and Spanish; some also provide their service in other languages.

Many other countries in all regions of the world have national news agencies of growing importance and a number of them maintain, individually or jointly, their own offices or correspondents abroad to collect or distribute news. Most national agencies have a network of correspondents in the country, while for external news they subscribe to or have exchange arrangements with two or more of the world agencies to receive foreign news and provide domestic news; many also subscribe to the services provided by smaller national agencies, either from neighbouring countries or from those with whom close ties exist. However, in a number of countries news services are not yet agencies in a proper sense, but more offices for collection and distribution of official information and a sort of gatekeeper for external news.

The total daily circulation of newspapers throughout the world is more than 400 million copies,[15] an increase of 20 per cent over the past ten years. Circulation per thousand inhabitants has increased even more on a world average: from 104 to 130. The total number of dailies is around 8,000. At the country level, the highest daily newspaper circulation (per 1,000 inhabitants) is in Sweden and Japan (nearly 600). Regionally, the highest circulation (per 1,000 inhabitants) is in the USSR (396) and the largest number of dailies is in North America (1,935). The lowest circulation is in Africa, with 14 copies per 1,000 inhabitants. Many local newspapers offer their readers little in the way of reporting in depth, foreign news, or the exchange of opinion. The small size of such papers is often cited as the reason, but some papers with only four or six pages manage quite successfully to keep their readers well-informed.

Available figures show that although circulation has grown constantly, the world-wide total of daily newspapers has remained about the same for years. This figure has remained static mainly because of mergers, the death of small local papers, and competition from radio and television, factors operating largely in North America and Western Europe.

The role of newspapers in circulating news is decreasing as broadcasting, particularly by television in developed countries, has stepped up its reporting and enhanced its appeal as a news source. But newspapers play an increasingly valuable role in explaining, interpreting and commenting upon events in society, especially when broad debates on major social objectives or world affairs are taking place that require expanded analysis as opposed to straight-forward reporting. When this is so, certain beliefs about the function of the press have to be revised,[16] and the need to specify the various functions of journalists reinforced.

The periodical press is such a diverse field that it is impossible to generalize about its structure, content or even to estimate accurately its size, and thereby its influence.[17] Magnitude aside, it is obvious the periodical press serves multiple audiences with an almost infinite variety of content. There are signs in many countries that the periodical press influence and appeal become a counter-weight and a corrective to the uniformity of mass messages.

Books are, as they have been in the past, an irreplaceable storehouse of knowledge and of cultural values. This century has seen a great and still accelerating increase in book production, which can be ascribed to the growth in the absolute number of literates, advances in education, the arrival of paperbacks, improvements in production and distribution techniques, and the spread of libraries and travelling libraries even to remote places. Between 1955 and 1975, world book production more than doubled, taking the number of titles published annually, and tripled in the number of copies printed. Eight billion books, and 590,000 new titles, now come from the presses every year. However, a high increase in book prices, largely due to paper cost, has impeded their necessary growth. The scene is also one of marked imbalance and dependence. Books are very unevenly distributed, both inside and among countries. Developing countries, with 70 per cent of the world's population, produce 20 per cent of the books published, and many of these are printed by subsidiaries of firms centred in developed countries. Imported books, sometimes unsuitable in various ways, have to be used in schools, and national literature is poorly represented in bookshops and libraries because of the inadequacy of publishing resources.

In all regions of the world, radio is the most ubiquitous of the mass media. Transmission capacity has more than tripled in the last quarter century. In 1950, some 50 countries in the world had no broadcasting facilities; 23 of these were in Africa. Around 1960, the number of countries with no radio transmitters had shrunk to 12, seven of which were in Africa. Around 1973, a world survey of 187 countries and territories showed only three of them with no transmitting facilities: Bhutan, Liechtenstein and San Marino. There are an estimated one billion receivers in the world, i.e. an average of approximately one for every four persons on earth. The proliferation of receivers around the world is an important indication of the long arm of radio, and developing countries have made particular use of this medium in the last two decades.

In developing countries, radio is the only medium that can really be labelled 'mass' where a large proportion of the population can be reached by radio broadcasts and possesses the means to receive them.

No other medium now has the potential to reach so many people so efficiently for information, educational, cultural and entertainment purposes. Radio can be used easily and economically to reach outlying regions and for communication in the many vernacular — often unwritten — languages existing in developing countries. Almost all countries have a certain capacity to produce radio programmes in line with their political needs, cultural patterns and basic values. Radio is perhaps today the least transnationalized communication medium both in terms of ownership and programme flows. Despite these advantages, radio is to an extent limited as an international medium of communication because of language and technical barriers, except in the field of

Estimated Number of Radio Receivers in Use

Continent	year	Total number (million)	Continent	Year	Total number (million)
Africa	circa 1960	4	Asia	circa 1960	22
	1970	16		1970	58
	1976	30		1976	113
America, North	circa 1960	184	Europe	circa 1960	136
	1970	326		1970	233
	1976	454		1976	284
America, South	circa 1960	14	Oceania	circa 1960	3
	1970	31		1970	8
	1976	58		1976	14

Source: *Unesco Statistics on radio and television 1960-1976,* Office of Statistics, Publication No. 23

music where it promotes a universal language. Music needs no interpreter, and radio has achieved a great deal in preserving, encouraging and popularizing the music of various countries, especially folk-music. For example, the Asia-Pacific Broadcasting Union has built up a major collection of folk-music recordings which are exchanged among broadcasting systems affiliated to the Union. The rise of television as a communication medium is obviously more striking since it started from a zero base only a few decades ago. Its phenomenal development has been not only in the proliferation of receiving sets but also in the quality of its output. Television has multiplied the amount of visual information and entertainment available to the public to a vast degree and has introduced new dramatic sensations which involve the viewer in far flung events. Television, more than any other medium, epitomizes the advances made in communication in the last 25 years.

The age of television dawned in 1936 when France and the United Kingdom began regular transmission of programmes. By 1950, five countries had a regular TV service and by 1955 the number was 17. This figure had increased fourfold by 1960. A decade later, more than 100 countries were transmitting television programmes and, today, television services exist around the world in a total of 138 countries. The number of television receivers, reaching a formidable 400 million throughout the world, is proof of the immeasurable impact this invention has had on the lives of millions and on the spread of information. The most recent available figures show that between 1960 and 1976 the number of countries with more than one million television receivers increased from 13 to 34. At least nine nations have more than 10 million receivers and, in most developed countries, the number of sets approaches the number of households.

However, in developing countries it is the possession of a minority, sometimes a tiny minority, and in certain countries the programme content reveals that it is there primarily to serve the local elite and the expatriate community. Despite its phenomenal growth, television reaches in some 40 countries less than 10 per cent of household units, and in more than half of the countries, less than half of the households have TV receivers. By contrast with radio, the cost of a television set is beyond the income of the average family; community sets, for example in village halls, have only partially mitigated this limitation. Also, its limited range means that it is available chiefly to city-dwellers and reaches only a fraction of the rural population. Again by contrast with radio, the production of television programmes is an expensive business, and poor countries naturally have other priorities. The screens are therefore filled for many hours with imported programmes, made originally for audiences in the developed countries; in most developing nations, these imports account for over half of transmission time. It is in the field of television, more than any other, that anxieties arise about cultural domination and threats to cultural identity.

All sorts of technological innovations have accompanied or had their roots in the explosion of mass media, which opened the doors to larger audiences, expanded sources and resources for information and entertainment and supported important cultural and social changes. While it is obvious that mass media have widespread positive effects, the phenomenon of their growth is of such importance that much more research is necessary, not only in developing but in developed countries, since the expansion of mass media and their orientation cannot be guided only by political decisions or available resources. Fundamental research in all countries should provide the framework for future development of communication.

7. SATELLITES

The growth of planetary satellite communication has been spectacular, as shown in these two tables:

GROWTH OF THE INTELSAT SATELLITE SYSTEM

Year	Countries with Antennas	Leased Half-Circuits
1965	5	150
1970	30	4,259
1975	71	13,369
1979	114	n.a.

Source: Intelsat Annual Report, 1979

GROWTH OF THE INTERSPUTNIK SATELLITE SYSTEM

Year	Countries with Earth-Based Stations	Satellites Type
1973	3	'Molnia' 2
1975	6	and 'Molnia' 3
1979	9	'Stationar'
1980	12	'Stationar'

Source: Document provided from the Intersputnik, 1979

   In the short time that satellites have been showering the planet with messages (since 1957 up to end 1979, around 2,100 satellites were launched) they have become an integral part of so many circuits — news agencies and the press, radio and television broadcasting, telephone and telecommunication links,[18] business, banking, commerce, agriculture, mining, aviation, navigation, meteorology, entertainment — that already their innumerable effects are directly and indirectly influencing the daily lives of the majority of human beings.[19]

   More than 33 communication satellite systems of national, regional or international scope are now functioning or are under construction in the world. A score more are on the drawing board. They can be divided into four categories by use:

(a) International satellite systems. Intelsat and Intersputnik are the only systems of this type existing today. The Intelsat system provides direct satellite communication for more than 100 member countries operating over the three oceans. Although primarily a domestic system, Intersputnik is also used by socialist and some other countries.

(b) Domestic and regional satellite systems. The USSR's Molnia and Ecran, Canada's Anik, Indonesia's Palapa and the USA's Westar, Comstar and RCA are operational examples. The West European, Arab and Nordic country regions are likely to be the next to possess operational systems.

(c) Marine and aeronautical satellite systems. Examples of these mobile communication satellites include the Marisat system for ships at sea, Aerosat (in the planning stage) for commercial aircraft use, and the European Space Agency's Marecs (a marine satellite spin-off).

(d) Military satellite systems. [...]

8. COMPUTERS

Last but not least among contemporary developments, informatics has advanced at a speed not anticipated even by those working in the field. The pulsed transmission of information (coded binary, or digital, information) has progressively extended the scope of the computer systems initially installed in centralized services of large organizations. This was first effected by earth links (co-axial cables and radio links) and later by satellite linkages around the earth. This evolution has taken different forms: multiple terminals making possible various forms of teleprocessing (star-shaped configurations); an increasing interlinkage of computers (data transmission); or various data-processing service networks (data bases,[20] customized data-processing, storage and filing). Thus computer networks and/or systems have entered the sphere of communication. However, three basic functions constantly recur, and are now becoming increasingly 'distributed': storage (memory), arithmetical and logical operational units (processing), peripheral input/output units (access). It is the latter which make communication between the user and the computer system possible. Constant improvements are being made in cost, performance, reliability and the size of computer hardware, as well as in the diversification of the capacities and the ways in which they may be used. Indeed, self-contained mini-systems are becoming increasingly numerous.

Computers are now capable of performing one billion

operations a second, or a million times more than the pioneer computer of 1944. The size of processing and storage units has shrunk by a factor of about 10,000 while the speed of these units (measured in the number of instructions or calculations processed per second) has increased by approximately 50,000. According to experts' predictions, these trends are expected to continue at least into the early 1980s. Electronic circuits can be manufactured as a unit known as a microcircuit on the surface of a silicon chip five

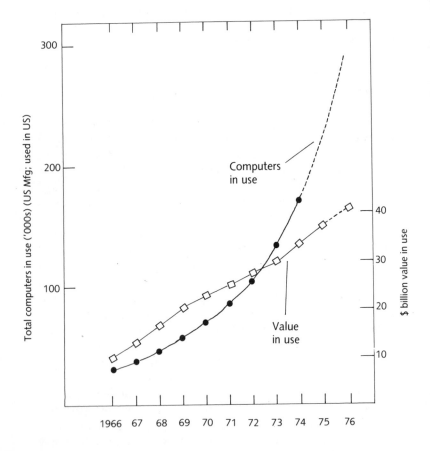

*Source: *High and Low Politics: Information Resources for the 80s*, Oettinger, Berman, Read; Pallinger Publishing Co., Cambridge, 1977.

millimetres in diameter. The number of components that a chip can carry has increased in recent years from ten to 64,000; manufacturers foresee a rise to a million by 1985. A wafer-thin element measuring 10 by 15 centimetres can store more information than the telephone directory of a large city. The speed of transmission from a computer or data bank to a terminal has similarly increased, thanks first to the analogue system — meaning the use of signals in a form analogous to the relevant information — and then to the digital binary system; the latter translates all information into numerical form, and is called binary because it uses only two symbols instead of the usual ten numbers. Information in words is transmitted in this binary form and decoded on arrival, so quickly that the process is almost instantaneous. By the use of repeaters, signals can be transmitted over great distances with little or no loss in quality. Several thousand signals, interleaved and then automatically separated, can be carried at the same time.

The cost of electronic processing and storage units has fallen dramatically over the past 25 years; e.g. the cost per computation has fallen 180 times. A computer which might have cost a million dollars in the early days can now be acquired for $300. The cost of performing one million calculations fell within a decade from ten dollars to two cents, and the cost of a component carried on a silicon chip from ten dollars to less than one-fifth of a cent. Informatics, once the privilege of wealthy corporations and major government departments, is thus brought within the reach of the small business, the neighbourhood school, and even the home.

The reduction in data processing costs is well illustrated by the chart on the preceding page, comparing the rise in the number of computers used and their value in the United States over the ten-year period 1966-1976.

Industrialized countries are steadily increasing their investments in computer development which is growing in fact faster than indicated below (p. 28) because the costs of computers have decreased so sharply over the years. This table shows investment in computers (as percentage of GNP) for a few developed countries.[21] ...

In addition to overall political development and economic growth the most recent advances have led to a massive expansion in the volume of communication facilities and activity, thanks to three developments: (a) the growth, extension and increasingly efficient organization of communication infrastructures; (b) the use of new forms of energy and machines to produce, transmit and

	1970	1979
USA	2.11%	3.2 %
Federal Republic of Germany	1.34%	2.45%
United Kingdom	1.55%	2.83%
France	1.18%	2.65%
Italy	0.77%	1.5 %
Benelux	1.15%	2.3 %

receive messages; (c) changes in the methods and signals used in communication (i.e. digital signals).

The use of digital data transmission methods can be regarded as the most important advance, in a technical sense, for it means the complete transformation of storage, retrieval and transmission of both oral and visual messages produced by 'computer' language which itself has recently made an exponential leap forward in practice and potential.

From the continuous and steady development of communication means, two main conclusions may be drawn: one, that these changes represent an irreversible trend in the development of communication; two, that basically there is interdependence and not competition between different media. Nations which choose to concentrate on one technique should not do so to the detriment or neglect of another. While it is often said that we are entering 'the electronic age', there is for instance no sign of the demise of the print media. Newspapers, magazines and books will continue for decades to be major sources of information, knowledge and pleasure; efforts should be made to ensure their continuity, to increase their quantity and to improve their quality. Radio and television also need further expansion and larger investment, above all in developing countries. The same is true of the newest innovations in technology; all nations need to plan for at least their gradual introduction. Developing nations in particular should make their plans as a matter of urgency, in order to share in the advantages of new technologies and adapt them to their special needs and conditions.

NOTES

1. N.B.: Throughout this review, some statistical data are presented, which call for a word of caution. First, available statistics in the many fields related to communication vary widely in their abundance and accuracy or verifiability. Second,

statistical presentations usually involve a selection, which by nature is necessarily subjective. Third, statistics often express aggregate totals or averages which sometimes mask wide variations in the separate units of the composite. Fourth, data published in a given year often refer to statistics assembled several years earlier which may be outdated. However, some relatively complete data are available in certain areas, allowing more or less valid assumptions or conclusions; in other fields or for different regions of the world, more selective, yet indicative, figures can be given. Despite these disclaimers, the data presented illustrate the situations examined and may help in understanding them.

2. E.g. facial expression, gesture, mime, dance, images, music, songs, drawings, paintings, sculptures, sport, etc. Of special value are lip-reading and sign languages used by millions of handicapped persons.

3. To give but one example of the order of magnitude of such activities, it is estimated that every year some two million scientists, technicians and specialists participate in international congresses alone; if national and regional scientific gatherings are taken into account, probably more than five million individuals are annually involved.

4. These figures (their source being *Languages of the World,* Kenneth Katzner, Toronto 1975) are only indicative, since they are contested on various grounds. The mapping of different languages has not yet been completed. Divergences in differentiation between languages and dialects are still common among scientists. General census has not yet covered large areas in several countries. Some political considerations have also made some distinctions rather difficult. In the current literature, for instance, the number of languages ranges from two thousand to around four thousand. As far as written languages are concerned, divergences also arise from the fact that out of 500 with a script, only 200 are judged to have written and literary traditions, another 200 to have only a written tradition, while around 100 have little more than alphabets and some form of primer.

5. It is estimated (by Unesco services) that more than two-thirds of printed materials are produced in English, Russian, Spanish, German and French.

6. It is estimated that about 60% of scientific communication is conducted in English. Even in French-speaking countries, according to some estimates, 70% of researchers use English sources.

7. It is interesting to note however that this did not effectively solve the problem of producing input output software, which in most computer printing still uses typewriter-like impact printing, a mechanism ill-suited to accommodate 2,000 characters. Now, new electromechanical, microprocessing technologies have been used to develop what is called 'ink-jet printing', in which each character is broken down into an array of minute drops of ink which have been squirted from a nozzle and electronically steered inflight to form the desired printed character. (Various methods of ink-jet printing have been devised; one device prints 45,000 lines per minute!)

8. 'Most people think of waste in physical terms, such as waste of resources, energy, or money. Indeed, the global problematique has focused attention on the wasteful misuse of non-renewable physical resources. .... But another kind of waste has an even more serious impact on the whole knot of global problems: the waste of human learning potential. In this context, waste can result not only from the misuse that relegates people to marginal positions, but also from the lack of use or neglect of human capacities. .... Unacceptably large numbers of people find themselves excluded from all but the most rudimentary, informal opportunities to develop their learning processes. .... Illiteracy, both a symptom and a cause of the downward spiral of ignorance and poverty, epitomizes the waste of human learning potential.' (*The Human Gap,* The Learning Project Report to the Club of Rome, 1979, pp. 106-7).

9. *Source* for figures on illiteracy: Unesco Office of Statistics. Particularly the recent publication *Estimates and Projections of Illiteracy,* Unesco, Sept. 1978

(figures do not include China, Democratic People's Republic of Korea and Vietnam).

10. As expressed by Paulo Freire, Brazilian educationist.

11. On the average worldwide there is one post office for every 7,000 persons; some European countries (e.g. Norway, Portugal), have fewer than 1,000 persons per post office, but in some African and Asian countries there is only one for hundreds of thousands (e.g. one per 300,000 in Rwanda (Source: *Encyclopaedia Britannica* 1974).

12. Because the telephone has become such a commonplace feature in industrialized societies, its vital role is often simply taken for granted and its socio-economic impact insufficiently analysed, particularly as a potentially powerful, indeed essential, tool for development in the Third World. It was quite rightly stated: 'How important was the telephone's specific technology in these processes of change? It is extraordinary how little has been written exploring this question. Social scientists have neglected the telephone not only along with, but also relative to, other technologies. As a cause of social change, transportation has been much more studied than communication. And among communication media, TV, radio, movies, even the telegraph have been studied more than the telephone.' (*The Social Impact of the Telephone,* Ithiel de Sola Pool, Editor, The MIT Press, Cambridge, Massachusetts, 1977.)

13. *The Role of Telecommunications in Socio-Economic Development,* Hudson, Goldschmidt, Parker and Hardy, Keewatin Publications, 1979.

14. A quote from a well-known expert in these issues may be relevant: 'As the focus of the development programme turns toward local activity, there will be more and more incentive for a developing country to concern itself with local rather than large-audience media. Such a country will not have to *choose* between big and little media, for it needs both, but it will have to display wisdom and foresight in balancing big against little, national radio against local radio, wall and mimeograph newspapers against national newspapers, and the like. Most such countries already have some big media, and they are not about to throw them down the drain. Indeed, such media will continue to have important uses. The essential questions are (1) how best to use them, when development strategy turns toward localities? (2) what priority should now be assigned to maintaining and strengthening the system of large media as against the demands of local communication?' (Wilbur Schramm, *Mass Media and National Development 1979,* CIC Document No. 42.)

15. Source: *Unesco Statistical Yearbook* (1977) and *World Communications* (Unesco, 1975). Data cited here do not include China, the Democratic People's Republic of Korea and the Socialist Republic of Vietnam. Latest data for China reported that in 1966 there were 1,908 dailies; circulation figures for 1,455 newspapers around 1960 were 20 million copies or about 27 copies per 1,000 persons.

16. The idea that reporters and newspapers have no further obligation than to present the news and the facts has often been challenged. In many Third World and socialist countries, leading authorities and journalists see the role of media as contributing to the solution of social, political and economic problems and needs. Many journalists understand their role in an analogous way in western developed countries. It may be relevant to quote here the voice of John Hughes, editor of *The Christian Science Monitor* and president of the American Society of Newspaper Editors, who said of their role: 'Newspapers have responsibility to prepare their readers for social change ... editors have a responsibility to produce newspapers that are more relevant to society's needs; that have more depth ...'

17. Statistics covering periodicals are grossly inadequate; data and estimates vary widely. The International Federation of the Periodical Press states that in 1975 there were approximately 410,000 periodical titles in existence. For the same year, reporting data from 137 countries, the *Unesco Statistical Yearbook* gives a figure of

123,000. The reliability of either figure is tenuous if one accepts estimates (Mountbatten Stammer) made in the 1960s of only scientific and technical periodicals, which place that single category around the 100,000 level.

18.   One example: In the past decade, the telephone capacity of international satellite communications has jumped from 150 to more than 10,000 circuits; the latest generation of satellite used for transmitting telephone messages can handle 6,000 calls simultaneously. In 1978, about 70 per cent of the 1 billion international calls were handled by satellite.

19.   This is apart from the military use of satellites — more than two-thirds of those now in orbit — which affects the whole world.

20.   A distinction must be drawn between 'data bases' and 'data banks'. It is now possible to establish and operate magnetic memories capable of representing billions of words, each of which is accessible in the computer system. These stocks of information are termed 'data bases' in the case of bibliographical references concerning actual documents located elsewhere which must then be retrieved and read in order to secure the information desired. What in fact is involved is the automation, generally via 'transnational' channels, of scientific and technical or similar documentation. The term 'data bank' tends to be reserved not for such indirect information but rather for direct information through immediate reading of computerized 'data'. Once access to the computer system is secured it is possible to call up instantly on one's terminal or computer numerical values, statistical series, descriptive attributes, etc. Interest in these data banks is growing particularly since their computerization makes them amenable to all subsequent forms of processing (sorting, amalgamation of files, statistical calculations). However, their rapid development is limited by three factors: the cost of data capture and validation; the costs of up-dating; lastly, the preservation of various secrets.

21.   Source: *A four-year programme for the Development of Informatics in the Community*, Commission of European Communities, 1976.

1.2 Human Communication and its History

RAYMOND WILLIAMS*

For century after century, through all the many fluctuations of human fortune and endeavour, a distinguishing characteristic of man's existence has been his desire — and his ability — to communicate, to exchange meanings with his fellow men. Nearly two-and-a-half thousand years separate us from the civilization of Classical Greece, yet we can still find meaning in these lines:

Language, and thought like the wind
And the feelings that make the town
Man has taught himself, and shelter against the cold,
Refuge from rain.

These English words represent lines written by Sophocles in 442 BC as part of a choral song, now commonly known as the Hymn to Man. Their general meaning comes through to us clearly. Men have taught themselves language, thought, the sense of society and the means of material shelter, as the bases of human life. But then consider what has happened since Sophocles composed those words to be sung and danced by a chorus in his tragedy *Antigone*. We cannot be sure how he originally wrote them down, if indeed that is what he did; perhaps with a pen made from a shaped split reed, using ink made from lampblack, gum and water, on material made from the stem of the paper reed, *Cyperus papyrus*. But he was not writing the lines for what is now meant by publication. The verses would have been learned, by oral repetition, perhaps directly from their author, and he and the fifteen members of the chorus, divided into two groups of seven and a leader, would have been working out, in relation to the metre, the music and the dance movements which would accompany their singing.

*Source: Raymond Williams (ed.), *Contact: Human Communication and its History* (Thames and Hudson, London, 1986), pp. 7-20.

We know that the lines became famous, by repeated public recitation and singing. Many years later, when there was a danger of the plays being forgotten or remembered only imperfectly, scholars and scribes, still reading aloud, made copies of seven of Sophocles' most famous plays; these seven are all we now have complete; more than a hundred others, which were not copied, are now lost and unknown. Yet the seven plays lasted, and can be read now in hundreds of editions. To bring them through to later times they have been translated and re-translated into all the major languages. What we now read as Sophocles has passed through this long and complex material and intellectual process.

We can reckon what we have lost along the way. We can also know what we have gained: this remarkable communication between a great poet of the ancient world and modern readers speaking languages and living in conditions which, even in the great Hymn to Man, he could not have imagined.

This is just one striking example of the extraordinary story of human communication. There are also more immediate contemporary examples. We can press a switch on a machine in our homes and find ourselves watching a battle that was fought yesterday in Asia or a football match that is being played today in South America. On another machine we can, with a little preparation, talk directly to a friend half way round the world, and hear his replies. It is not so long since we called these possibilities the marvels of modern communication. But we have got used to them and, rather than talking about marvels, we are likely, often, to find ourselves complaining about the quality of reception, the standard of the camerawork, the badness of the connection. What was once extraordinary, and as such would have amazed, if they could now see it, the most farsighted of our ancestors, is now literally an everyday business, beyond which we are already looking to new possibilities and new machines.

It is undoubtedly the scale and rapidity of changes in methods of communication, above all in the 20th century, which have led to some new questions about human communication as such, and, as ways of trying to answer these questions, to new branches of scientific and humane inquiry. Most of us in the developed industrial societies have got used to the machines. Some of us take both them and their uses for granted. But many of us, at this point or that, see questions that have to be asked and, when we try to answer them, feel the need for more information and for ways of interpreting the information we already have. For example, it is obvious, when we think about it, that we are not seeing that battle in Asia by chance, or as a necessary consequence of some property of the machine. There are people, other than those directly concerned in the battle, at the far end and at the near end of what we are watching. It is, that is to say, no miracle. There is a specific advanced technology, which we can all in general principle come to understand. At the same time there are many people, at different stages of its operation, who are in specific social, economic and political relations to each other and to us. For we do not watch this battle like gods. A moment's attention will show us that we are not watching the battle from a neutral position above it, or from both sides, but typically from one side, where it was both possible to take film cameras and to link their film to the transmission system which ends in the machine in our house. If we had been, say, in a house in another country, pressing a switch on a very similar machine, we might well have seen quite different film, from the other side of the same battle, where other cameras, linked to a different transmission system, could be put in position. Thus what begins, apparently, as a technical marvel has to be seen, in the end, within whole social and political systems.

There are particular reasons why, in a battle, a neutral camera position would be very difficult to obtain: reasons of danger and of battlefield control. But look again at that very different event, the football match, being played as we watch it, on the other side of the world. Here the cameras can be neutrally positioned. We can watch the game with equal attention to each side. But then notice how often, behind the running players, we see not only the crowd — the immediate audience — but as it were accidentally placed the name of a chocolate, a beer, a washing machine. The camera positions are such that we can only watch the game if we see also, at some level of attention or attempted inattention, these advertisement signs which have been placed, for a price, in exactly those positions. But this is only the most immediate problem. In what sense can we really say that we are watching the match as it is played? Are we seeing, as we might from a good position inside the stadium, the whole field and the patterns of play on it? Occasionally perhaps, but more often we are seeing, in varying degrees of close-up, selected local encounters, sometimes of several players, sometimes of just two, sometimes indeed of two or three disembodied legs or arms. What we actually see is being chosen, by cameramen or directors, of course with the intention that we should see what is most exciting. Yet, staring at their end-product, often putting aside our questions and other observations because we are interested in the game, we can easily forget this, falling back on our assumption of the everyday miracle.

Yet we do not all forget it, all the time. It is from the questions that arise when we see and remember what is actually happening that we have developed those new branches of scientific and humane inquiry that we can try to group as communications studies or the communications sciences. We shall see, as we look closer, that these branches of inquiry are often, in fact, very diffi-cult to group, because in their developed forms they have such apparently different emphases and methods. Indeed, to come across any one of these branches in isolation is often to feel that we have strayed into another country, where we may know with luck what is being discussed but cannot really follow it, since the language is so often unfamiliar. It is especially ironic that this should be the case in studies of human communications. Yet there are discoverable reasons for it. The story is often told of an inter-national conference of Latin scholars, at which it was innocently proposed that the language of the conference should be Latin, as the only language which all present could be expected to under-stand. The proposal failed, for an interesting reason. If all the conference papers had been in Latin, they would indeed have been readily understood. But since Latin is not now a language spoken by an actual people, and is indeed a language that has to be learned from written texts, there is no agreed or authoritative way of speaking it, and the variations between speakers having differ-ent mother tongues could be enough to prevent them understand-ing each other when they spoke.

In the case of communications studies, the irony is as deep but the reasons are different. Instead of diverging from an ancient field, which was once held in common, the study of com-munications, in its modern forms, is a convergence, or attempted convergence, of people who were trained, initially, in very different fields; in history and philosophy, in literary and cultural studies, in sociology, technology and psychology. What all these people have in common, ultimately, is a field of interest. But it is not only inevitable, it is also in the end useful and necessary, that they should study this field in what are, at least initially, very different ways. For the problems, when closely examined, are neither simple

nor special, and the necessary range of different kinds of knowledge and different kinds of analysis is beyond the scope of any
single approach. Yet while we need these specialized approaches,
we must obviously try, at times, to bring them together in the area
of interest which they share with all those who, though they may
not have studied communications, in any of its disciplines, have
thought and are thinking about one of the central activities of the
world. ...

WHY COMMUNICATIONS MATTER

Access and Action

As has already been said, it was the scale and rapidity of 20th-
century changes in the means of communication which led to the
intensive development of new kinds of communications studies.
The effect of these changes can indeed hardly be overestimated. It
is not only the provision of access, for hundreds of millions of us,
to quite newly direct versions of thousands of distant events. That
is the most commonly mentioned effect, often described as 'a
window on the world'. But it is of course a very curious window. It
is not the fixed view, from some place where we have chosen to
stand. As was noted in the examples of the war and the football
match, we are at once seeing and being shown. The window is not
plain glass but a very complex process of technical and social production. And we must then make further distinctions. The war, we
can presume, would have occurred whether or not there was
television to report it. Our access to a version of what it is like can
then range from simple spectacle — another thing to watch,
without any real involvement — to concerned information, in
which something of the reality of what is happening can be
connected not only to our sense of the world beyond our everyday
local experiences but also to our political perspectives and
decisions. Access, that is to say, *as a viewer*, is already too simple a
description. We can either rest content with this magic window or,
at the other extreme, break the glass and get involved, because of
what we have seen, in the actual events.

Events and Pseudo-events

But this is only a variation in response to events that would, we
suppose, have occurred in any case. The example of the football

match is already to some extent different. In a majority of cases it would no doubt have been played, whether television was available or not. But an increasing number of sporting events — in golf and boxing most evidently — have from the beginning been arranged as subjects for television. Moreover this trend is increasing, with very important effects on the organization and financing of most sports. The case is important in itself, but it is also an instance of those real processes which the description as 'access' — the 'window on the world' — obscures and is sometimes meant to obscure. A very high proportion of what is there to be seen was put there to be seen, and it is only when we consider communications as production, rather than reducing it to simple consumption, that we can at all understand its whole range.

In fact an emphasis on production is readily admitted, in certain specified areas. It is obvious that in the whole range of communications technologies — from publishing and the press through cinema to radio and television — most works are produced and, though then in highly variable ways, offered to others. A philosophical essay, a novel, a feature film, a radio play, a television variety show, are all in this sense manifestly produced. Moreover they are all forms governed by certain descriptions and conventions, which indicate, usually successfully, what kind of work is being offered. But there is then an initially simple contrast with another whole range of communications production, when what is being offered is not signalled as production at all, but as 'actuality'. Here the usual signals, of form and convention, which enable us to distinguish, on the whole successfully, between a novel and a biography, or a play and a recording of conversation, are not only not present; they are replaced by other signals, as most typically 'Here is the news', the explicit or implicit signal of newspapers and broadcast news bulletins.

It was the exceptional scale and intensity of this kind of communication that first attracted attention in the 20th century. Would not these new and powerful technologies offer opportunities for propaganda and brainwashing on a mass scale? Would they not slant and distort the news and monopolize opinion? These remain important questions. Nobody, looking at actual output, could simply dismiss them as hysterical. For we can see, if only in the contrast between different news and broadcasting services, a range of performance from some attempts at objectivity, especially in certain areas, to the most blatant distortion and propaganda. I say 'we can see', but in fact this contrast is only ever adequately available to people who have the means and take the trouble to compare different newspapers and different broadcasting services, especially — where the contrasts can jump at us — between different countries. Most of us, most of the time, have to make more internal comparisons, paying particular attention to reports of events of which we have some direct knowledge (the level of scepticism about these is significantly high) or to identifiable uses of words and images which carry or imply prejudice.

The Window Changes the World

But then the problem is deeper than this. It is not only a question of whether some independently occurring event is being reported with relative accuracy or with a decent range of opinions on its significance. It is also a question of the relations between such independently occurring events and specially arranged events. For it is not only in sport that events are arranged primarily so that they can be reported. In politics and in commerce such events are now regularly arranged. A camera does not happen to be present when a political leader happens to be taking what the French call a 'crowd bath' and what the British and Americans call a 'public walkabout' or 'meeting the people'. Elaborate schedules of time and logistics have in almost all cases made certain not only that the camera should be there but that the political leader and even, in some cases, the crowd should be there. What is then reported and shown may indeed be relatively accurate, and a claim to objectivity can be further staked if several alternative political leaders are shown in the same kind of crowd bath. Yet what is happening, beyond this, is a produced version of politics: that this, in at least one important way, is how leaders and people should relate, politically; indeed, structurally, and at a deeper level, that politics is wholly or primarily a matter of the relative generalized popularity of leaders or competing leaders. What is then happening, often without any local or immediate distortion, is the production of a version of politics, or of the electoral process, which in its repeated emphasis can override, or attempt to override, other versions: not just as a matter of opinion, but as a specific kind of produced event.

Medium as Market

Similar processes of communicative production are now widely evident in commerce. A whole branch of cultural production has developed, within modern communications systems, with quite new quantitative and qualitative effects. Paid advertisements, or commercials, are now a significantly large element of most newspapers and most broadcasting services, to an extent where, in a majority of cases, the financial viability of the presumably primary service — the newspaper or general broadcasting — is directly determined by its performance in this area. Yet it is not only a matter of this now huge area of cultural production as commercial persuasion. In its most visible forms, specific signals — that this is a 'commercial'; that what is being said or shown has, if you take the trouble to think about it, been arranged, scripted, directed and paid for — are indeed present. Yet beyond this there is a range, as in politics, of apparently independent events, which are in fact also produced. The most widespread type is the sponsored event, in which something that might have happened in any case is integrated with the naming of some basically irrelevant product, until the event and the product come to seem factually associated. Then there are other events which would never have happened unless they had been arranged to display or in association with the commercial product. One simple example is the increasing practice of 'product anniversaries' where what looks like news, that something or some name has been produced or marketed for some plausible number of years, over the available numerical range of ordinary social or personal celebration (the centenary, the jubilee, the twenty-first birthday), turns out, in most cases, to have been planned, paid for and in the fullest sense produced.

'Fact' and 'Fiction'

These are major modern instances of a necessary concern with communications. But, profoundly important as they are, we should not make the mistake of limiting or reducing communications studies to matters of this kind. For the social processes involved, in these and in other less noticed cases, are on closer examination very complex. Thus we can become so used to descriptions of modern communications in terms of political or commercial propaganda or manipulation that we can fail to notice some equally widespread and perhaps equally significant cultural processes of an apparently different kind. The case of drama is an exceptionally strong example. For dramatic performance has been an important cultural practice, in many different kinds of society, for some twenty-five centuries, yet it is only comparatively recently that it has become an everyday event for what are in effect whole populations. In most earlier periods, drama was performed only on special occasions, such as festivals, and even when it became more regularly available, in city theatres and in touring companies, it reached only comparative minorities. Today, many old and new kinds of dramatic performances, not only in theatres but in cinemas, on the radio and on television, are produced in a truly astonishing number and frequency. On television alone many people in industrial societies can find themselves watching several hours of dramatic performance on most evenings. Indeed more time can be, and often is, spent in watching some kind of dramatic performance than in, say, eating.

Such a phenomenon can be interpreted, quite correctly, as an instance of an expanding culture. Similar kinds of expansion can be observed in other cultural activities such as reading and music. But is this the only relevant kind of interpretation? May there not be important questions, of a different kind, about the social and cultural significance of so large and regular an involvement, as spectators, in dramatic performance and in other kinds of what we still, by habit, call 'fiction'; fiction as distinct from 'fact'? Faced by a social fact of this magnitude, that does not fit in easily with our ordinary thinking about communications as news and opinions, we have to recognize the need for a kind of inquiry which does not simply begin from existing categories, but which is capable of examining the categories themselves.

The History of Communications

One way of examining the categories, in practice, is to include, deliberately as I have said, the available historical range. The extraordinary developments of modern communications can so impress us that we isolate them, put them in a special field. And this is easily done if we adopt, uncritically, certain further current assumptions. Thus it is widely said that communications, in our time, are effectively 'mass communications', and that this is so because we live in a 'mass society'. Communication is thought of, within such definitions, in too functional and too secondary a way. The model of a small number of communicators using powerful technologies to address very large publics is obviously appropriate to many actual contemporary situations, especially in the cases of a heavily centralized press and of centralized broadcasting and cinema. But we may not be able to understand even this situation unless we have looked, very carefully, at the history of this kind of communication. The phenomenon of a minority addressing or controlling communication with a very large public can be quite quickly shown, when we have looked at the history, to be in no sense, a singular 20th-century phenomenon. Or if we say that the singularity is a consequence of the 20th-century technologies, we have at once to notice that there are radical differences between, for example, the very large television audience — millions of people watching a single programme, but mainly in small unconnected groups in family homes; the very large cinema public — millions of people seeing a single film, but in audiences of varying sizes, in public places, on a string of occasions; and the very large actual crowds, at certain kinds of event, who are indeed (but only in this case) physically massed. In general, as we shall see from the history, the dispersed large public is much more typical of modern communications technologies than the large crowds and audiences — ('masses') — of many periods before these technologies were invented. Thus, instead of rushing into easy descriptions, before the full range of the evidence has been admitted, we find ourselves faced with the need to rethink our customary interpretations as well as to inform ourselves about what is, when looked at directly, the truly extraordinary history of human communications systems. [...]

While it is possible to discuss communications — meanings and messages — at the level of simple *ideas*, it is impossible in the end to separate such discussion from that very important and indeed primary branch of social production which is the making of communications technologies and systems.

Communications in Society

Thus it can be wrongly assumed that it is only with the coming of 20th-century technologies that communication has been at once systematized and mechanized. The real relations between techniques and systems, from the earliest experiments in writing and in other kinds of sign, through the application of printing to writing but also to other kinds of graphic reproduction, to the extension and combined extension of sounds and images in modern electronic systems, are at once more complex and more interesting. We do indeed, along the way, find major qualitative changes, crucial transformations in the nature of social communications.

This is no simple history of continuity and expansion; within the systems and between the systems there are many kinds of unevenness, contradiction and mixtures of intended and unintended effect. But what most needs to be emphasized is that the communications systems have never been as it were an optional extra in social organization or in historical development. They take their place, as we read their real history, alongside other major forms of social organization and production, as they also take their place in the history of material invention and economic arrangement. It has been customary to think of communication as merely derived from other 'more practical' needs and arrangements. But while there are many such cases of applied communication, there are also, as we read the history, as many cases of the systems and the technologies becoming major elements in the nature and development of social orders as a whole. [...]

Messages, Meanings, Relationships

Thus we can begin to assess, in some new ways, the past, present and future significance of human communications as one of our central and decisive activities. However, to grasp the fullest significance, we have to add to this historical account and analysis a different kind of discussion. I have said that communication is often understood as if it were only something that occurred *after* other more important events. Thus it is suggested that we build settlements, plant crops, fight wars, have thoughts, and after all this we tell each other about them. But in fact, when we look at any of these human actions, we can hardly fail to notice that communication, if in different ways, is from the beginning involved in them, and is indeed in many cases their necessary condition. We do not simply pass messages to each other after such events; we often precede and organize them by messages, of many kinds.

Yet the truth is more than this. Much of the activity of human communication is not limited to the passing of messages, in the simple sense in which that term is often understood. What we say and write and show to each other is in no way limited to the passing of certain definite quantities of information in its everyday sense. For before even the passing of information can happen, let alone the passing of other material and other meanings, certain major processes must be available to us. Even the simplest communication depends on the existence or close possibility of significant relationships between those involved: sharing a language or certain gestures or some system of signs. Moreover these relationships are not merely available; in the course of communication they are themselves developed, and the means of communication with them. When this is realized we soon recognize that in all this vast complex of active communicating relationships we are doing more than speaking at or to each other; often, and indeed perhaps typically, we are speaking *with* each other, and the meanings that then emerge are often much more than some separable body of relayed information. Indeed, in the full sense, we cannot separate the relationships from this complex and active production and reproduction of meanings. In the same way, we cannot separate information — 'the facts' — or thought — 'our ideas' — from these basic processes through which we not only transmit or receive but necessarily compose what we have to say or to show.

Primary Resources of Communication

These basic processes are then of course necessarily complex. Since we are so deeply involved in them, it is easy to take them more or less for granted. But once we start thinking about the nature and processes of language, or of what we now call 'non-verbal' communication, or of the making of signs and symbols, we find that we are faced with some of the most difficult as well as the most central questions about ourselves. [...]

Each of these kinds of communication is so important, and also at once so fascinating and so difficult, that it requires a chapter to itself. Yet something can also be said about the full range of such processes and about their interrelations. Thus we can see that, apparently from the beginning of human societies, men and women have drawn on two kinds of communicative resource. First, we have used and continue to use the resources of our own bodies. How much we do this, and at the same time the difficult problems of interpreting many such uses, can be seen in the account of 'non-verbal' communication in its now specialized scientific sense. Movements of our bodies and parts of our bodies can be related to both messages and meanings, and though some of these are simple, others are not. Then, second, we have used and continue to use non-human material objects and forces, which we adapt and shape for communicative purposes. This ranges from very simple uses — the mark on a tree, the significantly placed stone — through systems of an increasing complexity of shape, line and colour to the full complexity of systems we can differentiate and specialize as the visual arts and design. Between them these two kinds of resources — movements of our bodies and parts of our bodies; adaptations and shapings of non-human material objects — are composed into a vast and complex range of human communications.

Combination and Elaboration of Resources

Yet while we can distinguish these two kinds of resource, each of which can be used very significantly on its own, the full range, and then much of the history, of communications includes an interactive area between them. Thus the masked and painted dancer, or the robed figure carrying the significantly shaped and marked piece of wood or stone or metal, are basic examples of a powerfully combined use of human and non-human resources. But the interactions go much further. Language, initially, is a direct use and development of our own physical resources, in speech and song. But we have then not only combined these with other, non-verbal, bodily movements and gestures, and either or both with shaped and adapted non-human resources. In one major and transforming stage, we have developed variable graphic systems which can be seen, at least initially, as notations of other, more direct, kinds of use. Written language is still the major example. It can be seen as a way of recording and substituting for our directly physical speech. But we do not have to look far into the relations between spoken and written language to realize that while these direct relations are always important, the systems of notation become, in practice, more than that; become indeed, though always in variable degrees, means of composition, apparently in their own right. Writers, for example, have learned the intricate practical differences between writing for speech, or for being read aloud, and writing to be silently read. In this major area of communicative development, there are not only simple transfers, between one kind of system and another, but genuine and active transformations. Written language is not the only such case. The complex systems of notation of sound, as in musical notation, can be usefully compared and contrasted with written language; they appear to remain more strictly notational. But the systems of notation of mathematical properties, for example, while retaining an important directly notational status, have long since passed the stage of simple transfer and include not only transformations but what appear to be new and irreplaceable means of direct intellectual composition.

Such interactions as these, in the combined use of human and non-human resources, are now central to human communicative activity. They raise, evidently, the most difficult questions: for example, about the relations between such material composition and the vital but extremely complex categories of 'thought' and 'experience', which can at one extreme be said to be merely 'expressed', as already formed wholes, by these means of composition, and at the other extreme be said to come into existence, or into substantial existence, only to the extent that they are articulated by systematic compositional means. These are, in varying forms, permanent philosophical questions, which underlie our thinking not only about communications but about many kinds of related human practices. ...

Magnification of Resources

But the full extent of these relations and interactions goes beyond the development of representational and notational systems. Over a long period, the interaction between human and non-human resources had to do, primarily, with material objects: wood, stone, metal; materials for writing and painting. From each of these uses of objects elaborate communicative systems were developed. But already in some of these uses what was happening was more than adaptation or application: shaping a stick, carving a stone, selecting this or that object for this or that conventional significance. There was the development of tools and instruments for these simple uses, and then beyond that the development of means of transforming the objects, for new uses; by fire, as in the use of new metals; by chemical interaction, as in the later pigments and inks. From these productive developments we learned the possibilities — in communications as in other kinds of production — of the use of non-human forces as well as non-human objects. There have been many stages of this development, but the application of steam power to printing and other graphic reproduction is one major example, with its extraordinary extension of range. The applications of electricity and magnetism have of course been even more extraordinary. For here there were not only more powerful ways of doing what had anyhow, by less developed means, already been done. In the extraordinary systems that were eventually developed from them, in the modern chemical, engineering and electronics industries, what seem not merely new devices, but new forms of communication were developed. ...

'Modern' Communications, 'Mass' Communications?

The simplest response, as I argued above, was to separate off these new means and systems, as a modern area, and by calling them mechanical and electronic and then mass communications convert all previous history of communications to their implied opposites: human, natural and personal. But if there is one thing which the detailed histories show, it is that from the beginning the processes of communication have involved the use of both direct and indirect — human and non-human — physical resources. Similarly, the development of 'impersonal' communications — as distinct from the model of direct 'face-to-face' exchanges — is at least as early as the development of writing systems and indeed, in their graphic predecessors, much earlier. There is no future in attempting to reduce the many problems of modern communications to falsely absolute contrasts of that familiar kind. On the other hand, to fail to recognize changes of degree, in just this respect, would be to underestimate the problems quite hopelessly. ...

Communication, as we have seen and can confirm in all the detailed accounts, is involved from the beginning in the whole range of human practice. But this does not prevent us from saying — indeed it shows us a way of saying — that as an integral element of human practice it has, in itself and in its relations, a history. And there can be little doubt that the significance of this history has never, in all our long record, been more important.

For the processes of modern communications indicate, in many respects, a qualitatively new social situation. It is in practice impossible to separate them, in their present stages, from other ways of describing our qualitatively distinct contemporary situation. Thus it is impossible to separate the development, along particular lines and through particular institutions, of a potential and in some cases actual world communications system from the development of what, again along particular lines and through particular institutions, has to be seen as a relatively integrated world economy. Earlier and still continuing processes of the national organization of communications systems relate, in comparable ways, to the older and continuing processes of the formation of nation-states. Many current communications problems are indeed centred on the complex relations between these national formations and the powerful international market.

The important current controversy, for example, about the legal status of transmitting satellite stations, with its difficult questions about national and other forms of sovereignty in the air space above a territory and about national and other forms of reception and control of reception, is an exact case in point. It is a central issue in communications, and in the development of communications technology, but it is also a central issue in international politics, in its potential effects on the sources and controls of news and opinion, and in international economics, in its relations to the activities of para-national companies and the whole contested area of imports and exports, not only in ordinary goods and services but in cultural products, services and influences. Already, by developments in radio, we can, in all parts of the world, listen to political news and opinion from sources not only different from our ordinary political authorities but also, if we choose, disapproved of by them. The example reminds us that communications technology is used not only to bridge distances but consciously to implant alternative views in other societies and of course also to interfere with and jam alternative kinds of reception. Thus an issue in communications technology, about which we certainly need to inform ourselves, is at the same time a complex — and as we continue to consider it a very difficult — issue in international politics and economics, and indeed in some of our most basic thinking about political and economic questions and principles.

But then this issue turns up, also, in matters much nearer home. The origins and the control systems of the most public kinds of communications are major issues within our own most immediate societies. Indeed they cannot be reduced to issues between nations, though in some areas they are undeniably that, since it is a crucial question of any modern social order as to how the press or broadcasting or cinema or publishing are politically and economically organized and in that sense, directly or indirectly, controlled. These are questions with a long history of discussion, dispute and struggle. But increasing degrees of extension and magnification now make them especially urgent.

All these processes and changes have been occurring, moreover, in relation to other processes and changes which we are still struggling to understand. Two of these need special mention. First, there is now extraordinary mobility, of a physical kind. More people can and do move often and regularly beyond and outside their familiar communities. This actual movement relates in complicated ways to the means of cultural mobility in the developed communications systems, where forms of contact, but here mediated contact, with other peoples and cultures are now common. The effects of these different kinds of mobility, inter-acting as they do with still very powerful and relatively stable communications and other systems, in homes and families and workplaces and local communities and national educational systems, seem to require, for their understanding, quite new kinds of social thinking. The excited, merely rhetorical stress on mobility, which new systems of transport and communications can suggest, and in their own terms correctly suggest, cannot be allowed to run to the point where we underestimate, or simply fail to notice, these relatively stable persistences, with their undoubted capacity, as in all working communications systems, to reproduce, often very powerfully because apparently naturally, existing forms and relations. We need many kinds of evidence and inquiry to be able to understand these now exceptionally complicated relations between practical mobility and effective social and cultural repro-duction, but clearly one essential area of any such inquiry is that of the communications processes through which so many of them are actually negotiated.

To this emphasis on the changing problems of mobility we can add an emphasis on the changing character of our labour processes. On the one hand a sizeable proportion of the working population, by any previous standards, is employed in the advanced industrial societies in communications in their tradition-ally differentiated form: in the press and publishing, radio and television, advertising, public relations and publicity, cinema, musical publishing, performance and recording, galleries, theatres and entertainment clubs, together with all those who produce machines and equipment for these sectors or are involved in distribution in them. It is then already the case that communica-tions is a very much more significant sector of the economy than it was in periods when (confirming an already established prejudice) it could be seen as, and in the practical economy was, peripheral.

But this visible differentiated area is only part of the change. At every level of the constitution and reproduction of the social order, and most notably in the continually expanding area of administra-tion, communications processes take an increasingly larger share of workers and working time. Further, in direct production of the traditional kinds, in areas well beyond the important sectors of communications manufacturing, not only internal administration but programmes aimed at influencing production and labour relations amount, even in this area, to a significant proportion of workers and working time. Again, within education, which in its primary practices can reasonably be differentiated from communications, though the links between them are obviously close, the use of all kinds of direct communications materials and techniques has rapidly increased.

In all these ways there has been what has to be seen as a qualitative change. All societies depend on communications processes and in an important sense can be said to be founded on them. But in advanced industrial societies, both in their scale and complexity and in their changes in productive and reproductive techniques, the dependence is central, and the elements of foundation, often in simpler societies in effect dissolved into other social relations, are manifest and crucial. Thus while it has always been necessary to understand a society in terms which include its communications processes and techniques, it is necessary in advanced industrial societies not only to emphasize their importance but to try to think through again, from what they are showing us, the nature of all, and especially of these, social relations.

But then as we enter these problems, necessarily in our own kind of world and in relation to a continually developing technology, we may hear at our side those old and still powerful words:

Language, and thought like the wind
And the feelings that make the town
Man has taught himself ...

SECTION 2

COMMUNICATIONS AND SOCIAL POWER

INTRODUCTION

In the first contribution to this section, Curran *et al.* set out to review liberal-pluralist and Marxist approaches to the study of the mass media. In their opinion, however, the most interesting arguments have not been between these two approaches, but have arisen within Marxism. Their survey, therefore, distinguishes between a number of contending Marxist approaches: 'structuralist', 'culturalist' and that of 'political economy'.

In its more sophisticated forms, Marxist analysis is likely to emphasize concepts like the media's 'cultural leadership' in the promotion of hegemony, a hegemony that is in accordance with dominant social interests. But whether sophisticated or otherwise, in the view of some academics the search for dominance — or at least the search to verify it empirically — 'has had a stultifying effect on British media studies' (Harrison, 1985, p. 126). This search is based on elaborating the supposed function of the media in an industrialized society. Though studies of this kind are preoccupied with investigating the content of media output, they can be readily subsumed under the wider heading of *media effects* with which McQuail is concerned. This relationship is especially relevant to the most recent era of effects research described by McQuail, in which attention has turned toward long-term change, cognition and structures of belief.

There are, in addition, other points of comparison. As McQuail points out, in the area of the media's role in long-term change there is an abundance of theory and speculation, but little firm evidence. Nevertheless, he sets out to develop an intelligent way to discuss issues such as agenda setting, diffusion of news and knowledge-gaps. Central to this discussion is deciding whether the media favours conservation or encourages change and, in either case, in whose interest? This, in turn, raises the question of the degree to which there is a pattern and a consistency in media output. According to McQuail, such consistency can depend just as much on what is absent as it can on what is present. He cites the work of the Glasgow Media Group (the GMG) as documenting some significant patterns of omission and a pattern of selection so consistent that a corresponding pattern of rejection can be inferred.

The GMG and others (for example Hall (1981) and Miliband (1969)) argue that the function of the mass media is to legitimize the state in capitalist society and, by extension, to delegitimize those forces or groups that can be seen to be actively or potentially in opposition to dominant interests. In their most explicit formulation, the GMG assert that industrial stories are depicted by TV news in a way that 'the hearer (sic) could only attribute their cause to the *unreasonable* because unexplained action of labour ((1980), PXIV, emphasis added). The actions of labour, they argue, are presented as a threat to the economy and to the national interest.

In *More Bad News*, the GMG say that despite criticism of the overall strategy of their work, whether from academics or from within the media, their 'evident detail' has remained unchallenged (1980, p. 398). With the publication of Harrison's book, *TV News — Whose Bias?* this is no longer so. On the basis of his study of all the relevant ITN scripts, Harrison argues that the GMG are guilty of the very crime of which they accuse ITN (and the BBC): 'in the face of contradictory evidence which, when it appears is either ignored, smothered, or at worst treated as if it supports' their inferential framework (Harrison (1985), p. 125 quoting the GMG (1976) pp. 267-8). Considerations of space preclude an examination of this debate in its entirety, but an adequate flavour may be obtained by reading first one of the GMG's original case studies, their analysis of coverage of the so-called 'Glasgow rubbish strike' which lasted from January to April, 1975, and then Harrison's review of their analysis.

Even if we discount the objections that Harrison raises about the validity of the GMG's content analysis, there remains the question of what evidence is there that the dominant view that is discerned by the GMG and by others, influences the audience to the extent that is often suggested? In fairness, we should say that this does not require a single or inescapable meaning as claimed by the GMG, but merely what is called a 'preferred' meaning. In short, is the reading of some critics of the media the same as that of the audience?

This is one of the questions that may be illuminated by employing a semiological analysis. As Berger explains, the basic concern of semiology is how meaning is generated and conveyed. By unlocking the structure of media messages semiologists might claim that we are in a better position to analyse their effects. Berger's article provides us with a valuable introduction to this type of analysis. We can, however, accept semiology as illuminating and as internally consistent, yet remain sceptical in other respects. For example, we may ask whether the structures discovered by semiologists are really there? And we may point to Eco's contention, elaborated by Berger, that 'aberrant decoding' is the rule in the mass media, that is to say that people bring with them to a given mass media message different codes, based on their ethnic or religious background, their value systems and so on, and so interpret it in different ways.

The final two contributions concretize some of the themes raised earlier in the section with particular reference to ideas of 'dominance' and 'hegemony'. Collins's analysis of the history of broadcasting in Canada belongs to the debate about the role of the mass media in the creation of cultural dominance and cultural dependency between nations, more often encountered in the context of developing countries and their relations with developed countries. He elaborates both sides of the argument between those who are content to let 'market forces' determine the flow of communications and those who insist that this flow must be restricted in order to safeguard national cultural sovereignty. He explains the importance that control over the means of communication has assumed in Canada as a means of national self-definition. Yet he reveals an enduring contradiction between stated policy and the provision of the means to achieve this policy. This is explained not just by Canada's proximity to the USA, but by relative production costs and the development of new communication technologies: 'Each new technological initiative accelerates the spiral of decline by sucking in more and more foreign production and thereby making ... Canadian production harder and harder to achieve' (p. 229). But for all this, Collins concludes that there is no evidence that even though Canadian broadcasting may be effectively American, this has caused a loss of Canadian national cohesion.

It might also be said that many elements of the new communication technologies are equally 'effectively American'. Thus Schiller reveals the extent to which American companies dominate world markets in, for example, mainframe computers and semi-conductors. An obvious conclusion to be drawn seems to be that the burgeoning information industry may fall under an American controlled 'global hegemony'. However, given the growth of pub-lically funded networks in Japan and Europe, Schiller does not see this as occurring. What may be deduced from Schiller's article is that the traditional concerns of media and communications analysts may need to change in order to take account of the grow-ing importance of computerized data based searching. In Schiller's view, only the widest participation in the preparation of data bases will permit what he terms 'meaningful autonomy', whether locally, nationally or internationally. The development of these tech-nologies, Schiller argues, raises the prospect of an increasing gap between information 'haves' and 'have nots' and between 'information users' and the 'information used'.

REFERENCES

Collins, R. (1985) 'Canada: Nation-building Threatened by US-dominated Media' in Kuhn, R. *Politics of Broadcasting* (Croom Helm, London, 1985) pp. 197-232.
Eco, U. (1976) *A Theory of Semiotics*, Indiana University Press.
The Glasgow Media Group (1976) *Bad News*, London, Routledge and Kegan Paul.
The Glasgow Media Group (1980) *More Bad News*, London, Routledge and Kegan Paul.
Hall, S. (1981) 'The Rediscovery of Ideology' in Guneritch, M. *et al. Culture, Media and Society*, Methuen.
Harrison, M. (1985) 'TV News: Whose Bias?' Policy Journals.
Miliband, R. (1969) *The State in Capitalist Society*, Weidenfeld and Nicolson.

2.1 The Study of the Media: Theoretical Approaches

JAMES CURRAN, MICHAEL GUREVITCH
and JANET WOOLLACOTT*

In this chapter we do not attempt to chart systematically all the different approaches to the study of the mass media, each set in their different intellectual, social and historical contexts. Instead we have chosen to examine selectively the way in which different researchers have perceived the *power* of the mass media and to point to the different theoretical conceptions and empirical enquiries that have informed some of those perceptions. In particular, we have focused on the clashes and common ground between different accounts of the power of the media in three areas; in the distinctions between liberal-pluralist and Marxist approaches, often conceived of in terms of a distinction between empiricism and theory; in different approaches to the analysis of media institutions and finally in the different accounts of media power located in contemporary Marxist studies of the media.

THE POWER OF THE MEDIA: THEORY AND EMPIRICISM

To a remarkable extent, there was a broad consensus during the inter-war period — to which many researchers, writing from a 'right' as well as a 'left' perspective subscribed — that the mass media exercised a powerful and persuasive influence. Underlying this consensus was (1) the creation of mass audiences on a scale that was unprecedented through the application of new technology — the rotary press, film and radio — to the mass production of communications; (2) a fashionable though not unchallenged view, that urbanization and industrialization had created a society that was volatile, unstable, rootless, alienated and inherently suscep- tible to manipulation; (3) linked to a view of urbanized man as

*Source: Michael Gurevitch, Tony Bennett, James Curran and Janet Woollacott (eds) *Culture, Society and the Media* (Methuen, London, 1982), pp. 11-29.

being relatively defenceless, an easy prey to mass communication since he was no longer anchored in the network of social relations and stable, inherited values that characterized settled, rural communities; (4) anecdotal but seemingly persuasive evidence that the mass media had brainwashed people during World War 1, and engineered the rise of fascism in Europe between the wars.

This encouraged a relatively uncomplicated view of the media as all-powerful propaganda agencies brainwashing a susceptible and defenceless public. The media propelled 'word bullets' that penetrated deep into its inert and passive victims. All that needed to be done was to measure the depth and size of penetration through modern scientific techniques.

A reassessment of the impact of the mass media during the late 1940s, 1950s and 1960s gave rise to a new academic orthodoxy — that the mass media have only a very limited influence. This view was succinctly stated by Klapper (1960) in a classic summary of more than a decade's empirical research. 'Mass communications', he concludes, 'ordinarily do not serve as a necessary and sufficient cause of audience effects' (p. 8). Underlying this new orthodoxy, was a reassessment of man's susceptibility to influence. A succession of empirical enquiries, using experimental laboratory and social survey techniques, demonstrated that people tended to expose themselves to, understand and remember communications selectively, according to prior dispositions. People, it was argued, manipulated — rather than were manipulated by — the mass media. The empirical demonstration of selective audience behaviour was further reinforced by a number of uses and gratifications studies which argued that audience members are active rather than passive and brings to the media a variety of different needs and uses that influence their response to the media.

Underpinning this reassuring conclusion about the lack of media influence was a repudiation of the mass society thesis on which the presumption of media power had been based. The view of society as being composed of isolated and anomic individuals gave way to a view of society as a honeycomb of small groups bound by a rich web of personal ties and dependences. Stable group pressures, it was concluded, helped to shield the individual from media influence. This stress on the salience of small groups as a buffer against media influence was often linked to a diffusionist model of power. In particular, it was stressed by a number of leading empirical researchers that the social mediation of media messages was not a hierarchical process. 'Some individuals of high social status apparently wield little independent influence', wrote Katz and Lazarsfeld (1955), 'and some of low status have considerable personal influence'. Wealth and power, it seemed, did not shape public opinion in the leading Western democracy.

Even the image of man as a natural prey to suggestion and influence was challenged by a number of persuasive theories of personality formation that apparently explained selective audience behaviour. In particular cognitive dissonance theory, which postulated that people seek to minimize the psychological discomfort of having incompatible values and beliefs, seemed to explain people's deliberate avoidance and unconscious decoding of uncongenial media messages.

In short, the conventional belief in the power of the media seemed to be demolished. A popular view based on flimsy anecdotal evidence had been confounded by systematic empirical enquiry. Even the assumptions about the nature of man and the structure of society on which the belief in media power had rested, had been 'revealed' as bankrupt and misguided.

During the late 1960s and the 1970s, the new orthodoxy was challenged from two quite different, indeed opposed, directions. Those working within the empirical effects tradition initiated what Jay Blumler has called the 'new look' in mass communications research. This has consisted partly of looking again at the small print of the pioneering studies into media effects obscured by the often polemically worded dismissals of media influence that are regularly cited in summary overviews of the literature. For although leading researchers like Katz, Lazarsfeld and Klapper reacted strongly against the conventional view of the omnipotent media in sometimes extravagantly worded generalizations, they were careful to qualify what they said by allowing a number of cases when the media may be or has been persuasive: when audience attention is casual, when information rather than attitude or opinion is involved, when the media source is prestigious, trusted or liked, when monopoly conditions are more complete, when the issue at stake is remote from the receiver's experience or concern, when personal contacts are not opposed to the direction of the message or when the recipient of the message is cross-pressured. More recently a number of scholars have also re-examined the empirical data presented in the early classic 'effects' studies and argued that they do not fully support the negative conclusions about media influence that were derived from them (Becker, McCombs and McLeod, 1975; Gitlin, 1978). Furthermore, it has been argued, social changes such as the decline of stable political allegiances and the development of a new mass medium in television require the conclusions derived from older empirical studies to be reassessed.

The limited model of media influence was also attacked by scholars in the Marxist and neo-Marxist critical tradition that became a growing influence on mass communication research during the 1970s. The initial response of many Marxist and critical writers was to dismiss out of hand empirical communications research as being uniformly uninteresting. The media, they argued, were ideological agencies that played a central role in maintaining class domination: research studies that denied media influence were so disabled in their theoretical approach as to be scarcely worth confronting (or indeed, even reading).

Some empirical researchers responded with evident exasperation to this sweeping dismissal by arguing that disciplined, rigorous empirical research had revealed the inadequacy of unsubstantiated theorizing about the mass media (e.g. Blumler, 1977). Indeed, a casual reader of exchanges between these two traditions might be forgiven for thinking that a new engagement had developed in which a view of the mass media as having only limited influence, grounded in empirical research within a liberal tradition, was pitted against an alternative conception of the mass media as powerful agencies, informed by an exclusively theoretical Marxist/critical perspective.

But while the two research traditions are, in some ways, fundamentally and irreconcilably opposed, they are not divided primarily by the differences highlighted in this debate. In fact, the classical empirical studies did not demonstrate that the mass media had very little influence: on the contrary, they revealed the central role of the media in consolidating and fortifying the values and attitudes of audience members. This tended to be presented in a negative way only because the preceding orthodoxy they were attacking had defined the influence of omnipotent media in terms of changing attitudes and beliefs. The absence of media *conversion* consequently tended to be equated with the absence of influence.

Ironically, Marxist and critical commentators have also argued that the mass media play a strategic role in reinforcing dominant social norms and values that legitimize the social system. There is thus no inconsistency, at an empirical level, in the two approaches. Indeed, as Marcuse has suggested, 'the objection that we overrate greatly the indoctrinating power of the "media" ... misses the point. The preconditioning does not start with the mass production of radio and television and the centralization of their control. The people entered this stage as preconditioned receptacles of long standing ...' (Marcuse, 1972). He could have added with justification, that a generation of empirical research from a different tradition had provided corroboration of the reinforcement 'effect' he was attributing to the media.

Differences between the pluralist and critical schools about the power of the mass media, at the level of effectiveness, are to a certain extent based on mutual misunderstanding (notably, an over-literal acceptance by some Marxist commentators of polemical generalizations about the lack of media influence advanced by some empirical researchers). This misunderstanding has been perpetuated by the tendency for researchers in the two different traditions to examine the impact of the mass media in different contexts as a consequence of their divergent ideological and theoretical preoccupations.

Consider, for instance, the vexed issue of media portrayals of violence. Most researchers in the Marxist tradition in Britain have approached this question in terms of whether media portrayals of violence have served to legitimize the forces of law and order, build consent for the extension of coercive state regulation and de-legitimize outsiders and dissidents (Hall, 1974; Cohen, 1973; Murdock, 1973; Chibnall, 1977; Whannel, 1979). They have thus examined the impact of the mass media in situations where mediated communications are powerfully supported by other institutions such as the police, judiciary and schools, and sustained by already widely diffused attitudes favourable towards law enforcement agencies and generally unfavourable towards groups like youth gangs, student radicals, trade union militants and football hooligans. The power of the media is thus portrayed as that of renewing, amplifying and extending the existing predispositions that constitute the dominant culture, not in creating them. In contrast, empirical researchers in the liberal tradition have tended to examine media portrayals of violence in terms of whether they promote and encourage violence in everyday life. They have consequently defined the potential influence of these portrayals of violence in a form that is opposed to deeply engrained moral

norms supported and maintained by a network of social relationships and powerful institutions actively opposed to 'anti-social
behaviour'. That a 'limited effects' model of media influence
emerged from such studies should come as no surprise: it was
inherent in the way in which media influence was defined in the
first place.

The same pattern of difference can be illustrated in relation to
the question of voting. Some Marxist commentators have
contended that media portrayals of elections constitute dramatized
rituals that legitimize the power structure in liberal democracies;
voting is seen as an ideological practice that helps to sustain the
myth of representative democracy, political equality and collective
self-determination. The impact of election coverage is thus
conceived in terms of reinforcing political values that are widely
shared in Western democracies and are actively endorsed by the
education system, the principal political organizations and the
apparatus of the state. In contrast, pioneering studies into the
effects of the media on voting behaviour by Lazarsfeld *et al.*
(1948), Berelson *et al.* (1954) and Trenaman and McQuail (1961)
concluded that the media had only marginal influence in changing
the way in which people voted. Their negative conclusions were
based on an analysis of media influence in a form that was strongly
opposed by powerful group norms, at a time when partisan
allegiances were stable. Significantly, their conclusions have been
modified as these contingent influences have weakened.

The alleged dichotomy between the 'grand-theoretical' and
'atheoretical' approaches to media study represented by the two
opposed traditions of Marxism and liberalism is also a little misleading. The liberal tradition in mass communications research has
been characterized by a greater attention to empirical investigation. But it does not constitute an 'atheoretical' approach: on the
contrary, empirical communications research is based upon
theoretical models of society even if these are often unexamined
and unstated.

Indeed, the conventional characterization of liberal and Marxist
traditions in mass communications research as constituting two
opposed schools tends to obscure both the internal differences
within each of these traditions and the reciprocal influence which
each has exerted upon the other. The shift from a perception of the
media as a stupefying, totally subduing force expressed, for
example, by Marcuse (1972), to a more cautious assessment in

which dominant meaning systems are moulded and relayed by the media, are adapted by audiences and integrated into class-based or 'situated' meaning systems articulated by McCron (1976), is characteristic of a significant shift within Marxist research that has been influenced, in part at least, by empirical communications studies. This has been accompanied by increasing interest within the Marxist tradition in empirical survey-based research into audience adaptation of media-relayed ideologies, exemplified recently for instance by Hartman (1979) and Morley (1980). At the same time, Marxist critiques have contributed to a growing recognition within empirical communications research that more attention needs to be paid to the influence of the media on the ideological categories and frames of reference through which people understand the world. Evolving from the relatively limited conception of media 'agenda-setting' (the ranking of issues, in terms of their perceived importance) in election studies, a new interest has developed in the wider 'cognitive effects' of the media that reflects a nearly universal dissatisfaction amongst researchers with the narrow conceptualization of media influence afforded by the classic effects studies.

MEDIA INSTITUTIONS

Shifting paradigms of the power of the media have had important implications for enquiry into media organizations. Clearly, recognition of the power of the media raises questions as to how and by whom this power is wielded. Answers to these questions have been sought through the investigation and analysis of the structures and practices of media organizations.

Concern with the study of media institutions, their work practices and their relationship with their socio-political environment, emerged as a mainstream feature of mass communication research only in the last two decades. Inasmuch as the early history of this field of research has been characterized by a preoccupation with the study of the effects of the media on their audiences, this new concern constituted a major shift of interest in the field. The reasons for this shift have been varied: in part it was prompted by some disillusionment with the capacity of 'effects research' to fully explain the power of the media. At the same time it also reflected an awareness of the relative neglect of media institutions as objects of study. But the more important stimuli came from theoretical developments outside the narrow confines of media research. At least three different sources of influence should be identified here: first, developments in the sociological study of large scale, formal organizations yielded theories of organizational structure and behaviour, as well as analytic tools, which were seen to be applicable to the study of media organizations and of their work practices and production processes. Secondly, the increasing influence of Marxist theorizing, with its challenge to pluralist models of power in society, prompted a reappraisal of the role of the media in society, and focused attention on the structure and the organization of the media. The media came to be seen, in this perspective, not as an autonomous organizational system, but as a set of institutions closely linked to the dominant power structure through ownership, legal regulation, the values implicit in the professional ideologies in the media, and the structures and ideological consequences of prevailing modes of newsgathering. Thirdly, increasing attention to the study of the role of the mass media in politics indicated the importance of examining the relationship between media institutions and the political institutions of society, and the ways in which political communication emerges as a subtly composite product of the interaction between these two sets of institutions.

These different influences resulted inevitably, not in a unified set of interests, but in examinations of different aspects of the institutions of the media. Having come to the study of these institutions from different perspectives and under different influences, researchers working in this field have developed at least four different foci of study, reflecting their interests in different aspects of these institutions. The four strands of interest discernible in the literature can be grouped under the following headings:

1. Institutional structures and role relationships;
2. The political economy of media institutions;
3. Professional ideologies and work practices;
4. Interaction of media institutions with the socio-political environment.

In spite of their different foci, the basic issue which underlies all four strands of study is the process of the shaping of media messages. Researchers working in this area share the assumption that an examination of the political, organizational and professional factors which impinge on the process of message production could shed considerable light on the question of the power of the media. Because different factors are selected for examination within each strand of studies, together they complement each other. When pulled together they provide a comprehensive view of the ways in which media messages are produced and shaped, and offer insights into the ways in which different influences on this process are combined in a single composite product.

Institutional Structures and Role Relationships

This strand of studies draws its inspiration primarily from work on formal organizations. Media organizations are seen as possessing the same attributes which characterize other large-scale industrial organizations. These include: hierarchical structures; an internal division of labour and role differentiation; clearly specified and accepted institutional goals, translated into specific policies and organizational practices; clear lines of communication and accountability which generally follow and represent the hierarchical structure; modes of peer and of superior-subordinate relationships which regulate the interaction between incumbents in different roles. Most of the emphasis of this approach is thus placed on intra-organizational structures and behaviour, although some recognition is given to extra-organizational factors which impinge on the organization, such as 'shareholders', 'clients', 'sources' etc.

The various 'gatekeeper' studies, which examined the flow of news materials through the stages of the selection and editing process, as well as studies of formal and peer control in media organizations are the clearest representatives of this approach.

These studies explained the products of the media as outcomes of the interaction amongst different members of media organizations. But the interaction is not random, nor is power equally distributed amongst the occupants of different organizational positions. Rather, power and control are structured along the lines of the organizational hierarchy. But according to these studies, control in media organizations was not exerted directly or crudely. It depended on social control via informal channels more than on direct control via formal channels. The mechanisms of social control were embedded in the provision (or withholding) of organizational and professional rewards to members of the organization. They ensured the consistency of media outputs and, more important, they produced conformity by media personnel to the overall goals, policies and 'editorial lines' of the organizations for which they worked. Control, thus, is exerted from the organizational top downwards, both through formal and informal channels. It functions, however, not in a coercive fashion, but through the acceptance by occupants of the lower echelons of the legitimacy of the authority of those occupying the top positions in the organization. The conclusion which these studies reach then, is that the power of the media is located at the top of the hierarchy of media organizations.

The Political Economy of Media Institutions

Resembling the preceding strand in its focus of interest, but diametrically opposed to it, is the perspective which searches for the answers to the question of the power of the media in the analysis of their structures of ownership and control. Adopting a fundamentalist-Marxist approach, studies conducted in this vein have been based on the assumption that the dynamics of the 'culture-producing industries' can be understood primarily in terms of their economic determination (Murdock and Golding, 1977; Curran and Seaton, 1981). Thus, the contents of the media and the meanings carried by their messages are according to this view primarily determined by the economic base of the organizations in which they are produced. Commercial media organizations must cater to the needs of advertisers and produce audience-maximizing products (hence the heavy doses of sex-and-violence content) while those media institutions whose revenues are controlled by the dominant political institutions or by the state gravitate towards a middle ground, or towards the heartland of the prevailing consensus (Elliott, 1977).

The precise mechanisms and processes whereby ownership of the media or control of their economics are translated into controls over the message are, according to the proponents of this approach, rather complex and often problematic. The workings of these controls are not easy to demonstrate — or to examine empirically. The evidence quite often is circumstantial and is derived from the 'fit' between the ideology implicit in the message and the interests of those in control. The links between the economic determinants of the media on the one hand and the contents of the media on the other must, according to this analysis, be sought in the professional ideologies and the work practices of media professionals, since these are the only channel through which organizational controls can be brought to bear on the output of the media. Studies of the political economy of media organizations must therefore be closely related to, and supplemented by, analyses of the professional ideologies and practices found in these organizations.

Professional Ideologies and Work Practices

Studies of the beliefs, values and work procedures of media professionals have their theoretical roots in the sociology of the professions. Early studies of professionalism in the media raised the question whether those employed in the media deserved the accolade of being described as a profession. The search for an answer was based on examining whether media occupations possessed the attributes of professionalism, which have defined the classic professions, such as medicine and the law. One of the attributes of professionalism has been the development of a professional ethos or ideology which defined the beliefs and values of the profession, laid down guidelines for accepted and proper professional behaviour and served to legitimate the profession's sources of control and its insistence on the right to regulate and control itself and its members. Examinations of professionalism in media occupations, particularly in journalism, identified a strong claim for professional autonomy, derived from the democratic tenets of freedom of expression and 'the public's right to know'. In addition, media professional ideology developed a commitment to values such as objectivity, impartiality and fairness.

Academic discussions of the ideologies of media professionals reveal the diametrically opposed conclusions which might be reached when the same body of evidence is looked at from competing theoretical perspectives. A strict pluralist interpretation would accept that media professionals' claims to autonomy and their commitment to the principles of objectivity and impartiality indeed operate as guidelines for their work practices and as regulators of their professional conduct. It would, therefore, see ultimate control of the production process in the media as resting in the hands of the professionals responsible for it, in spite of the variety of pressures and influences to which they may be subjected. Some Marxist interpretations, on the other hand, challenge the validity of the claims by media personnel and dismiss the notions of objective and impartial work practices as, at best, limited and societal, masking the professionals' subservience to the dominant ideology. Control of the production process by media professionals is confined, in this view, to the production of messages whose meanings are primarily determined elsewhere within the dominant culture.

The polarity of these interpretations allows ample space for intermediate positions. Thus some proponents of the pluralist approach acknowledge the limitations on the autonomy of media professionals, and concede that the prevailing socio-political consensus defines the boundaries and constrains the space within which media professionals can be impartial. Similarly, some Marxist interpretations stress the relative autonomy of the mass media — both in the sphere of professional organization and of signification.

Some observers of these trends have suggested that as further empirical evidence is gathered, pluralist and Marxist analyses of professionalism in the media will continue to influence each other, and to discover some areas of agreement. Thus, for example, researchers from both camps now share the view that powerful institutions and groups in society do have privileged access to the media, because they are regarded by media professionals as more credible and trustworthy, and because they have the resources to process information and to offer the media their views in a usable and attractive form, tailor-made to fit the requirements of the media. They also agree that the commitment of media professionals to the canons of objectivity and impartiality, however genuinely held, also serves to protect them from criticism of their performance as professionals, by partly removing their responsibility for the output of the media and placing it on their 'sources'. And they accept the analysis that this professional ideology also provides a basis for the profession's self-respect, and lays claim for respect from the public. We may tentatively conclude from this evidence of common denominators in the thinking of both schools that this strand of studies offers possibilities of further mutual influence and agreement, without necessarily leading to a convergence of the different perspectives.

Interaction of Media Institutions with the Socio-political Environment

A fourth direction which some studies of media institutions have followed has an extra-organizational focus, and examines the relationship between the media and the institutional structures and interests in their environment. This area of interest is somewhat akin to the domain of the 'political economy' approach, inasmuch as both strands of research examine the relationship between media institutions and the political and economic institutions of society. However, the macro-level at which the 'political economy' analysis is conducted leaves some micro-aspects of this relationship unexplored. In particular, questions concerning the interaction between media professionals and their 'sources' in political and state institutions appear to be crucial for understanding the production process in the media. Media organizations exist in a symbiotic relationship with their environment, drawing on it not only for their economic sustenance but also for the 'raw materials' of which their contents are made. The generation and shaping of these materials through interaction between media professionals and their sources of information, inspiration and support outside their own institutions take place at the 'interface' between the media and these institutions (Gurevitch and Blumler, 1977). Contacts at the interface, therefore, constitute a critical part of the production process, and an important area for investigating the ways in which external inputs into the production process are managed.

Here, too, it is interesting to note the differences between the pluralist and the Marxist analysis of this relationship. Pluralist analyses tend to emphasize the *mutual dependence* between media professionals and the representatives or spokesmen for other institutions. They argue that while the media are dependent on the central institutions of society for their raw material, these institutions are at the same time dependent on the media to communicate their viewpoints to the public. The capacity of the media to 'deliver' large audiences provides them, according to this analysis, with at least a semi-independent power base *vis-à-vis* other power centres in society. The implication is not that an *equality* of power obtains between the media and other powerful institutions, but rather that some measure of independent power enters into the dealings of the media with these institutions. Marxist analyses, on the other hand, regard media institutions as at best 'relatively' and marginally autonomous. The media are regarded as being locked into the power structure, and consequently as acting largely in tandem with the dominant institutions in society. The media thus reproduce the viewpoints of dominant institutions not as one among a number of alternative perspectives, but as the central and 'obvious' or 'natural' perspective.

Thus, again, competing interpretations are provided by rival perspectives, although the evidence deployed by both is similar. Questions about the power of media institutions are, therefore, less likely to be resolved empirically, than to generate further theoretical and ideological argument.

CHANGING PERSPECTIVES OF SOCIAL THEORY

In the preceding discussion, we have indicated some past shifts in the focus of interest in media studies, from a primary concern with effects to a concern with consequences which the operations of the media have for the shaping of the message. In both these areas different questions have been raised and different conclusions emerge when different theoretical frameworks are deployed. Such is the case when attempts are made to describe and define, for example, the media's relationship to their contents. One of the key issues here revolves around the degree to which the media are regarded as passive transmitters or active interveners in the shaping of the message. Probably the most familiar of the 'passive transmitter' theories is the one which employs the metaphor of the mirror to describe the role of the media in society. The notion that the media are a 'mirror to reality' could be traced to different sources. On the one hand, it is a reflection of the neutral stance implied in the concepts of objectivity and impartiality embedded in the dominant professional ideology in the media. At the same time it is rooted in a pluralist view of society, in which the media are seen to provide a forum for contending social and political positions to parade their wares and vie for public support. The media are thus expected to *reflect* a multifaceted reality, as truthfully and objectively as possible, free from any bias, especially the biases of the professionals engaged in recording and reporting events in the outside world. This view is based on the notion that facts may be separated from opinions and hence, that while comment is free, facts are sacred. Ironically, in view of this obvious source for the 'mirror of reality' image of the media, metaphors of reflection have been almost equally influential within the Marxist tradition, if in an inverted form. Here images and definitions provided by the media have been seen to be distorted or 'false' accounts of an objective reality which are biased because they are moulded by ruling political and economic groups. Media journalism is made to appear, in Connell's phrase, as a 'kind of megaphone' by which ruling-class ideas are amplified and generalized across society (Connell, 1979).

Increasingly, however, the last decade has seen some basic shifts away from this view of the media. Essentially classical Marxism conceived of the media in terms of the metaphor of base and superstructure and little attention was paid to the specific autonomy of the mass media and to the area of its effectivity. The power of the media was simply the power of contemporary ruling classes utilizing modern communications systems to pursue their interests in line with the much quoted description of ruling-class ideology, taken from *The German Ideology*:

> The ideas of the ruling class are in every epoch the ruling ideas: i.e. the class which is the ruling *material* force in society is at the same time its ruling *intellectual* force. The class which has the means of material production at its disposal has control at the same time over the means of mental production, so that thereby, generally speaking, the ideas of those who lack the means of mental production are subject to it. (Marx and Engels, 1970, p.64)

The effects of the mass media, in early forms of Marxist analysis were not seen as discrete and measurable but were important in the dissemination of ideologies opposed to the interests of working-class groups and the production of false consciousness in such groups. Changes in this view of the media arose in part because of internal developments in Marxism but also because of the influence of other theoretical traditions.

One of the most important shifts generally in more recent mass communications research, be it Marxist or pluralist, has been the redirection of attention to the formal qualities of media discourse. The influence of semiology and linguistics on the direction of mass communications research has been important not simply as an addition to existing studies of political effects, ownership and control and the internal workings of media organizations, but also because of the re-thinking of existing and often recognizably unsatisfactory accounts of media power which it brought about. It is worth examining the impact of structuralism on Marxist accounts of the media because, in a sense, it is around this area of theoretical convergence and contradiction that it is possible to plot some of the distinctive changes which have characterized media studies in the last few years. [...]

Recent developments in Marxist theory, in Britain for example through the 'cultural' traditions of Williams and Hall and through the importations of European 'structuralisms' (the theories of Lévi-Strauss, Althusser, Lacan and Gramsci), have meant that many of the important questions about the mass media and about 'culture' more generally are now posed within Marxism rather than between Marxism and other accounts (Johnson, 1979). Within contemporary Marxist studies of the media there are a number of different reflections in the conceptualization of the power of the media. Marxist theorists vary in their accounts of the determination of the mass media and in their accounts of the nature and power of mass media ideologies. Structuralism has played an important part in producing and illuminating distinctive differences in Marxist views of the media. The theoretical differences within Marxism have been variously described as 'three problematics' (Johnson, 1979) or the 'two paradigms' (Hall, 1980). The three different approaches which we identify here not only characterize the power of the media in different and sometimes contradictory ways but also, between them, provide the type of arena for disagreement and debate, which in the past has been a consistent feature of the differences between the pluralist and the Marxist tradition.

Structuralist Studies of the Media

Structuralist accounts of the media have incorporated many diverse contributions, including Saussurean linguistics, the structural anthropology of Lévi-Strauss, the semiotics of Roland Barthes and Lacan's reworking of psychoanalysis. The central and substantive concern has been with the systems and processes of signification and representation, the key to which has been seen to lie in the analysis of 'texts'; films, photographs, television programmes, literary texts and so forth. Structuralist studies in this area have been closely linked with some crucial reformulations of Marxist theories of ideology which, although bitterly attacked by those who have wished to remain on more traditional Marxist terrain, have played a positive part in by-passing and moving beyond certain impasses within Marxist accounts of the media associated with the idea of ideology as a reflection of the economic basis of media industries and society.

Althusser's reformulation of a theory of ideology, for example, clearly indicated an important shift in Marxist thinking. Althusser's view of ideology as a representation of the imaginary relationship of individuals with the real conditions of their existence moved the notion of ideology away from 'ideas' which constituted a distorted reflection of reality. Althusser's work stressed that ideology expressed the themes and representations through which men relate to the real world. For Althusser ideology always had a material existence. It is inscribed within an apparatus and its practices. Ideology operates here to interpellate individuals as subjects, 'hailing' individuals through the apparently obvious and normal rituals of everyday living. Ideology, rather than being imposed from above and being, therefore, implicitly dispensable, is the medium through which all people experience the world. Although Althusser retains both the overall form of the base/ superstructure metaphor and the notion of determination in the last instance by the economic he also emphasizes the irreducibility and materiality of ideology. Determination in the last instance by the economic is a necessary but not sufficient explanation of the nature and existence of the ideological superstructures. The media within an Althusserian framework operate predominantly through ideology: they are ideological state apparatuses as opposed to more classically repressive state apparatuses. Thus the effectivity of the media lies not in an imposed false consciousness, nor in changing attitudes, but in the unconscious categories through which conditions are represented and experienced.

The combination of Althusserian Marxism and semiotics provided the initial impetus for sustained work on media texts. By largely suspending the traditional Marxist concern with the external social and economic determinants of ideology, in favour of a focus on the internal relations of signifying practices, such as film or television, structuralist media research formed the theoretical space within which to carry out detailed textual analysis [....]

Structuralist studies have, however, moved beyond an Althusserian problematic in a number of ways. First, through attempting to combine the analysis of media-signifying practices with psychoanalysis, there has been an attempt to theorize the relationship of texts to subjects. The subject, constituted in language, in Lacanian terminology, is not the unified subject of the Althusserian formulation and traditional Marxist view, but a contradictory, de-centred subject displaced across the range of discourses in which he or she participates. Although this is a relatively undeveloped area in Marxist studies of the media and in Marxism generally, this line of development indicates some crucial absences both in Marxism and in earlier structuralist studies. A second movement within structuralism has involved a rejection of the base/superstructure model for a focus on the articulation of autonomous discourses. Hirst, for example, suggests that the idea of the 'relative autonomy' of ideology and the linked notion of representation is inherently unstable in its juxtaposition of ideas (the relative autonomy of the ideological and the determination of ideology by the economic base) which are logically opposed to one another. In this view there can be no middle ground between the autonomy of ideological practices such as the mass media and straightforward economic determinism.

'Political Economy'

If the structuralist paradigm has directed attention at and conceived the power of the media as ideological, there have been consistent attempts to reverse the structuralist views of ideology in favour of a 'political economy' of the media. This well-established tradition in media research, which we have already touched on in relation to the analysis of media organizations, has heavily criticized structuralist accounts of the media for their over-concentration on ideological elements.

> Instead of starting from a concrete analysis of economic relations and the ways in which they structure both the processes and results of cultural production, they start by analysing the form and content of cultural artefacts and then working backwards to describe their economic base. The characteristic outcome is a top-heavy analysis in which an elaborate autonomy of cultural forms balances insecurely on a schematic account of economic forces shaping their production. (Murdock and Golding, 1977, p. 17)

Similarly, Garnham characterizes the post-Althusserian position 'popular within film studies' as 'an evacuation of the field of historical materialism' for determination in the last instance by the 'unconscious as theorized within an essentially idealist' problematic (Garnham, 1979, pp. 131-2).

Of course, 'idealism' and 'economism' are terms which are readily exchanged in arguments between Marxists, each protagonist invoking the name of the master and the spirit of historical materialism. The 'political economy' account of the media argues for the location of media power in the economic processes and structures of media production. In a return to the base/superstructure metaphor, 'political economists' conceive of ideology both as less important than, and determined by the economic base. Ideology is returned to the confines of 'false consciousness' and denied autonomous effectiveness. Also, since the fundamental nature of class struggle is grounded in economic antagonisms, the role of the media is that of concealing and misrepresenting these fundamental antagonisms. Ideology becomes the route through which struggle is obliterated rather than the site of struggle. Murdock and Golding contend that the pressure to maximize audiences and revenues produces a consistent tendency to avoid the 'unpopular and tendentious and draw instead on the values and assumptions which are most familiar and most widely legitimated' (Murdock and Golding, 1977, p. 37). The role of the media here is that of legitimation through the production of false consciousness, in the interests of a class which owns and controls the media. The main concern of this form of media research is, therefore, the increasing monopolization of the culture industry, through concentration and diversification.

Valuable though such research may be in summarizing the evidence on the ownership of the media, there are problems with this return to the classic model of base and superstructure. As Hall suggests, the advocates of political economy 'conceive the economic level as not only a "necessary" but a "sufficient" explanation of cultural and ideological effects' (Hall, 1980, p. 15). Yet the focus on general economic forms of capitalism dissipates distinctions between different media practices and allows little in the way of specific historical analysis beyond the bare bones of ownership. There is obviously some justification in the arguments by political economists that ideology has been given priority at the expense of serious consideration of the economic determinants of the mass media. Yet political economy, in its present state of development, would return us to the view of the media as a distorting mirror, a window on reality, which misrepresents reality. This view of the media, combined with a predilection for empirical analysis in the area of ownership and media organizations, frequently seems to give political economy more in common with pluralist accounts of the media than with other Marxist accounts.

'Culturalist' Studies of the Media

Culturalist studies of the media could be said to stand in an uneasy and ambiguous position in relation to the theoretical concerns of structuralism and political economy. On the one hand the indigenous British tradition of cultural studies, initiated through the work of Williams, Thompson and Hoggart has always been opposed to economic reductionism. This position has been effectively summarized by Hall:

> It (cultural studies) stands opposed to the residual and merely reflective role assigned to the 'cultural'. In its different ways it conceptualises culture as inter-woven with all social practices; and those practices, in turn, as a common form of human activity; sensuous human praxis, the activity through which men and women make history. It is opposed to the base superstructure way of formulating the relationship between ideal and material forces, especially, where the base is defined by the determination by the 'economic' in any simple sense. It prefers the wider formulation — the dialectic between social being and social consciousness ... It defines 'culture' as both the means and values which arise amongst distinctive social groups and classes, on the basis of their given historical conditions and relationships, through which they 'handle' and respond to the conditions of existence: *and* as the lived traditions and practices through which those 'understandings' are expressed and in which they are embodied. (Hall, 1980, p. 63)

On the other hand, cultural studies incorporate a stress on experience as the 'authenticating' position and a humanist emphasis on the creative, which is very much at odds with the structuralist position outlined earlier. Where structuralism had focused on the autonomy and articulation of media discourses, culturalist studies seek to place the media and other practices within a society conceived of as a complex expressive totality.

This view of media power is present in recent work which attempts a combining of culturalist and structuralist views. *Policing the Crisis* (Hall *et al.* 1978), for example, although theoretically eclectic in its bold, if not entirely successful, compound of a theory of hegemony derived from Gramsci, a sociology of 'moral panics', and an account of the social production of news, retains a view of society as an expressive totality. The crisis in hegemony which the authors identify has its basis in the decline of the British economy after the post-war boom but is resonated in the production of popular consent through the signification of a crisis in law and order in which the mass media play the key role. The media play their part in combination with other primary institutional definers (politicians, the police, the courts) in 'representing' this crisis. In the area of news, however, media definitions are 'secondary'. The media are not the primary definers of news events but their structured relationship to powerful primary definers has the effect of giving them a crucial role in reproducing the definitions of those who have privileged access to the media as 'accredited sources' (Hall *et al.* 1978). They are partners in the signification spiral through which distinct and local problems, such as youth cultures, student protests and industrial action, are pulled together as part of a crisis in law and order. The framework again emphasizes the expressive interconnections of the culturalist position. There are, of course, some unresolved problems in this approach, not least of which is the unevenness of the theoretical synthesis achieved. Hence, while the media are represented as a 'key terrain where consent is won or lost', they are also in other formulations conceived of as signifying a crisis which has already occurred, both in economic and political terms (Hall *et al.*, 1978). ...

The theoretical perspectives on the mass media contained within Marxism share a general agreement that the power of the media is *ideological* but there are distinct differences in the conceptualization of ideology, ranging from the focus on the internal articulation of the signifying systems of the media within structuralist analysis, through to the focus on the determination of ideology in 'political economy' perspectives and to a culturalist view of the media as a powerful shaper of public consciousness and popular consent. Although disagreements about the role of the media as an ideological force within these approaches may be similar in their intensity to earlier debates on the nature of the power of the media, these are in no sense simple repetitions of earlier debates. The theoretical ground has shifted. Increasingly, work on the media has focused on a related series of issues: the establishment of the autonomy, or relative autonomy of the media and its specific effectiveness; tracing the articulation between the media and other ideological practices; and attempting to rethink the complex unity which such practices constitute together. The way in which questions in these areas have been posed does vary in relation to different Marxist and other perspectives, but it is in relation to these issues within Marxism that intellectual work on the nature of media power proceeds at present.

REFERENCES

Althusser, L. (1969) *For Marx*, London, Allen Lane.
Althusser, L. (1971) *Lenin and Philosophy and Other Essays*, London, New Left Books.
Althusser, L. (1976) *Essays in Self Criticism*, London, New Left Books.
Becker, L., McCombs, M. and McLeod, J. (1975) 'The development of political cognitions', in Chaffee, S. (ed.) *Political Communication: issues and strategies for research*, Beverley Hills, Sage.
Berelson, B., Lazarsfeld, P. and McPhee, W. (1954) *Voting: a study of opinion formation in a presidential campaign*, Chicago, University of Chicago Press.
Blumler, J. (1977) 'The political effects of mass communication', in DE 353, *Mass Communication and Society*, Milton Keynes, Open University Press.
Centre for Contemporary Cultural Studies (1978) *On Ideology*, London, Hutchinson.
Chibnall, S. (1977) *Law-and-Order News*, London, Tavistock.
Clarke, J., Critcher, C. and Johnson, R. (1979) *Working-class Culture*, London, Hutchinson.
Cohen, S. (1973) *Folk Devils and Moral Panics*, St Albans, Paladin.
Connell, I. (1979) 'Television, news and the social contract', *Screen*, Spring 1979, 20(1).
Curran, J. and Seaton, J. (1981) *Power Without Responsibility*, London, Fontana.
Elliott, P. (1977) 'Media organisations and occupations: an overview', in Curran, J., Gurevitch, M. and Woollacott, J. *Mass Communication and Society*, London, Edward Arnold.
Garnham, N. (1979) 'Contribution to a political economy of mass communication', *Media, Culture and Society*, 1(2).
Gitlin, T. (1978) 'Media sociology: the dominant paradigm', *'Theory and Society*, 6.
Gurevitch, M. and Blumler, J. (1977) 'Linkages between the mass media and politics', in Curran, J., Gurevitch, M. and Woollacott, J. *Mass Communication and Society*, London, Edward Arnold.
Hall, S. (1974) 'Deviance, politics and the media', in McIntosh, M. and Rock, P. (eds) *Deviance and Social Control*, London, Tavistock.
Hall, S. Critcher, C., Jefferson T., Clarke, J. and Roberts, B. (1978) *Policing the Crisis*, London, Macmillan.
Hall, S. (1980) 'Cultural studies: two paradigms', *Media, Culture and Society*, (2).
Hartman, P. (1979) 'News and public perceptions of industrial relations', *Media, Culture and Society*, 1(3).
Hirst, P.Q. (1976) 'Althusser's theory of ideology', *Economy and Society*, 5.
Johnson, R. (1979) 'Culture and the historians', Three problematics: elements of a theory of working-class culture', in Clarke *et. al. Working-class Culture*, London, Hutchinson.

Katz, E. and Lazarsfeld, P. (1955) *Personal Influence*, Glencoe, Free Press.

Klapper, J. (1960) *The Effects of Mass Communication*, Glencoe, Free Press.

Lazarsfeld, P., Berelson, B. and Gaudet, H. (1948) *The People's Choice*, New York, Columbia University Press.

McCron, R. (1976) 'Changing perspectives in the study of mass media and socialisation', in Halloran, J. (ed.) *Mass Media and Socialisation*, International Association for Mass Communication Research.

Marcuse, H. (1972) *One-Dimensional Man*, London, Abacus.

Marx, K. and Engels, F. (1970) *The German Ideology*, London, Lawrence and Wishart.

Morley, D. (1980) *The 'Nationwide' Audience: structure and decoding*, London, British Film Institute.

Murdock, G. (1973) 'Political deviance: the press presentation of a militant mass demonstration', in Cohen, S. and Young, J. (eds) *The Manufacture of News*, London, Constable.

Murdock, G. and Golding, P. (1977) 'Capitalism, communication and class relations', in Curran, J., Gurevitch, M. and Woollacott, J. *Mass Communication and Society*, London, Edward Arnold.

Trenaman, J. and McQuail, D. (1961) *Television and the Political Image*, London, Methuen.

Whannel, G. (1979) 'Football, crowd behaviour and the press', *Media, Culture and Society*, 1 (4).

Westergaard, J. and Ressler, H. (1975) *Class in a Capitalist Society: a study of contemporary Britain*, London, Heinemann.

2.2 Processes of Media Effects

DENIS MCQUAIL*

INTRODUCTION

The entire study of mass communication is based on the premise that there are effects from the media, yet it seems to be the issue on which there is least certainty and least agreement. This apparent uncertainty is the more surprising since everyday experience provides countless examples of small effects. We dress for the weather under the influence of a weather forecast, buy something because of an advertisement, go to a film mentioned in a newspaper, react in countless ways to television, radio or music. We live in a world where political and governmental processes are based on the assumption that we know what is going on from press and television or radio. There are few people who can trace no piece of information or opinion to a source in the media and much money and effort is spent in directing media to achieve such effects.

And yet it is true that much doubt exists about the degree, incidence and kind of effects and our knowledge is insufficient to make any but the most simple prediction about the occurrence of an effect in a given case. Even where we can make a prediction, it is usually based on experience and rule of thumb rather than on a precise knowledge of *how* a given effect has occurred or might occur. It is the availability of such pragmatic knowledge, based on experience, that enables the media and their clients to continue without too much self-questioning. There are many good reasons for scientific uncertainty and even common sense and 'practical knowledge' waver when faced with some of the possibilities of media effect in the contested areas of morals, opinion and deviant behaviour which attract most public notice. On many such matters there can be no question of the media being a primary cause and we have no real 'explanation' of patterns of thought, culture and behaviour with deep social and historical roots. Furthermore, it

*Source: Denis McQuail, *Mass Communication Theory — an introduction* (Sage Publications, London, Beverly Hills, New Delhi, 1983), Reproduced by permission of Sage Publications Ltd.

makes little sense to speak of 'the media' as if they were one thing, rather than an enormously diverse set of messages, images and ideas, most of which do not originate with the media themselves but come from society and are sent 'back' to society. It is thus not at all easy to name a case where the media can plausibly be regarded as the sole or indispensable cause of a given social effect. Despite the difficulties and the inevitable inconclusiveness, the question of media effects has proved as fascinating and unavoidable for social scientists as it has for the media themselves and the general public. If we did not fundamentally believe them to have important long term consequences, we could not devote so much time to their study.

THE NATURAL HISTORY OF MEDIA EFFECT RESEARCH AND THEORY

The development of thinking about media effects may be said to have a 'natural history', since it has been strongly shaped by the circumstances of time and place and influenced by several environmental factors: the interests of governments and lawmakers; the needs of industry; the activities of pressure groups; the purposes of political and commercial propagandists; the current concern of public opinion; the fashions of social science. It is not surprising that no straight path of cumulative development of knowledge can easily be discerned. Even so, we can distinguish a number of stages in the history of the field which indicate some measure of ordered progression and of cumulation. In the first phase, which extends from the turn of the century until the late 1930s, the media, where they were well developed, were credited with considerable power to shape opinion and belief, change habits of life, actively mould behaviour more or less according to the will of those who could control the media and their content (Bauer and Bauer, 1960). Such views were not based on scientific investigation, but on observation of the enormous popularity of the press and the new media of film and radio and their intrusion into many aspects of everyday life. These beliefs were shared and reinforced by advertisers and by government propagandists during the first world war. In Europe the use of media by dictatorial states in the interwar years appeared to confirm what people were already inclined to believe — that the media could be immensely powerful. It was in the context of such beliefs, and with an inclination to accept them, that research of a scientific kind, using the survey and experiment and drawing largely on social psychology, was begun.

This second phase, opened perhaps by the series of Payne Fund studies in the United States in the early 1930s (Blumer, 1933; Blumer and Hauser, 1933; Peterson and Thurstone, 1933), continued until the early 1960s. Many separate studies of the effects on types of content, particular films or programmes in whole campaigns were carried out. The range was wide, but attention concentrated on the possibilities of using film and other media for active persuasion or information (e.g. Hovland *et al.*, 1949; Lazarsfeld *et al.*, 1944; Star and Hughes, 1950) or for assessing, with a view to prevention, harmful effects in respect of delinquency, prejudice, aggression, sexual stimulation. What now seems like the end of an era was marked by some expression of disillusion with this kind of research (e.g. Berelson, 1959) and by a new statement of conventional wisdom which assigned a more modest role to media in causing any of their chosen or unintended effects. The still influential summary of early research by Joseph Klapper, published in 1960, set the seal on this stage of research by concluding that 'mass communication does not ordinarily serve as a necessary and sufficient cause of audience effects, but rather functions through a nexus of mediating factors' (p. 8). It was not that media had been shown to be, under all conditions, without effects but that they operated within a pre-existing structure of social relationships and in a given social and cultural context. These social and cultural factors have a primary role in shaping choice, attention and response by audiences. This new sobriety of assessment was slow to modify opinion outside the social-scientific community. It was particularly hard to accept for those who made a living out of advertising and propaganda and for those in the media who valued the myth of their own great potency. However, hardly had the 'no effect' conclusion been disseminated by social scientists than it was subject to a re-examination by those who doubted that the whole story had been written and who were reluctant to dismiss the possibility that media might indeed have important social effects (e.g. Lang and Lang, 1959; Key, 1961; Blumler, 1964; Halloran, 1965).

The third phase of theory and research, which is still with us, is one in which effects and potential effects are still being sought, without rejecting the conclusions of early research, but according to revised conceptions of the social and media processes likely to be involved. Early investigation had relied very heavily on a model in which correlations were sought between degree of 'exposure' to given content and measured change of, or variation in, attitude, opinion or information. The renewal of effects research was marked by a shift of attention towards: long term change; cognition rather than attitude and affect; the part played by intervening variables of context, disposition and motivation; collective phenomena such as climates of opinion, structures of belief, ideologies, cultural patterns and even institutional forms. Much of [. . . what] follows is taken up with a review of these newer theories of effect and developments of the early model of direct effect. [. . .]

LEVELS AND KINDS OF EFFECT

In speaking of 'media effects' we are necessarily referring to what has already occurred as a direct consequence of mass communication, whether intended or not. The expression 'media power', on the other hand, refers to a potential for the future or a statement of probability about effects, under given conditions. 'Media effectiveness' is a statement about the *efficiency* of media in achieving a given aim and can apply to past, present or future, but always denoting intention. Such distinctions can often be important for precision of speaking about the media, although it is hard to keep to a consistent usage. Even more essential for research and theory is to observe the distinction between 'level' of occurrence, distinguishing at least the levels of: individual; group or organization; social institution; whole society; and culture. Each or all can be affected by mass communication, and effects at any one level always imply effects at other levels. It happens that most research has been carried out at the individual level, with consequent difficulties for drawing conclusions about effects at collective or higher levels, as recommended in the current research phase.

Perhaps the most confusing aspect of research on effects is the multiplicity and complexity of the phenomena involved. Broad distinctions are normally made between: effects which are cognitive (to do with knowledge and opinion); those which are affectual (relating to attitude and feelings); effects on behaviour. These distinctions have been treated in early research as distinct and following a logical order, from the first to the third.

In fact it is no longer found easy to sustain the distinction between the three concepts or to believe in the unique logic of that particular order of occurrence. To add to the complexity, much of our evidence comes from replies to questionnaires which are themselves individual acts of verbal behaviour from which we hope to reconstruct collective phenomena, often with an inextricable mixture of cognitive and affectual elements.

A final word should be said at this point about another kind of differentiation — that of type and direction of effect. In his summary, Klapper (1960) distinguished between 'conversion', 'minor change' and 'reinforcement' — respectively: change according to the intention of the communicator change in form or intensity; confirmation by the receiver of his or her own existing beliefs and opinions. This three-fold distinction needs to be widened to include other possibilities, especially at the supra-individual level, leading to the following:

media may: cause intended change (conversion)
       : cause unintended change
       : cause minor change (form or intensity)
       : facilitate change (intended or not)
       : reinforce what exists (no change)
       : prevent change

The categories are mainly self-explanatory, but the facilitation of change refers to the mediating role of media in wider processes of change in society. Both of the last two named imply no effect, but involve different conceptions of media working. Reinforcement is an observable consequence of selective attention by the receiver to content which is congruent with existing views, aided perhaps by a generous supply of such content. The second, 'preventing change', implies deliberate supply of one-sided or ideologically-shaped content in order to inhibit change in a conforming public. The 'no change' effect from the media, of which we have so much evidence, requires very close attention because of its long term consequences. It is indeed a somewhat misleading expression, since anything that alters the probability of opinion or belief distribution in the future is an intervention into social process and thus an effect.

PROCESSES OF MEDIA EFFECTS: A TYPOLOGY

In order to provide an outline of developments in theory and research we begin by interrelating two of the distinctions which have already been mentioned; between the intended and the un-intended and between short term and long term. This device was suggested by Golding (1980) to help distinguish different concepts of news and its effects: thus deliberate short term effects may be considered as 'bias', short term non-deliberate effects fall under the heading of 'unwitting bias'; deliberate and long term effects indicate 'policy'; while long term and non-deliberate effects of news are 'ideology'. Something of the same way of thinking helps us to map out, in terms of these two coordinates, the main kinds of effect process which have been dealt with in the literature. The result is given in Figure 1. [...]

These entries in Figure 1 are intended to stand for processes of

Figure 1: A typology of media effects

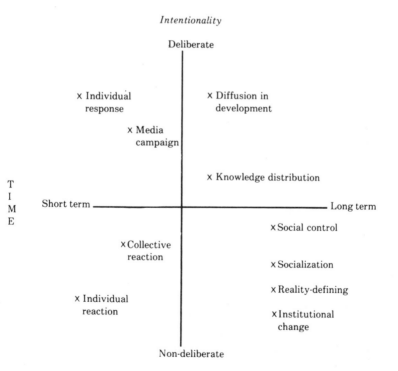

effect differentiated according to level, time-span, complexity and several other conditions. In some cases, the same basic model is sufficient to deal with more than one of the processes since the difference of specification is not fundamental. The discussion which follows deals with these effect processes in terms of a number of basic models, summarizing the current state of theory in relation to each.

INDIVIDUAL RESPONSE AND INDIVIDUAL REACTION

The S-R Model

These two entries in Figure 1 can be dealt with together since they share the same underlying model, that of stimulus response or conditioning. Its main features can be simply represented as follows:

Figure 1

Single message ⎯⎯⎯⎯►Individual receiver ⎯⎯⎯⎯►Reaction

It applies more or less equally to intended and to unintended effects although it does not show the difference between a response (implying some interaction with the receiver) and a reaction (which implies no choice or interaction on the part of the receiver). A more elaborated version of the basic process as it occurs in persuasion is indicated by McGuire (1973) in the form of six stages in sequence: presentation — attention — comprehension — yielding — retention — overt behaviour. This elaboration is sufficient to show why stimulus-response theory has had to be modified to take account of selective attention, interpretation, response and recall. The model, in whatever form, is highly pragmatic, predicting, *ceteris paribus*, the occurrence of a response (verbal or behavioural act) according to the presence or absence of an appropriate stimulus (message). It presumes a more or less direct effect in line with the intention of the initiator or built into the message.

In discussions of media effect, this has been sometimes referred to as the 'bullet' or 'hypodermic' theory, terms which far exaggerate the probability of effect and the vulnerability of the receiver to influence. Much has been written of the inadequacy of such theory and DeFleur (1970) has shown how this model has had to be modified in the light of growing experience and research. Firstly, account has had to be taken of individual differences, since even where expected reactions have been observed, their incidence varies according to difference of personality, attitude, intelligence, interest, etc. As DeFleur writes, 'media messages contain particular stimulus attributes that have differential interaction with personality characteristics of audience members' (1970, p. 122). This is especially relevant, given the complexity of most media messages compared with the kind of stimulus used in most psychological experiments. Secondly, it became clear that response varies systematically according to social categories within which the receiver can be placed, thus according to age, occupation, lifestyle, gender, religion, etc. Defleur notes, with some overstatement, that 'members of a particular category will select more or less the same communication content and will respond to it in roughly equal ways' (p. 123).

Mediating Conditions

[...]

The degree of motivation or involvement has been singled out as of particular importance in the influence process and in determining the sequence in which different kinds of effect occur (Krugman, 1965). According to Ray (1973) the normal 'effect hierarchy' as found, for instance, in the work of Hovland *et al.* (1949) is a process leading from cognition (the most common effect) to affective response (like or dislike, opinion, attitude) to 'conative' effect (behaviour or action). Ray argues, with some supporting evidence, that this model is only normal under conditions of high involvement (high interest and attention). With low involvement (common in many television viewing situations and especially with advertising) the sequence may be from cognition directly to behaviour, with affective adjustment occurring later to bring attitude into line with behaviour (reduction of dissonance, Festinger, 1957). In itself, this formulation casts doubt on the logic and design of many studies of persuasive communication which assume attitude as a correlate and indicator of behaviour.

. In any non-laboratory situation of mass communication, individual receivers will choose which stimulus to attend to or to avoid, will interpret its meaning variably and will react or not behaviourally, according to choice. This seriously undermines the validity of the conditioning model since the factors influencing selectivity are bound to be strongly related to the nature of the stimulus, working for or against the occurrence of an effect. Our attention should consequently be drawn away from the fact of experience of a stimulus and towards the mediating conditions described above, especially in their totality and mutual interaction. This approach to the effect problem is more or less what Klapper (1960, p. 5) recommends and describes as a 'phenomenistic' approach — one which sees 'media as influences working amid other influences in a total situation'.

Source-Receiver Relationships

There have been several attempts to develop theories which would account for different kinds of relationships at the individual level between sender (or message sent) and receiver, in addition to the thought already expressed that trust in — and respect for — the source can be conducive to effect. One framework is suggested by French and Raven (1953), indicating five alternative forms of communication relationship in which social power may be exercised by a sender and influence accepted by a receiver. The underlying proposition is that influence through communication is a form of exercise of power which depends on certain assets or properties of the agent of influence (communicator). The first two types of power asset are classified as 'reward' and 'coercion' respectively. The former depends on there being a gratification for the recipient from a message (enjoyment, for instance, or useful advice), the latter depends on some negative consequence of non-compliance (uncommon in mass communication). A third is described as 'referent' and describes the attraction or prestige of the sender, such that the receiver identifies with the person and is willingly influenced, for affective reason.

Fourthly, there is 'legitimate' power, according to which influence is accepted on the assumption that a sender has a right to be followed or obeyed. This is not very common in mass communication, but may occur where authoritative messages are transmitted from political sources or other relevant institutional leaders. Finally, there is 'expert power', which operates where superior knowledge is attributed to the source or sender and accepted by the receiver. This situation is not uncommon in the sphere of media information-giving and may apply to the influence of 'news' and the effects of experts used for comment or advice. This appears to be a further specification of the condition that messages from authoritative and respected sources are more effective than others, but these types of communicative power refer not just to a message or a source, but to a *relationship* between receiver and sender in which the former plays an active part and which gives rise to the necessary definitions of the situation. Such relationships are only established on a relatively long term basis and thus predate and survive any given instance of communication. One might add that more than one of these power sources is likely to be operative on any one given occasion. [...]

COLLECTIVE REACTION — PANIC AND DISORDER

Two main kinds of effect are here in question: widespread panic in response to alarming, incomplete or misleading information and the amplification or spreading of mob activity. The term 'contagion effect' describes one important aspect of both. The first kind of effect is instanced by the much-cited reaction to the Orson Welles radio broadcast of the 'War of the Worlds' in 1938 when simulated news bulletins reported a Martian invasion (Cantril *et al.*, 1940). The second is demonstrated by the hypothesized effect of the media in stimulating civil disorder in some American cities in the late 1960s. In the first case there remains uncertainty about the real scale and character of the 'panic', but there is little doubt that the conditions for panic reaction to news could well arise given the increase of civil terrorism and the risk of nuclear attack or, more likely, of nuclear accident. Rosengren (1976) reports an instance of alarm spread by media about the latter. We are dealing here with a special case of rumour (see Shibutani, 1966), but the media contribute the element of reaching large numbers of separate people at the same moment with the same item of news. The other related conditions for panic response are anxiety, fear and uncertainty. Beyond this, precipitating features of panic seem to be: incompleteness or inaccuracy of information leading to the urgent search for information, usually through personal channels, thus giving further currency to the original message.

Because of the threat to the established order, non-institutionalized and violent collective behaviour have been extensively studied and the media have been implicated in the search for causes of such behaviour. It has been suggested that the media, variously, can provoke a riot, create a culture of rioting, provide lessons on 'how to riot', spread a disturbance from place to place. The evidence for or against these propositions is very fragmentary although it seems to be acknowledged that personal contact plays a larger part than media in any on-going riot situation. There is some evidence, even so, that the media can contribute by simply signalling the occurrence and location of a riot event (Singer, 1970), by publicizing incidents which are themselves causes of riot behaviour, or by giving advance publicity to the likely occurrence of rioting. While the media have not been shown to be a primary or main cause of rioting (Kerner, 1968), they may influence the timing or form of riot behaviour. Spilerman (1976) lends some support to this and other hypotheses, on the basis of rather negative evidence. After failing, through extensive research, to find a satisfactory structural explanation of many urban riots in the United States (i.e. explanations in terms of community conditions) he concluded that television and its network news structure was primarily responsible, especially by creating a 'black solidarity that would transcend the boundaries of community'. In treating together the topics of panic and rioting, it is worth noting that the most canvassed solution to the dangers just signalled, the control or silencing of news (Paletz and Dunn, 1969) might entail a local panic through lack of interpretation of observable neighbourhood disturbances.

An interesting variant of this theme of media effect arises in the case of media reporting (or not) of terrorism. Much violence or disorder is either planned or threatened for political objectives, by persons seeking, however indirectly, to use the media, giving rise to a complex interaction between the two. In an analysis of this problem, Schmid and De Graaf (1982) argue that violence is often a means of access to mass communication and even a message in itself. The media are inevitably implicated in this process because of the weight they attach to reporting violence. An interesting example of possible effect is the sequence of aircraft hijacking crimes in 1971-72, which showed clear signs of being modelled on news reports. The same authors also show the existence of strong beliefs by police and a moderate belief by media personnel that live coverage of terrorist acts does encourage terrorism. More difficult to assess are the consequences of refusing such coverage. There has been other empirical support for the theory that press reports can 'trigger' individual but widespread actions of a pathological kind. Philips (1980) has reported empirical data showing that suicides, motor vehicle fatalities, commercial and non-commercial plane fatalities have a tendency to increase following press publicity for suicides or murder-suicides. On the basis of this evidence he argues for the need to develop a sociological theory of imitation and suggestion — the 'contagion' phenomenon mentioned at the outset. [...]

DISTRIBUTION OF KNOWLEDGE

As we enter a new 'area' of our media effect typology (Figure 1) we have to deal with a set of topics and concepts which are difficult to locate in terms of the two main variables of time and purposiveness. They are, however, united by a concern with cognition: each has to do with information or knowledge in the conventional sense. One has to do with a major media activity, news provision. Another deals with differential attention to issues and objects in the world: 'agenda-setting'. A third covers the general distribution of opinion and information in society, potentially leading to the 'knowledge gap' as an effect. These different kinds of media effect are included under the rather neutral label 'distribution of knowledge', since the media do actually distribute and the result can be expressed as a distribution in the statistical sense. Alternative terms such as 'control' or 'management' of information would imply a consciously directed effort. This would accord with some general theories of media but not with others and the evidence for 'manipulation' in this field is not conclusive (Weaver, 1981). The kinds of effect dealt with here cannot be accommodated within any of the models so far presented, but they can be considered as falling within the scope of the model which follows (Figure 2).

News Diffusion

The diffusion of news in the sense of its take-up and incorporation into what people 'know' is mainly a short or medium term matter, but with long term and often systematic consequences. It is also open to alternative formulations as to purpose: the media do intend in general that their audiences will learn about events but they do not try to teach people what is in the news. The question of how much people understand and remember from the news has only recently begun to receive much serious attention (e.g. Findahl and Höijer, 1981) and most research has so far concentrated on 'diffusion' — the spread of news as measured by the capacity to recall certain named events. Four main variables have been at the centre of interest here: the extent to which people know about a given event; the relative importance or salience of the event concerned; the volume of information about it which is transmitted; the extent to which knowledge of an event comes first from news or from personal contact. The possible interactions between these four are complex, but one model of the interaction is expressed by the J-curved relationship between the proportion who are aware of an event and the proportion who heard of the same event from an interpersonal source (Greenberg, 1964).

The J-shape expresses the following findings: when an event is known about by virtually everyone (such as the assassination of Kennedy in 1963), a very high proportion (over 50 per cent) will have been told by a personal contact (associated conditions here being high event salience and rapid diffusion). When events are known by decreasing proportions of the population, the percentage of personal contact origination falls and that of media source rises (associated conditions are lower salience and slower diffusion rates). However, there is a category of events which is known about ultimately by rather small proportions of a whole population. These comprise minorities for whom the event or topic is highly salient and the proportion of knowledge from personal contact rises again in relation to media sources, because personal contact networks are activated.

Theory about news diffusion is still held back by the bias of research towards a certain class of events, especially 'hard news', with a high measure of unexpectedness (Rosengren, 1973). In order to have a fuller picture of processes of news diffusion we would need more evidence about 'soft news' and more about routine or anticipated events. We are also limited by the difficulty of estimating event importance independently of amount of attention by the media, bearing in mind the differing interests of different sectors of the society. We can, nevertheless, reach a truistic conclusion that news learning does occur and much of it is a result of direct contact with media.

Agenda-setting

This term was coined by McCombs and Shaw (1972) to describe in more general terms a phenomenon that had long been noticed and studied in the context of election campaigns. An example would be a situation in which politicians seek to convince voters as to what, from their party standpoint, are the most important issues. This is an essential part of advocacy and attempts at opinion shaping. As a hypothesis, it seems to have escaped the general conclusion that persuasive campaigns have small or no effects. As Trenaman and McQuail (1961) pointed out: 'The evidence strongly suggests that people think *about* what they are told ... but at no level do they think what they are told'. The evidence at that time and since collected consists of data showing a correspondence between the order of importance given in the media to 'issues' and the order of significance attached to the same issues by the public and the politicians. This is the essence of the agenda-setting hypothesis, but such evidence is insufficient to show a causal connection between the various issue 'agendas'. For that we need a combination of party programmes, evidence of opinion change over time in a given section of the public, preferably with panel data, a content analysis showing media attention to different issues in the relevant period and some indication of relevant media use by the public concerned. Such data have rarely if ever been produced at the same time in support of the hypothesis of agenda-setting and the further one moves from the general notion that media direct attention and shape cognitions and towards precise cases, the more uncertain it becomes whether such an effect actually occurs.

Recent assessments (e.g. Kraus and Davis, 1976; Becker, 1982) tend to leave agenda-setting with the status of a plausible but unproven idea. The doubts stem not only from the strict methodological demands, but also from theoretical ambiguities. The hypothesis presupposes a process of influence from the priorities of political or other interest groups, to the news priorities of media, in which news values and audience interests play a strong part, and from there to the opinions of the public. There are certainly alternative models of this relationship, of which the main one would reverse the flow and state that underlying concerns of the public will shape both issue definition by political elites and those of the media, a process which is fundamental to political theory and to the logic of free media. It is likely that the media do contribute to a convergence of the three 'agendas' but that is a different matter from setting any particular one of them.

Knowledge Gaps

It has been a longstanding assumption that the press, and later broadcasting, have added so greatly to the flow of public information that they will have helped to modify differences of knowledge resulting from inequalities of education and social position. There is some evidence from political campaign studies to show that 'gap-closing' between social groups can occur in the short term (e.g. Blumler and McQuail, 1968). However, there has long been evidence of the reverse effect, showing that an attentive minority gains much more information than the rest, thus widening the gap between certain sectors of the public. Tichenor *et al.* (1970) wrote of the 'knowledge gap hypothesis' that it 'does not hold that lower status population segments remain completely uninformed (or that the poorer in knowledge get poorer in an absolute sense). Instead the proposition is that growth of knowledge is relatively greater among the higher status segments'. There is certainly a class bias in attention to 'information-rich' sources and strong correlations are persistently found between social class, attention to these sources and being able to answer information questions on political, social, or economic matters.

There are two aspects to the knowledge gap hypothesis, one concerning the general distribution of aggregate information in society between social classes, the other relating to specific subjects or topics on which some are better informed than others. As to the first 'gap', it is likely to have roots in fundamental social inequalities which the media alone cannot modify. As to the second, there are many possibilities for opening and closing gaps and it is likely that the media do close some and open others. A number of factors can be named as relevant to the direction of media effect. Donohue *et al.* (1975) put special emphasis on the fact that media do operate to close gaps on issues which are of wide concern to small communities, especially under conditions of conflict, which promote attention and learning. [...]

LONG-TERM CHANGE, PLANNED AND UNPLANNED: A MODEL

We enter an area where there is much theory and speculation but little firm evidence of confirmed relationships between the mass media and the phenomena under discussion: systems of values, beliefs, opinions, social attitudes. The reasons for this uncertainty are familiar: the matters are too large and complex to investigate reliably or fully; they involve broad historical and ideological judgements; the direction of influence between media and social phenomena can nearly always be two-way and is often unclear. Where evidence exists, it does little more than illustrate and add to the plausibility of a theory and it may be difficult ever to expect more. Nevertheless, we are dealing with one of the most interesting and important aspects of the working of mass communication and can at least try to develop an intelligent way of talking about what might happen.

Each of the effect processes to be discussed can occur in western liberal societies without intention being present in any significant, visible, or well-organized manner. Yet we should also recognize that these same processes are central to normative and ideological control, to the composition and maintenance of public belief systems, climates of opinion, value patterns and forms of collective awareness posited by many social theorists. It is hard to conceive of a society without such phenomena, however difficult they are to specify and quantify. Thus something of the sort is happening and the media are implicated. More important than determining the precise degree of intention is the question of direction. Do the processes favour conservation or change, and in either eventuality, in whose interest? Without some attention to this question, however provisional and beyond the scope of 'media theory' alone to answer, the discussion of these matters is rather pointless.

The model given in Figure 2 indicates some features common to various kinds of (variably) unplanned and long term effects which have been attributed to mass media, irrespective of purpose or direction.

Firstly, the outcomes of the various processes all posit some

Figure 2: Process model of social control and consciousness-forming

SOURCE →	CONTENT →	FIRST → EFFECT	SECOND → EFFECT	THIRD EFFECT
Unspecified multiple sources: media in general	Messages with stable and systematic structure	Available stock of knowledge, values, opinions, culture	Differential selection and response	Socialization Reality definition Distribution of knowledge Social control

pattern and consistency over time in media output. Secondly, they presuppose an initial cognitive effect, of the kind partly discussed. Thus the media provide materials for recognizing and interpreting reality beyond what is available from personal experience. What is termed in the model the 'second effect' refers to the encounter between what is made available and people in audiences. Here the set of 'filter conditions' signalled in the case of the campaign operate in much the same way, but especially those which have to do with social group and cultural environment. Beyond this, the processes listed as 'third effects' need to be discussed separately, having already paid attention to 'knowledge distribution'.

SOCIALIZATION

That the media play a part in the early socialization of children and the long term socialization of adults is widely accepted, although in the nature of the case it is almost impossible to prove. This is partly because it is such a long term process and partly because any effect from media interacts with other social background influences and variable modes of socialization within families (Hedinsson, 1981). Nevertheless, certain basic assumptions about the potential sociali- zation effects from media are present in policies for control of the media, decisions by media themselves and the norms and expect- ations which parents apply or hold in relation to the media use of their own children. An anomalous, but not contradictory, strand in the assumption of media as a socialization agent is the high atten- tion given to media as potentially de-socializing — challenging and disturbing the setting of values by parents, educators and other agents of social control.

The logic underlying the proposition that media do socialize or de-socialize involves a view of socialization as the teaching of established norms and values by way of symbolic reward and punishment for different kinds of behaviour. An alternative view is that it is a learning process whereby we all learn how to behave in certain situations and learn the expectations which go with a given role or status in society. Thus the media are continually offering pictures of life and models of behaviour in advance of actual experience. Studies of children's use of media (e.g. Wolfe and Fiske, 1949; Himmelweit *et al.*, 1958; Brown, 1976; Noble, 1975) confirm a tendency for children to find lessons about life and to connect these with their own experience. Studies of content also draw attention to the systematic presentation of images of social life which could strongly shape children's expectations and aspirations (e.g. DeFleur, 1964; Tuchmann *et al.*, 1978). These studies focus especially on occupation and sex roles, but there is also an extensive literature on political socialization (e.g. Dawson and Prewitt, 1969; Dennis, 1973).

McCron (1976) points to a basic divergence of theory, one strand emphasizing the consensual nature of social norms and values and another viewing media along with other agencies of social control as tending to impose on subordinate groups the values of dominant classes. The latter perspective emphasizes the central conflicts of society and the possibility of change through resistance and renegotiation of meanings. In this view, the media are neither 'pro-social' nor 'anti-social' but tending to favour the values of an established order and probably of a dominant class. In whichever formulation, the general theory that media have a socialization effect is hard to doubt, but only indirectly founded on empirical evidence, mainly concerning content and use.

REALITY DEFINING

That media offer many representations of the reality of society has already been argued and some aspects of the nature of this 'reality' have been discussed. One possible effect has been discussed under the heading of 'agenda-setting'. If the media can convey an impression about priorities and direct attention selectively amongst issues and problems they can do much more. The step from such a ranking process to wider opinion-forming is not a large one, and the theory of media socialization contains such an element. The basic process at work may be described by the general term 'defining the situation' and its importance rests on the familiar sociological dictum of W.I. Thomas that 'if men define situations as real they are real in their consequences'. [...]

Structuring Reality — Unwitting Bias

Common to much theory in this area is the view that media effects occur unwittingly, as a result of organizational tendencies, occupational practices and technical limitations. Thus Paletz and Entman (1981) attributed the propagation of a conservative myth mainly to 'pack journalism', the tendency of journalists to work together, arrive at a consensus, cover the same stories and use the same news sources. The notion that media 'structure reality' in a way directed by their own needs and interests has provided the theme for some research with strong implications for effect. An early example was the study by Lang and Lang (1953) of the television coverage of the return of McArthur from Korea after his recall, which showed how a relatively small scale and muted occasion was turned into something approaching a mass demonstration of welcome and support by the selective attention of cameras to points of most activity and interest. The reportage was seeking to reproduce from rather unsatisfactory materials what had been predicted as a major occasion. The reporting of a large demonstration in London against the Vietnam war in 1968 appeared to follow much the same pattern (Halloran *et al.*, 1970). The coverage was planned for an event predefined (largely by the media themselves) as potentially violent and dramatic and the actual coverage strained to match this pre-definition, despite the lack of suitable reality material.

The evidence from such tendencies of an effect on how people define reality is not always easy to find. However, in their study of how children came to define the 'problem' of race and immigration Hartman and Husband (1974) do seem to show that in this respect dominant media definitions are picked up, especially where personal experience is lacking. Another, different kind of effect is documented by Gitlin (1981) in relation to media coverage of the American student radical movement in the late 1960s. Here the media played a major part in shaping the image of this movement for the American public, partly according to their own needs (e.g. for action, stars, conflict) and caused the student movement itself to respond to this image and adapt and develop accordingly. Most of the effects referred to here derive from 'unwitting bias' in the media, but the potential to define reality has been exploited quite knowingly. The term 'pseudo-events' has been used to refer to a category of event more or less manufactured to gain attention or create a particular impression (Boorstin, 1961). The staging of pseudo-events is now a familiar device in many campaigns (McGinnis, 1969), but more significant is the possibility that a high percentage of media coverage of 'actuality' really consists of planned events which are intended to shape impressions in favour of one interest or another. Those most able to manipulate actuality coverage are those with most power, so the bias, if it exists, may be unwitting on the part of the media, but is certainly not so for those trying to shape their own 'image'.

Cultivation Theory

Among theories of long term media effect, some prominence should be given to the cultivation hypothesis of Gerbner (1973) which holds that television, amongst modern media, has acquired such a central place in daily life that it dominates our 'symbolic environment', substituting its message about reality for personal experience and other means of knowing about the world. The message of television is, in their view, distinctive and deviant from 'reality' on several key points, yet persistent exposure to it leads to its adoption as a consensual view of (American) society. The main evidence for the 'cultivation' theory comes from systematic content analysis of American television, carried out over several years and showing consistent distortions of reality in respect of family, work and roles, aging, death and dying, education, violence and crime. This content is said to provide lessons about what to expect from life and it is not a very encouraging message, especially for the poor, women and racial minorities.

The propagation and take-up of this 'television view' is essentially the 'cultivation' process referred to. The second main source of evidence in support of the theory comes from surveys of opinion and attitude which seem to support the view that higher exposure to television goes with the sort of world view found in the message of television. It is not easy to assess this part of the evidence and several authors have raised doubts about the interpretation of the television message (e.g. Newcomb, 1978) and about the causal relationship posited between television use data and survey data concerning values and opinions (Hughes, 1980; Hirsch, 1980 and 1981). There is also some reason to doubt whether the 'cultivation' effect would occur elsewhere than in the United States, partly because television content and use are often different and partly because the limited evidence from other countries is not yet very confirmatory. In relation to images of a violent society Wober (1978) finds no support from British data and Doob and McDonald (1979) report similarly from Canada. A longitudinal study of Swedish children (Hedinsson, 1981, p. 188) concluded, however, that evidence amounted to, 'if not a direct support, at least a non-refutation of Gerbner's theory'. However plausible the theory, it is almost impossible to deal convincingly with the complexity of posited relationships between symbolic structures, audience behaviour and audience views, given the many intervening and powerful social background factors.

A remaining point of uncertainty about the cultivation hypothesis has to do with the origin and direction of the effect. According to its authors, 'television is a cultural arm of the established industrial order and as such serves primarily to maintain, stabilize and reinforce rather than to alter, threaten or weaken conventional beliefs and behaviours' (Gross, 1977, p. 180). The statement brings the cultivation effect very close to that posited by the critical theorists of the Frankfurt School and not far from later Marxist analyses. While Gerbner has paid some attention to the institutional origins of content (e.g. Gerbner, 1969) and recognized the importance of 'institutional process analysis' (Gerbner, 1977), this work has remained largely undone and the two bodies of theory remain some distance apart. One seems over-'positivistic' and the other over-theoretical and one-sided. Perhaps cultivation theory really belongs towards the end of the section that follows.

SOCIAL CONTROL AND CONSCIOUSNESS-FORMING

A number of media effects have already been discussed which might belong under this heading, since the idea of socialization includes an element of social control and some, at least, of the reality-defining tendencies that have been discussed seem to work in favour of an established social order. The effects still to be considered are thus not so different in kind, nor are they always easy to assess in terms of their purposefulness: to know, that is, who is doing what to whom with what objective. There are varying positions to be taken up. One is the view that the media act generally, but non-purposively, to support the values dominant in a community or nation, through a mixture of personal and institutional choice, external pressure and anticipation of what a large and heterogeneous audience expects and wants. Another view is that the media are essentially conservative because of a combination of market forces, operational requirements and established work practices. A third view holds that the media are actively engaged on behalf of a ruling (and often media-owning) class or bourgeois state in suppressing or diverting opposition and constraining political and social deviance. This is essentially the Marxist view of media as an instrument for the legitimation of capitalism (Miliband, 1969; Westergaard, 1977).

These alternative theories vary in their precision, in their specification of the mechanisms by which control is exercised and in the attribution of conscious power. However, they tend to draw on much the same evidence, most of it relating to systematic tendencies in content with very little directly about effects. A good deal of the evidence concerning content has already been discussed. Most relevant here are those many assertions, based on systematic content analysis, to the effect that the content of media with the largest publics, both in news or actuality and in fiction, is supportive of social norms and conventions (an aspect of socialization and of 'cultivation'). It has also been shown to be distinctly lacking in offering fundamental challenges to the national state or its established institutions and likely to treat such challenges offered by others in a discouraging way. The argument that mass media tend towards the confirmation of what exists is thus based on evidence both about what is present and about what is missing. The former includes the rewarding (in fiction) of 'conformist' or patriotic behaviour, the high attention and privileged (often direct) access given to established elites and points of view, the observably negative or unequal treatment of non-institutional or deviant behaviour, the devotion of media to a national or community consensus, the tendency to show problems as soluble within the established 'rules' of society and culture.

The evidence of media omission is, in the nature of things, harder to assemble but the search for it was begun by Warren Breed (1958) who, on the basis of what he called a 'reverse content analysis' (comparing press content with sociological community studies), concluded that American newspapers consistently omitted news which would offend the values of religion, family, community, business and patriotism. He concluded that '"power" and "class" are protected by media performance'. Comparative content analyses of news in one or several countries have added evidence of systematic omission in the attention given to certain issues and parts of the world. Detailed studies of news content such as those by the Glasgow Media Group (1977; 1980) or by Golding and Elliott (1979) have documented some significant patterns of omission. More importantly, perhaps, they have shown a pattern of selection which is so consistent and predictable that a corresponding pattern of rejection can be inferred.

Golding (1980) wrote of the 'missing dimensions' of power and social process in the television news of more than one country. The absence of power is attributed to: the imbalance of media attention over the world; the concentration on individuals rather than corporate entities; the separation of policy options from the underlying relations of political and economic power. Social process is lost by concentration on short term, fleeting events rather than deeper, long term changes. In Golding's view, the outcome is a kind of ideology of showing the world as unchanging and unchangeable and one likely to preclude 'the development of views which might question the prevailing distribution of power and control' (p. 80). The explanation also lies in the complex demands of news production and its place within the media industry. Herbert Gans (1980) reached not dissimilar conclusions about the generally conservative tendencies of the main American news media and is inclined to attribute this to organizational and occupational demands rather than conspiracy. He also lays stress on the reflection in news of the characteristic outlook and social milieu of those who make the news and tend, in the absence of better information, to assume an audience much the same as themselves.

The view that media are systematically used for purposes of legitimation of the state in capitalist society has often to rely heavily on evidence of what is missing in the media. Stuart Hall (1977, p. 336), drawing on the work of both Poulantzas and Althusser, names those ideological processes in the media as: 'masking and displacing'; 'fragmentation'; 'imposition of imaginary unity or coherence'. The first is the failure to admit or report the facts of class exploitation and conflict. The second refers to the tendency to deny or ignore common working class interests and to emphasize the plurality, disconnection and individuality of social life. The third refers to the 'taking for granted' of a national consensus, common to all classes and people of goodwill and common sense. There is some evidence for the latter two of these processes and it would probably not be difficult to argue that the main mass media of western society are no more inclined to go critically into the fundamentals of capitalism than are the media of eastern Europe to question the justice underlying their forms of economy and society. Hall's own contribution to the theory has been to suggest that a view supportive of the capitalist order is 'encoded' or built into many media messages, so as to indicate a 'preferred reading' or interpretation which is not easy to resist.

An additional element in the theory of conservative ideological formation by the media lies in the observation that the media define certain kinds of behaviours and groups as both deviant from, and dangerous to, society. Apart from the obviously criminal, these include groups such as teenage gangs, drugtakers, 'football hooligans', and some sexual deviants. It has been argued that attention by the media often demonstrably exaggerates the real danger and significance of such groups and their activities (Cohen and Young, 1973) and tends to the creation of 'moral panics' (Cohen, 1972). The effect is to provide society with scapegoats and objects of indignation, to divert attention from real evils with causes lying in the institutions of society and to rally support for the agencies of law and order. It has also been suggested that the media tend to widen the scope of their disapprobation to associate together quite different kinds of behaviour threatening to society. In the pattern of coverage, the activities of some kinds of terrorism, rioting or political violence help to provide a symbolic bridge between the clearly delinquent and those engaged in non-institutionalized forms of political behaviour like demonstrations or the spreading of strikes for political reasons. In some kinds of popular press treatment, according to Hall *et al.* (1978), it is hard to distinguish the criminal outsider from the political 'extremist'. Within the category of anti-social elements those who rely on welfare may also come to be included under the label of 'welfare scroungers' (Golding and Middleton, 1982) and the same can happen to immigrants. The process has been called 'blaming the victim' and is a familiar feature of collective opinion forming to which the media can obviously make a contribution.

It is almost impossible to give any useful assessment of the degree to which the effects posited by this body of theory and research actually occur. Firstly, the evidence of content is incomplete, relating only to some media in some places. Secondly, it has not really been demonstrated that the media in any western country offer a very consistent ideology, even if there are significant elements of consistency both of direction and of ideology. Thirdly, we have to accept that many of the processes, especially those of selective use and perception, by which people resist or ignore propaganda apply here as well as in campaign situations, even if it is less easy to resist what is not specifically offered as

propaganda and not easy to opt for what is not there. The historical evidence since the later 1960s, when theories of powerful mass
media began to be revived, seems, nevertheless, to support the
contention that something, if not the media, has been working to
maintain the stability of capitalist societies in the face of economic
crises which might have been expected to cause disaffection and
delegitimation. The elements of society which seem inclined to disaffection are not the 'masses' or the 'workers' but the intellectuals
and other marginal categories who do not rely on the mass media
for their world view. It remains equally likely, however, that fundamental forces in society helping to maintain the existing order are
reflected and expressed in the media in response to a deeply
conservative public opinion.

Nevertheless, it would be difficult to argue that the media are,
on balance, a major force for social change, or to deny that a large
part of what is most attended to is generally conformist in
tendency. It is also difficult to avoid the conclusion that, insofar as
media capture attention, occupy time and disseminate images of
reality and of potential alternatives, they fail to provide favourable
conditions for the formation of a consciousness and identity
amongst the less advantaged sectors of society and for the organization of opposition, both of which have been found necessary in
the past for radical social reform. It should not be lost sight of that
the media are mainly owned and controlled either by (often large)
business interests or (however indirectly) the state — thus the
interests which do have political and economic power. There is a
good deal of *prima facie* evidence that such controlling power over
the media is valued beyond its immediate economic yield. In any
case, it is no secret that most media most of the time do not see it
as their task to promote fundamental change in the social system.
They work within the arrangements that exist, often sharing the
consensual goal of gradual social improvement. Gans's judgement
(1980, p. 68) that 'news is not so much conservative or liberal as it
is reformist' probably applies very widely. The media are committed by their own ideology to serving as a carrier for messages (e.g.
about scandals, crises, social ills) which could be an impulse to
change, even of a quite fundamental kind. They probably do
stimulate much activity, agitation and anxiety which disturb the
existing order, within the limits of systems which have some capacity for generating change. Ultimately, the questions involved turn
on how dynamic societies are and on the division of social power

within them and these take us well beyond the scope of media-centred theory. [...]

REFERENCES

Bauer, R.A. and A. Bauer (1960), 'America, Mass Society and Mass Media', *Journal of Social Issues* 10(3): 3-66.

Becker, L. (1982), 'The Mass Media and Citizen Assessment of Issue Importance: A Reflection on Agenda-Setting Research', in Whitney *et al.*, 1982: 521-536.

Berelson, B. (1959), 'The State of Communication Research', *Public Opinion Quarterly*, 23(1): 1-6.

Blumer, H. (1933), *Movies and Conduct*, New York, Macmillan.

Blumer, H. and P.M. Hauser (1933), *Movies, Delinquency and Crime*, New York, Macmillan.

Blumler, J.G. (1964), 'British Television: The Outline of a Research Strategy', *British Journal of Sociology*, 15(3): 223-233.

Blumler, J.G. and D. McQuail (1968), *Television in Politics: Its Uses and Influence*, London, Faber.

Boorstin, D. (1961), *The Image: A Guide to Pseudo Events in America*, New York, Athenaeum.

Breed, W. (1958), 'Mass Communication and Socio-Cultural Integration', *Social Forces*, 37: 109-116.

Brown, J.R. (ed.) (1976), *Children and Television*, London, Collier-Macmillan.

Cantril, H., H. Gaudet and H. Hertzog (1940), *The Invasion from Mars*, Princeton, Princeton University Press.

Cohen, S. (1972), *Folk Devils and Moral Panics*, London, McGibbon and Kee.

Cohen, S. and J. Young (eds.) (1973), *The Manufacture of News*, London, Constable.

Curran, J., M. Gurevitch and J. Woollacott (eds.) (1977), *Mass Communication and Society*, London, Arnold.

Dawson, R.E. and K. Prewitt (1969), *Political Socialization*, Boston, Little Brown.

DeFleur, M.L. (1964), 'Occupational Roles as Portrayed on Television', *Public Opinion Quarterly*, 28: 57-74.

DeFleur, M.L. (1970), *Theories of Mass Communication* (2nd ed.), New York, David McKay.

Dennis, J. (ed.) (1973), *Socialization to Politics*, New York, Wiley.

Donohue, G.A., P.J. Tichenor and C.N. Olien (1975), 'Mass Media and the Knowledge Gap', *Communication Research*, 2: 3-23.

Doob, A. and G.E. McDonald (1979). 'Television Viewing and the Fear of Victimization: Is the Relationship Causal?', *Journal of Social Psychology and Personality*, 37: 170-179. Reprinted in Wilhoit and de Bock, 1980: 479-488.

Festinger, L.A. (1957), *A Theory of Cognitive Dissonance*, New York, Row Peterson.

Findahl, O. and B. Höijer (1981), 'Studies of News from the Perspective of Human Comprehension', in Wilhoit and de Bock, 1981: 393-403.

French, J.R.P. and B.H. Raven (1953), 'The Bases of Social Power', in D. Cartwright and A. Zander (eds.), *Group Dynamics*, London, Tavistock.

Gans, H.J. (1980), *Deciding What's News*, New York, Vintage Books.

Gerbner, G. (1969), 'Institutional Pressures on Mass Communicators', in Halmos, 1969: 205-248.

Gerbner, G. (1973), 'Cultural Indicators — The Third Voice', in G. Gerbner, L. Gross and W. Melody (eds.), *Communications Technology and Social Policy*, New York, Wiley: 553-573.

106   DENIS McQUAIL

Gerbner, G. (1977), 'Comparative Cultural Indicators', in G. Gerbner (ed.), *Mass Media Policies in Changing Cultures*, New York, Wiley.

Gitlin, T. (1981), *The Whole World is Watching — Mass Media in the Making and Unmaking of the New Left*, Berkeley, University of California Press.

Glasgow Media Group (1980), *More Bad News*, London, Routledge and Kegan Paul.

Golding, P. (1980), 'The Missing Dimensions — News Media and the Management of Social Change', in Katz and Szecskö, 1980: 63-81.

Golding, P. and P. Elliott (1979), *Making the News*, London, Longman.

Golding, P. and S. Middleton (1982), *Images of Welfare — Press and Public Attitudes to Poverty*, Oxford, Basil Blackwell and Martin Robertson.

Greenberg, B.S. (1964), 'Person-to-Person Communication in the Diffusion of a News Event', *Journalism Quarterly*, 41: 489-494.

Gross, L.P. (1977), 'Television as a Trojan Horse', *School Media Quarterly*, Spring: 175-180.

Hall, S. (1977), 'Culture, the Media and the Ideological Effect', in Curran *et al.*, 1977: 315-348.

Hall, S.J. Clarke, C. Critcher, T. Jefferson and B. Roberts (1978), *Policing the Crisis*, London, Macmillan.

Halloran, J.D. (1965), *The Effects of Mass Communication*, Leicester, Leicester University Press.

Halloran, J.D., P. Elliott and G. Murdoch (1970), *Communications and Demonstrations*, Harmondsworth, Penguin.

Hartman, P. and C. Husband (1974), *Racism and the Mass Media*, London, Davis Poynter.

Hedinsson, E. (1981), *Television, Family and Society — The Social Origins and Effects of Adolescent TV Use*, Stockholm, Almquist and Wiksel.

Himmelweit, H.T., P. Vince and A.N. Oppenheim (1958), *Television and the Child*, London, Oxford University Press.

Hirsch, P.M. (1980), 'The "Scary World" of the Non-viewer and Other Anomalies — A Reanalysis of Gerbner *et al.*'s Findings in Cultivation Analysis', Part I, *Communication Research*, 7(4): 403-456.

Hirsch, P.M. (1981), 'On Not Learning from One's Mistakes', Part II, *Communication Research* 8(1): 3-38.

Hovland, C.I., A.A. Lumsdaine and F.D. Sheffield (1949), *Experiments in Mass Communication*, Princeton, Princeton University Press.

Hughes, M. (1980), 'The Fruits of Cultivation Analysis: A Re-examination of Some Effects of TV Viewing', *Public Opinion Quarterly*, 44(3): 287-302.

Kerner, O. *et al.* (1968), *Report on the National Advisory Committee on Civil Disorders*, Washington, DC, GPO.

Key, V.O. (1961), *Public Opinion and American Democracy*, New York, Alfred Knopf.

Klapper, J. (1960), *The Effects of Mass Communication*, New York, Free Press.

Kraus, S. and D.K. Davis (1976), *The Effects of Mass Communication on Political Behavior*, University Park, Pennsylvania State University Press.

Krugman, H.E. (1965), 'The Impact of Television Advertising: Learning without Involvement', *Public Opinion Quarterly*, 29: 349-356.

Lang, K. and G.E. Lang (1953), 'The Unique Perspective of Television and its Effect', *American Sociological Review*, 18(1): 103-112.

Lang, K. and G.E. Lang (1959), 'The Mass Media and Voting', in E.J. Burdick and A.J. Brodbeck (eds.), *American Voting Behavior*, New York, Free Press.

Lazarsfeld, P.F., B. Berelson and H. Gaudet (1944), *The People's Choice*, New York, Duell, Sloan and Pearce.

McCombs, M.E. and D.L. Shaw (1972), 'The Agenda-setting Function of the Press', *Public Opinion Quarterly*, 36: 176-187.

McCron, R. (1976), 'Changing Perspectives in the Study of Mass Media and Socialization', in J. Halloran (ed.), *Mass Media and Socialization*, Leicester, IAMCR: 13-44.

McGinnis, J. (1969), *The Selling of the President*, New York, Trident Press.

McGranahan, D.V. and L. Wayne (1948), 'German and American Traits Reflected in Popular Drama', *Human Relations*, 1(4): 429-455.

McGuire, W.J. (1973), 'Persuasion, Resistance and Attitude Change', in I. de Sola Pool *et al.* (eds.), *Handbook of Communication*, Chicago, Rand McNally: 216-252.

Miliband, R. (1969), *The State in Capitalist Society*, London, Weidenfeld and Nicolson.

Newcomb, H. (1978), 'Assessing the Violence Profile of Gerbner and Gross: A Humanistic Critique and Suggestion', *Communication Research*, 5(3): 264-282.

Noble, G. (1975), *Children in Front of the Small Screen*, London, Constable.

Paletz, D.L., and R. Dunn (1969), 'Press Coverage of Civil Disorders: A Case-study of Winston-Salem', *Public Opinion Quarterly*, 33: 328-345.

Paletz, D.L., and R. Entman (1981), *Media, Power, Politics*, New York, Free Press.

Peterson, R.C. and L.L. Thurstone (1933), *Motion Pictures and Social Attitudes*, New York, Macmillan.

Philips, D.P. (1980), 'Airplane Accidents, Murder and the Mass Media', *Social Forces*, 58(4): 1001-1024.

Ray, M.L. (1973), 'Marketing Communication and the Hierarchy-of-Effects', in P. Clarke (ed.), *New Models for Communication Research*, Beverly Hills and London, Sage Publications: 147-176.

Rosengren, K.-E. (1973), 'News Diffusion: An Overview', *Journalism Quarterly*, 50: 83-91.

Rosengren, K.-E. (1976), 'The Barseback "Panic" ', Lund University (mimeo).

Schmid, A.P. and J. De Graaf (1982), *Violence as Communication*, Beverly Hills and London, Sage Publications.

Shibutani, T. (1966), *Improvised News*, New York, Bobbs-Merrill.

Singer, B.D. (1970), 'Mass Media and Communication Processes in the Detroit Riots of 1967', *Public Opinion Quarterly*, 34: 236-245.

Spilerman, S. (1976), 'Structural Characteristics and Severity of Racial Disorders', *American Sociological Review*, 41: 771-792.

Star, S.A. and H.M. Hughes (1950), 'Report on an Education Campaign: The Cincinatti Plan for the UN', *American Journal of Sociology*, 55:389-400.

Tichenor, P.J., G.A. Donohue and C.N. Olien (1970), 'Mass Media and the Differential Growth in Knowledge'. *Public Opinion Quarterly*, 34: 158-170.

Trenaman, J.S.M. and D. McQuail (1961), *Television and the Political Image*, London, Methuen.

Tuchman, G. (1978), *Making News: A Study in the Construction of Reality*, New York, Free Press.

Weaver, D.H. (1981), 'Media Agenda-setting and Media Manipulation', *Massacommunicatie*, 9(5): 213-229. Reprinted in Whitney *et al.* 1982: 537-554.

Westergaard, J. (1977), 'Power, Class and the Media', in Curran et al., 1977: 95-115.

Wober, J.M. (1978), 'Televised Violence and Paranoid Perception: The View from Gt. Britain', *Public Opinion Quarterly*, 42: 315-321.

Wolfe, K.M. and M. Fiske (1949), 'Why they Read Comics', in Lazarsfeld and Stanton, 1949: 3-50.

2.3 Down to Cases

THE GLASGOW UNIVERSITY MEDIA GROUP*

'AND NOW, RUBBISH'[1]

In the confused debate over the news, one of the commonest charges made against the media is that of 'superficiality' in industrial coverage. Dispute reporting, it is said, concentrates on the 'effects' of union action to the neglect of its underlying causes. The result is that in the absence of essential background information the activities of strikers, which might otherwise appear quite rational and reasonable, are presented to the public as sensational. Underlying such complaints is perhaps a fear of 'trial by television', and the trial analogy is not inapt, especially since such media 'trials' tend to ignore the motives of those publicly accused.

The characteristic inferential framework, used by television journalists in reporting disputes, is to utilise limited aspects of a dispute to create a dominant view. A strike has its roots in grievances or demands but it also has human protagonists and visible results and ramifications. All of this, as in the events in Glasgow, is 'news'. Michael Edwards, industrial correspondent of the *Daily Mail*, remarked in a television discussion: '... the background is a fairly static thing, it doesn't change, the background is always the same ... after that the situation is a moving situation and people want to know what's going on.'

The balancing of these elements is an essential professional task of the journalist. This is not just for the sake of impartiality but also to achieve a literate, easily comprehensible and interesting level of reporting.

'The Glasgow rubbish' or the 'Glasgow rubbish strike'[2] was one of the biggest stories featured in the bulletins during the recording period, covered in 102 bulletins over 3 months from 11 January to 14 April 1975.[3] As regards the coverage given, it could be seen as one of the most important television news stories of the first half of

---

*Source: The Glasgow University Media Group, 'Down to Cases', first part of chapter 7 of *Bad News* (Routledge & Kegan Paul, London, 1976), pp. 244-300.

the year. The Heavy Goods Vehicle (HGV) licence holders, working for Glasgow Corporation (over half of them drivers of dustcarts), went on strike. The most public result of this action was that the uncollected refuse was eventually partially cleared by the army. This was the first time in some 25 years that troops had been used in an industrial dispute.

The coverage began with the strike decision and continued periodically as new angles were highlighed until the drivers returned to work on 14 April. The dispute was treated by the Glasgow Corporation and the government as a matter of extreme importance. Yet despite the extensive national television coverage of the issues raised, the actual case of the men on strike was neglected.

The weak position of unofficial strikers in the 'hierarchy of access' to the media contributed to the television news definition of the issues raised by the dispute. Thus the framework used concentrated on issues other than the conflict between Glasgow Corporation and their employees. The focus of the coverage became from the outset a 'health hazard'. Whilst it is in no way suggested that a serious problem did not come to exist as a result of many thousands of tons of refuse lying untreated on open dumps, it seems reasonable to question the manner in which this aspect was established as the initial focus of the coverage, even before the dumps had been created.

The threatened health hazard became the dominant theme of all three news services, being established on the very first day of coverage (11 January). Each of the six bulletins that reported the decision to strike on this day (a Saturday, the following Monday being the first day on which the drivers failed to turn out for work), used library film of piles of uncollected refuse from a strike of some four weeks' duration in the autumn of the previous year. The early evening bulletin on BBC1 included a film report from Glasgow in which Bill Hamilton *voiced over* film of men leaving a meeting with some details of the strike decision. Continuing over *library* film of last October's rubbish piles, he reported: 'It was only last October when rubbish piled up in the city streets for four weeks since Glasgow's dustmen [sic] staged their last strike for higher wages.' All other BBC bulletins on this day used only various cuts of the library footage of autumn's refuse, and in each case the newscaster said that 'the decision to stop work from Monday was bringing fears of a repeat of the situation last October when rubbish piled up in the streets causing a health hazard'. This was seven weeks before 4 March, when Glasgow Corporation themselves announced that a health hazard existed.

ITN bulletins, whilst using only their own library film of the October dispute, were not so explicit in suggesting the hazard. 'The strike means that Glasgow faces another pile-up of rubbish on the pavements as happened for four weeks last autumn' (newscaster *voice-over* film: both bulletins identical). ITN's *News at Ten* on the following day (12 January) repeated the showing of last October's rubbish, as did BBC1's *Nine O'Clock News* on the 13th. In order to maintain the 'health hazard' angle as the dominant view, this latter bulletin was still for the third day juxtapositioning the library-film of rubbish with the current film, by then available, of parked dustcarts. Emphasis was also placed on the fact that this was the second strike by Glasgow dustcart drivers within three months.

That this was the second strike by Glasgow's dustcart drivers within three months of their previous strike was emphasised in 13 of the 14 bulletins covering the strike.[4] This fact was still being reported in ITN bulletins on 24 January (Early Evening Bulletin and *News at Ten*). There was no coverage of the strike on either BBC1 or BBC2 during this week.

There were other disputes in Scotland, indeed in Glasgow, some affecting local authority services, and from the second day of coverage of the dustcart strike, reporting often linked them in bulletins: principally all five bulletins covering the dustcart strike on 13 January (3 ITN bulletins, 2 BBC1 bulletins), BBC1's *Nine O'Clock News* on the 12th, BBC1 Early Evening Bulletin on the 15th, and BBC2 *News Review* on 19 January. For example, 'Another strike is due to start in Scotland tomorrow. Yesterday Glasgow dustcart drivers voted to come out. Today, ambulance officers from all over Scotland decided to stop work over a pay dispute' (BBC1. 21.50, 12 January).

Following a lead report of the ambulance controllers' strike, ITN's *News at Ten* added that 'there will be no rubbish collected either in Glasgow tomorrow when 350 dustcart drivers start another pay strike ...' (12 January). This packaging led Robert Kee to remark the next day 'they are having a bad time with things in Scotland this morning' (ITN, *First Report*, 13 January). Other bulletins during the next few days, used phrases such as these: 'Still in Scotland ...'; 'In Scotland ambulance controllers and Glasgow

dustcart drivers have gone on strike, in both cases over pay': 'And
still in Scotland, strikes by hospital engineers, dustmen [sic] and
ambulance controllers continue.'[5]

In fact, as indicated in Chapter 1, eventually the frame was reinforced for many of the industrial events in the UK during that
week. 'The week had its share of unrest. Trouble in Glasgow with
striking dustmen and ambulance controllers, short time in the car
industry, no *Sunday Mirror* or *Sunday People* and a fair amount of
general trouble in Fleet Street ...' (*News Review*, BBC2, Sunday
19 January).

The story lapsed until the Corporation transformed the media's
supposed health hazard by actually declaring that one existed
nearly two months later. BBC's *Nine O'Clock News* reported the
declaration of the health hazard by the Medical Authority on 4
March. The cause of the hazard was reported to be the piles of
rubbish accumulated 'during the strike by dustmen' (not dustcart
drivers) and further reference was made only to 'the strikers' in
this bulletin. When ITN ran the story for the first time since 25
January, they too were confused as to who was actually on strike,
reporting, 'In Glasgow where the dustmen's strike, or rather the
strike by dustcart drivers ...' (*First Report*, 10 March).

On 14 March, BBC1 5.45 p.m. news had reported a meeting of
350 dustcart drivers. But BBC1 Lunchtime Bulletin and the *Newsday* bulletin on BBC2 reported 'the dustmen's strike' and referred
to a meeting of '550 men' and '550 dustmen' respectively. *Nine
O'Clock News* the same day spoke only of a 'dustmen's strike'
(twice). On the *Nine O'Clock News* of 18 March their number had
become 500, all of them dustcart drivers. When the BBC1 Lunchtime News the next day reported the arrival of the troops to clear
up the rubbish, no mention was made of the strike except via a
reference to 'the dustmen who aren't involved in the strike'.

The other BBC1 bulletins, BBC2 *Newsday* bulletin and all ITN
bulletins, did however report a 'dustcart drivers' strike' and,
further, BBC1 Early Evening Bulletin and *Nine O'Clock News*
reported the work of the dustmen 'who haven't been involved in
the strike'. The strike is reported as being 9 weeks old on the Early
Bulletin and 10 weeks old in the *Nine O'Clock News.*

BBC1's Early Evening Bulletin and ITN *News at Ten*, on the
20th, reported the problems facing the troops in clearing the
rubbish, without mentioning the strike. Both the ITN evening bulletins on this day reported these same aspects of the story, but the

rubbish in question is that 'accumulated during the unofficial strike by dustcart drivers'. On 22 March the settlement of the similar Liverpool dustcart drivers' strike, after an interim pay award, was reported. Here BBC1's *Nine O'Clock News* mentioned the possibility that 'a similar settlement could be found for the Glasgow strike'. Their Early Evening Bulletin had reported the urging of an interim award 'for the dustcart drivers'. As the bulletins covered the developing, 'moving situation', the selection of information was determined by the new events on each day. Reports were increasingly dominated by meetings of the Corporation, with union representatives, with government officials, and the army and then when the troops finally arrived, by rats and rubbish piles. The dispute itself figured less and less in reports and the information, when it *was* given, varied from bulletin to bulletin, from day to day on the same channel.

On Sunday 16 March, when news was dominated by the expected arrival of the army, BBC1's Lunchtime Bulletin did not mention a strike in Glasgow. The Early Evening Bulletin reported both 'striking dustmen' and some '500 dustcart drivers' — this report also appeared on *News Extra*. The main evening news spoke of 'striking dustmen'. *News Review* accounted for the rubbish pile-up by reference to the 'long unofficial strike by dustmen'.

But before the cause of the strike slipped even further from view, it would be as well to recall how much reporting had been devoted to cases on both sides. For example, on the first day all bulletins which reported that the strike was to occur indicated its consequences in terms of inconvenience and hazard by reference to the previous strike. BBC bulletins reported the decision of a mass meeting to strike from the following Monday. ITN did not report this meeting. BBC1 Early Evening news reported that 350 dustcart drivers had voted unanimously; the other BBC bulletins said simply that dustcart drivers, along with other Corporation drivers, 'decided' at 'a mass meeting'. In these bulletins no numbers were mentioned. Both ITN bulletins on this day reported the request to the TGWU for official backing for the strike, whereas only BBC1's Early Evening Bulletin reported this.

But ITN did not mention the involvement of other Corporation drivers. Both ITN bulletins reported 350 dustcart drivers, only the Early Evening Bulletin of BBC1 reported this number. All BBC bulletins reported the pay claim as 'at least another £3.50 a week', while ITN bulletins reported 'an extra £3.35 pence'. The cause of the demand on all BBC bulletins being 'to bring them into line with private haulage drivers' and on ITN 'to reduce the differential between their pay and that of heavy vehicles drivers working for private companies'.

The dustcart drivers' basic demand for parity appears in all six bulletins on 11 January, but is dropped from both the bulletin reports (BBC1 *Nine O'Clock News*, and ITN *News at Ten*) on the 12th. On the 13th, BBC1 Early Evening Bulletin reported the dispute as one 'over pay', the other bulletins on this day (BBC1 *Nine O'Clock News* and all three ITN news bulletins) reported the parity claim. The BBC bulletins on 15 and 19 January contained no mention of parity. ITN's *News at Ten* on 23 January has it as 'pay strike' and on ITN's Early Evening Bulletin and *News at Ten* on 24 January the strikers want 'another 14 per cent', 'a further 14 per cent' and they are on strike 'for more pay'. The BBC did not run the story on this day.

Taking the coverage as a whole, out of 40 bulletins, covering the dispute on BBC1 only 4 contained reports of the parity claim. Some 7 other bulletins contained references to an 'interim offer' or an explanation such as 'over pay', etc. Of a total of 19 reports in BBC2 bulletins, only 2 explicitly mention a parity claim. Three others report the issue as 'over pay' and one other 'over a regrading structure'. Of the 43 ITN bulletins, 8 report the parity issue and 11 others restrict their reporting of the dispute's cause to simple questions of 'pay', etc. Thus the cause of the dispute is not inevitably reported and, in the minority of cases when it is, almost always characterised as being a pay claim with some references to 'parity' and one reference to 'regrading'.

The confusion of nomenclature and the lack of reference to the unofficial nature of the dispute has to be added to this assessment of the television coverage of the story.

The HGV drivers employed by Glasgow Corporation went on strike in the autumn of 1974 in furtherance of a demand for an extra payment to give them parity with the minimum wage earned by HGV licence holders in other industries. The drivers returned to work after four weeks with the issue unsettled but on an understanding on the part of the drivers that the Corporation would be willing to negotiate a local agreement on the parity issue if the national negotiations, still in progress at that time, did not produce a satisfactory settlement. When the HGV drivers went on strike again in 1975, one of their spokesmen appeared on the regional news programmes reading a statement giving the reasons for their action.

> The committee are still firmly of the opinion that they have a genuine grievance. They believe that the Corporation clearly promised to discuss the issue of a suitable payment at local level if national negotiations failed to provide an acceptable solution. The basic wage of HGV drivers with Glasgow Corporation is £32.50, the earnings referred to in last night's programme included bonus and at least 10 hours overtime payment. And there are Corporation drivers who only receive minimal bonuses. The lowest rate for a HGV driver in road haulage is £37.00. The committee are conscious of the effect of the strike on the public and would hope that the discussions they are now engaged in can provide the possibility of rapidly clearing the mountains of refuse now lying around the city.
> Dan Duffy

This statement appeared on *Scotland Today*, and *Reporting Scotland*, 11 March. The STV programme edited out the sentence 'And there are corporation drivers ... minimal bonuses.' STV followed with an interview with Duffy; the BBC programme did not on this day. The BBC had mentioned this claim on the *Nine O'Clock News* on 13 January: 'The men say their basic pay is £2.50 less than road haulage drivers *and accuse the corporation of going back on a promise to negotiate a local agreement*' (Campbell Barclay, voice over film of parked dustcarts in shed; author's italics).

Thus as reported on regional television and on the occasion noted above, the essential question was one of a claimed promise made by the Corporation to the dustcart drivers to make a local HGV parity agreement. The dominant view of the strike did not generally allow this alternative view to be put. At its most dramatic, this can be seen in the fact that during the whole of the strike, not one of the strikers was interviewed on the national news. Only from the day that the strike ended were the drivers allowed to comment on their lost cause.[6] During the course of the strike and the army clearance operation, 10 other people were interviewed in bulletins on the 3 news services, some of them appearing in several bulletins (the interviews were shown in 20 bulletins in all). The interviewees were as follows: Professor Gordon Stewart, Professor of Community Medicine, University of Glasgow (BBC2, *News Extra*, 4 March 1975; ITN *First Report* (live), 10 March 1975; BBC1, Early Evening Bulletin and *Nine O'Clock News*, 10 March 1975). J. Flockhart, Fire Brigade Officer (BBC1, *Nine O'Clock News*, 10 March 1975). Councillor Dick Dynes, Glasgow Corporation Labour group (ITN, *First Report*, 11 March 1975). Sir William Gray, Lord Provost of Glasgow (BBC1, *Nine O'Clock News*, 14 March 1975; *Nine O'Clock News*, 15 March 1975). William Ross, Secretary of State for Scotland (BBC1, *Nine O'Clock News*, 14 March 1975; BBC2, *News Extra*, 15 March 1975; and ITN, *News at Ten*, 15 March 1975; BBC1, Early Evening Bulletin, 15 March 1975). Mr McElhone MP (Labour) (BBC1, Early Evening Bulletin, 15 March 1975). Lt Colonel Campbell (BBC1, *Nine O'Clock News*, 14 March 1975; BBC2, *News Review*, 23 March 1975), Alex Kitson, TGWU official (BBC1, *Nine O'Clock News*, 14 March 1975; BBC1, Early Evening Bulletin, 14 March 1975; ITN, Early Evening Bulletin, 14 March 1975). George McGredie, TGWU official (BBC1, Early Evening Bulletin, 18 March 1975), 2nd Lt Milne (ITN, *News at Ten*, 1 March 1975).

In addition, 4 bulletins on 19 March showed snatches of conversation between pickets and soldiers (BBC1, Early Evening Bulletin and *Nine O'Clock News*: and ITN Early Bulletin and *News at Ten*). BBC2's *News Review* showed this film on 23 March. Also, following the interview with the Lieutenant, ITN *News at Ten* screened vox pop comments of four soldiers (1 April).

Neither of the TGWU officials interviewed could properly be said to speak for the strikers in an unofficial dispute. Their comments in the bulletins concerned are particularly unrevealing.

Alex Kitson of the TGWU appeared first on BBC1 Early Evening Bulletin and later on *Nine O'Clock News*, giving his reactions to the prospect of the arrival of troops:

I would hope personally that there will be a great deal of deep thinking before that decision is taken and in fact it will be my responsibility to contact the powers that be, and that's the Glasgow Corporation, on this question.'
Reporter: 'So what will happen now then, Mr Kitson?'
Alex Kitson: 'Well we're polarised at the moment, I mean I've got to admit that, but we've been in this situation before and

we'll have to make arrangements to try and get out, I mean we'll start now to see what we can do to get out of it.

However, the interview with the same official shown in one ITN bulletin the same day (ITN, Early Evening Bulletin, 14 March), gave information on the strikers' claim, and though the questions put to Alex Kitson are not shown in the bulletin, it is rather more meaningfully integrated into a report of the issues of the strike. A film report began:

> The strikers were defiant this morning as they left their mass meeting with only one of them voting against the decision to stay out. They'd been offered bonus rates to clear up the mess which had been agreed with Glasgow Corporation, but the central issue of extra pay for men with heavy goods licences remained unresolved and so the men stay out. Glasgow Corporation insist that this is a national not a local issue. Alex Kitson: 'What's got to happen now is that the Corporation and ourselves as a union have got to pressurise for this situation to be cleared up at national level or they go back and fulfil the promise that if it wasn't satisfactorily dealt with at national level they'll negotiate locally, and I think they've got a responsibility to the citizens of Glasgow and in the light of the circumstances, they should get off this hobby horse and take into consideration the problems that the citizens of Glasgow are going through.'

The strain between strikers and their union, since the dispute was unofficial, was not an element of the dominant view. The interviews with the union officials were angled within the dominant view towards the arrival of the troops. Thus follow-up questions as to what action might ensue elicited opaque responses because the officials were referencing a framework otherwise unreported.

The selection of interviewees that appeared in the national news reflects those chosen aspects of the story within which the television bulletins organised their coverage. But the fact that the strikers themselves were not interviewed is not the only reason the dispute was not adequately reported. Those involved in the strike were, on occasions, named, and statements paraphrased by the reporter were attributed to them: 'one shop steward told me today', etc. When the decision was made to send in troops, the Corporation's view was balanced by a clear quote from the strikers, but significantly no mention of the claim is made:

Tonight Mr Archy Hood, the convener of the drivers' shop stewards' committee, threatened to ask for support from every other trade unionist in the country to protest at the move; he said: 'It's a pretty shocking thing when a Labour Government is using troops for strike-breaking in this way. I've never known a Labour Government to act like this; I think they are trying to starve us out.' (ITN, *News at Ten*, 15 March 1975)

Even given the fact that only officials of various kinds were interviewed during the strike, questions as to the nature of the dispute, the strikers' claim and the Corporation's refusal to meet it, could have been asked.

One film report on BBC1 did come near to the cause of the dispute in summarising the situation:

The strike began almost 13 weeks ago when the drivers walked out demanding parity with the drivers in the private sector. But the Corporation refused to listen. They have, in fact, all along. The men were told that there would be no local pay deals. If they wanted more money then this would have to come at national level. (BBC1, Early Evening Bulletin, 3 April 1975)

But there was no mention of the claimed promise that had been reported so briefly in the *Nine O'Clock News* of 13 January. The Corporation's case is put very clearly, not the men's understanding of it. Despite the library film used in the early coverage, the basis of the autumn return to work was largely ignored. Only on the day that the strike ended was a striker quoted in a way that related the two disputes on the matter of the promise.

Dan Duffy, one of the strikers' leaders, said that the men had been starved into submission. He said that the Corporation had ratted on an undertaking they gave last October to hold local negotiations, and Mr Duffy warned that the Corporation's behaviour had done no good to Glasgow's future industrial relations. (ITN, *First Report*, 9 April 1975)

However, ITN bulletins later in the day reported only the defeat of the strikers: 'One shop steward convenor said "there's no future in banging our heads against a brick wall"' and then 'One shop steward said the strike had been no use because they had been up against the government, the Corporation and the troops' (ITN,

Early Evening Bulletin and *News at Ten*).

News at Ten also included an interview with Dan Duffy, the first with a dustcart driver, saying that the decision to return to work was taken 'in view of the fact that the Corporation were not prepared to honour any agreement and were continuing to welsh on the agreements they had made with us.'

On the same day the BBC reported at lunchtime, 'One of the leaders of the unofficial strike claimed they had been starved into submission.' This forced submission was an angle chosen by the BBC to put to Dan Duffy in an interview in the Early Evening Bulletin. Duffy said: 'The Corporation have shown that they're not prepared to honour any commitment that they gave to us, they have welshed on us all along.' This interview was also shown on the *Nine O'Clock News*. The lack of reporting of any 'commitment' or 'agreement' during the strike must, we would suggest, render Duffy's statements rather meaningless for the viewer on the day it ended.

The arrival of the troops 3 weeks before, moved the story away from the dustcart drivers' case. Trade-union opposition to the troops was forthcoming with a demonstration organised by the Glasgow Trades Council on 21 March. *First Report*, transmitted at 1.00 p.m., had no film. The newscaster reported,

> And in Glasgow, the use of the troops to clear the rubbish there has brought a protest march by trade unionists from Glasgow and the West of Scotland. About 500 of them marched through the city centre, this morning. The march was organised by Glasgow's Trades Council. And the spokesman said the army was being used to break the dustcart drivers' strike. The march passed off peacefully though it did meet a certain amount of heckling and abuse from passers-by.

By the time of transmission of the Early Evening Bulletin 5.50 p.m., film of the demonstration was available. Six different shots were included in footage of the Glasgow report, five different shots of the marchers passing by, the third shot in the sequence showing several women standing passively on the pavement. The newscaster read the commentary over the film:

> In Glasgow shop stewards representing 50,000 Scottish workers marched to the City Chambers to protest against troops being

used to clear away refuse built up by the 10 week old dustcart drivers' strike and Glasgow's 800 firemen have decided on a policy of non-co-operation with the army. They'll only tackle fires in rubbish heaps if there is a danger to life and property and not while the army are there.

No comment was made on the nature of the march, peaceful or otherwise, or on the way it was received by onlookers.

The importance of actuality film is demonstrated by *News at Ten* on this day. In this bulletin the report of the demonstration is organised around a theme of the public's hostile reaction to the marchers. Reading to camera, the newscaster's introduction to the report emphasised a new interpretation of the demonstration: 'Earlier today shop stewards representing 50,000 Scottish Workers marched to the city centre to protest against the use of the troops, but as Trevor MacDonald reports, they got little sympathy from the public.'

The film sequence over which the reporter read his commentary now included two shots of people on the pavement as the demonstration passed by: the first in which several women shouted comments (4th shot in sequence), and the second showed two children shouting at the edge of the pavement in front of the onlookers (5th shot in sequence). The 6th shot showed an army landrover passing: shots 1, 2, 3 and 7 in the sequence were of the silent marchers.

> MacDonald: 'If the purpose of today's march was to rally support for the strikers, their demonstration was a disaster. At several points on the three mile route to the city centre, the marchers were shouted at, booed and jeered by people whose rat-infested rubbish has been lying in backyards now for 10 weeks. (shouting) Before the march began the shop stewards warned off members of activist groups who have become increasingly visible on the picket lines since the troops moved in.'

The peaceful march reported at 1.00 p.m. which met 'a certain amount of heckling and abuse from passers-by', and the demonstrations that at 5.50 p.m. simply 'marched to the City Chambers' is presented to the viewers of *News at Ten* as 'a disaster' whose participants 'were shouted at, booed and jeered'.

This demonstration was not covered by BBC1. BBC1's Early Bulletin reported the health problem in Liverpool created by uncollected rubbish arising out of a similar dispute between 300 dustcart drivers and the Corporation there. Shown in interview on film, the Medical Officer of Health warned of the possible dangers of disease. ITN's 3 bulletins covered the Liverpool situation as well in *First Report. News at Ten* (immediately preceding the Glasgow report) and following a Glasgow report in the Early Evening Bulletin. BBC1 and 2 bulletins did not report any of the events surrounding the dispute on 21 March 1975. BBC2's *News Review* however did made reference to the Trades Council march at the end of a report of the Glasgow situation: 'The strikers have made several calls for support in their stand against the use of the army but with little result. One demonstration met with bitter hostility from housewives.' This was read over film of soldiers working at a rubbish tip.

When the drivers began work again on 14 April ITN bulletins reported only that the 350 men were back at work 'after their abortive 13 week strike'. One of the drivers was interviewed and said, in the reporter's words, that he would 'happily go through it all again':

Tom Docherty: I would go on strike for the same cause again because we're qualified drivers.... We're experienced and we're professionals ... we are entitled to this money....

Rep.: But going on strike doesn't appear to have achieved anything because the army can come in and do your work?

Docherty: Certainly, because we didn't have union backing this time.

Rep.: So why go on strike again?

Docherty: We'll go on strike on principal and we're still entitled to this money. And there's nobody saying we won't go on strike, we definitely will, if it comes to the cause again, and it's a justful cause, we must go on strike for it again.

The public hardly had a chance to discover from the bulletins what this 'justful cause' was.

NOTES

1. Reginald Bosanquet introducing reports of both the Liverpool and Glasgow drivers' disputes. Item 10, *News at Ten*, 21 March 1975.

2. BBC1, 5.15 p.m., 15 March 1975 and BBC1, 17.45, 14 March 1975 respectively.

3. A total of 96 bulletins (ITN 43, BBC2 17 and BBC1 36) were recorded between 11 January and 14 April. A further 6 bulletins from the BBC were obtained from BBC microfilm to fill the gaps in the coverage analysis caused by machine failure, etc. (16 March 1975, 2 BBC2 bulletins and 3 BBC1 bulletins, and 1 BBC1 bulletin on 14 March 1975). However, as ITN microfilm or other transcript material was not available, it was not possible to check those few ITN bulletins that may have been missed. Thus the sample for analysis was 102 bulletins, 40 bulletins on BBC1, 19 on BBC2 and 43 on ITN.

4. On 11 January, in 2 ITN bulletins, 2 BBC1 and 2 on BBC2. On 12 January, in 1 ITN bulletin, on 13 January in 3 ITN bulletins, 2 BBC1 bulletins, and on 15 January, 1 BBC1 bulletin.

5. In a film report from Glasgow in this bulletin, Michael Buerk tells us that 'Glasgow dustmen [sic] are on strike again'.

6. Dan Duffy was interviewed on 9 April 1975 after a mass meeting decision to end the strike. This was shown on BBC1 Early Evening bulletin and *Nine O'Clock News* and similarly on ITN's *First Report*. When the dustcart drivers returned to work on 14 April, all 3 ITN bulletins contained interviews with one of the drivers, Mr Docherty, and a binman who said of the strikers that they should have returned to work long ago.

2.4 The Glasgow Dustcart Drivers' Strike

MARTIN HARRISON*

The closing chapter of *Bad News* comes 'Down to Cases'. Given the authors' frequent invocations of their 'findings' and 'evidence', and their damning conclusions, it comes as a surprise to find that they provide extended analysis of the coverage of only two strikes. The first is the Glasgow dustcart drivers' strike (News Scripts 4). This featured in 44 ITN bulletins between 11 January and 14 April — nine times in First Report (totalling 13'35"), 15 in the Early News (13'15"), and 20 on the Late News (27'02").

In the autumn of 1974 heavy goods vehicle drivers employed by Glasgow Corporation struck in furtherance of a claim for parity with rates that private drivers in Scotland had won that summer. The Corporation argued that it was bound by national agreements, and that the knock-on effects of conceding the claim would be unacceptably high. The men returned to work when the Corporation promised that if national negotiations, then in progress, did not produce a settlement, they would be willing to reach a local agreement. With national negotiations still under way, the drivers came out in January. Most were dustcart drivers, though smaller numbers were employed on other duties such as delivering school meals or driving handicapped children to and from school. In March the Army was called in to shift the rubbish. In April, after attempts to spread the strike had met only limited success, the strikers returned to work without winning their demands, though they negotiated bonus payments for clearing the backlog of rubbish.

Such were the bones of the affair. Fuller accounts would have to say something about the industrial history of Clydeside, and about the apparent ineptitude of the Corporation in making a pledge (or allowing the drivers to believe it had done so) without adequate

*Source: Martin Harrison, *TV News: Whose Bias?* (Policy Journals, 1985), pp. 83-92.

reflection on its consequences, and in failing to make clear that it considered the promise nullified when the men came out. More would also need to be said about the failure of local union officials to bring home to the men that London was unlikely to recognise a strike which threatened the whole system of national pay awards, and which also, arguably, contravened the 'social contract'. Again, the drivers undoubtedly had a deep sense of grievance; but whether their case had any great merit, and whether they allowed the Corporation enough time for national negotiations are other matters.

The *Bad News* commentary on the Glasgow dispute opens with the assertion that: 'The characteristic inferential framework, used by television journalists in reporting disputes, is to utilise limited aspects of a dispute to create a dominant view' (244). In the Glasgow strike 'The focus of the coverage became from the outset a "health hazard"' (245). Acknowledging that a serious problem did come to exist, the authors assert that 'it seems reasonable to question the manner in which this aspect was established as the initial focus of the coverage, even before the dumps had been created' (245). They add, 'The threatened health hazard became the dominant theme of all three news services, being established on the very first day of the coverage' (245). Later they note that the story soon lapsed 'until the Corporation transformed the media's supposed health hazard by declaring one existed nearly two months later' (247).

What really happened? ITN ran the following story in the Early News and *News at Ten* on 11 January:

Glasgow's 350 dustcart drivers are to go on indefinite strike from Monday.
The strike means that Glasgow faces another pile-up of rubbish on the pavements as happened for four weeks last autumn. The drivers have asked the national executive of the Transport & General Workers' Union to make the strike official. They want an extra £3.35 to reduce the differential between their pay and that of heavy-vehicle drivers working for private companies.[1]

From about the word 'pavements' the report was spoken over library film of the piles of rubbish that accumulated during the earlier strike. Coverage the next day was similar but slightly shorter.

The *Bad News* comment that these ITN reports were 'not so explicit' in suggesting the hazard as the BBC's (246) is worth savouring as a way of conceding that there was in fact no explicit reference at all. To assert so flatly that ITN coverage established a 'dominant frame' around the health hazard from the very start calls for an unusual blend of fertile imagination linked to sheer audacity.

Richard Hoggart, while not challenging the Group's account of the coverage in his foreword to *Bad News*, suggests that in using library film the intention was not 'any sinister desire to put the strikers in a bad light; it was much more likely ... to have been inspired by the trivial notion that this was a "good news angle", "good visual stuff" ...' (xii). By contrast, a former editor of ITN, Sir Geoffrey Cox, notes that 'only three months earlier Glasgow had faced a strike of dustmen which had produced piles of uncollected garbage, infected by rats. This film was used by the BBC and ITN to inform viewers that they could be in for another such experience' — and, one might add, to show the rest of the country what Glasgow might be in for.[2] It is also possible that, as a way of providing visual variation on the newsreader's 'talking head', ITN editors took the opportunity to run some relevant recent film. There is no conclusive proof of any of these explanations, and at this date we are unlikely to get one. What *is* clear is that among several possible explanations the Group opted unhesitatingly and without qualification for one which, while most straining credulity, showed television news in the worst light of all.[3]

While BBC coverage is not generally under consideration here, it is worth noting that their report, also over library film, stated that the strike decision brought 'fears of a repeat of the situation last October when rubbish piled up in the streets causing a health hazard' (*Bad News* 245). Scarcely a 'dominant frame'! Be that as it may, the Group's reference to 'the media's supposed health hazard' implies that this was pure invention. Quite apart from the fact that newsmen were perfectly capable of recalling the previous strike and realising that similar problems could readily recur, it is remarkable that, presumably living and working in the city at the time of the strike, the Group failed to notice that the convenor of the Corporation's establishment committee predicted *at the very outset* that it seemed 'certain to last several weeks at least, with the city facing again the health and fire risks of rubbish stored in plastic bags piled up in the streets'.[4] Even more interesting is the

fact that on 4 March one of the strikers' stewards said that they
had been 'warning for weeks about the potential health risks in the
city'.[5] So much for 'the media's supposed health hazard' (247).

The BBC's initial reference to a potential hazard (not an actual
one) seems fully vindicated. When ITN did mention the health risk
for the first time in the Early News on 23 February they were
scarcely rushing in prematurely. Their report featured a warning by
Professor Stewart of the Department of Community Medicine at
the University of Glasgow that the strike was creating a serious
health hazard. He did not criticise the strikers but accused 'the
local health authorities of playing down the seriousness of the situation "for political reasons".[6] The Group make no reference to
this report. Indeed, they seem to have missed it completely, since
in commenting on the handling of the story by First Report on 10
March they say that 'When ITN ran the story for the *first time
since 25 January*, they too were confused as to who was actually
on strike' (*Bad News* 247; emphasis mine). Later they refer again
to a 'confusion of nomenclature' (249). The 'confusion' lay in the
fact that Robert Kee opened the item with the words, 'In Glasgow
where the dustmen's strike, or rather the strike by dustcart drivers
...' Having worked through the reports on the dispute the Group
should have been aware that this was the only time ITN described
the strikers in these terms on the air, and they should also have
recognised that the phrasing was not in normal news style. The
most likely explanation is that Kee, who often worked without a
script, made a slip of the tongue. At all events, he corrected
himself in the next breath. Clearly the Group are prepared to seize
on the most trivial slip to make an adverse point — and ironically
their correction itself contained an error.

As we have seen, *Bad News* considers the Glasgow dispute as a
particularly bad example of television's failure to provide basic
information and to report the strikers' case. Yet the initial ITN
reports stated clearly who was on strike, and mentioned the
TGWU, the application for the strike to be made official, and the
essence of the men's demands. In all, 37 reports identified the
strikers as dustcart drivers, and where the number on strike was
mentioned it was in every case given as 350. Only three mentioned
the other services provided by the drivers (thereby passing up the
chance of reporting the 'effects' of the strike on handicapped
children!). Five reports named the TGWU; ten indicated that the
strike was unofficial. Eight mentioned the parity issue in some

form, two referred to a 'review of pay grading', and eleven simply identified the issue as 'pay' or 'extra pay for men with HGV licences'. The sums at stake were variously stated as £3.35 twice, £2.50 twice, 14 per cent twice and £5 once. The differing versions of the claim look untidy, but in this case reality itself was untidy. Initially the men were said to be £2.50 behind private drivers of vehicles of between five and ten tons. TGWU regrading proposals would have been worth between £1.27 and £2.16. Later the leader of the city's ruling Labour group, Councillor Dynes, said that the men were seeking '£5 outwith the NJC agreement and outwith the TGWU demand'. At the National Joint Industrial Council the TGWU called for improvements of from 38 pence to £3.29. Later the gap between the drivers and the corporation contractors was put at £5 per week.[7] One possible way of achieving the parity the men were seeking was through regrading rather than a straight pay increase. So it was not surprising that ITN put varying figures on a demand which itself appears to have varied, and which meant different amounts to different people.

The Group contend that there was 'a lack of reference to the unofficial nature of the strike' (*Bad News* 249). Yet although ITN can be criticised for insufficient recapitulation, ten indications that the strike was unofficial scarcely amounted to an unqualified 'lack of reference'. How much happier would the Group have been if the status of the strike had been carried in all 44 reports? Notwithstanding the status of the strike, the drivers were throughout supported by local TGWU officials, who continued to act on their behalf.[8]

'The essential question', says the Group, was a 'claimed promise made by the Corporation to the dustcart drivers to make a local HGV parity agreement' (*Bad News* 250). They omit to mention the condition attached to the promise, and therefore any consideration of whether the men allowed the Corporation enough time for the national negotiations. Certainly the feeling that the Corporation had broken its word fuelled the drivers' sense of grievance. Whether this was therefore 'the essential question' is debatable; what about the merit of the men's claim or the integrity of national wage agreements? As the authors say, ITN alluded to the pledge only twice and then indirectly in an interview with Alex Kitson of the TGWU (*E,L 14 March), and again at the end of the strike (F 9

---

*E = Early News, L = Late News, F = First Report.

April). But then, the few references to the national negotiations (E, L 3 April) and to the problem of the National Joint Industrial Council agreement were not very revealing. ('Glasgow says it can't pay until new national negotiations are complete'; E, L 24 Feb.) ITN also said nothing about the City's fears of a knock-on effect if it conceded the claim, about the refusal of the dustmen to support the drivers, the unwillingness of the TGWU to back a strike in breach of a national agreement, the attempt by the Scottish Trades Union Congress to get the strike called off, or the appeal from the city's eleven Labour MPs for the strikers to return to work.[9]

At one point the Group question the 'adequacy' of television coverage (*Bad News* 252), only to revert immediately to their narrower concern with the presentation of the strikers' case. But the two are not necessarily interchangeable. ITN's treatment of the strike left many details unreported, but as the examples just cited show these included developments which told against the strikers and not just material which might be thought to favour them. ITN is open to criticism for failing to explore the complicated background to this exceptionally protracted strike more thoroughly, and for not recalling the basic information about the dispute sufficiently frequently. The extent to which it should have done this is a matter of legitimate challenge — providing the pressures of time constraints are faced more squarely than in *Bad News*.

One of the main complaints is that 'during the whole of the strike not one of the strikers was interviewed on the national news' (*Bad News* 250; Trade Unions and the Media 133). The words are carefully chosen. Strikers *were* interviewed at the end of the strike and on regional television. Their appearances on Scotland Today and Reporting Scotland are dismissed as irrelevant to the discussion of national television output (*Bad News* 56-7) — although in view of the authors' argument that the 'unvarying frame' of coverage tends to exclude such groups, they might have been expected to explain why the frame apparently did not operate in regional coverage by the same broadcasting organisations. Nevertheless, it is true that ITN did not interview any striker until Dan Duffy appeared after the vote to return to work (L 9 April; also quoted F, E 9 April). There was also an interview with a driver on the day work resumed, saying that he would be prepared to do it again for 'a justful cause' (F, E, L 14 April). Although they came at the end of the dispute both interviews contributed something to the understanding of shopfloor opinion, and they cannot therefore be dismissed completely.

But what did the imbalance amount to in practice? Up to the decision to end the strike ITN carried interviews with only five people. One was Professor Stewart on the health hazard; he refused to allocate blame for the situation (F 10 March). Another was a single sentence from the Scottish Secretary, William Ross, on the likely reaction from other trade unionists to the decision to bring in the troops:

> This is an unofficial strike, but I think everyone in Glasgow appreciates that you've got to take into account, and the Government must take into account, the whole question of the health risk involved (L 15 March).

In a third, 2nd Lt. Milne of the Royal Highland Fusiliers spoke for about eleven seconds on the work of the troops (L 1 April). And there was a decidedly soggy interview with Councillor Dynes. After he had been asked whether there was any alternative to calling in the troops the interviewer put the point to him:

> OK, it's fine if the Army clear it up, but surely the only long-term solution is to get the men back to work.
> DYNES: Oh, we're entirely in the hands of the men, but it's coming through to me. I've gained certain knowledge that the men haven't had a mass meeting for the best part of two months now, if my information is correct. But the men have been isolated by everyone — government, Members of Parliament, the public and the Corporation, and by their own union, and we're really in their hands, and I'm sure that at the end of the day, when [ever?] that day is, they'll see sense and return to work. I don't think there's any alternative there either for themselves. They've lost a great deal of money from all of this, and I'm sure that they're quite anxious to return. I would hope so anyway (L 13 March).

Another unhappy man, the Lord Provost, who had earlier been reported as 'appalled and distressed' by the decision to ask for the troops to be sent in, gave the impression of being overtaken by events (E, L 14 March). He said nothing about either the strikers or the issues apart from passing responsibility for finding a solution to the government or the National Board for Prices & Incomes. On the same programme Alex Kitson commented in terms which appeared as embarrassed as they were ambiguous:

> What's got to happen now is that either Glasgow Corporation, and ourselves as a union, have got to pressurise for this situation to be cleared up at a national level, or they go back and fulfil the promise that if it wasn't satisfactorily dealt with at national level, they'll negotiate locally, and I think they've got a responsibility to the citizens of Glasgow, and in the light of the circumstances they should get off this hobby-horse and take into consideration the problems that the citizens of Glasgow are going through (L 14 March).

However, ITN also reported his earlier, more trenchant warning that to bring in the troops would be an 'act of folly' (F, L 14 March), criticism by the Scottish Trades Union Congress (L 17 March) and the Glasgow Trades Council (L 17 March; L 19 March), and the reaction of the drivers' convenor, Archie Hood: 'It is a pretty shocking thing when a Labour Government is using troops for strike-breaking in this way. I have never known a Labour Government to act like this. I think they are trying to starve us out' (L 15 March). It also carried an assurance by a drivers' shop steward, Fergus Hilton, that they would not interfere with the Army (F 19 March), and specifically mentioned the pickets'good-humoured behaviour when the Army did move in (F, L 19 March).

The strikers' case did not go unreported, as the Annan Committee was led to believe, and examination of the content of the various interviews shows the imbalance to be less culpable than the crude figures suggest.[10] Nevertheless, it would have been appropriate to have interviewed the strikers, and ITN's failure to do so can fairly be criticised. What the Committee apparently did not know was that the strikers were not the only interested parties whose position received little direct attention. Apart from the inconclusive Dynes interview, ITN carried no statements about the merits of the dispute from the Corporation either, and its position never emerged as clearly as that of the strikers'. Nor were there interviews with the more numerous dustmen who refused to support the drivers, or from ordinary Glaswegians troubled by the smells, rats, fires and general squalor of the dumps.[11] It would seem more profitable to consider the absence of the strikers as part of a wider discussion of the general adequacy of the coverage rather than as an example of specific discrimination against labour. One may well feel that neither Glasgow City Council, nor the strikers, nor the TGWU and the National Joint Industrial Council came out of the dispute with credit. More enquiring coverage might have shed fuller light on their failure.

Initially the Glasgow strike was reported briefly and routinely as one of a clutch of disputes on Clydeside; eight of the first nine reports ran less than 40 seconds. Nevertheless they presented the essentials of the dispute clearly, competently and fairly. A claim for 'parity' has a legitimate sound to it; certainly workers striking for parity are not being taxed with 'irrational' or 'futile' behaviour. Coverage might well have stayed on that very modest scale, as it did with a comparable stoppage in Liverpool around the same time (News Scripts 17). What lifted the Glasgow strike to prominence was the decision to send for the Army. As the first occasion on which troops had been used as strike-breakers for a quarter of a century, this obviously warranted extensive reporting. But ITN's preoccupation with the military angle led to the substance of the strike's being pushed into the background during the later stages. It may be no coincidence that at least ten different people appear to have 'subbed' the story at one time or other, and it was covered from Glasgow by five different journalists, four of them general reporters on brief visits to the city. None was a member of ITN's industrial staff. While the individual reports were competent and fair, the overall handling of the story could have been more coherent, more comprehensive and more inquisitive. Few strikes drag on as long as this one, and the very tenacity of the two sides merited more investigation and explanation. ITN creditably reported what happened; the 'why' was handled less satisfactorily. All the same, there was a greater professionalism to ITN's coverage than to the Glasgow critique of it.

NOTES

1. According to *Bad News*, TV10 'emphasised the fact that this was the second strike in three months.' Whether reports such as this amounted to 'emphasis' is a matter of judgment; technically the reference was probably inserted to explain the library film.
2. Sir Geoffrey Cox, 'Bad News — Or Poor Scholarship?'. Independent Broadcasting, December 1976.

3. Where use of the library film seems more open to criticism is in introducing a 'vision track' which may have distracted viewers and therefore impeded assimilation of the spoken text.

4. *Glasgow Herald*, 13 January 1975.

5. *Glasgow Herald*, 5 March 1975.

6. See also *Glasgow Herald*, 24 February 1975. On 1 March the *Herald* reported the city's director of environmental health as saying that 'come the breeding season I cannot be responsible for anything that might happen.' On 3 March the *Herald* said that sanitary officials had warned of the danger of a plague of rats, and there had been increasing claims of a health hazard by medical officials. On 5 March, in addition to the shop steward's warning, it carried a report that the city's corporate policy committee had been told that the potential health hazard could become an actual one in two to three weeks if action was not taken. Reports from council officers referred to rats breeding and the possibility of a plague of flies, with the consequential danger of dysentery and food poisoning. On 7 March the Minister of State at the Scottish Office, Bruce Millan, was reported as appealing to the strikers to return to work because of the very serious potential health hazard. With the exception noted ITN reported none of these.

7. *Glasgow Herald*, 10 January 1975, 4 and 11 March 1975, 4 and 10 April 1975.

8. *Glasgow Herald*, 22 January, 28 February 1975.

9. *Glasgow Herald*, 1, 3, 4, 18 March 1975; 3, 4 February 1975; 27 January, 8 March, 4 April 1975; 10, 11 March 1975.

10. Report of the Committee on the Future of Broadcasting. Cmnd. 6753, HMSO, 1977, 272.

11. *Glasgow Herald*, 3, 4 February 1975.

2.5 Semiological Analysis

ARTHUR ASA BERGER*

Semiology — the science of signs — is concerned, primarily, with how meaning is generated in 'texts' (films, television programs, and other works of art). It deals with what signs are and how they function. In this chapter, after discussing the most essential semiological concepts and some related concerns, we apply them to an episode of a television program. We then deal with codes, formulas, and the 'language' of television.

I face this assignment — explaining semiology and showing how it can be applied to television and popular culture to those who know little or nothing about the subject — with a certain amount of apprehension. I'm not sure whether semiology (also sometimes called semiotics) is a subject, a movement, a philosophy, or a cult-like religion. I do know that there is a large and rapidly expanding literature on the subject and that many of the writings by semiologists are difficult and highly technical.

So my mission, if not impossible, is quite challenging. For not only am I to explain the fundamental notions or elements of semiology, I am also to apply them to television and television productions as well as to popular culture in general. It is a large undertaking, but I think it can be done.

The price I must pay involves a certain amount of simplification and narrowness of focus. I'm going to explain the basic principles of semiology and apply them. I hope that after reading this chapter and the annotated bibliography provided, those interested in the matter can probe more deeply into it at their own convenience.

Although an interest in signs and the way they communicate has a long history (medieval philosophers, John Locke, and others have shown interest), modern semiological analysis can be said to have begun with two men — Swiss linguist Ferdinand de Saussure

*Source: Arthur Asa Berger, *Media Analysis Techniques* (Sage Publications, Beverly Hills, California and London, 1982), pp. 14-43.

Figure 1.1: Three aspects of signs

	Icon	Index	Symbol
signify by	resemblance	causal connections	conventions
examples	pictures, statues	smoke/fire, symptom/disease	words, numbers, flags
process	can see	can figure out	must learn

(1857-1913) and American philosopher Charles Saunders Peirce (1839-1914).[1]

Saussure's book, *Course in General Linguistics*, first published posthumously in 1915, suggests the possibility of semiological analysis. It deals with many of the concepts that can be applied to signs and that are explicated in this essay. Saussure's division of the sign into two components, the signifier, or 'sound-image,' and the signified, or 'concept,' and his suggestion that the relationship between signifiers and signified is arbitrary were of crucial importance for the development of semiology. Peirce, on the other hand, focused on three aspects of signs — their iconic, indexical, and symbolic dimensions (see Figure 1.1).

From these two points of departure a movement was born, and semiological analysis (I will use that term exclusively, henceforth) has spread all over the globe. Important work was done in Prague and Russia early in the twentieth century, and semiology is now well established in France and Italy (where Roland Barthes, Umberto Eco, and many others are doing important theoretical as well as applied work). There are also outposts of progress in England, the United States, and many other countries. [...]

THE PROBLEM OF MEANING

In what follows we are going to be learning a new language — a number of concepts that enable us to look at films, television programs, fashion, foods — almost anything — in ways somewhat different from the manner in which we generally look at these things. *Our basic concern will always be how meaning is generated and conveyed,* with particular reference to the films or television programs we will be examining. (Henceforth we will focus on television programs, which will be called 'texts.')

But how is meaning generated?

The essential breakthrough of semiology is to take linguistics as a model and apply linguistic concepts to other phenomena — texts — and not just to language itself. In fact, we treat texts as being like languages, in that relationships are all important, and not things *per se*. To quote Jonathan Culler (1976: 4):

> The notion that linguistics might be useful in studying other cultural phenomena is based on two fundamental insights: first, that social and cultural phenomena are not simply material objects or events but objects or events with meaning, and hence signs; and second, that they do not have essences but are defined by a network of relations.

Signs and relations! They are two of the key notions of semiological analysis. A text such as *Star Trek* can be thought of as a system of signs, and the meaning in the program stems from the signs and from the system that ties the signs together. This system is generally not obvious and must be elicited from the text.

In semiological analysis we make an arbitrary and temporary separation of content and form and focus our attention on the system of signs that makes up a text. Thus a meal, to stray from television for a moment, is not seen as steak, salad, baked potato, and apple pie, but rather as a sign system conveying meanings related to matters such as status, taste, sophistication, nationality, and so on.

Perhaps it is best now to quote from one of the founding fathers of semiology, Swiss linguist Ferdinand de Saussure (1966: 16):

> Language is a system of signs that express ideas, and is therefore comparable to a system of writing, the alphabet of deaf-mutes, symbolic rites, polite formulas, military signals, etc. But it is the most important of all these systems.
>
> *A science that studies the life of signs within society* is conceivable; it would be a part of social psychology and consequently of general psychology; I shall call it *semiology* (from Greek *semeion* 'sign'). Semiology would show what constitutes signs, what laws govern them. Since the science does not yet exist, no one can say what it would be; but it has a right to existence, a place staked out in advance.

SEMIOLOGICAL ANALYSIS   135

This is the charter statement of semiology, a statement that opens the study of media to us, for not only can we study symbolic rites and military signals, we can also study commercials, soap operas, situation comedies, and almost anything else as 'sign systems.'

Saussure offered another crucial insight that is relevant here — that concepts have meaning because of relations and the basic relationship is oppositional. Thus 'rich' doesn't mean anything unless there is 'poor,' or 'happy' unless there is 'sad.' 'Concepts are purely differential and defined not by their positive content but negatively by their relations with the other terms of the system' (Saussure, 1966: 117). It is not 'content' that determines meaning, but 'relations' in some kind of a system. The 'most precise characteristic' of these concepts 'is in being what the others are not' (Saussure, 1966: 117). We can see this readily enough in language, but it also holds for texts. Nothing has meaning in itself!

So where are we now? I have suggested that semiological analysis is concerned with meaning in texts, that meaning stems from relationships, and, in particular, the relationship among signs. But what, exactly, is a sign?

SIGNS

A sign, Saussure tells us, is a combination of a concept and a sound-image, a combination that cannot be separated. But because these terms are not quite satisfactory for him he modifies them slightly:

> I propose to retain the word sign [signe] to designate the whole and to replace concept and sound-image respectively by *signified* [signifié] and *signifier* [signifiant]; the last two terms have the advantage of indicating the opposition that separates them from each other and from the whole of which they are parts [Saussure, 1966: 67].

The relationship between the signifier and signified — and this is crucial — is *arbitrary*, unmotivated, un-natural. There is no logical connection between a word and a concept or a signifier and signified, a point that makes finding meaning in texts interesting and problematical.

Saussure uses trees as an example. He offers a diagram of the sign in general (see Figure 1.2), and then of the *sign* tree (Figure 1.3).

The difference between a sign and a symbol, Saussure (1966: 68) suggests, is that a symbol has a signifier that is never wholly arbitrary.

> One characteristic of the symbol is that it is never wholly arbitrary; it is not empty, for there is a rudiment of a natural bond between the signifier and signified. The symbol of justice, a pair of scales, could not be replaced by just another symbol, such as a chariot.

We now can start looking at texts differently and can start thinking about how it is that signifiers generate meaning.

How do signifiers generate meaning? And how is it that we know these meanings? If the relationship between a signifier and signified is arbitrary, the meanings these signifiers hold must be learned somehow, which implies that there are certain structured associations, or *codes*, we pick up that help us interpret signs. (I will deal with this subject in more detail shortly.)

Let's look at the television program *Star Trek* in terms of its signifiers and what is signified. Anyone who has seen the program knows that it is a space adventure/science fiction series. We know this because we are 'told' so at the beginning of each episode,

Figure 1.2: Saussure's diagram of a sign

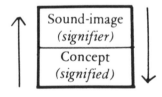

Figure 1.3: Saussure's diagram of the sign and symbol 'tree'

when the Starship Enterprise is sent on a mission in outer space —
to explore new worlds and seek out new civilizations, to 'boldly go
where no man has gone before.' We can say that science fiction
adventure is the general 'signified' and that numbers of signifiers
are given to show this. For example, we find rocket ships, futuristic
uniforms, ray guns, advanced computer technology, extrater-
restrials with strange powers (such as Mr Spock, whose pointy ears
signify that he is only partly human), and magic/science, among
other things.

Figure 1.4

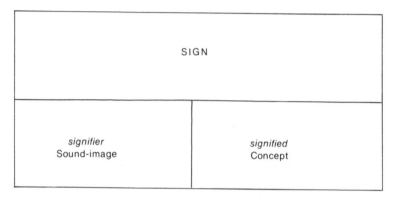

It is precisely the fact that the program is so rich in signifiers that
enables the legions of 'Trekkies' to hold conventions, wear
costumes, sell 'phasers,' and so on. For when you have appropriated the signifiers, you have 'captured,' so to speak, the signified. This, I might point out, is how many commercials work.
People purchase the 'right' products and assume (or hope) that
these products will signify a certain social class, status, lifestyle, or
what you will.

All of this is based on associations we learn and then carry
around with us. Anyone who communicates uses these associations
between signifiers and signifieds all the time. Since in real life the
relationships are arbitrary and change rapidly, one must be on
one's toes all the time. Signifiers can become dated and change
their significance all too quickly. In a sense, then, we are all
practicing semiologists who pay a great deal of attention to signs —
signifiers and signifieds — even though we may never have heard
these terms before.

LANGUAGE AND SPEAKING

Earlier I suggested that texts (such as films, television programs, commercials, and so on) are 'like languages,' and that the rules of linguistics can be applied to them. What languages do is enable us to communicate information, feelings, ideas, and the like by establishing systems and rules that people learn. And just as there is grammar for writing and speaking, there is also a grammar for various kinds of texts — and for different media.

Saussure made a distinction that is useful here — between *language* and *speaking*. Language is a social institution, made up of rules and conventions that have been systematized, that enables us to speak (or, more broadly, communicate). Each person 'speaks' in his or her own manner, but this speaking is based on the language and rules that everyone learns. A television program such as *Star Trek* — and I must point out that most of what I'm dealing with involves narratives — can be looked upon as speech that is intelligible to its audience because the audience knows the language. That is, we know the signs and what they signify, we know the conventions of the genre or what is acceptable and unacceptable. We know the codes!

Sometimes there is confusion and the code of the creator of a program isn't the code of the members of the audience. In such cases there is bad communication. What makes things complicated is the fact that, *generally speaking, people are not consciously aware of the rules and codes and cannot articulate them*, though they respond to them. A scene in a program that is meant to be sad but which occasions laughter is an example of this kind of mix-up.

It is obvious, then, that people are 'speaking' all the time, even when they aren't saying anything. Our hairstyles, eyeglasses, clothes, facial expressions, posture, gestures, and many other things about us are communicating or 'speaking' (that is, signifying continually, for those who are sensitive to such things and who are mindful of signs and signifiers). Speech always implies, as Saussure (1966) tells us, an established system, though this system is also evolving continually. Let me offer a brief summary here:

(1) Our concern is how *meaning* is created and conveyed in texts and, in particular, narratives (or stories).
(2) Our focus is upon the *signs* we find in these texts, understanding signs to be combinations of *signifiers* and *signifieds.*

(3) Since nothing has meaning in itself, the *relationships* that exist among signs are crucial. An analogy can be made with words and grammar here; it is the way the words are combined that determines what they mean. *Language* is a social institution that tells us how words are to be used and *speaking* is an individual act based on language.

(4) *Texts* can be looked upon as being similar to speech and implying grammars or languages that make these texts meaningful. There are codes and conventions that make the signs in a narrative understandable and that also shape the actions.

THE SYNCHRONIC AND THE DIACHRONIC

This distinction is yet another legacy from Saussure. As he uses the terms, 'synchronic' means analytical and 'diachronic' means historical, so a synchronic study of a text looks at the relationships that exist among its elements and a diachronic study looks at the way the narrative evolves. Another way of putting this is that a synchronic analysis of a text looks for the pattern of paired oppositions buried in the text (the paradigmatic structure) while a diachronic analysis focuses upon the chain of events (the syntagmatic structure) that forms the narrative.

Figure 1.5 shows these relationships more clearly. Claude Lévi-Strauss and Vladimir Propp are offered here as exemplars of each method. Their ideas will be explained in the sections that follow.

Figure 1.5: Elements of synchronic analysis and diachronic analysis

SYNCHRONIC	DIACHRONIC
simultaneity	succession
static	evolutionary
relations in a system	relations in time
paradigmatic	syntagmatic
Lévi-Strauss	Propp

SYNTAGMATIC ANALYSIS

A syntagm is a chain, and a syntagmatic analysis of a text looks at it as a sequence of events that forms some kind of a narrative. I will be dealing with the ideas of a Russian folklorist, Vladimir Propp, who wrote a pioneering book in 1928, *Morphology of the Folktale*. Morphology is the study of forms — that is, the component parts of something and their relationships to each other and to the whole.

Propp (1968: 19) did his work on a group of fairy tales and describes his method as follows:

> We are undertaking a comparison of the themes of these tales. For the sake of comparison we shall separate the component parts of fairy tales by special methods; and then, we shall make a comparison of the tales according to their components. The result will be a morphology (i.e., a description of the tale according to its component parts and the relationship of these components to each other and to the whole).

The essential or basic narrative unit that Propp (1968: 21-23) used was what he called a 'function.'

Function is understood as an act of a character, defined from the point of view of its significance for the course of the action.

The observations cited may be briefly formulated in the following manner:

1. *Functions of characters serve as stable, constant elements in a tale, independent of how and by whom they are fulfilled. They constitute the fundamental components of a tale.*
2. *The number of functions known to the fairy tale is limited.*
3. *The sequence of functions is always identical.*
4. *All fairy tales are of one type in regard to their structure.*

Propp's work has great significance to us, for we can adopt and adapt his ideas to films, television stories, comics, and all kinds of other narratives. Whether or not Propp was correct in all his assertions is not of great importance to us here. His concept of functions can be applied to all kinds of texts with interesting results.

Propp gives a summary of the essence of each function, an abbreviated definition of it in one word, and a conventional sign for it. Some functions are rather complicated and have numerous subcategories, all of which fulfill the same task.

Propp's first function is quoted below so that you can see what a simple one is like and how he develops each:

1. ONE OF THE MEMBERS OF A FAMILY ABSENTS HIMSELF FROM HOME. (Definition: *absentation.* Designation: β.)

1. *The person absenting himself can be a member of the older generation* (β_1). Parents leave for work (113). 'The prince had to go on a distant journey, leaving his wife to the care of strangers' (265). 'Once, he (a merchant) went away to foreign lands' (17). Usual forms of absentation: going to work, to the forest, to trade, to war, 'on business.'
2. *An intensified form of absentation is represented by the death of parents* (β_2).
3. *Sometimes members of the younger generation absent themselves* (β_3). They go visiting (101), fishing (108), for a walk (137), out to gather berries (244) [Propp, 1968: 26; the numbers in parentheses refer to specific fairy tales studied by Propp].

This is one of Propp's briefer functions; for instance, number 8 (about a villain doing harm or injury to a member of family) has 19 subcategories.

Even though we do not possess all the subcategories of each function, it is still possible to use Propp's 31 functions to make syntagmatic analyses of selected texts (Figure 1.6 presents these functions and a brief description of each.) What will become obvious to you as you use these functions is the degree to which many contemporary stories contain many of Propp's functions. His definition of the hero as 'that character who either directly suffers from the action of the villain ... or who agrees to liquidate the misfortune or lack of another person' is also worth considering (Propp, 1968: 50). Heroes also, he tells us, are supplied with magical agents or helpers that they make use of in difficult situations.

Figure 1.6 (which contains a simplification and slight modification of Propp's list) gives each function and describes it briefly.

Figure 1.6: Propp's functions

α	Initial situation	Members of family or hero introduced.
β	Absentation	One of the members of a family absents himself from home.
γ	Interdiction	An interdiction is addressed to the hero.
δ	Violation	An interdiction is violated.
ϵ	Reconnaissance	The villain makes an attempt at reconnaissance.
ζ	Delivery	The villain receives information about his victim.
η	Trickery	The villain attempts to deceive his victim.
θ	Complicity	The victim submits to deception, unwittingly helps his enemy.
A	Villainy	The villain causes harm or injury to a member of a family.
a	Lack	One member of a family lacks something or wants something.
B	Mediation	Misfortune is made known, hero is dispatched.
C	Counteraction	Seekers agree to decide on counteraction.
↑	Departure	The hero leaves home.
D	1st function of donor	Hero is tested, receives magical agent or helper.
E	Hero's reaction	Hero reacts to actions of the future donor.
F	Receipt of magic agent	Hero acquires the use of a magical agent.
G	Spatial transference	Hero led to object of search.
H	Struggle	Hero and villain join in direct combat.
J	Branding	Hero is branded.
I	Victory	Villain is defeated.
K	Liquidation	Initial misfortune or lack is liquidated.
↓	Return	The hero returns.
Pr	Pursuit	A chase: the hero is pursued.
Rs	Rescue	Rescue of hero from pursuit.
O	Unrecognized arrival	The hero, unrecognized, arrives home or in another country.
L	Unfounded claims	A false hero presents unfounded claims.
M	Difficult task	A difficult task is proposed to the hero.
N	Solution	The task is resolved.
Q	Recognition	The hero is recognized.
Ex	Exposure	The false hero or villain is exposed.
T	Transfiguration	The hero is given a new appearance.
U	Punishment	The villain is punished.

W	Wedding	The hero is married and ascends the throne.

There are seven dramatis personae in Propp's scheme and they are listed below and described:

1.	Villain	Fights with hero.
2.	Donor	Provides hero with magical agent.
3.	Helper	Aids hero in solving difficult tasks, etc.
4.	Princess and her father	Sought-for person. Assigns difficult tasks.
5.	Dispatcher	Sends hero on his mission.
6.	Hero	Searches for something or fights with villain.
7.	False hero	Claims to be hero but is unmasked.

I will now apply Propp's functions to an episode of the television program *The Prisoner* to show how Propp helps us uncover the morphology of a narrative text. *The Prisoner* is a remarkable 'existential' television series first broadcast a number of years ago. It is regarded by many people as a classic. It is about a spy who resigns from some mysterious organization, returns to his apartment, where he is gassed, and then wakes up in a strange, resort-like, island prison, the Village, where everyone is called by a number. The hero, 'the prisoner,' is locked into battles with various adversaries, each playing Number Two, in the 17 episodes of the series. At the end of the series, the prisoner (Number Six) escapes from the Village, which he destroys, and returns to his apartment in London.

A synopsis of the first episode, 'Arrival,' follows:

The program opens with a scene in which the hero, unnamed, is shown resigning. He is in an office with some officials; he pounds the table and leaves. He returns to his apartment and begins packing. As he does this, he is gassed and passes out. He wakes in the Village, a resort-like prison (and a totalitarian society) where everyone has numbers instead of names. He is told that he is Number Six and is pitted against Number Two, who wishes to find out why Six resigned. Six tries to escape by running along the seashore but is 'captured' by a huge and terrifying rubber sphere, Rover,that is kept beneath the sea and is controlled by Number Two. Six is sent to the Village hospital, where he finds himself sharing a room with an old friend, also a spy. While Six is being examined by a doctor there is a commotion. Six rushes to his room and is told that the friend has committed suicide. After Six is released from the hospital he notices a woman acting strangely at the friend's burial procession. Six talks with the woman, who tells him she was the friend's lover and that they were planning to escape from the island. She has a watch with a special device that will enable Six to evade Rover and steal a helicopter. Six takes the watch and 'escapes' via the helicopter, but shortly after he has left the island he discovers the helicopter is rigged and controlled by Number Two. The episode ends with the helicopter returning to the Village and the spy friend, who has supposedly committed suicide, telling Two that Six is an unusual person who will need special treatment.

Although *The Prisoner* is not a fairy tale, *per se*, it contains many elements of the fairy tale. Many contemporary narrative texts are, it can be argued, modified and updated fairy tales that, to a considerable degree, resemble the tales Propp described. Figure 1.7 lists a few of the Proppian functions that can be applied to events in 'Arrival.' This analysis could have been extended and made more detailed by citing some of the subcategories Propp (1968) uses in *Morphology of the Folktale*, but I only want to suggest the possibilities of this kind of analysis here.

There are several important things to be learned from a syntagmatic analysis. First, narratives, regardless of kind or genre, are composed of certain functions (or elements) that are essential for the creation of a story. Propp leads us, then, to understanding the nature of formulas. Second, the order in which events take place in a narrative is of great importance. There is a logic to narrative texts and the arrangement of elements in a story greatly affects our perception of what anything 'means'. That, in fact, is what editing is.[2]

Figure 1.7: Proppian functions in 'Arrival' episode of *The Prisoner*

Propp's Functions	Symbol	Events in "Arrival"
initial situation	∝	hero shown resigning
interdiction violated	δ	(implicit) spies can't resign
villain causes injury	A	hero abducted to the Village
receipt of a magical agent	F	woman gives Six watch with device
false hero exposed	Ex	friend shown with Two

PARADIGMATIC ANALYSIS

The paradigmatic analysis of a text involves searching for a hidden pattern of oppositions that are buried in it and that generate meaning. As Alan Dundes writes in his introduction to Propp's *Morphology of the Folktale*, the paradigmatic form of structural analysis

> seeks to describe the pattern (usually based on *a priori* binary principle of opposition) which allegedly underlies the folkloristic text. This pattern is not the same as the sequential structure at all. Rather, the elements are taken out of the 'given' order and are regrouped in one or more analytic schema [Propp, 1968: xi].

There is a reason we search for binary or polar oppositions. It is because meaning is based upon establishing relationships, and the most important relationship in the production of meaning in language is that of opposition.

We return here to Saussure's (1966) notion that 'in language there are only differences.' Or, as Jonathan Culler (1976: 15) has put it: 'Structuralists have generally followed Jakobsen and taken the binary opposition as a fundamental operation of the human mind basic to the production of meaning.' Thus in all texts (whether narrative or not) there must be some kind of a systematic and interrelated set of oppositions that can be elicited. Many people are not conscious of these polar oppositions — and sometimes they are implied, and not given — but without differences there is no meaning.

Some people argue that the oppositions and other structures that semiologists 'elicit' from texts are not really there. These critics assert that semiologists do not *discover* systems of relationships but, instead, *invent* them. This controversy is sometimes known as the 'hocus-pocus' versus the 'God's truth', problem. I believe that the bipolar oppositions that semiologists find in texts are actually there; not only that, but they *have* to be there. Finding meaning without discerning polar oppositions is like listening to the sound of one hand clapping.

Since I've used *The Prisoner* already, let me offer a paradigmatic analysis of 'Arrival.' The most important opposition found in this episode is between freedom and control and I use these two concepts at the head of my list of oppositions (Figure 1.8). This brief listing shows the ideational structure upon which the narrative is hung.

Claude Lévi-Strauss, the distinguished French anthropologist, suggests that the syntagmatic analysis of a text gives the text's manifest meaning and that the paradigmatic analysis of a text gives its latent meaning. The manifest structure involves what happens and the latent structure involves what a text is about. Or, to put it another way, we are not so much concerned with what characters *do* as we are with what they *mean* when we use the paradigmatic approach.

What Lévi-Strauss is interested in is the way narratives are organized or structured and how their organization generates meaning. He has done a great deal of work (much of it highly controversial) on myths, kinship systems, and related matters. There are, he believes, fundamental or minimal units of myths, 'mythemes,' which combine in certain ways to give messages. These mythemes can be expressed in short sentences that express important relationships. For example, in the Oedipus myth, Lévi-Strauss offers mythemes such as 'Oedipus kills his father, Laius' or 'Oedipus marries his mother' or 'Oedipus immolates the Sphinx.' These mythemes and their rules of combination (what he calls 'bundles' or relations) are the stuff of which myths are made. Myths are important because they not only function as charters for the groups that tell and believe them, but also because they are the keys to the ways in which the human mind works.

What is most significant about myths is the stories they tell, not their style. Thus the structured relationships among the characters and what these relationships ultimately mean should be the object of one's attention, not the way a story is told. Myths, Lévi-Strauss

Figure 1.8: Polar oppositions in 'Arrival'

Freedom	Control
Number Six	Number Two
the individual	the organization
willpower	force
escape	entrapment
trust	deception

believes, give coded messages from cultures to individuals, and the task of the analyst is to discover these masked or hidden messages by 'cracking the code,' so to speak. In the final analysis this involves eliciting the paradigmatic structure of a text.[3]

In making a paradigmatic analysis of a text several errors should be avoided. First, make certain you elicit true oppositions (as opposed to mere negations). I would suggest that 'poor' is the opposite of 'rich,' and should be used instead of something such as 'unrich' or 'nonrich.' And second, be sure that your oppositions are tied to characters and events in the text.

If I had offered a more detailed synopsis of 'Arrival' I would have been able to offer more detailed syntagmatic and paradigmatic analyses of this story, and my lists of Proppian functions and polar oppositions (Figures 1.7 and 1.8) would have been longer. I might add that it is useful to explicate the terms used in the list of oppositions and explain to the reader why each paired opposition is used.

METAPHOR AND METONYMY

Metaphor and metonymy are two important ways of transmitting meaning. In metaphor a relationship between two things is suggested through the use of *analogy*. Thus we might say, 'My love is a red rose.' One of the most common metaphoric forms is the simile, in which 'like' or 'as' is used and a comparison is suggested. For example, we find similes in statements such as 'He's as sharp as a razor,' or 'She's as good as an angel.'

In metonymy a relationship is suggested that is based on *association*, which implies the existence of codes in people's minds that enable the proper connections to be made. As James Monaco writes in *How to Read a Film* (1977: 135):

> A metonymy is a figure of speech in which an associated detail or notion is used to invoke an idea or represent an object. Etymologically, the word means 'substitute naming' (from the Greek meta, involving transfer, and onoma, name). Thus in literature we can speak of the king (and the idea of a kingship) as 'the crown.'

A common form of metonymy is a synecdoche, in which a part stands for the whole or vice versa.

A good example of metaphor in film is the famous scene in
Chaplin's *The Gold Rush* in which he cooks his boots and eats the
shoelaces the way one eats spaghetti. A good example of metonymy in *The Prisoner* would be the monstrous balloon, Rover,
which symbolizes the oppressive regime that runs the Village.
Figure 1.9 compares and contrasts metaphor and metonymy and
should help to clarify the two concepts.

Generally speaking we find metaphor and metonymy all mixed
together, and sometimes a given object might have both
metaphoric and metonymic significance. The distinction is important because it enables us to see more clearly how objects and
images (as well as language) generate meaning. And, in the case of
metonymy, it becomes obvious that people carry *codes* around in
their heads, highly complex patterns of associations that enable
them to interpret metonymic communication correctly. Just as you
can't tell the players without a program, you can't understand the
meaning of most things without knowing the codes.

CODES

Codes are highly complex patterns of associations we all learn in a
given society and culture. These codes, or 'secret structures' in our

Figure 1.9: Metaphor and metonymy contrasted

Metaphor	Metonymy
resemblance based on *analogy*	resemblance based on *association*
meta — transfer, beyond *phor* — to bear	*meta* — transfer *onoma* — name
Chaplin eats shoelaces like spaghetti	Rover kills one of the villagers on command of Number Two
simile: important subcategory in which comparison is made using "like" or "as"	*synecdoche:* important subcategory in which part stands for the whole or whole for a part
"No man is an island . . ."	red suggests passion
costume of Spiderman	Uncle Sam "stands for" America
long, thin objects can be seen as penises	"bowler" implies Englishman; cowboy hat implies the American West

minds, affect the way we interpret signs and symbols found in the media and the way we live. From this perspective, cultures are codification systems that play an important (though often unperceived) role in our lives. To be socialized and be given a culture means, in essence, to be taught a number of codes, most of which are quite specific to a person's social class, geographical location, ethnic group, and so on, though these, subcodings may exist within a more general code, such as 'American character,' for example.

We all recognize that in order for one to be able to drive on the highways a code is needed. This code is a collection of rules that tells us what to do in all conceivable situations. In like manner, we are all taught (often informally) other codes that tell us what to do in various situations and, when we think of television, what certain things 'mean.' Quite obviously we carry over our rules and understandings about life to media productions or, as we now put it, 'mass-mediated culture.'

It is quite possible, then, for misunderstandings to arise between those who create television programs and those who view them. In his essay, 'Towards a Semiotic Inquiry into the Television Message,' Umberto Eco (1972: 106), the distinguished Italian semiologist, suggests that 'the aberrant decoding ... is the rule in the mass media.' This is because people bring different codes to a given message and thus interpret it in different ways. As Eco (1972: 115) puts it:

> Codes and subcodes are applied to the message [read text here] in the light of a general framework of cultural references, which constitutes the receiver's patrimony of knowledge: his ideological, ethical, religious standpoints, his psychological attitudes, his tastes, his value systems, etc.

Eco offers some examples that suggest how these aberrant decodings might have taken place in the past: foreigners in strange cultures who do not know the codes or people who interpret messages in terms of their codes rather than the codes in which the messages were originally cast. This was, he tells us, before the development of mass media, when aberrant decodings were the exception, not the rule. With the development of mass media, however, the situation changed radically and aberrant decoding became the norm. According to Eco, this is because of the wide gap that exists between those who create and generate the material carried by the media and those who receive this material.

The transmitters of messages, because of their social class, educational level, political ideologies, world view, ethos, and so on, do not share the same codes as their audiences, who differ from the message transmitters in some or even most of the above respects and who interpret the messages they receive from their own perspectives. [...]

It has been said that the United States and Great Britain are two nations separated by a common language. In the same manner, the different classes in Britain, with their different codes, seem to be separated. When you move from language to the media, where there are aesthetic codes, iconic codes, and more separating people, the fact that the media can communicate with any degree of effectiveness becomes quite remarkable.

There are a number of aspects of codes and questions related to them that I would like to mention (but not deal with in any detail here) and that anyone interested in codes would do well to consider and investigate:

Characteristics of codes: coherence, covertness, clarity, concreteness, continuity, comprehensiveness, and the like.

Manifestations of codes: personality (in psychology), social roles (in social psychology), institutions (in sociology), ideologies (in political science), rituals (in anthropology).

Problems: creation of codes, modification of codes, conflicting codes, countercodes, codes and rules.

Codes in popular culture: formulas in spy stories, detective stories, westerns, science fiction adventures, pop music, fanzines, girly fiction, horror stories, gothic novels, advertisements, sitcoms, and so on.

Ritual: meals, drinking in bars, gift giving, dating, watching television, supermarket shopping, behaviour in elevators, sports contests, making love, dressing, and so on.[4]

Codes are difficult to see because of their characteristics — they are all-pervasive, specific, and clear-cut, which makes them almost invisible. They inform almost every aspect of our existence (I've listed some of their manifestations) and provide a useful concept for the analyst of the popular arts and media. For not only do genres such as the western or the sitcom follow codes, which are commonly known as formulas, but so do the media in general. It is to this subject I would like to turn now, specifically, with a discussion of codes in television.

SEMIOLOGY OF THE TELEVISION MEDIUM

I have, to this point, been concerned with the way in which semiological analysis can explicate programs carried on television, with a specific focus on the television narrative. A medium carries various genres of the popular arts, as the list below demonstrates:

Media	*Popular Art Forms*
radio	soap operas
television	advertisements/commercials
films	westerns
comics	police dramas
records	variety shows
posters	musicals
newspapers	talk shows
magazines	news
telephone	spy stories
books	documentaries
billboards	love stories

Each medium, because of its nature, imposes certain limitations on whichever popular art form or genre it carries. Because of the small screen and nature of the television image, for instance, it is difficult to do huge battle scenes. Television is a 'close-up' medium better suited to revealing character than to capturing action.

In applying semiology to television, then, it makes sense to concern ourselves with aspects of the medium that *function* as 'signs,' as distinguished from carrying signs. What is most interesting about television, from this point of view, are the kinds of camera shots employed in the medium. The list below shows the more important kinds of shots, which function as signifiers, defines them, and suggests what is signified by each shot.

Signifier (shot)	Definition	Signified (meaning)
close-up	face only	intimacy
medium shot	most of body	personal relationship
long shot	setting and characters	context, scope public distance
full shot	full body of person	social relationship

We can do the same for camera work and editing techniques:

Signifier	Definition	Signified (meaning)
pan down	camera looks down	power, authority
pan up	camera looks up	smallness, weakness
zoom in	camera moves in	observation, focus
fade in	image appears on blank screen	beginning
fade out	image screen goes blank	ending
cut	switch from one image to another	simultaneity, excitement
wipe	image wiped off screen	imposed conclusion

The above material represents a kind of grammar of television as far as shots, camera work, and editing techniques are concerned. We all learn the meanings of these phenomena as we watch television and they help us to understand what is going on in a given program.

There are other matters that might be considered here, also, such as lighting techniques, the use of color, sound effects, music, and so on. All of these are signifiers that help us interpret what we see on television (and also what we hear). Television is a highly complex medium that uses verbal language, visual images, and sound to generate impressions and ideas in people. It is the task of the television semiologist to determine, first, how this is possible and, second, how this is accomplished. [...]

A CHECKLIST FOR SEMIOLOGICAL ANALYSIS OF TELEVISION

In the material that follows I suggest some activities that should be undertaken in making a semiological analysis of a television program. I have concentrated on the narrative in this chapter, but much of what I've discussed is applicable to all kinds of programs.

(A) *Isolate and analyze the important signs in your text.*
(1) What are the important signifiers and what do they signify?
(2) What is the system that gives these signs meaning?
(3) What codes can be found?
(4) What ideological and sociological matters are involved?

(B) *What is the paradigmatic structure of the text?*
(1) What is the central opposition in the text?
(2) What paired opposites fit under the various categories?
(3) Do these oppositions have any psychological or social import?

(C) *What is the syntagmatic structure of the text?*
(1) What functions from Propp can be applied to the text?
(2) How does the sequential arrangement of elements affect meaning?
(3) Are there formulaic aspects that have shaped the text?

(D) *How does the medium of television affect the text?*
(1) What kinds of shots, camera angles, and editing techniques are used?
(2) How are lighting, color, music, and sound used to give meaning to signs?

(E) *What contributions have theorists made that can be applied?*
(1) What have semiological theorists written that can be adapted to television?
(2) What have media theorists written that can be applied to semiological analysis?

I hope that the contents of this chapter will give you a sense of the semiological approach and enable you to apply this fascinating — and powerful — analytical tool. You can apply semiology to television, film, the comics, advertisements, architecture, medical diseases, artifacts, objects, formulas, conventions, organizations, friends, enemies, and just about anything in which communication is important — and in which there is signification.

NOTES

1. Peirce's system is called 'semiotics' and differs somewhat from semiology, which has a linguistic base. But, for our purposes, we will consider them essentially the same.
2. For example, consider the difference order makes in the following two phrases, each of which contains the same words: 'My husband was late . . .' and 'My late husband was . . .'
3. Space does not permit me to dwell any longer on Lévi-Strauss. Readers interested in pursuing this subject are referred to the annotated bibliography that accompanies this chapter for works by and about Lévi-Strauss.
4. For an explication of these matters, see Berger (1976).

ANNOTATED REFERENCES

Barthes, Roland. *Mythologies.* Hill and Wang, 1972. A collection of short essays on everyday life topics, such as wrestling, soap powders, margarine, and steak and chips, and a long essay on semiological aspects of myth. A fascinating book and one of the most interesting examples of applied semiological analysis.
Barthes, Roland. *Writing Degree Zero and Elements of Semiology.* Beacon Press, 1970. Barthes deals with the basic concepts used in semiological analysis. He makes reference to some of the work he's done on food, fashion, furniture, and automobiles.
Coward, Rosalind and John Ellis. *Language and Materialism: Developments in Semiology and the Theory of the Subject.* Routledge & Kegan Paul, 1977. An important theoretical work that deals with semiological thought and its relation to Marxism, the work of French post-Freudian Lacan, and other topics.
Culler, Jonathan. *Structuralist Poetics: Structuralism, Linguistics and the Study of Literature.* Cornell University Press, 1976. An excellent discussion of the basic principles of semiological analysis and application to literature. Another book by Culler, *Ferdinand de Saussure*, in the Penguin Modern Masters series, is also highly recommended.
Eco, Umberto. *A Theory of Semiotics.* Indiana University Press, 1976. Important theoretical analysis of semiotics that deals with its range of applications. An advanced text for readers with a good background in the subject. See also Eco's *The Role of the Reader.*
Fiske, John and John Hartley. *Reading Television.* Methuen & Company, 1978. This is one of the most useful applications of semiological theory to television to be found. The authors devote a good deal of attention to codes and to specific texts.
Guiraud, Pierre. *Semiology.* Routledge & Kegan Paul, 1975. A very brief but interesting explication of semiological principles, originally published in the French 'Que sais-je?' series. Focus is on functions of media, signification, and codes.
Leach, Edmund. *Claude Lévi-Strauss.* Viking Press, 1970. One of the more

successful attempts to make Lévi-Strauss understandable to the general reader. Has some biographical material as well as chapters on myth, kinship, and symbolism.

Lévi-Strauss, Claude. *Structural Anthropology.* Doubleday & Co., 1967. A collection of essays on language, kinship, social organization, magic, religion, and art by the distinguished French anthropologist, an original mind and a great literary stylist.

Propp, Vladimir. *Morphology of the Folktale.* University of Texas Press, 1973. A classic 'formalist' analysis of fairy tales that has implications for the analysis of all kinds of other mass-mediated culture.

Saussure, Ferdinand de. *Course in General Linguistics.* McGraw-Hill, 1966. One of the central documents in semiological analysis and the source of many of the concepts used in the field.

Scholes, Robert. *Structuralism in Literature.* Yale University Press, 1974. An introduction to structuralist thinkers, with a focus on the analysis of literary texts but with obvious implications for other kinds of texts. The ideas of thinkers such as Jakobson, Lévi-Strauss, Jolles, Souriau, Propp, and Barthes are dealt with.

Sebeok, Thomas A. (ed.) *A Perfusion of Signs and Sight, Sound and Sense.* Indiana University Press, 1977 and 1978. Two important collections of applied semiological theory. Topics dealt with include clowns, medicine, faces, religion, nonsense, architecture, music, and culture.

Wright, Will. *Sixguns and Society: A Structural Study of the Western.* University of California Press, 1975. An ingenious application of the ideas of Lévi-Strauss, Propp, and others to the western.

2.6 Canada: Nation-building Threatened by the US-Dominated Media

RICHARD COLLINS*

Canada offers students of broadcasting a site for investigating a number of general problems of broadcasting policy as well as a distinctive broadcasting formation of some complexity but great fascination. For Canada has the problems of both a large and a small country, of an advanced and a developing society, but above all of a nation whose identity is always in question. What holds Canada together?

The country has two official languages and substantial linguistic minorities speaking Italian, German, Ukranian, native Indian and Inuit languages, Greek and Chinese. It is the second largest nation state in the world stretching nearly three thousand miles north–south and four thousand miles east–west, spanning seven time zones, with a population of almost 23 million largely dwelling in a strip two hundred miles deep north of the US/Canadian border embracing three metropolises but with a substantial scattered rural population. The geography of Canada is such that although east–west water communications stretching from the Atlantic to the Rocky Mountains facilitated early exploration and exploitation of a large land area, in much of the country north–south connections are as convenient as east–west. Physical communications with the United States are, in western and Atlantic Canada, as easy or easier than they are with central Canada.

Perhaps most importantly the economic interests of the Canadian regions diverge and one of the enduring tasks of the Federal government has been to mediate between these interests, though that mediation has often, though not invariably, been in the interests of central Canada, i.e. the two most populous provinces of Ontario and Quebec. [...]

---

*Source: Richard Collins 'Canada: Nation-building Threatened by US-dominated Media' in Kuhn, R. *Politics of Broadcasting* (Croom Helm, London, 1985) pp. 197-232.

To say that the unity of Canada is in crisis is a truism: in Quebec and Alberta separatist politicians have entered office, the provinces take each other and the Federal government to court and the passage to bilingualism in Ontario and Manitoba is exceeded in conflict only by Quebec's passage to monolingualism. [...] Yet Canada survives. The 1976 victory of the Parti Quebecois (PQ) with its sails set for separatism has been followed by the rejection of this policy by the population of Quebec in the 1980 referendum. Recent polls in Quebec indicate substantial Francophone dissatisfaction with the provincial government's hard-line policy towards the use of the English language in Quebec and Anglophone institutions. Provinces fight out their disagreements with each other and with the Federal government in Canadian courts — within a Canadian institutional framework. There is substantial popular assent to nation-building investments and policies; whilst westerners may be alienated and resent central hegemony, they still fly Maple Leaf flags outside their homes.

Canadian identity may be problematic, but it is less problematic than would be Albertan, United States, British colonial or even Quebec national identity, even though Canadian identity is characteristically defined by what it is not: not American, not British, not French. As Wilden puts it, Canada is 'Notland': a country whose limits of action, identity and geography are defined by others — nowhere more so than in communications.[1]

Given the centrifugal forces at work in Canada, a consistent theme in Canadian history and public policy has been that of nation-building: the construction of an infrastructure, an economic and political regime and ideology that will establish and maintain the imaginary unity of the Canadian nation. In this constant activity of national construction and self-definition, communications and the activity of the state — principally at Federal but also at provincial level — in facilitating inter-Canadian communications have long been central.

For example, the construction of the Inter Colonial Railway (opened 1876) between the Atlantic provinces and central Canada was part of the Confederation agreement and the accession of British Columbia to the Canadian confederation was conditional on the construction of an east–west transcontinental railway to link British Columbia to central Canada. The alignment of these railways was determined by military and economic judgements regarding the threat to Canadian interests from the United States as well as by geography. In the judgement of Sir John A MacDonald, the first Prime Minister of the Dominion of Canada, a condition of Canada's existence was the assertion of east–west transcontinental links and the construction of a communication infrastructure to realise them.

Since confederation, efficient communications and the state's role in communication have been consistently regarded by Canadian policy makers and scholars as a condition of Canada's continued existence. Whether the concern is with physical communication (the Canadian Pacific and National railways, the Trans Canada Highway or the development of Trans Canada Airlines, later Air Canada, as a Crown Corporation) or with the communication of information (the regulation of the telephone and telegraph systems, the establishment of the National Film Board of Canada and the Canadian Broadcasting Corporation or the dollar-for-dollar matching grants from Federal government to newspapers establishing news bureaux outside their home provinces or abroad), Canada has always had communication as a matter of great importance on the public policy agenda. Canada is exceptional in having a Ministry of Communications and Federal (and provincial) resources are devoted to the production of, in general very good quality, research and communication policy formation.

The historical importance of communications infrastructure in the formation of the Canadian state, the primary ceded to communication in Canadian political and academic discourse following Harold Innis and Marshall McLuhan, combined with the technological fix exposure to Daniel Bell's prophecies of a post-industrial information society, have created in Canada a kind of national obsession with communication policy and Canadian communication sovereignty. Whether one considers this obsession to be rooted in a correct apprehension of a real threat or in an imaginary fear that irrationally strikes residents of 'Notland'. depends on one's judgement as to the importance of communications in the maintenance of the Canadian state and Canadian sovereignty. In any event there can be no doubt that historically broadcasting in Canada has been used for nation-building purposes. In particular, this concern with the establishment and maintenance of a Canadian identity has manifested itself in a fear of cultural domination via the broadcasting media by Canada's powerful southern neighbour, the USA.

The provisions of the 1968 Broadcasting Act are particularly revealing in this respect. For example, under the terms of section 3, 'Broadcasting Policy for Canada', it is stated that

> The Canadian broadcasting system should be effectively owned and controlled by Canadians so as to safeguard, enrich and strengthen the cultural, political, social and economic fabric of Canada; ... the programming provided by each broadcaster should be of high standard, using predominantly Canadian creative and other resources; there should be provided, through a corporation established by Parliament for the purpose, a national broadcasting service that is predominantly Canadian in content and character; and the national broadcasting service should ... contribute to the development of national unity and provide for continuing expression of Canadian identity.[2]

Despite these provisions, however, broadcasting in Canada is, and has been since its inception in Montreal in 1919, surbordinated to foreign interests. The global trends identified by Schiller,[3] Tunstall[4] and Smith[5] of US dominance in world information flows are nowhere more potently exemplified than in Canadian broadcasting. The history of Canadian broadcasting (we shall use this somewhat misleading term in the absence of a comprehensible alternative that embraces the phenomena of cable, satellite, terrestrial microwave and broadcast distribution of audiovisual information signals) from 1919 to 1983 is one of subordination to the United States. Moreover, the lack of communication sovereignty experienced by Canada in its relations with the United States is reproduced within Canada where the problem is always with the bigger neighbour next door: Anglophone Canadian culture dominates Francophone, Ontario dominates Atlantic and western Anglophones, the native Indian and Inuit people are subordinated to the dominant Francophone or Anglophone culture and broadcasting systems, and so on. To help understand the Canadian fear of US domination and the concomitant normative emphasis on nationbuilding in Canada through broadcasting, indeed to comprehend fully the contemporary nature of Canadian broadcasting, we must first look at the history of radio and television in this North American society.

THE HISTORICAL DEVELOPMENT OF BROADCASTING IN CANADA

Radio broadcasting began in Canada in 1920 when the Canadian Marconi Company began service from its Montreal station XWA (later CFCF). [...] From the inception of broadcasting in Canada to the present day the Canadian experience has been decisively shaped by developments south of the border. By 1932, the year of the establishment of the Canadian Radio Broadcasting Commission (CRBC) under the Canadian Radio Broadcasting Act of the same year (the first step taken by the government of Canada to direct the development of broadcasting), the combined radiated power of US broadcasters was 680,000 watts, while that of Canadian broadcasters was less than 50,000 watts.[6] Peers instances the popularity of US stations with Canadian listeners:

> Nine tenths of the radio fans in this Dominion hear three or four times as many United States stations as Canadian. Few fans, no matter in what part of Canada they live, can regularly pick up more than three or four different Canadian stations; any fan with a good set can 'log' a score of American stations.[7]

In 1928 the first Royal Commission on broadcasting in Canada, the Aird Commission, was appointed and it reported in 1929, a decade after the licensing of Canada's first radio station. Many of the concerns of the Aird Commission have become perennials in Canadian broadcasting policy, but of particular interest is the Commission's concern with the two major paradigms of broadcasting organisation: the US model of, supposedly, free competition among stations for audiences and revenue on the one hand and the European public service model of state licensed and funded monopoly on the other. In their analysis of the Canadian situation the members of the Aird Commission found themselves drawn to the European solution (particularly to the instances of Germany which offered a model of Reich/Land relations that had potential for Federal/provincial relations and the UK's monopoly incorporated in the BBC). However, the Commission was reporting on a system that had developed on essentially American lines, of competition among stations in profitable markets for audiences and advertising revenue, and which was in danger of becoming wholly American in nature. In their visit to NBC (National Broadcasting Company) in New York members of the Commission were disturbed by NBC management's reassurance that the company intended to extend its service, and the same quality of service as that enjoyed in the United States, to Canada. In 1929 the two principal Toronto stations joined US networks: station CFRB joined CBS (Columbia Broadcasting System) and station CKGW responded by joining the NBC Red network. In Montreal station CKAC similarly joined CBS in 1929 and the pioneer Canadian station CFCF (owned by Canadian Marconi in which RCA — Radio Corporation of America — had an interest) affiliated to NBC in 1930. Radio stations serving the two great Canadian metropolises, Toronto and Montreal, accounted for half the total radiated power of transmitters in Canada.

The Aird Report led — in the teeth of opposition from the vested interests of Canadian commercial broadcasters represented by their trade association the CAB (Canadian Association of Broadcasters) — to the establishment of a national system of broadcasting in Canada. Statements made by one of the members of the Commission (C. Bowman) argued that only a national publicly financed system could be genuinely Canadian:

The drift under private enterprise is tending towards dependence upon United States sources. Contracts are being made between Canadian broadcasting agencies and the more powerful broadcasting interests of the United States. Increasing dependence upon such contracts would lead broadcasting on this continent into the same position as the motion picture industry has reached, after years of fruitless endeavour to establish Canadian independence in the production of films.

For

privately owned Canadian broadcasting stations, with nothing like the revenue available to the larger stations in the United States, cannot hope to compete beyond a very limited audience which in itself would be insufficient to support broadcasting worthy of Canada ... The cost of equipping Canada with radio stations to compare with the most popular stations in the United States would be more than Canadian radio advertising would support.[8] [...]

The report of the Aird Commission was followed by a period of intense debate, lobbying and political action which resulted in the promulgation of the Broadcasting Act of 1932, the establishment of the first public body concerned with broadcasting in Canada, the Canadian Radio Broadcasting Commission, and a much quoted statement by the Prime Minister that exemplifies the enduring contradiction in Canadian communications policy between the noble articulation of intelligent policy and a refusal of the necessary changes in the status quo required to realise the stated policy goals.

> This country must be assured of complete control of broadcasting from Canadian sources, free from foreign interference or influence. Without such control radio broadcasting can never become a great agency for communication of matters of national concern and for the diffusion of national thought and ideals, and without such control it can never be the agency by which national consciousness may be fostered and sustained and national unity still further strengthened. Secondly, no other scheme than that of public ownership can ensure to the people of this country, without regard to class or place, equal enjoyment of the benefits and pleasures of radio broadcasting. Then there is a third factor, ... the use of the air ... that lies over the soil or land of Canada is a natural resource over which we have complete jurisdiction under the recent decision of the privy council (referring to the confirmation of federal prerogatives in broadcasting challenged by provincial governments — *author*). I cannot think that any government would be warranted in leaving the air to private exploitation and not reserving it for development for the use of the people.[9]

Bennet's lofty sentiments notwithstanding, the CRBC was established for the fulfilment of compelling national goals with a budget insufficient to construct an adequate network of transmitters for the proposed national service or to induce private broadcasters to sell airtime for the broadcast of CRBC programmes. Dissatisfaction with the regime established for the CRBC was orchestrated and articulated by the Canadian Radio League, which had been established by a number of patriotic and influential young Canadian activists to press for a broadcasting order through which the goals of Canadian nationalism could be realised. The Radio League, now called the Broadcasting League, was established 'to create a radio broadcasting system which can draw the different parts of Canada together, which can use the air not only for indirect advertising but more essentially for educational and public purposes.'[10] The opposition of the Radio League, articulated in political attacks on the Liberal party by the Conservatives, resulted in the newly elected Liberal government for 1936 legislating to establish the Canadian Broadcasting Corporation, the CBC.

The Canadian Broadcasting Act of 1936 established a corporation modelled on the BBC. [...] Support for the public service ethos was further evidenced by the appointment of Alan Plaunt, the President of the Canadian Radio League, to the first board of the CBC.

The first priority for the new corporation was the establishment of an effective national distribution system for Canadian reception of Canadian radio programming. The daunting and costly task of achieving coverage of 84% of the population of the nation was completed in 1939. Comprehensive coverage (if coverage excluding 16% of the population can be called comprehensive) was achieved in partnership with some commercial broadcasters, whereby the private stations became affiliates of the CBC network and sold advertising and served audiences with CBC programmes. In addition, the programming for the extended network included programmes sponsored by advertisers and much American production which could be purchased at a price far below that required to produce Canadian material of comparable appeal and production values. Thus CBC was in competition with Canadian commercial broadcasters both as a purchaser of programmes from third parties (principally the United States) and of Canadian talent, as well as for advertising revenues and audiences. Programming and purchasing policy, though in parts distinctive, was forced into a convergence with that of the private broadcasters, with the commercial broadcasters seeking to maximise audiences for the least expenditure on programming (and therefore affiliating to the US radio networks and securing programmes from the USA) and thus maximise profits, while CBC was compelled to programme its schedules at the lowest cost (tending similarly to seek products from the USA) because of the constraints imposed by a shortage of funds resulting from heavy expenditure in constructing and operating its national transmission and distribution system.

The CBC thus developed as a public sector and public service broadcaster heavily influenced by the model of Reith's BBC though in a distinctively different fashion. In many ways CBC's initial development was one following the model of the US radio networks: a central organisation owning and operating transmitters in major metropolitan areas making available programming produced at the centre to remote, affiliated, privately-owned stations that themselves produced some of their own programming. Unlike the US networks though, CBC (although drawing some of its revenues from the sale of audiences to advertisers) was publicly financed and charged with the achievement of national political and cultural goals both through its own programming and through the powers to regulate the commercial broadcasters of Canada.

The recurrent criticism of the CBC from the commercial broadcasters in Canada was that it was both 'cop and competitor', for the new corporation retained a feature inherited from its predecessor, the CRBC, of regulating the whole of the Canadian broadcasting system as well as participating as a major state funded element within that system. The anomaly of cop and competitor was not rectified until 1958 with the establishment of the Board of Broadcast Governors separate from the CBC. Essentially what now appears as anomalous was an expression of the ideology of broadcasting in Canada as a *single* system, a viewpoint reiterated by the 1968 Broadcasting Act. 'Broadcasting undertakings in Canada ... constitute a single system, herein referred to as the Canadian broadcasting system, comprising public and private elements.'[11] No government, however, was prepared to fund the national service and curb the power of the commercial broadcasters in order to realise such a single system. Moreover, while the notion of a single system has persisted, acting as a rallying flag for nationalists who have sought to orchestrate the whole of Canadian broadcasting, public and private, for the achievement of nationalist goals, in fact Canadian broadcasting has never been a single system and this is even more true of the post-television era. [...]

In 1949 a commission of enquiry into the arts and culture in Canada including broadcasting, the Massey Commission, was established. Its report, published in 1951, largely supported the CBC for its achievement of three pre-eminent goals: 'An adequate coverage of the entire population, opportunities for Canadian talent and for Canadian self-expression generally, and successful resistance to the absorption of Canada into the general cultural pattern of the United States.'

The inadequacies of the CBC were those of insufficiently rigorous regulation of commercial broadcasting and of 'reticence' as to publicising itself. Massey therefore substantially endorsed the notion of the single national system, approved CBC's practice as a broadcaster and only condemned CBC as a regulator. For Massey it seems CBC's faults were those of being too soft a cop and too quiet a competitor. However, Massey's endorsement of the CBC (qualified by the minority report of one member, Dr. Surveyor) and his argument for the extension of the CBC's hegemony over radio in Canada were based on assumptions that a new broadcasting technology, television, was to expose as erroneous. The Massey Commission argued that; 'the principal grievance of the private broadcasters is based ... on a false assumption that broadcasting in Canada is an industry. Broadcasting in Canada in our view is a public service directed and controlled in the public interest by a body responsible to Parliament.'[12] Television was to demonstrate that the private broadcasters were correct. Even if their truth was not the whole truth, it was part of the truth. Broadcasting is an industry, an industry of a particular kind, a cultural industry with many differences to the steel or shoe industry, but an industry nonetheless.

The commercial broadcasters and other Canadian interests were anxious to establish television in Canada as early as possible. CBC, however, helped by the support given it by the Massey Commission, was able to block private television broadcasting, but was until 1952 unable to command the revenues to initiate its own television service. Its pious priorities were set out in the late 40s:

> The Board believes that in line with fundamental radio policies laid down by Parliament for radio broadcasting, television should be developed so as to be of benefit to the greatest possible number of people, so that public channels should be used in the public interest and with the overall aim of stimulating Canadian national life and not merely of broadcasting non-Canadian visual material in this country. The Board will strive for the maximum provision of Canadian television for Canadians.[13]

CBC's inability to command public funds adequate to the

achievement of the national goals it espoused, combined with its political influence and licensing power enabling it to block the development of commercial television, created a vacuum into which, of course, the cross border signals of the US TV networks flowed. Thus, television in Canada characteristically began before Canadian television. At the inception of CBC's services in September 1952 — in Toronto and Montreal only — there were 146,000 television receivers in Canada tuned to American stations and the first cable network was established in London Ontario to distribute US signals to subscribers.

The history of radio in Canada was replicated by television. American signals were imported over the air from powerful transmitters in US border settlements like Buffalo, Burlington and Bellingham built to deliver Canadian audiences to US advertisers and by cable to Canadians in towns unable to receive a satisfactory signal with a home aerial. Again the resources made available by government to the CBC to institute a national system of Canadian television were inadequate for the task and substantially less than those committed by private capital to the commercial section of the supposedly single Canadian broadcasting system. [...]

CBC's achievements satisfied few Canadians. Sections of the population lacked a television service, others had access to only one channel, and in the border areas and those served by the growing cable system Canadian channels and programming were outweighed by productions from the USA. The commercial broadcasters were to be excluded from establishing a television service, the Massey Commission had recommended, until after CBC had developed national programming in the two official languages available. But in order to make available a national television service as rapidly as possible, the government instituted a policy of licensing private broadcasters in areas unserved by CBC and declining to license second stations in markets already served by a Canadian television broadcaster until national single channel coverage had been achieved. The effect of this attempt to shotgun a national network based on co-operation between CBC and commercial broadcasters was disastrous. CBC were excluded from extending their services to a number of provincial capitals (because private broadcasters had the initial licence) and private interests were excluded from the major metropolitan markets. Absence of service in major Canadian centres of population, the existence of competition for audiences from the US networks in border areas,

the conflict of interests between CBC, the commercial broadcasters and advertisers and the continuing anomaly of CBC acting
as 'cop and competitor' provided fecund provocations for dis-
content.

The Fowler Royal Commission on Broadcasting, appointed in
1955, reported in 1957. The report recommended the establishment of a regulatory board independent of the CBC — the Board
of Broadcast Governors (BBG) appointed by the government. It
also favoured funding mechanisms for CBC that would separate its
funding from direct influence by government and which would,
hopefully, provide CBC with the resources necessary to establish a
national television distribution infrastructure and to fill its
schedules with substantial amounts of quality Canadian
programming. Fowler also reiterated the pious, orthodox litany of
a single national broadcasting system of mixed ownership with
CBC assuming the role of 'central factor' in the system.

Implementing or not the Fowler report was to become the
prerogative of a new Conservative government returned in 1958
with close links to a number of commercial broadcasting interests.
Essentially the elements of Fowler that were appropriated by the
Conservatives were those that enlarged the rights of commercial
broadcasting and reduced those of CBC. The 1958 Broadcasting
Act established a Board of Broadcast Governors, maintained
CBC's direct financial dependence on government and removed
from the provisions of the Broadcasting Act referring to CBC's
aims and objectives any responsibility for the fulfilment of national
purposes and responsibilities. [...]

In order to protect the Canadian production industry, and even
more importantly, national, cultural, political and ideological ends,
the BBG promulgated the first 'Canadian content' regulations,
attempting to inhibit by regulation the tendency, which it had
fostered by the licensing of an expanded television distribution
system, to secure television programming from the US rather than
Canadian sources. The first Canadian content requirements of the
BBG were for a minimum of 45% rising by April 1962 to a
minimum of 55% home-produced content. The long story of
negotiation between a regulator charged with maintaining a
Canadian element in Canadian broadcasting and a commercial
television industry with strong financial incentives to minimise the
exposure of its audiences to Canadian programming had begun.
The structural processes that the BBG had initiated with the

licensing of second stations and the CTV network were, in the coming decades, to be amplified by the growth of cable distribution of broadcast television in Canada and the consequential penetration of the US networks into markets that the technology of terrestrial broadcasting had not permitted them to enter.

The customary retrospect of broadcasting historians on the BBG is to regard it as a classic instance of a regulatory agency 'captured' by the interests it was supposed to police. This view though is one that proceeds from the axiom that Canadian national interest and identity are dependent on an effective policy of Canadian content and control in communications. Through that optic the era of the BBG is one of a regulator complicit with a group of traitors within the gates — the commercial broadcasters — in constituting the Canadian broadcasting industry as a channel for the distribution of US programming. This analysis of the commercial broadcasting interest and its regulatory lapdog as comprador capitalists profiting from the delivery of their compatriots' attention and identity to foreign interests is open to a number of challenges. For instance, it could be argued that Canadian national interest and identity are not vitally dependent on communication policy — Canada and Canadian nationalism have survived in robust health in spite of the substantial non-Canadian presence and interest in the Canadian broadcasting system since 1919. Indeed Canadian communication policy may be seen from a standpoint different to that of the customary cultural nationalist one as having consistently commanded the assent of Canadians for a broadcasting system based on the profit motive and the importation of programming for consumption by Canadians at substantially less than the economic cost of production. In other words, the policy has been one of consumers and distributor enjoying an abundant supply of information goods free of the task of paying an economic price for them.

Hull rather argues that the BBG mediated relatively successfully between the interests of commercial broadcasters and those of the national interest and that deficiencies in its stewardship stemmed from inadequacies in the Broadcasting Act of 1958 and the lack of ministerial concern with communications issues, rather than from the BBG itself.[14] Moreover, the promulgation of Canadian content regulations, even though softened by the BBG under pressure from commercial broadcasters, was definitely not in the interests of the commercial television and radio industry. The controversial nature of the regime of the Board of Broadcast Governors is due to the board presiding over, and in part promoting, a crucial divide in Canadian broadcasting. The shift was from a national system dominated by the CBC to a system where commercial interests — at first the commercial broadcasters, but latterly and increasingly the cable industry — achieved dominance in Canadian broadcasting as, essentially, distribution conduits for American programming checked only by the modest inhibitions enjoined by the regulator. That such a fundamental shift had taken place was recognised by the appointment of Robert Fowler (who had chaired the Royal Commission of 1955-7) to head an advisory committee on broadcasting in 1964. The second Fowler report urged — in a somewhat Utopian fashion — that government define clearly its intentions for broadcasting and create effective instruments for the promulgation of its policies: 'In the past Parliament has not stated the goals and purposes for the Canadian broadcasting system with sufficient clarity and precision, and this has been more responsible than anything else for the confusion in the system and the continuing dissatisfaction which has led to an endless series of investigations of it.'[15] The twin thrusts of Fowler's recommendations identified by Ellis — clear policy objectives and regulatory restructuring — were taken into the government's 1966 Broadcasting White Paper and the 1968 Act.

The 1968 Act is clearly based on the assumption that Canadian identity and nationhood are dependent on the Canadianness of its communication systems. The minister's statement introducing the Bill in Parliament included the following passage:

The most important of these principles is surely that which established that the air waves, which must be shared between public and private broadcasters, are public property and that they constitute a single broadcasting system. It is impossible to exaggerate the importance of broadcasting as a means of preserving and strengthening the cultural, social, political and economic fabric of Canada.[16]

A new regulatory agency was created to enforce the goals enjoined on broadcasters by the 1968 Act — the CRTC, Canadian Radio Television Commission (later the Canadian Radio-Television and Telecommunications Commission), which replaced the BBG. In setting out a broadcasting policy for Canada and by creating the CRTC, the 1968 Act fulfilled the recommendations of Fowler, but broadcasting in Canada and in particular the relations of the new regulator with its clients have been no less troubled post-68 than they were previously. For the Act, reflecting the minister's analysis and intention, was based on the fallacious theology of a single broadcasting system — the view that Canadian national integrity necessitates a Canadian communication system and that regulation and legislation can prescribe and control the forms of Canadian communication development. Fortunately or unfortunately, communications in Canada have been extremely hard for government to control because of Canada's proximity to the United States and its ability readily to import communication goods, coupled with the rapid development of communication technologies unforeseen by legislators. The 1968 Act for instance does not consider a technology that had been in place in Canada for sixteen years — cable television — let alone those developments, like broadcasting satellites, which are now exercising the minds of Canadian policy makers.

CABLE TELEVISION

Cable television in Canada developed as a system for the distribution of broadcast television signals from the United States to subscribers unable to receive these signals over the air with a domestic receiving aerial. There are markets in which local topography precludes reception of any television signals (including Canadian) with a domestic receiving aerial, but the most important reason for the general penetration of cable distribution in Canada is its delivery of foreign signals. The countries that vie with Canada for the status of being the most extensively cabled in the world (the small countries of Europe: Belgium, the Netherlands, Switzerland) share a common experience: a small population relative to neighbouring countries with a common language, which means that domestic broadcasters have low revenues for programme production compared to those enjoyed by the neighbouring broadcaster. Thus CBC, supported from the state budget and a share in the revenues from the sale of television advertising in Canada with a tenth of the population of the neighbouring United States, has much in common with the Dutch broadcasting authority NOS neighbouring West Germany. Dutch and Canadian viewers can, by subscribing to cable, enjoy television funded by revenues approximately ten times larger than the domestic service. Thus, audiences in the Netherlands for the German ARD and ZDF services are as high as those in Canada for the American CBS and NBC.[...]

Given then that cable offers benefits, why is it frequently identified in Europe and Canada as a major problem? Many regard trans-border flows of television programming as a kind of pollution of the airwaves — an involuntary and unwelcome import like acid rain. For any provision of new services, and hence any extension of choice, fragments the audience and diminishes the revenue base for existing services. Thus revenues available for production and programming tend to decline unless either more television is consumed (and viewing hours tend to be fairly inelastic — even in a Canadian winter only so much time can be devoted to television viewing, with Canadians already watching an average of 23 hours per week)[17] or premium rates are paid as in the renting of cassettes or videodiscs or for pay television. This rationale lies behind the licensing of pay television in Canada in 1982. Given this general tendency for revenues accruing to each station to decline with additional services, broadcasters are compelled to procure their programming from sources that provide the highest appeal to viewers at the lowest costs — in most cases from United States producers. [...]

The typical programme imported from the US by the Canadian networks during the 1974/75 season (and the situation has not changed since[18]) could be purchased for about $2000 per half hour, although the cost to the US producer would be about $125,000. With a much smaller market the Canadian producer spends about $30,000 on a similar type of programme. It is scarcely surprising that Canadian viewers regard a programme costing $30,000 to produce as inferior to one costing $125,000. When two specific programmes of the same type are compared, we find examples such as *Excuse my French*, a Canadian situation comedy, with an estimated revenue of $16,000 and production costs of $30,000 per episode and *M*A*S*H* which brought in an estimated revenue of $24,000 for a purchase cost per episode of about $2,000.[19] [...]

Cable television then has expanded the distribution capacity of the Canadian television industry, fragmented audiences and the revenue base of Canadian broadcasters and amplified the long term structural imbalance between US and Canadian broadcasting.

In 1977, 62.35% of Anglophone Canada had access to four *US* television channels, while only 45.61% of Anglophone Canada had access to 4 *Canadian* television channels.[20] Broadcasting interests — whether CBC or commercial broadcasters — have customarily deplored this state of affairs. The Canadian Association of Broadcasters (CAB), the trade association of commercial broadcasters, stated: 'The critical source of funding for commercial broadcast programmes depends on advertising revenue and the generation of this revenue is seriously affected by growing numbers of alternative viewing opportunities, notably those represented by US stations and other programming services carried by cable.'[21]

The CAB's protests and its playing the nationalist cause are more than slightly disingenuous, for the commercial broadcasters are themselves major carriers of US programming. A variety of regulations — the deletion of commercials on US signals carried by cable, the passing of bill C58 removing tax deductible benefits for Canadian corporations advertising on US stations and the simultaneous substitution policy whereby when a programme is scheduled by both Canadian and US stations a cable operator is required to substitute the Canadian for the US signal — have been promulgated to protect the revenues from the sale of advertising accruing to Canadian broadcasters.

Canada has, as the Minister of Communications Francis Fox said in *Towards a New National Broadcasting Policy:*

> The finest technical infrastructure for broadcasting in the world. Canada also has the world's most advanced system of domestic communications satellites which is employed to distribute radio and television programming. Satellite, microwave and cable technologies have made possible major achievements in extending broadcasting services in both official languages to all but a small minority of Canadians.

More debatably he argued,

> And this elaborate technical infrastructure, which on a per capita basis is more extensive than that of any country in the world, is effectively owned and controlled by Canadians.[22]

This distribution system has been created by the two interests operating in the supposedly single, national system. The public sector — notably CBC, but in recent years a number of the provinces as well (principally Ontario and Quebec but also Alberta, Saskatchewan and British Columbia) — has created a transmission and distribution system for the pursuit of public service and Canadian (or Quebec) goals. The private sector, whether the commercial broadcasters or the cable industry, have created subject to the market and regulation by the CBC, BBG or CRTC their transmission and distribution system for profit generated largely by the delivery of American production — the US networks by the cable operators and US programming by the commercial broadcasters. American and other foreign, principally British, programming is by no means absent from public sector stations, whether CBC owned and operated, CBC affiliates or run by the provinces (the latter are nominally educational but increasingly, particularly TV Ontario and Radio Quebec, provide a genuine alternative service). The public sector, however, exists for the achievement of goals unattainable by scheduling exclusively foreign programming, whereas the goals of the private sector could best be met by scheduling entirely programming produced outside Canada.

The Federal Cultural Policy Review Committee (the Applebaum Hebert or Applebert report) argues that broadcasting policy is the most developed expression of a pervasive Canadian condition:

> Cultural policy has not been entirely successful in encouraging the best use of the human creative resources Canada has in abundance. As a democratic and cosmopolitan country we have thrown open our borders to foreign cultural products and not given ourselves sufficient opportunity to enjoy the fruits of our own cultural labour. It is a telling state of affairs that our broadcasting system boasts the most sophisticated transmission hardware in the world — satellites, interactive cable, teletext — while Canadian viewers spend 80% of their viewing time watching foreign programmes on television. Broadcasting may provide the most striking illustration of this point, but it is by no means the only one. Our response to this dilemma is not, however, to come down on the side of protectionism, but rather to press home the point as forcefully as we can that federal cultural policy has largely favoured physical plant and organisational development over artistic creativity and achievement.[23] [. . .]

The principal strategy for the achievement of the ends of the 1968 Broadcasting Act — 'to safeguard, enrich and strengthen the cultural, political, social and economic fabric of Canada' through the notionally 'single system' — is the Canadian content regulations of the CRTC. Other potential powers, such as the granting and withdrawal of licences, have not been much used, though the CRTC, in an innovatory decision of potentially enormous importance in 1979, renewed the network licence for the CTV commercial, national, Anglophone network on the condition that it scheduled 26 hours of original Canadian drama in 1981-82. This decision of the CRTC, the subject of appeal by the CTV through the courts, was vindicated as an implementation of Section 3 of the 1968 Broadcasting Act by the Supreme Court in 1982.

Canadian content regulations were introduced by the BBG in 1959 and changes are currently being proposed by the CRTC. The regulations now provide that 60% of all programming broadcast on television be Canadian and that between 6 p.m. and midnight, the main viewing hours, 60% of CBC and 50% of private broadcasters' programming be Canadian. Canadian content is broadly defined: co-productions with Commonwealth or Francophone countries qualify as Canadian if 30% of the budget is spent in Canada or on Canadian participation, while other co-productions qualify if 50% is spent on qualifying expenditure (these percentages have varied at different periods of Canadian content regulations). Programmes of 'general interest to Canadians' qualify as Canadian content, including the world series and the United States President's State of the Union message. An off-the-record unattributable and possibly apocryphal story told to the author by a Canadian broadcaster in 1981 concerned another broadcaster who fulfilled Canadian content requirements by training a camera on an aquarium of swimming fish — Canadian fish and so Canadian content! [...]

In January 1983 the CRTC published a policy statement of its intentions for Canadian content in television. The CRTC notes that CBC exceeds its Canadian content requirements and intends to raise its Canadian content to 80%. But there has been:

An unacceptable decline in the amount of Canadian programming scheduled by a number of private television broadcasters serving major markets during the hours of heavy viewing between 7.30-10.30 p.m. In addition there is an under-representation of some forms of programming particularly in the areas of entertainment and children's programming. Canadian dramatic productions are virtually non-existent on private English language television, which is dominated by foreign entertainment programs and this is particularly the case during the mid-evening hours. Drama currently accounts for 49% of all viewing time on English language television and 66% of the viewing time between 7.30 p.m. and 10.30 p.m. However only 5% of drama scheduled is Canadian produced, and Canadian drama represents only 2% of the total time spent by Canadians viewing dramatic productions.[24]

To meet these problems (which are much less marked for Francophone television than for Anglophone) the CRTC proposed to introduce a points system which would give 'weighted points for the contribution of actors, singers and other performers' and 'take into account the various contributions of the production team, from the producer and editor to the set designer and camera operator.'[25] It is also considering introducing a 35% quota for the mid-evening hours, changing the annual period over which Canadian content is assessed to two semi-annual periods (to avoid the practice of filling the low viewing summer months with Canadian programmes and filling the high viewing winter months with foreign production) and to give a 50% Canadian content credit to programmes made outside Canada and not in French, English, Inuktitut or Canadian Indian languages which are then dubbed or lip synchronised in Canada. [...]

SATELLITE BROADCASTING

In the early 1970s the government of Canada created Telesat Canada. Owned by the government and the principal tele-communications carriers of Canada, Telesat operates the domestic communication satellite system of Canada which is used *inter alia*, for the distribution of television signals across Canada by CBC for re-broadcasting by terrestrial transmitters. In 1981 the CRTC licensed Canadian Satellite Communications (CANCOM) to provide a satellite to home television and radio distribution systems. The licensing of CANCOM was influenced by three principal factors: the desire to stimulate the communications satellite industry in Canada for reasons of industrial policy; the existence of an estimated 800,000 homes that can only be adequately provided with television services by DBS (Direct Broadcasting Satellites) because they are in small communities, isolated farms or in remote areas[26]; and the perceived need for a Canadian service to compete with the unauthorised reception of US satellite 'superstation' programmes. This reception of US satellite signals has become extremely common in Canada even when strictly illegal. Bars, hotels and motels in urban areas attract clients on the basis of offering viewing of US satellite signals, principally from the Satcom 1 satellite.

CANCOM was licensed to deliver four Canadian television signals (3 Anglophone and 1 Francophone) and eight radio signals (2 native language, 2 French and 4 English); but in 1983 the CRTC licensed CANCOM to add the 3 + 1 package to its services (3 + 1 is the United States CBS, NBC, ABC networks and PBS). The CRTC's rationale for this decision was that licensing CANCOM to deliver US television signals (the principal market being cable operators hitherto unable to offer them due to the high cost of terrestrial microwave transport of the signals) would enable CANCOM to keep the cost of its Canadian services low. Essentially CANCOM has been licensed as a 'cable in the sky' system with a potential franchise of 800,000 subscribers delivering both Canadian and US signals to subscribers. The major difference is that some markets served by CANCOM may have already been consuming US production but were unable to receive Canadian television. Yet the net effect of the 1981 and 1983 CANCOM decisions seems to have been to deliver US television to Canadians who have hitherto been unable to receive it and to expose Canadian broadcasters and programme makers to sharpened foreign competition. As Lyman points out:

> The outcome of major technological evolution can be a negative one for Canada's cultural industries. Too much emphasis on technology and the implementation of new delivery infrastructures may direct investment away from programming, i.e. investment in Canadian production. A specific example is the licensing of the Atlantic regional pay-TV network whose potential subscriber base is so small that the CRTC imposed as a condition of licence a very low proportional commitment to Canadian programming (15% of gross revenues as opposed to

50% for the Ontario regional license holder).[27]

Just as radio, television and cable offered distribution technologies that enabled new markets to be served with cultural goods and created market relationships that favoured non-Canadian producers of those goods, so too are broadcasting satellites. The Canadian state has invested heavily in satellite production and development and has a technology that may potentially lower broadcasting distribution costs dramatically, but it seems likely that the cultural goods that will circulate through the new low cost distribution systems will not be principally Canadian. In his presentation to the CRTC seeking approval (in the event denied) for a second CBC national television channel, CBC 2 — Télé 2, Al Johnson talked of the large economies available from the new distribution technologies: 'We propose ... to use the new mode of distribution — by satellite to cable. Not, by the way, simply because this is the new technological mode, but because the construction of parallel conventional distribution systems would cost over $80 million while satellite to cable distribution costs only $3.5 million per year.'[28]

The economies of the new distribution technology are evident enough. However, they are not being applied to existing services, but rather to make possible additional services. The CRTC's '3 + 1' decision recognises that by now a necessary condition of delivering Canadian signals to Canadians (in the absence of public funding further to the $477 million of the Federal budget for CBC, the $20 million for TV Ontario, $36 million for Radio Quebec and the more modest funding for provincial broadcasting in Alberta, British Columbia and Saskatchewan) is the supply of American signals. Audiences will pay for US services, but are less ready to pay for their Canadian equivalent.

PAY TELEVISION

The PAY TV licensing decision of the CRTC in 1982, referred to by Lyman above, is one that institutes a system for delivering cultural goods to consumers by completely eschewing the broadcasting distribution system which has been dominant in radio and television in Canada since 1919. Similarly it institutionalises a wholly new kind of financial relationship between consumers and distributors of cultural goods. Pay TV is available only to cable subscribers (though actually and potentially there is a very high penetration of cable in Canadian markets). In 1981 4,593,015 households were cable subscribers out of a total of 6,190,560 households wired in franchised areas covering 6,600,375 households.[29] Unlike broadcast radio and television, reception of which incurs no direct costs after purchase of the receiving apparatus, the PAY TV system delivers programmes only to those who pay a separate subscription. Pay TV was licensed: (a) to contribute to the realisation of the objectives set out in the Broadcasting Act and to strengthen the Canadian broadcasting system; (b) to increase the diversity of programming available to Canadians; and (c) to make available high quality Canadian programming from new programming sources by providing new opportunities and revenue sources for Canadian producers currently unable to gain access to the broadcasting system.[30]

To achieve these goals the CRTC licensed a 'national general interest service' *First Choice Canadian Communications Corporation* in French and English; 'regional general interest services' in Alberta *(Alberta Independent Pay Television)*, Ontario *(Ontario Independent Pay Television)* and the Atlantic Region *(Star Channel Services)*; a 'speciality' (performing arts) service, the *Lively Arts Market Building* (LAMB), for national distribution from Toronto; and a regional multilingual service, *World View Television*, for British Columbia.

The CRTC's decision has attracted hostile comment — both at the time of its delivery and subsequently in the light of the activities of the successful licensees. Much of the initial adverse comment was directed at the Commission's reversal of its conclusion in its Report on Pay Television that a single national pay television network be established.[31] The judgement of the report and of commentators (see *inter alios* Audley[32], Woodrow and Woodside[33] and the minority opinion of CRTC Commissioners Gagnon and Grace[34]) is that too many birds have been launched and that a plurality of pay services will fragment audiences and revenues, bid up the costs of programming (again largely emanating from the United States), siphon programming from broadcast television to Pay TV and prefer audiences in some regions of Canada at the expense of others. Lyman succinctly expresses the central proposition of the critics:

> The fundamental flaw in the CRTC's licensing scenario lies in
> the incomplete economic equation that seems to lie behind it.
> While the objectives are laudable in terms of support of
> Canadian programming ... it will prove almost impossible for
> Pay TV operators both to live up to the conditions of licence
> and to stimulate competitive Canadian programming — unless
> either the national or regional licence-holder drives the other
> out of the market in a particular geographic area. It appears that
> pay-TV in Canada will continue the tradition of broadcasting as
> a conduit for American entertainment programming.[35]

Experience supports the critic's judgement and not that of the
CRTC. For example, the arts channel went into receivership in
June 1983. The Alberta and Ontario regional pay systems now
operate under a common title, *Superchannel,* offering competition
to the supposedly national system in two crucial Anglophone
markets. In the other major Anglophone market, British
Columbia, *First Choice's* competition is not so fierce, but *World
View* is permitted to offer 40% of its total scheduling time and of
prime time in English. There seems no reason to suppose that
World View will be less successful than the commercial broadcasters in fulfilling the CRTC's requirements while still maximising
audiences and revenues on US programming. *First Choice* is
required to offer national distribution of Anglophone and Francophone programming. West of Winnipeg it is reported to have
subscribers to its Francophone services measured in double figures,
the revenues from whom are trifling when set against the costs of
satellite transponders for ensuring national availability of Francophone programming. In licensing Pay TV operations the CRTC
recognised the differences in the licencees' abilities to programme
Canadian content whilst maintaining economic viability. Accordingly the Atlantic region licensee, *Star Channel,* was required to
commit only 15% of gross revenues to Canadian content, while
the Ontario licensee, *Ontario Independent Pay Television,* was
required to commit 50%. *First Choice* was required to commit not
less than 45% of total revenues to Canadian programmes and is
partially fulfilling that requirement by co-producing in Canada
with Playboy Enterprises Canadian 'adult' (i.e. pornographic)
programmes — *First Choice* promotes itself as the 'Playboy

Channel.' The development is logical enough, since only porno-
graphy can command sufficient revenues from the fragmented
Canadian audience to make Canadian programming economically
viable for *First Choice*. Pay TV, no less than the development of a
plurality of Canadian broadcast television channels or the importation and distribution of US television signals by cable or satellite,
fragments the potential audience and lowers the revenue base for
programming. It exemplifies the persistence of the condition of
'Technopia Canadensis' diagnosed by the ex-minister of Communications, David MacDonald: 'A condition of intense focus on
hardware and new technologies causing an inability to see long
range effects.'[36]

CONCLUSION

The most recent developments in the Canadian broadcasting
system, CANCOM and Pay TV, will exemplify MacDonald's diagnosis. It is clear that there is a continuing contradiction between
the aspirations defined by the Canadian state in legislation for
Canada and its broadcasting system on the one hand, and those of
the Canadians who (outside the public sector) own and operate the
broadcasting system on the other. The CRTC, charged by the
Federal government with the responsibility of creating a broadcasting system that serves the national objectives prescribed in the
Broadcasting Act, sets out in the Pay TV Decision an explicit set
of objectives for Pay TV. However, the system that the CRTC
sanctions by its licenses cannot realise those objectives nor, given
that its role is reactive and regulatory, can the CRTC set in place a
Pay TV or broadcasting order which could realise the objectives of
the 1968 Broadcasting Act and Decision 82-240. The broadcasting system has overexpanded its distribution capacity, reducing
the revenues per hour available for programming finance and
necessitating the purchase of production from sources offering the
highest audience gratification for the lowest cost.

Each new technological initiative accelerates the spiral of
decline by sucking in more and more foreign production and
thereby making the conditions of existence of Canadian production harder and harder to achieve. However, it has to be recognised that this process has been remarkably consistent; perhaps it
is what Canadians want. Certainly there is no evidence that

suggests a regime necessary to achieve the aims of the Broad-casting Act would enjoy popular support. Such a regime would involve reducing the number of signals available to Canadians, ceasing the importation of US signals and the purchase of US programming, directing the revenues generated in the broadcasting system into production not shareholders' pockets and increasing the allocations from the public purse for broadcasting. Of the measures in the latest Canadian Federal policy statement in *Towards a New National Broadcasting Policy,* only increased allocations from the state budget is proposed. The other measures are directed towards stimulating the hardware industries and removing restrictions on programme reception. Probably no more could be done — the structural inhibitions to establishing a *Canadian* broadcasting system in Canada are by now too strong. All that can be done is to recognise that the notion of a single national system is an antique fiction and to continue support for the public sector and those parts of the private sector that can be recruited or coerced into serving the laudable ends of the 1968 Broadcasting Act.

At the same time, although one may recognise that hegemony in its own national culture and communications system is a legi-timate political goal for any state, there is no evidence offered by the case of Canada that loss of national cohesion and identity attends the absence of that hegemony. From outside the dominant, Innis-inspired Canadian approach, the history of broadcasting in Canada can be seen very plausibly as evidence that national sover-eignty, indeed nationhood itself, is not dependent on a distinctive national orientation in the communication system. Canadian broadcasting may effectively be American, but Canada is not thereby a part of the United States. 'Notland' is still somewhere.

NOTES

1. A. Wilden, *The Imaginary Canadian,* Vancouver, 1980.
2. 1968 Broadcasting Act, Section 3.
3. H. Schiller, *Mass Communications and American Empire,* New York, 1969.
4. J. Tunstall, *The Media are American,* London, 1977.
5. A. Smith, *The Geopolitics of Information: How Western Culture Dominates the World,* London, 1980.
6. D. Ellis, *Evolution of the Canadian Broadcasting System,* Hull, 1979, p. 2.
7. Elton Johnson, October 15 1924, quoted in Peers, *The Politics of Canadian Broadcasting 1920-51,* p. 20.

8. C. Bowman, articles in the *Ottawa Citizen*, December 27-31 1929, quoted in Peers, *The Politics of Canadian Broadcasting 1920-51*, pp. 53-54.

9. House of Commons debate, May 18 1932, quoted in Ellis, *Evolution of the Canadian Broadcasting System*, p. 8.

10. F. Peers, *The Politics of Canadian Broadcasting 1920-51*, Toronto, 1969, p. 65.

11. 1968 Broadcasting Act, Section 3.

12. Massey Report, p. 283, quoted in Ellis, *Evolution of the Canadian Broadcasting System*, p. 31.

13. F. Peers, *The Public Eye: Television and the Politics of Canadian Broadcasting 1952-68*, Toronto, 1979, p. 10.

14. W. Hull, 'Captive or Victim? The Board of Broadcast Governors and Bernstein's Law 1958-68', paper presented to the annual meeting of the Canadian Political Science Association, June 1983.

15. Ellis, *Evolution of the Canadian Broadcasting System*, p. 60.

16. House of Commons debate, October 17 1967, quoted in Ellis, *Evolution of the Canadian Broadcasting System*, p. 69.

17. Canadian Broadcasting Corporation, CB2/Télé 2, 'A proposal for national non-commercial satellite delivered CBC television services', 1980, p. 7.

18. Department of Communications, 'Towards a New National Broadcasting Policy', Ottawa, 1983.

19. CRTC background paper, 'The Economics of Canadian Television Production', Ottawa, 1976, quoted in McFadyen, Hoskins and Gillen, *Canadian Broadcasting*, p. 197.

20. CRTC, 'Canadian Broadcasting and Telecommunications: past experience and future options', 1980, p. 23.

21. Canadian Association of Broadcasters, 'Brief to the Federal Cultural Policy Review Committee', 1981, p. 49.

22. Department of Communications, 'Towards a New National Broadcasting Policy', Ottawa, 1983.

23. L. Applebaum and J. Hebert, *Report of the Federal Cultural Policy Review Committee*, Ottawa, 1982, p. 6. CRTC, 'Canadian Broadcasting and Telecommunications: past experience and future options', 1980, p. 23. A. Johnson, 'Canadian Programming on Television. Do Canadians want it?' Talk to the Broadcast Executives Society, February 1981, CBC mimeo.

24. CRTC, 'Policy Statement on Canadian Content in Television', 1983, pp. 6-7.

25. CRTC, 'Policy Statement on Canadian Content in Television, p. 14. CRTC, 'Survey of the Community Channel', 1979, p. 4. CRTC, 'Survey of the Community Channel', p. 38.

26. A. Curran, 'Canada Goes for the Middle Range in Television Satellites', *Intermedia*, vol. 9 no. 4, July, 1981.

27. P. Lyman, *Canada's Video Revolution*, Toronto, 1983, p. 95.

28. A. Johnson, 'CBC 2 and Télé 2', CBC documents, Ottawa, 1981, p. 5.

29. CRTC, 'Annual Report', Ottawa, 1982, p. 61.

30. CRTC, 'Decision 82-240 Pay Television', March 1982, p. 1.

31. CRTC, 'Report on Pay Television', March 1978.

32. P. Audley, *Canada's Cultural Industries*, Toronto, 1983.

33. R. Woodrow and K. Woodside, *The Introduction of Pay TV in Canada*, Montreal, 1982.

34. CRTC, 'Decision 82-240 Pay Television', March 1982.

35. P. Lyman, *Canada's Video Revolution*, p. 79.

36. R. Woodrow and K. Woodside, *The Introduction of Pay TV in Canada*, p. 161.

Note: The author wishes to acknowledge his particular debt to the work of Ellis and Peers in the writing of this chapter.

2.7 The Infrastructure of the 'Information Society'

HERBERT I. SCHILLER*

What is called the 'information society' is, in fact, the production, processing, and transmission of a very large amount of data about all sorts of matters — individual and national, social and commercial, economic and military. Most of the data are produced to meet very specific needs of super-corporations, national governmental bureaucracies, and the military establishments of the advanced industrial state.

New technology, new industries, new products and new services have come into being which derive profit from these data and which assist, as well, in their production and circulation. Already, institutional patterns have developed to facilitate these many activities. An examination of the communication structures, processes, and relationships currently in place may help to put in perspective the larger forces now at work in advanced capitalist society.

The complexity of the new information technology is beyond simple exposition. Many of the developments are difficult to ascertain because of the private nature of most of the arrangements and the technical sheath that conceals many of the socioeconomic factors. Additionally, the field is new, changing rapidly, and has not yet congealed into hard and fast relationships — though, as will be evident, this does seem to be occurring relatively quickly. For these reasons, what follows is intended to be exploratory, suggestive and certainly not definitive. One issue will remain central: How is the information dependency that now afflicts peoples and nations likely to be affected with the advent of the new instrumentation and its control mechanisms? [...]

*Source: Herbert I. Schiller, *Who Knows: Information in the Age of the Fortune 500* (Ablex Publishing, 1981, Norwood, New Jersey), pp. 25-45.

THE MAINFRAME COMPUTER INDUSTRY

The singular institutional attribute of the new communication technology, and especially of the big computers, is that almost all the hardware is produced by a very small number of companies. There is one corporation that dominates domestically and internationally.[1] One account describes this condition: Watching the movements made by companies and governments in the industry worldwide is like watching 15 chess matches going on at the same time. Every match has one thing in common though. IBM seems to control both queens on every board.[2]

Or, as the *un*authorized biographer of IBM writes: 'IBM is not just a major international company in the area of computing, it is the international environment.'[3] Currently, IBM operates 44 plants in 15 countries. In 1979, it received about half of its revenues from business outside the United States. In most of the major, developed countries in the world, its share of the communication markets starts at 50 percent.[4] In 1978, IBM had 53.8 percent of Western Europe's market for general purpose computers and nearly 60 percent of the West German market.[5]

IBM also constitutes the domestic computational environment. In 1979, 'IBM shipped 65.5 percent of the general-purpose computers and their related peripherals — a market share that in any other industry would be considered startling.' As several smaller firms produce equipment that ties into IBM's offering, 'one finds that IBM's decisions affect 74.5 percent of the nations's users ... To borrow a line from E.F. Hutton [the stockbrokerage firm] — when IBM speaks, *everybody* listens.'[6]

Actually, they do more than listen. They often disappear. In 1979, *Itel* Corporation 'become another victim of IBM's entrenched position in the marketplace.' It joined four other firms forced out of the business in the last ten years, 'and all have left primarily because of IBM's dominance in that market.'[7]

The size of the market for computers already is impressive. Its near term potential, projecting current installation trends, suggest that computers will constitute one of the world's largest industries. The power these developments confer on a corporation that now dominates the field, therefore, can hardly be overestimated.

MINICOMPUTERS

How specific market shares in this sector will evolve is difficult to predict. What is certain is the direction of its evolution. Further concentration, and consolidation into the domains of a few powerful businesses already on the scene, is the likely development.

SEMICONDUCTOR INDUSTRY

The integrated circuit or semiconductor industry constitutes a third and critical sector in the communication hardware category. Its product, the silicon chip containing miniaturized circuits, is the basis for the entire electronics industry — a field which 'is growing so fast that [it] could be a $400 billion industry by the late 1980s, a figure that puts electronics in the same league with oil, automobiles, and other giants of the business world.'[8] The chip is the basic element of computers, telecommunications items, pocket calculators, industrial process control equipment, scientific instruments, and defense systems.

The semiconductor industry has received heavy publicity in recent years as an example of dynamic capitalism. [...]

Taken out of historical and social context, it does seem as if the semiconductor industry has given a remarkable performance and demonstrated at the same time what capitalism, in its youth, was supposed to be all about: invention, application, risk, rapid growth, and product improvement. Overlooking the large element of myth surrounding what actually happened during capitalist development, capitalism is certainly not now in its youth. The semiconductor industry is better appreciated as a revealing example of late capitalist development. For this industry came into existence on the basis of huge governmental research funds allocated to maintain and expand the American corporate and military global presence. One example of many, 'the Minuteman missile program in particular ... greatly aided the development of integrated circuits by providing a market for the devices when they were just getting off the ground.'[9] Military support for the microcircuit industry has by no means abated. [...]

The high technology firms that sprouted in this period offered the publicists of American enterprise still another chance to glamorize a system that badly needed restoration. Yet this too has lapsed quickly. As a *Science* article reported: 'Great Corporations from Tiny Chips Grow ... microelectronics companies are changing in character from small, high-technology ventures of the 1950s and 1960s to large, mature corporations.'[10]

They are changing so because the capital required to start a microelectronic company in the current state of the art has jumped from $5 million in the 60s to at least $100 million currently. Further, to keep up with the advancing technology, increasingly expensive equipment is required. As has happened throughout capitalist development, the independents and the smaller firms are disappearing: being pushed out, bought up, or merged.

Actually, the semiconductor industry is made up of two kinds of manufacturers: the independents, who are disappearing; and those companies that are already included as divisions of vertically integrated firms. Examples of this second kind are IBM, TI (Texas Instruments), Motorola, and RCA.

The importance of semiconductors continues to grow, with *Business Week* noting that 'virtually every US manufacturer will soon be dependent on this technology',[11] and the international market for integrated circuits has become a scene of ferocious competition. United States' companies now hold two-thirds of the world market, but this apparently commanding position has been shrinking. It had been 88 percent in the 1960s; the Japanese offensive to take over a large chunk of the market grows more fierce.[12] The 1980 break-down of world market shares on a national and company basis is seen in Table 1.

However the world market for semiconductors may be re-divided in the years ahead, one development is assured. The small-scale, independent manufacturer will be gone and the integrated circuit industry will be absorbed into some subdivisions of a few transnational corporations. One of the early innovators in the industry predicted that 'in the 1980s there may be only about ten firms worldwide that remain as major suppliers of microcircuits.'[13]

SOFTWARE AND TRANSMISSIONS

While the hardware side of computer communication is being rationalized and transnationalized, similar developments are occurring on the less observable though no less important software side. This part of the computer communication industry includes

Table 1: Dividing the World's Market for Microchips

Share of world market	United States	European	Japanese
10% +	Texas Instruments IBM*		
5% to 10%	National Semiconductor Motorola Intel	Philips	
2% to 5%	Fairchild Camera Western Electric Mostek RCA	Siemens	Hitachi Toshiba NEC
1% to 2%	Hewlett-Packard Harris General Instruments Rockwell ITT	Thomson-CSF	Mitsubishi Fujitsu
Total share	67%	10%	15%

*Company makes integrated circuits for its own use only.
Source: Philips, *New York Times*, January 29, 1980.

the instructions (programs) for organizing, processing, and transmitting the data, as well as the data themselves and the prepared packages of data that are customized to meet individual specifications.

One of the most important categories of software is the data base. Data bases are constructed for many purposes, the most familiar of which is the academic/technical/scientific base. This is a set of data in a specific category or area — chemistry, physics, medicine, education, sociology — which has been stored in some suitably accessible form. The size of a base varies, but it may contain millions of records.

Other data bases are organized for the production, planning, and marketing needs of large, private corporations (for payrolls, raw material flows, property accounting, and customers) and for governmental and private administrative units (social security rolls, credit ratings, police records, and health statistics and information). This type of data base presently accounts for the preponderant utilization of computer communications. However, most of these are unavailable for systematic analysis and review because they are regarded as proprietary. Information searches by computer, already widespread, are likely to become standard tools in much of the scientific community's future research activity, to say nothing of their application to everyday business and government operations.

As computerized data base searching becomes the dominant mode of information acquisition, nothing less than the widest participation in the creation of the data base would be a prerequisite for meaningful information autonomy, locally, nationally, and internationally. This means the fullest opportunity for the user to know what is and what is not in the data base, the criteria for data selection and classification, and how changes may be introduced. [...]

Paralleling developments in the production and marketing of hardware, the software industry (apart from the totally proprietary intra-company computer systems) is being integrated rapidly into socioeconomic control structures. This follows in part from the considerable costs of assembling information. 'Putting [a data base] into operation requires the equivalent of 30 man years of work, an initial cash outlay of $0.8 to $1 million and an annual operating expenditure of between $120,000 and $200,000.'[14]

In a market economy, the questions of costs and prices inevitably play the most important, if not determining, roles in what kind of base will be constructed and the category of user the base is intended to serve (and by which it is to be paid for). The selection of material that goes into a data base is closely linked to the need for, and the marketability of, the information service. If corporate and government bureaucracies are the intended users — which happens most often because of their needs and ability to pay — their informational requirements will strongly influence the items put into the base, as well as the classifications adopted for easy retrieval of the information.

Currently, for example, financial data base services are largely the province of three Anglo-American corporate subsidiaries. Chase Econometrics (Chase Manhattan Bank), Reuters (English news agency) and AP-Dow Jones 'supply most of the world's demand for financial information.'[15] [...]

With respect to *organized* data — the essential prerequisite for utilization is an information-based economy — the United States in 1979 was ahead of other industrialized nations; almost two-thirds of the records held in organized data banks were located in US data bases. Of these, the US Government accounted for 25 percent and the private sector for 75 percent. Of that 75 percent, for-profit organizations have 44 percent and the not-for-profit organizations have 31 percent.

One other characteristic of these existing data bases in the United States, Canada, Japan and Europe is worth mentioning. It is striking that science-technology, science, and technology-related records accounted for 95 percent of the data held. One European study suggests that this reflects the development of publicly available computer-based information services that have been spin-offs from the massive US Government investment in defence and aerospace. These government agencies developed a methodology and technique of information handling to satisfy their own information needs. This methodology, updated to capitalize on advances in computer technology, is used by all the major international information services, such as System Development Corporation (SDC), Lockheed, the Space Documentation Service of the European Space Agency, and, also the major European operations.[16] Moreover, much of the assembled data originated in US military and military-related research and development after World War II.

Other developments are occurring that are rapidly transforming the organization and availability of data in the United States. There is, on one side, an uninterrupted assemblage of bases into ever larger aggregations of data available for a price. At the same time, new data base providers are appearing that are markedly different from the first data generators: the academic, scientific, and governmental producers. And, super corporations now are offering data amassed often for their own operations and made available for customized reworking, which they also will provide.

Considering the aggregation of existing data bases first, already a few corporations or corporate subsidiaries have emerged as significant data base organizers and data suppliers. Lockheed, for example, with its DIALOG information and retrieval system, contends that it is 'the largest and most extensive collection of on-line [interactive] data bases in the world.'[17] In 1980 it offered some 100 different data bases to its customers, including Foreign Traders Index (FTI), a data base prepared by the US Department of Commerce's Export Information Division.[18]

The FTI data base 'contains information on 150,000 firms in 130 countries, specifically with regard to the firms' contacts for international trading purposes. The file is designed to produce lists of potential foreign contacts for US businessmen and corporate executives.' Of some additional interest, especially to those professing attachment to the free flow of information, is that 'access to this file is being restricted to US organizations under terms of Lockheed's agreement with the Commerce Department.'[19] [...]

The main developments in data organization and supply are now coming from a new direction. *Fortune 500* corporations are moving into the field in a massive way. Already possessing sizable computer and data processing facilities, they are selling some of the information they produce for their international operations, also selling time on their computers and increasingly offering data processing operations to the specifications of interested customers. These developments allow new sources of profitmaking, assist diversification, and assure a place in the emerging arena of information control on a large scale.

Some of the business giants now entering the data processing and supply field move only a short distance from previous activities. McGraw-Hill Corporation, for example, is regarded still as a major publisher of books and magazines. Among its holdings are Standard & Poor's Stock Index, the Dodge construction index, Platt's Oilgram Price Report, and Data Resources, Inc. These and other information activities have permitted McGraw-Hill to become 'a world leader in the booming business of providing information to industry, government, and individuals.'[20] The voluminous data flows that supply the many familiar publishing enterprises of the company now are being organized and packaged for electronic distribution.

Another, different kind of entry into the electronic information processing and supply field is exemplified by *Citibank*, the second largest commercial bank in the United States. *Citibank* began to make its considerable in-house computer capacity available to non-banking customers in 1976. Additionally, it has been offering special services to the public such as a credit analysis system, an on-line financial data base, a securities data base, investment and economic planning, software, and related items. These services are being sold in 174 cities in the United States and around the world.[21]

Citibank, a mammoth financial enterprise with 'virtually no limit to the potential scope of [its] new burgeoning enterprise,'[22] is not alone in its data supply options. *Exxon*, the largest oil corporation in the world, has also moved into information processing and is expected to have subsidiaries in this field producing $10 to $15 billion in revenues by the end of the 1980s.[23] Still to be taken into account are the enormous resources of A T & T. [...]

INFORMATION NETWORKS: THE ULTIMATE SYNTHESIS

Summing up the discussion thus far: The manufacture of computers and the vital components of computers, the microcircuits, have become the business of a few giant companies. The use of computers to process data is being concentrated into huge service systems increasingly linked to conglomerate corporations which have large in-house computer facilities. At the same time, the data that are generated publicly by scientific, academic, and governmental bodies are being assembled into hundreds of data bases, distributed by a few corporate vendors. Other bodies of the data are being organized inside the business system itself, in the big banks and elsewhere. These data bases are being processed, packaged, and sold by firms many steps removed from communications in their alternate activities.

These movements and changes are occurring across several industries involving thousands of firms. At the same time, communication technology continues to develop and each generation of equipment far exceeds the capability of its predecessor. New models make existing facilities and processes obsolete. Not surprisingly, in such a period industrial stability and control are difficult to achieve, much less to maintain. One of the expectations arising out of these multitudinous shifts is for a new equilibrium to emerge that affords the information industry and its American managers, a continued opportunity for global hegemony. But for the moment, the scene bears a closer resemblance to Schumpeter's vision of the gales of 'capitalist creative destruction.'[24]

Yet with all this turbulence and uncertainty, a breathtaking and overarching synthesis seems to be, if not already emergent, at least present in some dim recognizable form. It takes the shape of *networks* — national and international systems linking powerful computational units, data bases, and transmission circuits. In the United States, unlike Western Europe, the network organizers are private corporations, most of which are already active and influential in one or another of several realms of modern communication. IBM, the dominant force worldwide in computers, leads the way in creating an all-embracing communications network. A new combinatory enterprise, Satellite Business Systems (a joint venture of subsidiaries of the International Business Machines Corporation, the Comsat General Corporation, and the Aetna Life and Casualty Company) has secured data transmission satellites through which it hopes to manage much of the rapidly expanding data transmission requirements of corporate business.[25] Charles P. Lecht, the President of Advanced Computer Techniques Corporation, predicts that IBM 'will eventually evolve into a "gigantic service bureau", providing computer power to users much the same way that utilities provide electricity today.'[26] [...]

IBM's path to becoming a planetary regulator is no smooth highway. As we shall find, international opposition from other industrial empires, private and public, is still to be confronted. At home, powerful corporate rivals already have indicated their willingness to challenge IBM for control of the electronic information environment. A T & T has announced plans for an Advanced Communication Service (ACS) network. Xerox Corporation has proposed Xerox Telecommunications Network (Xten). And Exxon Corporation has its Qwip-based network.

The struggle between the giants is bound to provide space for some public interest. How much will depend mainly on how well organized and how broad the anti-monopoly front will be. Internationally, some foresee massive confrontations in the 1980s between United States' private international communication networks and the public networks organized in Europe and Japan to defend national (and private) interests.[27]

The *domestic* outcome of these emerging structures — termed by some a 'network marketplace'[28] — is by no means a completed reality. All the same, some immediate consequences of what is happening are already observable.

As concentration and monopoly in communication hardware manufacturing and information-gathering, processing, and transmission have grown, so too has the gap widened in America between the information 'haves' and 'have nots'. The appearance of powerful corporate networks which integrate all levels of the informational field — from generation to dissemination — promises to deepen the existing gap into a chasm. In an article aptly titled 'Information Inequality',[29] the authors foresee a network marketplace that 'will be fragmented and serve only the needs of the major multiplant businesses and industries. Most of the *Fortune 500* companies and about one-third of the medium-size industries in the nation will account for almost 80% of network usage ... most of the smaller businesses and almost all consumers will still find the network marketplace too expensive.'[30] Already 'two classes of people and businesses: the information users and the information used,' are distinguished. By the mid-90s, 'the issue of information inequality,' the same authors believe, 'is likely to become one of some significant public concern, hence of political action.'

[...] For the moment, the private, corporate sphere of information control waxes as the public sphere wanes. But the public has scarcely understood the developments that are underway and that are further depriving it of its informational independence. As that recognition grows, and grow it must as one of the many results of the many rivalries that cannot be contained, what now seems an inexorable push toward a totally privatized, corporative, informational environment may not in fact, be the outcome which now appears inevitable.

NOTES

1. It is a mark of IBM's standing in the national economy that the Carter Administration contained nine persons with IBM connections in high-ranking positions. Three IBM board directors were in the cabinet. (*Computerworld*, June 25th and October 15, 1979). In the Reagan Administration, IBM promises to be at least as well represented. *Computerworld* (November 10, 1980) noted that 'The IBM board in fact has almost served as a "mini government in waiting" between elections.'

2. Angeline Pantages, 'The international computer industry,' *Datamation*, September 1976, p. 56.

3. Rex Malik, *And tomorrow the world?* London: Millington, 1975, p. x.

4. Angeline Pantages, *op. cit.*, p. 59.

5. *Business Week*, December 17, 1979, pp. 76 B & G.

6. *Computerworld*, editorial, 'When IBM speaks ...', March 31, 1980, p. 28.

7. *Computerworld*, editorial, 'The latest victim', October 8, 1979, p. 20.

8. Arthur L. Robinson 'Giant corporations from tiny chips grow,' *Science*, May 2, 1980 *208*, pp. 480-484.

9. Arthur L. Robinson, 'Perilous times for U.S. microcircuit makers,' *Science*, May 9, 1980, *208* pp. 582-586.

10. Arthur L. Robinson, 'Great corporations ...', *op. cit.*

11. 'Can semi-conductors survive big business?', Special Report, *Business Week*, December 3, 1979, p. 66.

12. 'Dividing the world market for microchips', *The New York Times*, January 29, 1980, p. D1.

13. Arthur L. Robinson, 'Great corporations ...', *op. cit.*

14. *Information Hot-Line* October 1976, *8* (9).

15. Cees J. Hamelink, 'International finances and the information industry,'

paper presented at the Conference on *World Communications: Decisions for the Eighties*, May 12-14, 1980, Annenberg School of Communications, Philadelphia.

16.   Gordon Pratt, (Ed.), *Information economics*. London: Association of Special Libraries and Information Bureaus (ASLIB), and European Association of Scientific Information Dissemination Centres (EUSIDIC) 1976, p. 1.

17.   *Advanced Technology/Libraries*, 6(1), January 1977.

18.   Walter Kiechel III, 'Everything you always wanted to know may soon be on-line', *Fortune*, May 5 1980, *101* (9), p. 227.

19.   *Online Review*, 1979, *3* (1) p. 7.

20.   Edwin McDowell, 'A data conglomerate,' *The New York Times*, September 3, 1979, p. 1, Section III.

21.   Association of Data Processing Service Organizations, Inc., *et al.* plaintiffs, against Citibank, N.A., *et al.* defendants. United States District Court for the Southern District of New York, Adapso brief, March 26, 1980. Also, Jake Kirchner, 'Adapso fighting Citibank offerings.' *Computerworld*, April 7, 1980.

22.   Adapso brief, *op. cit.*

23.   'Exxon's next prey: IBM and Xerox,' *Business Week*, April 28, 1980, p. 95.

24.   Joseph A. Schumpeter, *Capitalism, socialism and democracy*, New York: Harper Brothers & Row, 1950.

25.   Victor McElheny, 'Technology', *The New York Times*, August 17, 1977.

26.   Jeffry Beeler, 'IBM may become service bureau,' *Computerworld*, March 10, 1980, p. 1.

27.   Philip A. Tenkhoff, 'The networks face off,' *Computerworld*, June 16, 1980, p. 1 (Special Section 'In Depth')

28.   Herbert S. Dordick, Helen G. Bradley, & Burt Nanus, 'Information • inequality', *Computerworld*, April 21, 1980. See also (same authors), *The emerging network marketplace*, Norwood, N.J.: Ablex, 1981.

29.   *Ibid.*

30.   *Ibid.*

SECTION 3

MEDIA 'FORMS' AND THEIR EFFECTS

INTRODUCTION

Popular interest in the effects of the communications media tends to focus on their most manifest, perhaps most startling contents: e.g. sex, violence, bad language. Contributions to section 2 have indicated the dangers of inferring effects from content, and the difficulties of establishing that alleged effects have actually occurred. It is difficult even for researchers to be neutral in their assumptions about effects, for example to describe content without using language which in itself signals that certain effects are anticipated. The decision as to what should count as a discrete item of 'content' may disguise researchers' assumptions about what a viewer is likely to regard as significant. In the study of television violence for instance, does it make sense to look just at the gun firing, or should we take into account the heroism, shall we say, of the person who fired — perhaps to save the life of a friend at risk to his own? Or one can ask whether violence in cartoons carries equivalent weight to violence in more naturalistic portrayals. What in any case *is* content? Does it include the very structure of the narrative as well as its surface unfolding, or the dramatic strategies which contrive to grab our attention, keep us in suspense, play for our sympathy? Is the gun firing to the accompaniment of loud music and high-pace action of equivalent weight to a silent shot of smoke curling upwards from the gun barrel?

The term 'forms' is used sometimes to refer to the myriad of non-linguistic features of media that reside at levels other than those of the most manifest content. It is also sometimes used to refer to those general characteristics of a given medium which transcend the specific contents and which in combination distinguish it from other media. These considerations are relevant to education because the forms of a medium (the lay-out of a page, the juxtaposition of photographs with text, the angle and direction of a camera shot, etc.) may reinforce or even subvert the manifest message, or they may call upon particular cognitive skills for their interpretation and enjoyment and in so doing even cultivate and perfect those skills.

In the study of media forms is found fresh germination of a way of thinking about media that was once widely celebrated in the work of McLuhan and has now found new vigour within a surprisingly positivistic branch of educational psychology. Though often tentative, the findings have great significance for the improvement of our understanding of how the different media may be conducive to effective learning in distinctive ways.

In his chapters on graphic design Michael Twyman establishes a matrix categorization of the range of possible styles of text presentation within which most examples of page lay-out can be pigeonholed. Its relevance lies in the way it focuses our attention on formal aspects of print media usually taken for granted, and which can be regarded as important aids in improving the accessibility of a given text to its reader. Such forms often convey meanings in their own right by dint of well-established popular associations (e.g. the use of an Old English type-face to connote such things as age, tradition and craftsmanship). There is always an element of arbitrariness, in other words, to the distinction drawn between 'form' and 'content'.

How might form affect the educational potential of different media? Olson and Bruner draw a distinction between learning from direct experience and learning through media (with their heavy reliance on symbols). It is wrong, they say, to assume that the same content knowledge draws on the same mental or physical skills no matter how it is presented. This position may be a basis for arguing that different media call on different processing skills, but does not rule out the possibility that it is the form of presentation that is most important, regardless of medium: a picture of a cat may call on the same skills of mental processing whether it is in a book or on television. However Salomon argues that different media utilize unique mixes of symbol systems which in turn cultivate unique mental skills by either activating or overtly supplanting them (e.g. as when a particular filmic operation, such as zooming in or rotating in space, provides a model for thinking which a viewer with poor mastery of, say, detailed focus, or of imagining the unseen dimensions of an object, can adopt and internalize).

Detailed consideration of media forms seems to multiply the number of possible variables to be considered in any effects research and perhaps to further defer the possibility of consensus as to what effects can be attributed to media. But it has also added greatly to our understanding of what the media are and the language in which they may be described. More rigorous conceptualization of the different components of the form and content of media does offer further scope for manipulation of variables in experimental and field research to investigate aspects of comprehension, attention and memory. While the study of forms may have drawn back from McLuhanesque grand theory, at least temporarily, it has a lot to offer at a more modest level to the development of working guidelines for practitioners in production and education. This is demonstrated in relation to television by Rice *et al.* who distinguish between literal and symbolic portrayals, and find that some symbol systems employed by television are unique to that medium (e.g. the 'dissolve') while others are held in common with other media (e.g. many linguistic features). Within each of these categories are a diverse range of different forms with different potential effects, although one must query how far the significance of these may be diminished when considered in conjunction with manifest content. Successful educational and children's television, as the Rice chapter suggests, usually involves the manipulation of forms appropriate to the age, experience and understanding of children. In common with Olson and Bruner, and with Salomon, Rice *et al.* clearly see the relevance of theories of child development to an understanding of the learning potential of television.

3.1 A Schema for the Study of Graphic Language

MICHAEL TWYMAN*

[...] While all of us use graphic language as originators and consumers, very few of us are aware of how it should be planned so that it can be most effective. In this respect, as in many others, graphic language differs from oral language, which is either not consciously planned at all — as in most conversational situations — or is planned by those who engage in public speaking with a reasonable understanding of what they are doing. Our experience of planning graphic language — unless we have special problems, such as those presented by the preparation of a table for a scientific paper or a hand-made notice for a jumble sale — probably ended at school when we learned how to organize a letter, address an envelope, or set out a sum in mathematics. Most of those who use graphic means of communication professionally in everyday situations involving continuous prose merely pass on their problems to their typist who does the planning for them. In more complex areas of graphic communication, particularly when messages are non-linear, originators have less control over the graphic presentation of their messages and frequently rely on specialist draughtsmen, cartographers, or typographers. Such situations have few parallels in oral language.

OUTLINE OF OBJECTIVES

The principal objective of this paper is to demonstrate by means of a schema the wide range of approaches open to us in graphic language. The proposed schema, which is presented in the form of a matrix, draws attention to the different modes and configurations

*Source: P. Kolers, M.E. Wrolstad, H. Bound (eds), *Processing of Visible Language*, vol. 1 (Plenum Publishing Corporation, New York, 1979). (The version presented in this current volume has been edited and partly rewritten.)

of graphic language and is firmly rooted in practical applications. It is relevant to consider a schema of this kind — though not necessarily the one proposed — for both practical and theoretical reasons. In practical terms it is important because a schema which presents graphic language as a whole has the value of drawing attention to the variety of approaches available when using graphic language and defines those areas where decisions have to be made. All this is made necessary because our training and experience, whether primarily verbal, numerical, or visual, tends to predispose us towards particular approaches to graphic communication. In more theoretical terms, the overall pattern presented by the schema enables us to see points of connection between different areas of graphic language that are normally seen as discrete and that our traditional attitudes and terminology encourage us to keep separate.

The schema does not pretend to be watertight, and some of the boundaries between the cells of the matrix are drawn subjectively. The fact that some kinds of graphic language do not fit perfectly within the matrix serves only to highlight the subtlety and flexibility of graphic language. This should not invalidate the schema itself, which is intended as a device for directing our thinking and not as an end in itself.

FRAGMENTATION OF THE STUDY OF GRAPHIC LANGUAGE

Over the last few years I have attempted to develop approaches to the description of graphic language. In this respect I have taken a leaf out of the book of linguistic scientists, many of whom believe that description is a necessary prelude to understanding. Certain aspects of graphic language have, of course, been extremely well covered from a descriptive standpoint. The characters of the Latin alphabet, for instance, have been minutely studied: there are numerous classification systems designed to accommodate thousands of different styles of letterforms (most of which are not even noticed by the layman), and a precise language has been developed to describe the various parts of letters and their related characters. All this can perhaps be compared with phonetics as a branch of linguistics. There is also a vast literature which focuses on the iconography of that part of graphic language we call art, and traces subtle stylistic influences of one artist or school on another. This activity might be seen, at least in some respects, as akin to literary criticism.

These two aspects of graphic language have been chosen to highlight the diversity of the field and of the activities of those who work within it. Those who study letterforms in the manner described above are likely to be practising typographers or historians of printing; those who study the iconography of paintings are likely to be art historians. Though related to one another in that both are concerned with forms of graphic language, the two disciplines hardly interact. To a large degree the same must be said of other fields of scholarship concerned with graphic language within a theoretical framework, such as semiology, psychology, topology, anthropology, palaeography, linguistic science, and cartography.

THE MATRIX

The proposed schema is based on the matrix (Figure 1) which presents a number of theoretical possibilities in terms of approaches to graphic language. The column headings describe what have been called methods of configuration, by which is meant the graphic organization or structure of a message which influences and perhaps determines the 'searching,' 'reading,' and 'looking' strategies adopted by the user. There is no accepted terminology in this field, apart from the headings 'list,' 'linear branching,' and 'matrix', which will be readily understood. The division between the two headings to the extreme right of the matrix, 'non-linear directed viewing' and 'non-linear most options open' (shortened henceforth to 'non-linear directed' and 'non-linear open') is highly subjective and is therefore indicated by a dotted line. In reality the two categories, which are shown as discrete items in the matrix, form a continuum. There are elements of linear reading in some of the 'non-linear directed' categories, but the heading serves to emphasize that the principal searching strategy is non-linear. The most important general characteristic presented by the column headings is that they show a transition from pure linearity on the left to extreme non-linearity on the right.

Column headings have been limited to major categories since the main aim of this paper is to concentrate attention on a few central issues. It would not have been difficult to subdivide some of these major categories. For instance, the heading called 'linear

Method of configuration

Mode of symbolization	Pure linear	Linear interrupted	List	Linear branching	Matrix	Non-linear directed viewing	Non-linear most options open
Verbal/ numerical	1	2	3	4	5	6	7
Pictorial & verbal/ numerical	8	9	10	11	12	13	14
Pictorial	15	16	17	18	19	20	21
Schematic	22	23	24	25	26	27	28

Figure 1: The matrix

interrupted' could be further divided according to whether all reading was in the same direction (i.e., left to right, or right to left), or whether it was to be done boustrophedon (as the ox ploughs). Within each of these categories the interruption of the linear flow may be made on the following grounds:

1)   semantically (with the lines broken only after linguistic units, the smallest such unit being the word)
2)   quasi-semantically (with the lines broken only between words or within words according to etymology)
3)   partially semantically (with the lines broken between words or within words either phonetically or arbitrarily)
4)   mechanically (with words broken at the most convenient point, regardless of meaning).

Even within these four categories there are different ways in which these line endings may be achieved, and most of these can be found in everyday use. It is clear, however, that little is to be gained by producing a matrix of such complexity that it would be understood only by its originator or those prepared to spend an inordinate amount of time studying it.

The row headings describe, in a fairly crude way, the different modes of symbolization. The subject is one that has attracted considerable attention from semiologists over the last few decades, particularly in relation to iconic and symbolic images, but such issues are not central to the theme of this paper, which is more concerned with the relation between mode of symbolization and method of configuration. It should be said that it is more difficult to establish a distinction between pictorial and schematic modes than between the other categories on this axis; for this reason the division between them is indicated by a dotted line. A number of additional headings could also have been introduced on the axis of the matrix. A 'numerical' mode might have been included as a separate category from 'verbal/numerical'; in addition, it might have been valuable to introduce a combined 'schematic and verbal/numerical' category and to distinguish between discrete pictorial symbols and unified synoptic pictures. However, it was felt that such additions to the matrix would have blurred an important issue — the conflict in reading/viewing strategies that arises from the linearity of the verbal mode and the non-linearity of both the pictorial and schematic modes.

In other respects, too, emphasis has been placed on ease of understanding. Most obviously the matrix, as presented, takes no account of sequences in time as seen in film and television; nor even of the interrupted sequences in time presented by pages of a book or sets of slides. Such approaches could have been accommodated by adding a third dimension to the matrix, but at the expense of clarity. Similarly, a number of the graphic variables isolated by Bertin (1967) — such as size, tone, texture, colour, and shape are not specifically catered for. These can, and should, be considered in relation to all the combinations of modes of symbolization and methods of configuration presented in the matrix.

The Cells of the Matrix

The cells of the matrix have been numbered for ease of reference, even though this approach reinforces one particular reading strategy at the expense of others. These numbers have been included in parentheses in the text of this paper where relevant.

The examples chosen to fill the cells of the matrix are mainly from this century and from those parts of the world using the roman alphabet. However, the matrix has validity in relation to other linguistic conventions and other periods of time, and culturally and historically based approaches to it would probably prove fruitful.

It is important to emphasize that each cell of the matrix offers a relatively wide range of graphic possibilities. The most effective way of presenting the essential characteristics of each cell would be to show numerous examples, but clearly a printed paper does not lend itself to this approach. There is the danger, in showing a single example, or even a limited number of examples, that this might lead to the formulation of a narrow set of definitions for the cells. It should be said therefore that the prime reason for presenting the matrix is neither to define nor confine graphic language, but to find a way of talking about its variables. The cells define characteristics of graphic language which can be found in innumerable mixes, and many items of graphic language display the characteristics of more than one cell of the matrix. What is more, such characteristics should not be seen as residing solely in the item itself; they have to do with the relationship between the item and its users. For example, they may well be determined by a user's background, skills, and expectations, or by such factors as the purpose of the communication and the circumstances under which

Cell 1. These examples come as close to pure linearity as a limited two-dimensional format will allow. On the left is the Phaistos disc (Minoan, c.1700BC) and on the right a recent handwritten letter. Both examples read from the outside to the centre.

Cell 2. In practice, linear flow of text is nearly always interrupted, as in the Codex Sinaiticus from the fourth century AD (top left). The reasons for this practice are various (ergonomic, perceptual, practical) and apply throughout the world whether the direction of reading is left to right, right to left, or top to bottom (centre). Normally, line breaks do not relate to semantic units. Lines are usually more or less of the same length within a single passage of text, but linear interrupted text may take other forms (top right). The methods used to make sequences of lines conform to predetermined arrays are too numerous to describe here.

Cell 3. Lists differ from 2 above in that the items presented on each line form discrete semantic units. On the left is the order of the coronation procession of George IV, 1821. On the right is a restaurant guide in which entries are distinguished from one another by occupying separate lines, though each entry consists of two parts which are distinguished from one another typographically.

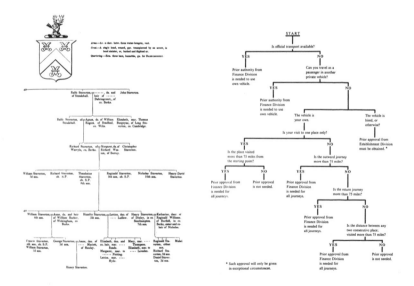

Cell 4. On the left is a traditional family tree of 1833, with many branches; on the right is an ordinary language algorithm, which is a binary branching structure.

FIRST DIVISION

		Home					Away					
	P	W	D	L	F	A	W	D	L	F	A	Pts
Leeds	13	5	1	0	12	4	3	3	1	8	5	20
Arsenal	13	6	1	0	21	2	1	3	2	6	11	18
Man. C	12	3	3	0	12	4	3	2	1	5	4	17
Spurs	13	4	1	1	9	4	2	4	1	10	6	17
Cryst P	13	5	0	2	10	5	2	3	1	5	4	17
Chelsea	13	3	3	0	11	8	2	3	2	5	5	16
Wolves	13	3	1	2	12	13	4	1	2	14	14	16
L'pool	12	4	2	0	12	2	1	3	2	3	4	15
Stoke	13	4	3	0	13	1	0	2	4	5	15	13
Cov C	13	3	1	2	6	3	2	2	3	6	8	13
Newc U	13	1	4	1	6	6	3	1	3	9	10	13
S'hmptn	13	3	2	1	8	3	1	2	4	7	10	12
Everton	13	2	3	1	9	6	2	1	4	9	15	12
Derby	13	3	1	3	11	9	1	2	3	7	11	11
WBA	13	3	3	1	13	9	0	2	4	9	21	11
Man. U	13	2	3	2	6	4	1	2	3	7	14	11
Notts F	13	3	2	1	12	6	0	3	4	1	12	11
H'field	13	3	3	1	9	5	0	2	4	3	12	11
Ipswich	13	3	2	2	13	7	0	1	5	1	8	9
W Ham	13	1	4	2	9	10	0	3	3	6	11	9
B'pool	13	1	3	2	6	9	1	1	5	4	14	8
Burnley	13	0	2	5	4	12	0	2	4	2	10	4

Investments in operating subsidiary companies

Name of company	Description of shares held	% of shares held	Country of registration
BRITISH IRON & STEEL CORPORATION LIMITED	Ordinary shares of £1 each	100	England
British Ore Investment Corporation Limited	Ordinary shares of £1 each	100	England
B.I.S.C. (Investments) Limited	Ordinary shares of £1 each	100	England
B.I.S.C. (Ore) Limited	Ordinary shares of £1 each	100	England
B.I.S.F. Pensions Limited	Ordinary shares of £1 each	100	England
British Magnesite Corporation Limited	'A' Ordinary shares of £1 each 'B' Ordinary shares of £1 each	60 2	England
BRITISH STEEL AND TUBE LIMITED (formerly Dorman Long and Company Limited)	D.L. Ordinary shares S.D. Ordinary shares S & L Ordinary shares 5½% Cumulative Preference shares	100 100 100 100	England
The British Structural Steel Company Limited	Shares of £1 each	100	England
Dorman Long & Amalgamated Engineering Limited (Incorporated in Nigeria)	Shares of N£1 each	83	Nigeria
Dorman Long (Bridge & Engineering) Limited	Ordinary shares of £1 each	100	England
Dorman Long (Chemicals) Limited	Ordinary shares of £1 each	100	England
Dorman Long (Engineering Holdings) Limited	Shares of £1 each	100	England
Dorman Long (Ghana) Limited (Incorporated in Ghana)	Shares of 2 new Cedis each	58	Ghana
Dorman Long (Steel) Limited	Ordinary shares of £1 each	100	England
Dormanstown Tenants Limited	Shares of £1 each	100	England
'Galvameta' Cia-Argentina Galvanizadora Y Metalurgica S.R.L. (Incorporated in Argentina)	Shares of 100 Pesos each	52	Argentina
The Middlesbrough Exchange Company Limited	Shares of £1 each	100	England
Redpath Dorman Long Limited	Ordinary shares of £1 each	100	Scotland
Richard Lees Limited	Ordinary shares of £1 each	100	England
TA Holdings Limited	Ordinary shares of £1 each	87	England
Teesside Bridge & Engineering Limited	Ordinary shares of £1 each	100	England
Tees Import Company Limited	Ordinary shares of £1 each	100	England
Zetland Road Trust Co Limited	Shares of £1 each	100	England
BRITISH STEEL CORPORATION (HOLDINGS) LIMITED	Ordinary shares of £1 each	100	England
The Glamorgan Hematite Iron Ore Company Limited	Ordinary shares of £1 each	100	England
South Wales Refractories Limited	Ordinary shares of £1 each	100	England
COLVILLES LIMITED	Ordinary shares of £1 each 5½% Preference shares of £1 each	100 100	Scotland
Blanchland Fluor Mines Limited	Ordinary shares of £1 each	100	England
The Clyde Alloy Steel Company Limited	Ordinary shares of £1 each	100	Scotland
Clyde Reinforcements Limited	Ordinary shares of £1 each	100	Scotland
Colvilles Constructional and Engineering Company Limited	Ordinary shares of £1 each	100	Scotland
Fullwood Foundry Company Limited	Ordinary shares of £1 each	100	Scotland
The Lanarkshire Steel Company Limited	Ordinary shares of £1 each	100	Scotland
Metal Gas Company Limited	'B' shares of 2/-d each 'C' shares of £1 each	100 100	Scotland
Scottish Fine Steels Limited	Ordinary shares of £1 each	100	Scotland
Shapfell Limestone Limited	Ordinary shares of £1 each	100	Scotland
Smith & McLean Limited	Ordinary shares of £1 each	100	Scotland
The Steel Company of Scotland Limited	Ordinary shares of £1 each	100	Scotland

Cell 5. Both these matrices would normally be called tables: the football league table (left) is primarily numerical, the page from a company report (right) is primarily verbal.

from 10s.; gents suits from £2; gents overcoats from £1; gents raincoats from 10s.; and hundreds of other bargains at The Tradin' Post, 1a, Whitley Street.—Reading 82972. C—26.9

TYPEWRITER, Underwood, manual, modern. Price £12 10s. — Phone Woodley Park 4960. C—26.9

CYCLE TYRES. 26 by 1⅜, 26 by 1¼, 27 by 1¼, from 11s. Tubes 5s. 6d. —K. Lovegrove, 181, Oxford Road, Reading. Tel. 51436. P—19.12

WEE BELLING Electric Cooker, £5; Tricycle, chain driven, age 4 to 6, £2 10s.; Cot and Mattress, £5; Boy's Sports Cycle, 3-speed, for age 12 onwards, £9 10s.; Pram Seat £1.—Reading 64297. P—26.9

MARPARTS open all day Sundays and late night Fridays. 5B—26.9

SOLID FUEL BOILER, Ideal Marquis, 45,000 b.t.u., with flue. £15. —Reading 21330. P—26.9

MARPARTS open all day Sundays and late night Fridays. 5B—26.9

GARDEN MASTER two-stroke rotovator, 25 gns. — Phone Reading 882386 C—26.9

GAS REFRIGERATOR recently converted, £8. View evenings after 6.30 p.m.—168, Kingfisher Drive, Woodley. C—26.9

SLOUGH CYCLE STORES.—Cycles

Cell 6. The boundary between Cells 6 and 7 is subjectively drawn. 'Non-linear directed' has traditionally been the language of advertising. Examples shown range from a consistent method of directing the viewing (left), where it is assumed that the bold headings will be scanned vertically as a first operation as in a list, to others (centre and right) where it is most unlikely that reading strategies will bear much relation to those adopted in relation to 'linear interrupted' language.

Cell 7. In the 'non-linear open' configuration, verbal language usually breaks down in terms of precise communication. In concrete poetry, however, it may take on other dimensions of meaning.

Cell 8. The Bayeux Tapestry is probably the nearest approach to a 'pure linear' image in this mode that can be found. It is not purely linear, however, as the verbal image is divided into discrete units and the picture is not a continuous narrative.

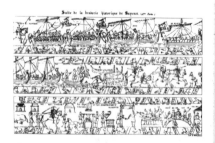

Cell 9. When presented in book form the Bayeux Tapestry (left) is usually divided into units of equal length as in traditional text setting. A well-tried application of the linear interrupted configuration using words and pictures is the comic strip (right), where the interruptions to the story are usually made on the basis of what will fit into the line.

car
adult } figures in these columns are
caravan } charges per night
tent
swimming (see L, P, R, S, and ⊖)

grass
sand
stone
little shade
partly shaded
mainly shaded
shower (cold only)
shower (hot and cold)
shop (see ⊖)
café
restaurant (see ⊖)
electric points for razors
electric points for caravans

E
Etr
exch
FDM
GC
h
junc
km
L
LC
lt
m
N
n/c
P
Pi

One small camera and/ or a pair of binoculars

Een kleine camera en/ of een verrekijker

One overcoat or wrap

Een overjas of mantel

One blanket

Een deken

One umbrella or walking-stick

Een parapluie of wandelstok

Cell 10. Combinations of pictures and words are found in list form in such things as keys to maps and guides (left) and travel regulations (right).

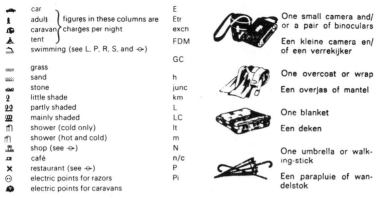

Cell 11. This is an unusual example of a multiple tree presented in the combined 'pictorial & verbal/numerical' mode.

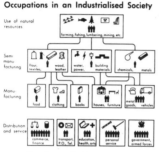

Cell 12. In the example on the left pictures are used as column and row headings to identify the numerical information in the cells of the matrix. In the example on the right, prepared for *The Sunday Times*, the actual content of the matrix is presented in pictorial terms and the user 'reads off' the information by assessing the length of the mini-skirts.

Cell 13. In the exhibition catalogue (left) the user's viewing is directed in a number of ways: horizontally along the row of pictures; horizontally from one column of text to another; and vertically so that each picture is read in conjunction with the passage of text beneath it. This scheme of organization is a rational one that has some of the characteristics of a matrix, whereas the directed viewing associated with advertising and popular journalism (right) is more intuitive and open to a wider range of reading/viewing strategies.

Cell 14. This early example of football reporting is probably as near as one can get to a graphic image in this mode, in which most options of viewing and reading are left open.

Cell 15. The story in relief sculpture spiralling up Trajan's Column of AD 112 in Rome (left), and panoramic views of coastlines and rivers (right) are examples of the linear presentation of pictures.

Cell 16. Wall paintings and mosaics have traditionally been presented in series of discrete scenes. The individual scenes of Giotto's fresco cycle in the Scrovegni Chapel, Padua (left and centre) of the early fourteenth century have been arranged, in so far as the structure of the building will allow, in much the same way as one reads text. A closer parallel with the 'verbal/numerical' mode is provided by the illustration of the funeral procession of Lord Nelson, 1806 (right), in which the rows of pictures have been 'justified' by putting variable amounts of space between the pictorial units.

Cell 17. Amongst the simplest pictorial lists are arrays of symbols designed to facilitate international travel (left). A more complicated example is provided by the sequence of pictures (right), each of which represents a separate stage in the narrative.

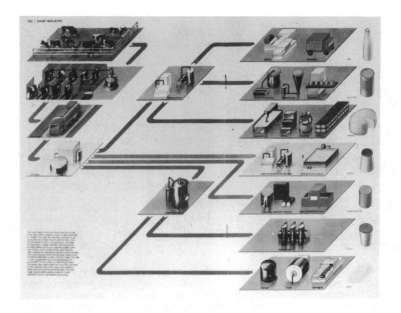

Cell 18. This pictorial tree from a pictorial encyclopaedia illustrates the structure of the dairy industry. The original is colour coded.

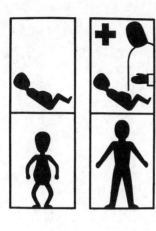 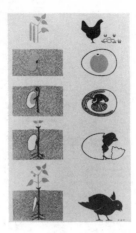

Cell 19. Matrices are rarely presented in the pictorial mode. In the example on the left the viewer has to deduce the headings from the content of the pictures (Column headings: no medical man/medical man. Row headings: swollen stomach/after swollen stomach). The example on the right shows the parallel life cycles of a bean and a chicken.

Cell 20. Most consciously-designed pictures fall into the category of 'non-linear directed', since it is usually the intention of an artist or photographer to direct our viewing. The difficulty lies in determining whether viewers do respond to images in the intended manner. It has been assumed that this perspective projection of the Great Exhibition building of 1851 provides a strong directive force in viewing.

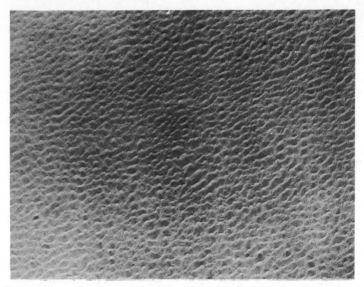

Cell 21. For the reasons given in relation to cell 20, it is almost impossible to find an example of 'non-linear open' in this mode. Even when a photograph is taken more or less at random there will be aspects in the organization of the image that influence our viewing. The example given is an aerial photograph of the North Sea.

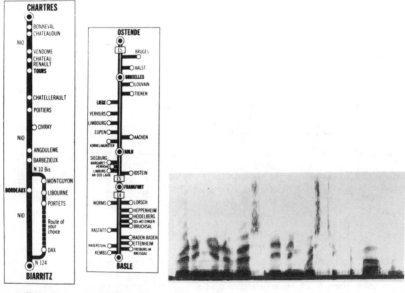

Cell 22. Route maps (left) and traces from graph plotters such as the spectrogram (right) provide well used examples of pure linear schematic language.

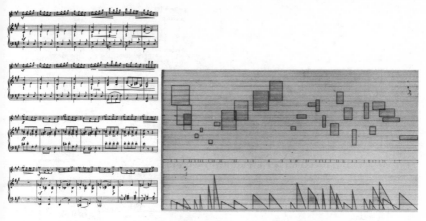

Cell 23. Traditional musical notation (left) and, more obviously schematic, modern form of notation (right), follow the 'linear interrupted' method of configuration.

Cell 24. No example has yet been found for this cell.

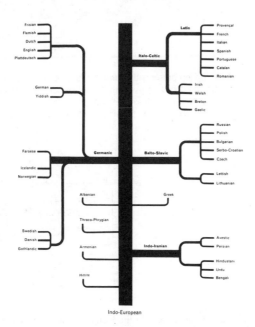

Cell 25. This schematic display of the relationship of the languages of the world follows a tree structure. The thickness of the lines relates to the evolutionary position of the languages shown.

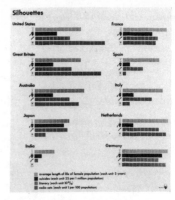

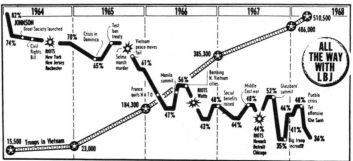

Cell 26. The example on the top left presents the range of spacing units available in letterpress printing using the Didot system. As with the set of bar charts (top right) it requires the user to make searches about two axes. Line graphs (centre) fall into this cell because they represent schematically the plotting of points on a matrix.

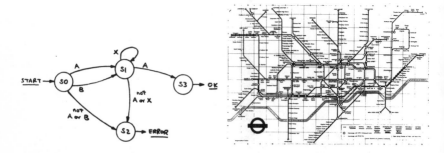

Cell 27. Most network diagrams (left) fall into the 'non-linear directed' category because only certain routes in them are regarded as legal. Some maps take the form of network diagrams: the London underground diagram, originally designed in 1933 (right), is perhaps the most influential network diagram ever produced.

Cell 28. Surface maps, such as this detail of a Canadian city, differ from network diagrams in that they leave most options open to the user. Some element of direction is provided for the user by such devices as colour coding and categories of labelling.

an item is used. The examples shown here should be considered with these comments in mind; they are presented in list form in the numbered sequence of the cells of the matrix, together with a brief commentary.

The following items have been provided as a visual footnote to the examples shown above in order to emphasize the point made above that the schema presented in this paper is a device for directing thinking about graphic language rather than a schema for the language itself. While there are many variants of graphic language that do not fit precisely within a single cell of the matrix, most such variants can be accommodated by it in that they combine the characteristics of a number of cells.

Abram Mrs V.E, 11 Midcroft,Slough ....**Farnham Com** 3601	Aczel Michael,
Abramowicz A, 15 Longwater Rd,Finchampstead ....**Eversley** 2677	Aczel Dr T, St.
Abrashve Specialities Ltd, 17 London Rd ....**Ascot** 23923	Adach Eliz, 44
Abrey G.A, 105 Vine Rd ....**Farnham Com** 4409	Adage Enginee
Abrey & Gerratt Ltd,Engs,	Adair C, 156 H
208 Bedford Av,Trading Est...**Slough** 32727	Adair D, 19 Sw
Abrey M, Glengariff,Altwood Bailey ....**Maidenhead** 26937	Adair Ian, The
Abrey M.J, 30 Southdown Rd,Emmer Gn ....**Reading** 471416	Adair J, 100 B
Abrey O.& F,Grcrs, 19 The Broadway.................**Thatcham** 3302	Adair J.R, 16 (
Absolom A.R, 6 South St,Caversham ....**Reading** 472236	Adair J.R, 29 I
Absolom D.W.A, 17 Romany La,Tilehurst............**Reading** 28247	Adair Maj P.R,
Absolom E.W, 25 Blagdon Rd ....**Reading** 85961	Adair R.M, 11 /
Absolom L.F, 2 Rifle Range Cotts,Berkley Av ......**Reading** 53377	Adam Brian, 1(
Absolom Oban G, The Maltsters Arms .....**Rotherfield Greys** 400	Adam D.J, 14 /
Absolom Peter F, 20 Northumberland Av ....**Reading** 82141	Adam E.W, 30
Absolom R.B, Yasume,Firs Rd,Tilehurst...............**Reading** 25853	Adam H, 11 Fr
Absolom R.B, 31 St. Johns Rd ....**Wallingford** 3561	Adam House Li
Absolom R.W,	Adam J, Timbe
Holly Cott,Layters Av,Chalfont St. Peter....**Gerrards X** 86158	Adam J.C, 8 B(
Absolom S,	Adam J.E, 37 I
2 Stonehouse Cotts,Highmoor,Henley...**Rotherfield Greys** 522	Adam M.J, 5 N
Absolon S.I, 42 Cromwell Rd ....**Maidenhead** 22028	Adam Peter—
Aburrow Brian R,	Shooting Loc
1, Eastwood Ct Eastwood Rd,Woodley...**Woodley Pk** 6212	(Gdnrs Res
Aburrow F.Leslie, 50 Western Elms Av ....**Reading** 52929	Adam P, Folly
Academy Hair Fashions,	Adam Miss S.J
126 Ashridge Rd,Wokingham...**W Forest** 6595	1 (
Accord Marine Ltd, 43 Vauxhall Dv,Woodley ....**Reading** 64580	Adam W.F,
Accounting,Bookeeping & Administrative Services,	Cotsw
38 Duke Rde...**Crowthorne** 2587	Adam W.L, 1C
Accounting & Secretarial Services,	Adamant Engin
131, Stoke Poges La...**Slough** 32223	
ACCURACY Ltd,Toolmkrs Injection Moulders,	Adamant & We
Factory 1 Weldeck Ho Weldeck Rd...Maidenhead 24396	
Ace Car Hire & Taxi Service—	Adamowicz M,
71 Kings Rd ....**Reading** 580911	Adams A,Saddl
Do. ....**Reading** 582143	Adams A, Oakn

Display 29. This detail from a telephone directory shows a sequence of lines composed of three discrete items in terms of content (name, address, number). However, only two distinctions are made typographically (the number is distinguished from the other two items by space and by the fact that part of it appears in bold type). This is not a simple list, because it has matrix characteristics. However, further typographic distinctions might need to be made for most people to regard it as a matrix.

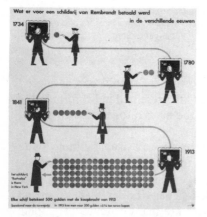

But when a boy leaves school for university or college, he learns, if botany be a branch of his studies, that the word tea is a corruption of the Chinese *Tsia* or *Tcha, Cha*. This is right enough ; but he is also taught that there are three distinct species of the tea plant, all belonging to the natural family Ternströmiaceæ, namely *Thea viridis*, or green tea ; *Thea Bohea*, which yields the black tea ; and *Thea Assamensis*, which gives us the teas of India, including Assam. At most examinations he would run the risk of being plucked, if

Displays 30 and 31. The pictorial chart (left) is particularly complex in its characteristics. It shows the growth in value of Rembrandt's paintings from top to bottom. In one sense it is purely linear in that viewing is directed in boustrophedon manner (as the ox ploughs) along a single drawn line; but there is a change in the orientation of the image on alternate rows as in some boustrophedon printing (right). Does this make it 'purely linear' or 'linear interrupted'? In any event, each row displays only one semantic unit, so that the chart has some of the characteristics of a list.

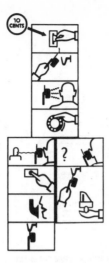

Display 32. This example can be seen as a cross between a pictorial list and a binary branching tree. In the original the two routes of the bottom half are printed in different colours. This is a very simple example of its kind, but the possibilities for the development of the approach are obvious.

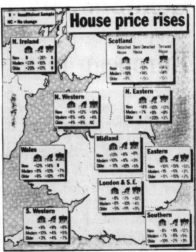

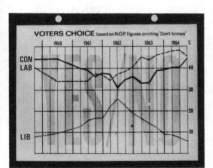

Displays 33 and 34. Many examples of everyday language we are presented with combine different modes of symbolization and methods of configuration. The example on the left combines a simple statement in the verbal mode with a more complex message stated schematically. The example on the right is a map within which discrete units of verbal, numerical and pictorial information are presented in matrix configurations.

222 MICHAEL TWYMAN

from Study I. However, because of the inclusion of a larger number of passages, it was necessary to use a somewhat more complicated order of presentation.

The passages consisted of six excerpts from the Davis Reading Test.[a] Six orders of presentation were used. These orders were arranged so that each passage appeared in each possible position (i.e., first, second, third, etc.) at least once. Within each order of presentation, half the passages were typed with proportional spacing and half with standard spacing, in counterbalanced order.

A total of 198 men and women were tested. As in Study I, the sampling procedure consisted of recruiting adult passers-by from a suburban shopping center. The demographic characteristics of the final sample are shown in Table IV.

TABLE IV. Demographic Characteristics of Sample: Study II

Characteristic	Men	Women	Total	Characteristic	Men	Women	Total
Age				**Income**			
21 to 25 years	27	46	73	Under $5,000	2	10	12
26 to 35 years	33	24	57	$5,000 to $9,999	35	30	65
36 to 45 years	19	19	38	$10,000 to $14,999	46	31	77
46 to 55 years	16	6	22	$15,000 to $19,999	11	13	24
56 years and older	4	3	7	$20,000 or more	6	4	10
Refused	1	—	1	Refused	—	10	10
Educational				**Occupation**			
High school some	20	36	56	Clerical	6	38	44
Some college	26	32	58	Sales	24	12	36
College graduate	52	17	49	Teacher	6	15	21
Graduate study	22	13	35	Engineer	19	—	19
				Manager	20	4	24
				Professional	23	21	44
				Refused	2	—	2
				Housewife	—	8	8

In both studies, the sampling procedures produced fairly heterogenous groups of adult subjects. However, there were some significant differences in the demographic composition of the two samples. The

[a] In Study II, one of the easy passages ("Finland") and one of the hard passages ("Economics") from Study I were used again. Two passages were added which were judged to be even easier than "Finland"—"Waldo" (366 words, Form 2-B, 11 questions), and "Johnson" (253 words, Form 1-C, 7 questions). Two others were added which were judged to be even harder than "Economics"—"Clocks" (334 words, Form 2-A, 10 questions), and "Lacquer" (236 words, Form 1-C, 10 questions).

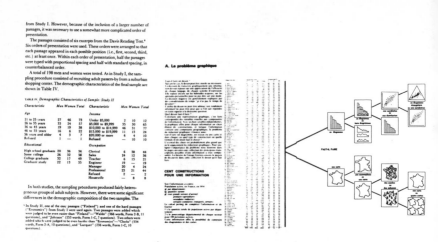

Displays 35 and 36. It is also common practice for a single sheet or other display of information to contain a variety of configurations such as tables with text (left), or text, lists, tables, and trees (right). When other variables of graphic language are taken into account (such as size, tone, texture, colour, orientation, form, and projection) the range of graphic language becomes considerable.

What Does the Matrix Reveal?

A full discussion of the matrix and the way in which graphic language relates to it would clearly be a major undertaking, and beyond the scope of this paper. On a general level it seems valuable to approach each row, column, and cell of the matrix from the point of view of both the originator and consumer of graphic language. It scarcely needs stating that some of the cells of the matrix that are widely used by people when in the role of consumer are hardly used by them at all when in the role of originator. Few people produce pictures, though most make use of them. The matrix can also be approached from the standpoint of specialist and non-specialist users of graphic language (the term specialist here applies to anyone who in a particular situation adopts, or has to respond to, an approach to graphic language not held to be in general use). Clearly there are degrees of specialism and no clear line of demarcation exists between specialist and non-specialist users. Nevertheless, some cells of the matrix include approaches to graphic language that are frequently used by specialists, but hardly at all by non-specialists.

In a practical situation (that is, when a designer has to make decisions with regard to graphic language) it would be useful to consider the cells of the matrix in relation to such factors as ease and cost of production, user capabilities, interests, and training, and the effectiveness of various approaches in connection with specific learning tasks. In order to make valid decisions without running special tests, a designer would need to know what empirical research reveals about the effectiveness of different approaches to graphic language in various circumstances. The matrix might therefore be considered as a useful aid for reviewing empirical research in the field of graphic language. But above all the matrix reveals the inescapable fact that in every graphic design situation choices have to be made concerning the method of configuration and mode of symbolization to be used. [...]

CONCLUSION

The matrix presented as the focal point of this paper reveals something of the scope and flexibility of graphic language. But how flexible is the human response to graphic language? The matrix invites us to ask how the readers/viewers are expected to respond to the variety of graphic language they are bombarded with in everyday situations. Do they face up to images on a page or VDU in the same way that they respond to real-world situations with their multiplicity of visual stimuli? It is reasonable to assume that there is usually no great problem in identifying the mode of symbolization being used in graphic language; but how is the reader/viewer to determine the method of configuration of a graphic display of information? Various writers have emphasized the importance of prediction in the reading process; but how does prediction apply when the rules of the game keep changing, or when there appear to be no rules? In any event, how do readers/viewers develop an appropriate strategy for extracting information once they have identified the method of configuration? What problems are presented by the apparent conflict between the linearity of the verbal mode and the non-linearity of the pictorial mode? This is a particularly important question since the two modes are being combined more regularly now, and at all levels of language, than at any time since the Middle Ages. What are the consequences of switching from one mode to another and one configuration to another on both eye movements and cognitive processes? Are there essential differences between absorbing information and ideas through discrete verbal statements (words, clauses, sentences), discrete pictorial symbols (pictographs, arrays of pictographs), and unified, synoptic pictures? How do all these questions relate to training in basic skills and working methods? Questions of this kind appear to be fundamental in relation to the processing of visible language. They can be formulated relatively easily; but how are they to be answered?

Many of the illustrations used in this paper are, strictly speaking, protected by copyright. It would have been virtually impossible to trace the sources for some of the illustrations used and if, through oversight or other circumstances, material has been reproduced without appropriate acknowledgments apologies are presented here. Those to whom acknowledgments should be made include the Automobile Association, The British Steel Corporation, the *Daily Mirror,* Mouton Publishers, Her Majesty's Stationery Office, Isotype Institute Ltd., Kimberly-Clark Limited, KLM Royal Dutch Airlines, the Kynoch Press, London Transport Executive, Macdonald & Co (Publishers) Ltd., Marlborough Fine Art (London) Ltd., Marshall Cavendish Ltd., G.J. Matthews, Penguin Books Ltd., Phaidon Press Ltd., and *The Sunday Times.*

REFERENCES

Bertin, J. *Sémiologie graphique: les diagrammes, les réseaux, les cartes* (2nd ed.). Paris, The Hague: Mouton and Gauthiers-Villars, 1967.

Feinberg, B.M. and Franklin, C.A. *Social Graphics Bibliography.* Washington, D.C.: Bureau of Social Science Research, 1975.

Feliciano, G.F., Powers, R.D. and Kearl, B.E. 'The presentation of statistical information'. *AV Communication Review,* 1963, 11, 32-39.

Goldsmith, E. *Research into Illustration: an Approach and a Review.* Cambridge: University Press, 1984.

Jones, S. *Design of Instruction.* London: Her Majesty's Stationery Office, 1968.

Kennedy, J.M. *A Psychology of Picture Perception.* San Francisco: Jossey-Bass, 1974.

Lewis, B., Horabin, I.S. and Gane, C.P., *Flowcharts, Logical Trees and Algorithms for Rules and Regulations,* London: HMSO, 1967.

Macdonald-Ross, M. 'How numbers are shown: a review of research on the presentation of quantitative data in text.' *AV Communication Review,* 1977, 25, 359-409.

Macdonald-Ross, M. and Smith, E. *Graphics in Text: a Bibliography.* Milton Keynes: The Open University, Institute of Educational Technology, Monograph No. 6, 1977.

Neurath, O., *International Picture Language* (Psyche Miniatures, General Series,

83), London: Kegan, Paul, Trench, Trubner, 1936.

Spencer, H., Reynolds, L. and Coe, B. *The Relative Effectiveness of Ten Alternative Systems of Typographic Coding in Bibliographical Material.* London: Royal College of Art, Readability of Print Research Unit, 1973.

Tinker, M.A. *Bases for Effective Reading.* Minneapolis: University of Minnesota Press, 1965.

Twyman, M., 'Using pictorial language: a discussion of the dimensions of the problem' in T. Duffy and R. Waller, *Designing Usable Texts,* Orlando, Florida: Academic Press, 1985.

Twyman, M. 'Articulating graphic language' in P. Kolers, M. Wrolstad, H. Bouma, *Processing of Visible Language,* vol. 3, New York: in press.

Wright, P. 'Writing to be understood: Why use sentences?' *Applied Ergonomics,* 1971, 2, 207-209.

Wright, P. 'Presenting technical information: A survey of research findings'. *Instructional Science,* 1977, 6, 93-134.

Wright, P. and Fox, K. 'Presenting information in tables.' *Applied Ergonomics,* 1970, 1, 234-242.

Wright, P. and Reid, F. 'Written information: Some alternatives to prose for expressing the outcomes of complex contingencies.' *Journal of Applied Psychology,* 1973, 57, 160-166.

3.2 Learning through Experience and Learning through Media

DAVID OLSON and JEROME BRUNER*

This paper is concerned broadly with the consequences of two types of experience which may be designated as direct experience and mediated experience, their partial equivalence and substitutability, and their differing potential roles in the intellectual development and acculturation of children. Our analysis will begin with the problem of the nature of direct experience and its effect on development. A clearer conception of the processes involved in direct experience will permit us to better examine the manner and extent to which mediate experience may complement, elaborate, and substitute for that direct experience.

Much of a child's experience is formalized through schooling. Whether for reasons of economy or effectiveness, schools have settled upon learning out of context through media which are primarily symbolic. Schooling generally reflects the naïve psychology which has been made explicit by Fritz Heider.[1] The general assumption of such a naïve psychology is that the effects of experience can be considered as knowledge, that knowledge is conscious, and that knowledge can be translated into words. Symmetrically, words can be translated into knowledge; hence, one can learn, that is, one can acquire knowledge, from being told.

Congruent with this is the belief that what differentiates child from adult is also knowledge and that the chief mission of school is to impart it by the formal mode of pedagogy. Concern for 'character' or 'virtue' centers not upon the school, but upon the home and the child's more intimate surroundings, the sources that provide models.

The assumptions that knowledge was central to the educational enterprise and that it was independent of both the form of experience from which it derived and the goals for which it was used had

*Source: David R. Olson, *Media and Symbols: the Forms of Expression, Communication and Education* (University of Chicago Press, Chicago, Illinois, 1974), pp. 125-50.

several important and persisting effects on educational thought. First, it led to a certain blindness to the effects of the *medium* of instruction as opposed to the content, a blindness that McLuhan has diagnosed[2] well; and, secondly, it led to a deemphasis of and a restricted conception of the nature and development of *ability*. As the effects of experience were increasingly equated to the accumulation of knowledge, experience was considered less and less often the source of ability. Since knowledge was all, ability could be taken for granted — simply, one *had* abilities that could be used to acquire knowledge. Abilities were, then, projected rather directly into the mind in the form of genetic traits. Culture and experience were both ignored as possible candidates to account for the development of abilities. The effect of this strange turn has been to downgrade the task of cultivating abilities in students, often thereby making schooling a poor instrument for the performance of this important task.

Education critics have, of course, long attacked educational goals formulated in terms of the simple acquisition of knowledge. Dewey's[3] concern with the relationship between knowledge and experience has much in common with contemporary reanalysis. In his view, genuine experience involved the initiation of some activity and a recognition of the consequences that ensued. Experiences of this sort would result, Dewey argued, in the natural and integrated development of knowledge, skills, and thinking. Schooling, on the other hand, attempted to develop the three independently of each other and with little regard for the experience of which they were products. No surprise, then, that schools frequently failed to achieve any of them. Dewey's revised conception of the relation between experience and knowledge reappears in the current attempts at educational reform which emphasize the role of process rather than content, or, more specifically, emphasize activity, participation, and experience rather than the acquisition of factual information.[4] The contemporary critic and Dewey alike would attack the assumption that knowledge is acquired independently of the means of instruction and independently of the intended uses to which knowledge is to be put.

That knowledge is dependent on or is limited by the purpose for which it was acquired has been illustrated in experiments by Duncker,[5] by Maier,[6] and by many other students of thinking and problem-solving. The conventional use of a pliers as a gripping instrument makes them difficult to perceive as a pendulum bob.

Knowledge *per se* does not make it possible to solve problems. The same appears to be true of verbally coded information. Maier, Thurber, and Janzen[7] showed that information which was coded appropriately for purposes of recall was, as a consequence, coded inappropriately for purposes of solving a problem. Information picked up from experience is limited in important ways to the purpose for which it is acquired — unless special means are arranged to free it from its context. But this conclusion is at odds with the naïve view that one can substitute 'instruction' for 'learning through experience.'

We must, then, reexamine the nature of direct experience and its relation to both knowledge and skills or abilities. Of course, the term 'direct' experience is somewhat misleading in that all knowledge is mediated through activity, and the resulting knowledge is not independent of the nature of those activities. But, if we consider both the knowledge of objects and events that results from experience and the structure of activities involved in experiencing, we may come closer to an adequate conception of 'direct experience'. We will then be in a better position to contrast it with mediated or, more accurately, the symbolically encoded and vicarious experience that is so important in acculturation.

DIRECT EXPERIENCE

Psychology, mirroring an earlier physics, often begins an account of the nature of experience with the concept of the 'stimulus.' What occurs in behavior is thought to be a reflection of the stimulus acting upon the organism. At a more abstract level of analysis, the shape of the effective stimulus is seen as the result of certain physical filterings or transformation of the input given by the nature of the nervous system and its transducers. This conception is much too passive and nonselective with respect to what affects organisms. Living systems have an integrity of their own; they have commerce with the environment on their own terms, selecting from the environment and building representations of this environment as required for the survival and fulfillment of the individual and the species. It follows that our conception of physical reality is itself achieved by selective mediation.[8] The search for a psychological account of behavior must begin with the organism's activities and then determine the nature of the 'reality' sustained by that type of activity. It is a point that is explicit and central to Piaget's conception of adaptive behavior in general and intelligence in particular: objects and events are not passively recorded or copied but, rather, acted upon and perceived in terms of action performed.[9]

What does this view imply about the nature and consequence of experience? As we have said, we have a picture of reality that is biased by or coded in terms of our actions upon it; knowledge is always mediated or specified through some form of human activity. But note that any knowledge acquired through any such activity has two facets: information about the *world* and information about the *activity* used in gaining knowledge. In an aphorism: from sitting on chairs one learns both about 'chairs' and about 'sitting'. This distinction is reflected in ordinary language in the terms *knowledge* and *skill* or *ability*. There are, therefore, two types of invariants that are specified through experience. The set of features that are more or less invariant across different activities may be considered as the structural or invariant features of objects and events that constitute our *knowledge* about those objects and events. Similarly, the set of operations or constituent acts that are invariant when performed across different objects and events may be considered as the structural basis of the activities themselves — that which we call *skills and abilities*. It is our hypothesis that 'knowledge' reflects the invariants in the natural and social environment while 'skills or abilities' reflect the structure of the medium or performatory domain in which various activities are carried out (see figure 1). Obviously, major significance must be attributed to *both* facets of experience.

Consider more specifically how both facets are realized in practice. The performance of any act may be considered a sequence of decision points, each involving a set of alternatives. These decision points are specified jointly by the intention motivating the act, the goal or end point, and the structure of the medium or environment in which the act occurs. A skilled performance requires that the actor have information available that permits him to choose between these alternatives. Problem-solving is a matter of trying out various means and assessing their contribution to the achievement of the end state. He must assess the means while keeping the end criteria in mind. It is a universal routine — in love, in war, in writing a paragraph or solving an equation, or, indeed, in managing to get hold of objects during the initial phases of the infant's mastery of reaching.

From this point of view, mastery depends upon the acquisition of information required for choosing between alternative courses of action that could lead to a sought-after end. The most obvious way to acquire such information is through active attempts to achieve various goals in a variety of performatory domains. The most obvious way to learn about a country is to walk its streets, read its poets, eat its foods, work in its fields, and so on. In so doing, one will learn both about the country (*that* the country is poor or hilly, etc.) and how to proceed in the activities required to be of that country (*how to* mend a net or tell a story). This is surely what is meant by learning through one's own direct contingent experience.

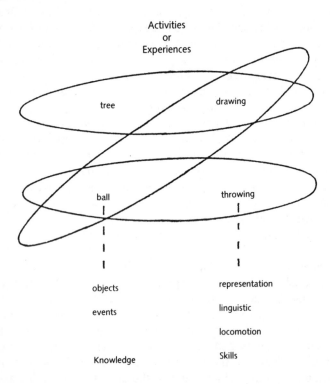

Figure 1: The relation of knowledge and skills to physical activity

MEDIATE EXPERIENCE

But there are other ways to acquire information. From seeing a man struggle with his load, one can make some estimate of its weight. That is, one can experience vicariously or mediately. Psychological studies have repeatedly shown that learning can occur when neither of the primary conditions for learning through contingent experience — self-initiated action or direct knowledge of its results — is fulfilled. Bandura[10] has summarized a wide range of data showing how behavior can be modified and new behavior patterns acquired by exposing the learner to modeling stimuli even in rather artificial laboratory situations. An illustrative experiment was performed long ago by Herbert and Harsh.[11] Two groups of cats learned to pull strings and open doors by observing other cats. One group of cats saw only the final errorless performances of cat models while the other group saw the early error-filled performances as well as the correct performances. Both groups of cats learned to solve the problems more quickly than the control cats, who learned only from their own contingent experience. But the cats that saw the error-filled performances learned more readily than those who saw only the error-free performances.

Another alternative to learning directly is through symbolically coded information, that is, the information that is transmitted through the media — the spoken or printed word, film, diagram, and so on. It is learning through these symbolic systems that most readily substitutes for direct experience in formal schooling. Vygotsky[12] and Bruner[13] have emphasized the extent to which language provides the means par excellence for teaching and learning out of context, out of a situation in which action is in process and contingent consequences are most direct. Language, as we shall see, provides an opportunity for acquiring knowledge which, while it is less useful for any particular line of action, has the advantage of ordering knowledge in a form compatible with the rules of abstract thought.

We have, therefore, three modes of experience which map roughly onto the three forms of representation discussed elsewhere[14] as enactive, iconic, and symbolic: the first is related to direct action, the second to models, and the third to symbolic systems.

More important to our purposes is the fact that these three modes of experience map onto evolutionary development.[15] While all animals learn from contingent experience, primates are distinctive in their capacity for learning by observation — there is an enormous amount of observation of adult behavior by the young, with incorporation of what has been learned into a pattern of play. The human species is, of course, marked by its reliance on symbolically coded experience — so much so that the development of language is taken as the distinctive characteristic of the human species and the development of literacy in various symbolic codes is the primary concern of formalized schooling. It follows that these three forms of experience differ greatly in the assumptions they make about the organism; that is, they differ primarily in terms of the skills they assume and develop in the learner.

ON THE ACQUISITION OF KNOWLEDGE

To this point, the burden of our argument has been to show that one can learn from three very different forms of experience and that these forms of experience, whether mediate or direct, qualify what is learned. This section of the paper is directed to an examination of what is common to different forms of experience; the next section is concerned with what is distinctive about them. Our conclusion will be that different forms of experience converge as to the knowledge they specify, but they diverge as to the skills they develop.

The assertion to be examined here is that different forms of experiencing an object or an event can be mapped onto a common underlying structure — a coherent and generalized conception of reality. Information about a particular event, regardless of the activity or medium through which it is obtained, has in common the property that it permits the differentiation of that event from the alternatives with which it is in danger of being confused. Consider the experience of actually seeing a zebra with that of hearing the instructional statement 'A zebra is a striped, horse-like animal.' The same features detected in the act of discrimination are specified in the statement; hence, they are informationally equivalent and they can both be mapped onto an underlying conception of zebras, horses, animals, and so on. This is not to deny that each mode has a residual uniqueness, but only to point out that they share a common structure as well. The range of topographically dissimilar forms of experience, including various forms of instruction, may be considered as various 'surface structures' which relate in their special ways to a common underlying structure of knowledge. Indeed, it is the very fact that information relevant to action can be acquired through means *other* than direct action itself that makes instruction possible. Thus, one can learn to sail, perhaps only to a limited extent, through watching films and reading books. There is considerable evidence from controlled laboratory experiments to show that common learning results from different types of experience. A child can learn to construct a diagonal either through activity coupled with reinforcement, through an appropriate demonstration, or through verbal instruction. Others have shown that children can learn difficult-to-teach Piagetian conservation tasks through quite different training techniques.[16] And it is well known that there is almost an infinite number of ways to teach reading.[17] The problem is to specify as far as possible the structure of information in these various instructional forms or surface structures and to see how they each relate to the underlying structure described above. Once these forms of instruction have been specified, it may be possible to indicate how each of them relates to the various technologies involved in their production and distribution. These relationships are set out in a preliminary way in figure 2. This figure indicates that there are three basic forms of instruction: through arranged contingent experience, observational learning, and symbolic systems, all of which have their effect by providing information relevant to the acquisition of both knowledge and skills.

All three forms of *instruction* can only be extensions of basic forms of interaction with the world and its symbols. They may be characterized as 'instructional' only when their use is marked by the intent of another person who for some reason, usually institutionally derived, accepts responsibility for the learner. *Learning from one's own contingent experience* can be regarded as instruction only in special circumstances, such as when the environment is intentionally prearranged by another person. The learner's role in this process is readily described as 'learning by doing', and the instructor's role is primarily that of selecting, simplifying, or otherwise ordering the environment so as to make the consequences of the action, the reinforcement, both obvious and safe. The second form of instruction may be designated *observational learning*. The learner's role may be described as 'learning by matching,' and the instructor's role is primarily that of providing a demonstration or

Figure 2: The acquisition of knowledge and skills and the forms of experience from which they are derived

Cognitive development		Categories of behaviour from which information may be extracted	Technological realizations
Knowledge	Skills		
chair	sitting		
	drawing	Information	
	describing	Extraction Processes	
		Direct	—Structured environments
		Contingent Directed	—Laboratory experiments
		experience (instructional)	—Simulations
objects	locomotive		—Educational toys
			—Automatizing devices
events	prehensive	Observation	—Films and animations
space	linguistic	Observational learning	
time	mathematical	Modeling (instruction)	—Demonstrations
causality	iconological		—Modeling
		Communication	—Print
		Symbolic systems	—Drawings
			—Diagrams
		Instruction	—Models
			—Graphs
			—Maps

model and perhaps some feedback. The third form of instruction involves the *use of various symbolic systems*, including a natural language. The learner's role is primarily that of 'learning by being told' and the instructor's role is that of telling — providing facts, descriptions, and explanations.

The three categories of instruction depend (as do the modes of learning on which they are based) upon the three modes of representing experience, namely, enactive, iconic, and symbolic.[18] In our view, these forms of instruction and the related modes of representation reflect different surface structures of experience that share an underlying informational or *knowledge* structure. To see how each of these surface structures relates to the common underlying knowledge structure, we must determine what information is invariant to all instruction and how information is coded in the instructional programs we have considered to this point. We shall accordingly examine reinforcement, modeling, and verbal instruction.

REINFORCEMENT

Firstly, consider the instructional effects of contingent experience, that is of reinforcement. Reinforcement broadly conceived is knowledge of the consequences of an act.[19] Reinforcement assures a means of determining when an appropriate choice among alternatives has been made. Reinforcement, by its universality across species, provides a medium of information exchange whereby a Skinner can communicate with a pigeon, and vice versa, for organisms are potent sources of consequence for the actions of other organisms. This assumes that organisms respond systematically to the responses of others — though not necessarily by a simple calculus of good and bad outcomes. And, obviously, reinforcement mediates much interacting with the inanimate environment. But while the discovery of new knowledge may be dependent on our direct contingent experiences with nature and with other organisms, reinforcement has the limitation of being ambiguous in outcome. When a teacher reinforces a child for asking a question, the child may not know if it was the question-asking that she approved or the merits of that specific question. Reinforcement can rarely indicate the critical alternatives but can indicate the consequences of the final performance. Guthrie's[20] cats, for example, did not know what aspect of their action in the puzzle box was critical for obtaining their release; hence they preserved many irrelevant ones. And given the fact that other human beings — with their obvious variability — are often the principal source of reinforcement, the ambiguity is confounded. It is surprising how uncritically many people accept the idea of control of behavior by reinforcement, in view of the constrained circumstances necessary for it to be effective at all. And more important for instruction, a child obtains no relevant information from a reinforcement if he happens not to be considering the critical alternatives. Modern theories of discrimination learning move increasingly in the direction of distinguishing between feature selection (attention) and reinforcement to deal with this point.[21] Given such considerations, one can account not only for the effects of this type of instruction but also for some of the anomalies in reinforcement theory.[22]

Three devices are widely used to render reinforcement less ambiguous. One is by immediacy: tagging the reinforcement directly to the act. The second is by disambiguating the feature of the stimulus to be attended to by placing it in a context that differentiates it from an alternative.[23] The third is through 'scientific method,' by unambiguously assigning certain sequelae to certain prior events so that the necessity of the conceptual link cannot be overlooked. This is typically the way of 'guided discovery' which, as with the other two techniques, relies on control of attention. In time, one who must learn by direct encounter comes to control his own attention in one of the three ways suggested: by keeping an eye 'peeled' for immediate results, by being selective in his scanning of features, and by attending to necessity and regularity of relationship. Obviously, there is a technology and a form of materials that must go with the learning of such 'discovery or reinforcement skills.' It would be foolish to assume that such learning is not crucially dependent on education. If such were not the case, there would be far more learning from direct experience than there seems to be.

MODELLING

One of the more transparent instructional approaches is that of modeling or providing demonstrations, an approach that makes up an important part of Montessori programs. How is information conveyed through modeling? Complex acts cannot be imitated unless the performer already knows how to carry out the act. That is, modeling may initiate or instigate known behavior but not, in any simple manner, produce learning. Yet, learning does occur in some situations.

How can information be conveyed appropriately through modeling? In line with the general theory advanced above, information permits a choice between alternatives. That is, consciousness of the alternatives is a necessary prerequisite for the pickup or acquisition of new information. In another context it was reported that a Montessori teacher successfully modeled, for a three-year-old child, the process of reconstructing a diagonal pattern, a task that is normally solved only by four- or five-year-olds.[24] The demonstration consisted of showing the child each of the choice points, that is, the critical alternatives, and then indicating how to choose between them. The demonstration of *where not to go* or *what not to do* is important to the extent that those alternatives are likely to mislead the child. In this light, it is possible to understand the finding of Herbert and Harsh,[25] mentioned earlier, that the cats who saw the error-filled performance learned more than those who saw the error-free performance. The latter performance deleted what the critical choice points or critical alternatives were. A final skilled performance does not render observable the critical alternatives; hence, the observer does not detect the information required to choose between them.

Good instruction through modeling depends upon the sensitivity of the instructor to the alternatives likely to be entertained by the child. Modeling or providing demonstrations is, therefore a skill to which most pedagogic theories are blind. I.A. Richards[26] provides an illustration of the pedagogic implications of such a theory:

A teacher should know how to demonstrate the meanings of sentences and other things in ways which are at once unambiguous, memorable, and easily imitated. ... For instance, with a ball and a table, a skilled teacher can in two minutes make the primal opposition of *on-off* evident. ... A careless teacher in the same minutes can generate potential confusions with other distinctions to be handled with *to* and *from* and *up* and *over*, confusions which may later on make the learner's tasks far harder than they need be.

Just as providing clear demonstrations involves skill, it seems possible *that learning from demonstrations itself demands a skill*; depending upon its generality and utility, it may be a skill worth including in our educational aims (aside from the knowledge conveyed by that means). Elsewhere it has been argued that learning through modeling depends precisely on the capacity not so much to imitate directly as to construct behavior from already mastered constituent acts in order to match selected features of the model — a procedure more like paraphrasing than imitating.[27]

To summarize, any skilled performance, be it doing, saying, or making something, requires perceptual information for the guidance of each component of the act, that is, for selecting between all possible alternatives at each choice point in the performance. Modeling as an instructional technique is successful to the extent that it creates an awareness both of the critical alternatives and of how to choose between them. To this extent a good demonstration is different from skilled performance.

VERBAL INSTRUCTION

Finally, consider language as an instructional medium. It is an instructional device *par excellence*, by virtue of the fact that a word indicates not only a perceived referent but also an excluded set of alternatives. Words function contrastively — they differentiate alternatives. The ordinary claim that 'words name things' overlooks the fact that words indicate or point to objects or events *in the implied context of the excluded alternatives.*[28] This point may be grasped by noting that the name or the description of an event is determined by the contrasting alternatives. Thus, a large white block in the context of a small white block is called 'the large one,' while the same block in the context of a large black block is called 'the white one.' Reciprocally, hearing such a sentence, or any other instructional sentence, the listener knows about both the intended referent *and the likely alternatives*. That is, language is structured precisely in the way that is required for instructional purposes in general. For this reason, the instruction of literate subjects almost always involves language; when experimentally tested, such instruction competes favorably with that making use of reinforcement and ordinary demonstrations; language coding is less ambiguous, that is, it conveys more information than those other media of instruction. (This, too, accords with the results obtained by Masters and Branch[29] and with those of many of the discovery-expository studies reported in the literature.)[30]

But there are many ways in which language can specify an intended referent, and these ways provide a microcosm for examining the major premises of the instructional model presented in this paper. The point is that certain very different sentences convey the same information and hence are generally called paraphrases of each other, or synonymous sentences. Consider these simple examples:

1. (a) George is here.
   (b) My father's brother is here.
   (c) My uncle is here.
2. (a) The stick is too short.
   (b) The stick is not long enough.

The sentences in (1) all designate the same intended referent and in some contexts are informationally equivalent. The specific sentences in each case differ, however, in the way the information is coded and in the specific mental processes involved in arriving at their meaning. They also differ in the assumptions they make about the listener; the first could be used only if the listener already knew who George was, and so on. This picture is complicated by the fact that different sentences frequently appear to arrive at a common effect without having a common meaning. Thus, Sheila Jones[31] gave subjects sheets of paper filled with the randomly ordered digits *1* through *8*. Some subjects were given the instruction in (3a) while others were given that in (3b).

3a. Mark the numbers 3, 4, 7, and 8.
3b. Mark all the numbers except 1, 2, 5, and 6.

Subjects found the latter more difficult, a result implying that information is more easily processed when coded one way than when coded another way. This example raises the question of the nature of the equivalence of sentences which are superficially different. It may be noted that in the context in which they were given, both of these sentences convey the same information: it is the *3, 4, 7,* and *8* that are to be marked. Hence, in this specific context they are paraphrases of each other, as may be a very dissimilar sentence such as (3c).

> 3c.   Beginning at the right side of the sheet, mark the first, third, seventh ... numbers.

These sentences are paraphrases of each other only in this immediate context, however. A new context would render them non-equivalent. Given the choice between two equivalent instructional sentences, one would choose between them on the same basis as between two instructional forms in general, that is, in terms of the complexity of the demands they make upon the learner and their generalizability to new but related problems.

The last point warrants an additional comment. In teaching children to find the perimeter of a particular rectangle, two instructional sentences which would convey the same information are the following:

> 4a.   Add the 7 to the 5 and multiply by 2.
> 4b.   Add the length to the width and multiply by 2.

Yet these two statements differ radically in their demands upon the listener, the latter statement being more complex than the former, and, in terms of their generality, the latter being more generalizable than the former. Generalizability refers to the fact that the second statement could apply to many different rectangles while the first could apply only to the particular given rectangle. It is interesting to note that the greater the generalizability of an instructional sentence (roughly, its instructional value), the greater the intellectual demand it makes (roughly, its difficulty or comprehension).

The teaching of rules and strategies falls into a similar position; they are difficult to comprehend but they have wide generality. There is always a trade-off between these two factors, a trade-off that is reflected in an instructional rule of thumb formulated by Carl Bereiter (personal communication) to the effect that if the rules are easily stated and have few exceptions, teach the rule and let the learners practice applying it to various problems; if the rules are not easily stated or have many exceptions, simply give practice on the problems and let the learners extract what rules they can for themselves.

The major limitation of language as an instructional medium, along with all cultural media such as graphs, diagrams, numbers, mime, and so on, is that the information is conveyed through a symbolic system that places high demands upon literacy in that medium. Further, the meaning extracted from those symbolic systems will be limited to the meaning acquired by the use of that symbol in the referential or experiential world.[32] Stated generally, this limitation of language implies an ancient point that no new information can be conveyed through language. If the information intended by the speaker falls outside the listener's 'competence' the listener will interpret that sentence in terms of the knowledge he already possesses. It follows that instruction through language is limited to rearranging, ordering, and differentiating knowledge or information that the listener already has available from other sources, such as modeling, or through his own direct experiences. Parker has illustrated this point by showing the impossibility of verbally explaining perspective to the blind. In spite of this dependence of language upon perception, perception does come to be shaped in a way to permit easier comment, for reasons examined in the remainder of this essay.

ON THE ACQUISITION OF SKILLS AND ABILITIES

Having said that knowledge from different forms of experience can map onto a common deep structure, we must now make plain that there are also differences. The most important non-equivalence among experiences of events in the three forms is manifest not so much in the knowledge acquired, but in the skills involved in extracting or utilizing that knowledge. It is true that common knowledge of zebras may be obtained from actual experience and from appropriate sentences, but the skills involved in the two cases are entirely different; it is obviously a skill to extract symbolically coded knowledge from a sentence, but it is no less a skill to discriminate zebras from horses, albeit a skill so overlearned that we fail to recognize it as such until we are faced with a subtler but equally 'obvious' discrimination such as that between Grant's gazelle and an impala. However combinable the outcomes, the skill of obtaining information by perceptual discrimination is a radically different skill from that of extracting the same information from language. The crucial issue for instruction, then, becomes one of deciding which skill one wishes to cultivate.

What of these skills? As we pointed out earlier, they are frequently rendered invisible by our habitual focus on the knowledge specified through the activity. As we examine a rock by turning it over in our hand we are aware of the fact that we acquire knowledge about the rock, but the skilled manipulation that gave rise to the knowledge of the rock is transparent to us. Our earlier example suggested that in carrying out any activity, such as kicking a ball, we are learning not only about the ball, but about the act of kicking. Carrying out that act across widely divergent objects or events would be responsible for the development of a skill of wide applicability. But if we look at the general skills that make up our cognitive or intellectual ability, we see that they are marked by the same property. Verbal, numerical, and spatial abilities reflect skills in such cultural activities as speaking and writing, counting, and manipulating Euclidean space.

Consider these skills in more detail. It is enormously to Piaget's credit to have insisted and demonstrated that the structure of any ability must be conceptualized in some major part in terms of 'internalized activity'. Activities one carries out in the physical world — rotating an object in space, lining up objects to form a straight line, ordering objects serially — come to be internalized or carried out mentally. There is not only an internalization of operations, but an increasingly economical representation of diverse events operated upon. A face looked at from various angles comes to be represented as a single face. Even more important are the temporal ordering operations, which permit an appreciation first of physical order and then of logical relations. Once we can convert back from a changed state to our original one, we come to appreciate that such reversibility is a logical possibility or property of events and not simply an act one performs. In turn, such operations make it possible to transform a novel event into a standard or base event or to convert some base event into a new structure more appropriate to novel contexts.

The operations specified by Piaget were largely those appropriate to the manipulation of real objects in the physical environment. His basic premise is that their internalization not only produces the groundwork for logic, but assures that logic will be appropriate to the state of the world one experiences. Such operations, consequently, have a wide range of applicability and appear to be almost universally relevant to problem-solving.

But internalized activity related to the physical environment does not begin to describe the range of activities of the human mind. Specifically, it leaves out of account how we learn to cope with the cultural or symbolic environment. 'Learning from the culture,' like learning from physical activities, involves the act of picking up information to decide among alternatives; it also involves skills, and it also results, finally, in a biased knowledge of reality. Sentences, for example, to the extent that they are about something, carry information common to the other forms of experiencing and are comprehended and spoken in terms of those general underlying structures of knowledge we discussed earlier. But the skills involved in using sentences are unique to the particular mode of expression and communication. The skillful use of a symbolic system involves the mastery of both its structure and its rules for transformation. Once mastered, these skills may be considered to be 'intelligence,' primarily because the range of their applicability is virtually open.

This wide and expanding range of applicability is further indicated in the arts, which may be viewed in part as creative attempts to expand the limitations of a particular medium or symbolic system. These expanded symbolic systems may then be applied to nature, if appropriate, much as the binomial distribution was found to be an appropriate description of the range of human variability. In this way, our use of symbolic systems, like our practical activities, results in a version of 'reality' appropriate to the activity. There is no objective reality to 'copy' or to 'imitate', but only a selection from that reality, expressed in terms of the kinds of practical and symbolic activities in which we engage. Thus, Nelson Goodman is led to say that 'the world is as many ways as there are correct descriptions of it.'[33] Similarly, Cezanne pointed out that the artist does not copy the world in his medium but, rather, re-creates it in terms of the structure of that medium. So too with the ordinary man operating in the various symbolic systems of his culture. Whorf was among the first to argue that we 'dissect nature along lines laid down by our native language.' But the process probably goes even beyond that, to something comparable to Gide's advising young poets to follow the rhymes and not their thoughts.[34] For the child, as for the creative artist, the uses of the culture involve processes of expanding and refining the code, of defining 'lawful' or 'comprehensible' or 'possible' options as he goes. This is the heart of skill in the use of symbolic codes. Even our failures in understanding new media, as McLuhan[35] has pointed out, come from a failure to recognize that they require different skills than does the medium they replace — as in going from an oral to a written code, or in going from print to television.

Man in culture, like the artist, is in continual search for ways of applying symbolic systems to his ordinary experience. Translation into a symbolic code such as logic or mathematics is even taken as the criterion for 'understanding' a phenomenon; to express the relation between temperatures, pressure, and volume in the form of an equation is to explain that relation. Hansen[36] goes so far as to say that scientific knowledge consists of statements known to be true.

But can one affirm that translation of experience into any one medium has more validity than translation into any other? A historical account of the intellectual roots of the industrial revolution may be of a different symbolic system but not necessarily of greater validity than Yeats's famous epigram:

Locke sank into a swoon;
The garden died;
God took the spinning jenny
Out of his side.

Yet a scientific and technological culture like our own has put a premium on translation into a few symbolic systems — written language as in literature and explanations, in logical and mathematical statements, and in spatial systems such as maps, models, graphs, and geometry.

We would argue that it is not only scholars, poets, and scientists who seek constantly to cast experience into symbolic codes. Our conjecture is that there is a form of metaprocessing that involves the constant reorganization of what we know so that it may be translated into symbolic systems. It is a matter of 'going over one's past experiences to see what they yield'[37] both for the purpose of facilitating the communication that is required for the survival of the culture and for the purposes of rendering one's own personal experience comprehensible. We may label this form of activity as 'deuteropraxis,' or second-order information processing. Deuteropraxis is elicited not only by failed communication but also by a conflict and difficulties in attempting to carry out an action or solve a problem. It occurs whenever there is information-processing capacity available not demanded by the task in hand. Deutero-praxis is involved in all translations of specific experience into general accounts. It can occur in any mode but it is clearly repre-sented both by the poet's or essayist's search for the appropriate phrase or the summarizing aphorism and by the scientist's search for the most general mathematical statement. Merleau-Ponty[38] has this in mind when he suggests that all intention wants to complete itself in saying. It is deuteropraxis that is responsible for the radical economization of the experience of the tribe or nation in a few great myths and, more generally, for the world view implicit in one's native language. It should not, however, be assumed that this process is simply one of translation. It more generally requires that the creator have more information available than was required for the ordinary experience of the event. This can easily be seen in the difficulties one encounters in an attempt to draw a map of a well-known territory or to give a description of a friend's appearance. New requirements, new purposes, or new activities alter our perceptions of events; this is no less true when these activities involve those that have been shaped or evolved by the culture, as in the arts, than when they involve various practical or physical acts. It follows that such symbolic activities as drawing an object, describing an object, or photographing an object require somewhat different information about that object than does the manipulation of that object. To the extent that these new forms of cultural or symbolic activity require previously undetected information about the world, the media of expression and communication are *explor-atory devices* — a point of immense importance to an understand-ing of the child's acquisition of knowledge.

Finally, deuteropraxis makes possible the organization of information into a form that is particularly appropriate for cultural transmission to the young. Since it is often difficult for the child (or an adult for that matter) to link an action with the consequences that follow, he is greatly aided by the deuteropraxis account of the event. Such accounts, whether in the form of an abstract equation, a principle, a noiseless exemplar, or an appropriate model, have the effect of 'time-binding' or virtually simultanizing temporal events and thereby surpassing ordinary experience.[39]

It is such deuteropraxis accounts that are examined in more detail in other chapters of this volume in terms of their instruc-tional potential. The very accounts that render experience compre-hensible render it instructible. But there are limits in the degree to which such representations, whether in language or other symbolic systems, can substitute for or extend ordinary experience. As a summary of experience they are indeed powerful; as an alternative to experience they are sometimes woefully inadequate. One can learn or memorize the summary without having a grasp of the information summarized. In *Portrait of the Artist as a Young Man*, Joyce tells how his teachers taught the young the aphorism 'Zeal without prudence is like a ship adrift' to show how instruction often falls wide of the mark. To some adult no doubt such a statement has meaning; it summarizes his own experience in a simple code. To the young it summarizes nothing. In large measure, the same is true of the great myths; to the extent that they summarize no experience, they convey little or no information. On the other hand, it is also true that aphorisms, like new vocabulary items, may serve as pointers from which experience is progressively assimilated. At an appropriate level, such instruction may be successful in aiding the assimilation of experience. Experience in this case instantiates the categories created through the symbolic code. Frye[40] makes a parallel point in regard to literature: 'criticism ... is designed to reconstruct the kind of experience we could and should have had, and thereby *to bring us into line with that experience*' (p. 27).

TECHNOLOGICAL REALIZATIONS

We return for the last time to the scheme offered in figure 2. The column headed 'Technological Realizations' indicates, in a rough manner, the media appropriate to each of the modes of experiencing the world. Learning through contingent experience may be facilitated through rearranging the environment to render the consequences of activity more obvious. Laboratory experiments are prototypic attempts to simplify direct experience. Structured environments, simulations, toys, and automatizing devices of various sorts have the advantages of both extending the range of a child's experience and making the relations between events observable or otherwise comprehensible.

Observational learning is realized through the provision of a model — 'This is how you break out a spinnaker.' As we pointed out earlier, carrying out a performance for its own sake and carrying it out so as to instruct another are not identical. A good demonstration makes explicit the decisions made in the course of the activity — thus a good demonstration shows the student what not to do as well as what to do; a skilled performance makes these same decisions invisible. Technological media can greatly facilitate these processes by highlighting in various ways the critical points in the performance; slow motion or stopped action as well as descriptions and drawings (including caricatures) may have this effect. Such instruction, while it may convey some of the same information that would be apprehended through direct contingent experience (by virtue of its shared deep structure), is never complete in itself but, rather, specifies some of the major features to be looked for when actual performances are attempted. That is, these forms of instruction rely heavily on prior or subsequent experience to instantiate the information.

The instructional effects of a model are greatly increased by tying that demonstration to an appropriate symbolic representation as in the provision of a few mnemonic rules. The words 'keep your weight on the downhill ski' coupled with a demonstration will render the demonstration more comprehensible — the observer knows what to look for. But even this will not perfect the novice's performance; direct contingent experience is required to 'instantiate' the instruction. Indeed, it is probably not until such instantiation occurs that the proposition is fully comprehended. One says (after the first fall), 'So that's what he meant.' Hence, all modes of instructing are in some sense incomplete or inadequate for achieving full performatory power or efficiency, and knowledge in the last analysis is tied to one's own experience.

Learning through the various symbolic systems, including language, graphs, mathematics, and the various systems of visual representation, is realized through books, graphs, maps, models, and so on. These media make strong assumptions about the literacy of the learner. The properties of a 'good' explanation, description, or portrayal are complex subjects worthy of study in their own right. But to untangle the educational effects of these symbolic systems we again have to differentiate the knowledge of the world conveyed through the system from the skills involved in the mastery of the structure of the medium itself. Recall our aphorism: instructional means converge as to the knowledge conveyed but they diverge as to the skills they assume and develop. As to the knowledge conveyed, different systems are useful for the partitioning of alternatives or the conveying of information in a way that is fundamentally compatible with the information picked up from other types of experiences. You may learn that the stove is hot by touching it, by seeing someone recoil from touching it, and by being told that it is hot. Granted some level of literacy and granted that the learner has had some experience to instantiate the experience, the three forms are essentially equivalent, as we pointed out in the first part of this essay.

However, as to the skills they develop, each form of experience, including the various symbolic systems tied to the media, produces a unique pattern of skills for dealing with or thinking about the world. It is the skills in these systems that we call intelligence. The choice of a means of instruction, then, must not depend solely upon the effectiveness of the means for conveying and developing knowledge; it must depend as well upon its effects on the mental skills that are developed in the course of acquiring that knowledge.

We return, then, to our point of departure. The acquisition of knowledge as the primary goal of education can be seriously questioned. The analysis we have developed points to the contingent relationship between the knowledge acquired and the intellectual skills developed. To neglect the skills is to forget that they are the primary tools for acquiring and using knowledge — tools that are critical for the child's further self-education.

NOTES

1. A.L. Baldwin, *Theories of Child Development* (New York: John Wiley & Sons, 1967).
2. M. McLuhan, *Understanding Media, the Extensions of Man* (New York: McGraw-Hill Book Co., 1964).
3. J. Dewey, *Democracy and Education* (New York: MacMillan Co., 1916).
4. J.S. Bruner, *The Process of Education* (Cambridge, Mass.: Harvard University Press, 1960); *Living and Learning*, Report of the Ontario Provincial Committee on Aims and Objectives of Education in the Schools of Ontario, Cochairmen, E.M. Hall and L.A. Dennis (Toronto: Ontario Department of Education, 1968).
5. K. Duncker, 'On Problem Solving,' *Psychological Monographs* 58 (1945): 270.
6. N.R.F. Maier, 'Reasoning and Learning,' *Psychological Review* 38 (1931): 332-46.
7. N.R.F. Maier, J.A. Thurber, and J.C. Janzen, 'Studies in Creativity: The Selection Process in Recall and in Problem Solving Situations,' *Psychological Reports* 23 (1968): 1003-22.
8. This central point appears in several related disciplines, including psychology, psychophysiology, and biology. See E.C. Tolman, *Purposive Behavior in Animals and Man* (New York: D. Appleton-Century Co., 1932); K.H. Pribram,

Languages of the Brain: Experimental Paradoxes and Principles in Neuropsychology
(Englewood Cliffs, N.J.: Prentice-Hall, 1971); E.N. Sokolov, 'The Modeling
Properties of the Nervous System,' in *A Handbook of Contemporary Soviet
Psychology*, ed. I. Maltzman and M. Cole (New York: Basic Books, 1969); E. von
Holst, 'Vom Wesen der Ordnung im Zentral Nerven System,' *Die
Naturwissenschaften 25* (1937): 625-31, 641-47.

9. J. Piaget, *Biology and Knowledge* (University of Chicago Press, 1971).

10. A. Bandura, *Principles of Behavior Modification* (New York: Holt,
Rinehart & Winston, 1969).

11. J.J. Herbert and C.M. Harsh, 'Observational Learning by Cat,' *Journal of
Comparative Psychology 37* (1944): 81-95.

12. L.S. Vygotsky, *Thought and Language* (Cambridge, Mass.: M.I.T. Press,
1962).

13. J.S. Bruner, R. Olver, and P.M. Greenfield, *Studies in Cognitive Growth*
(New York: John Wiley & Sons, 1966).

14. Ibid.

15. J.S. Bruner, 'Nature and Uses of Immaturity,' *American Psychologist 27*
(1972): 687-708.

16. P.E. Bryant, 'Cognitive Development,' *British Medical Bulletin 27* (1971):
200-5; G.S. Halford, 'A Theory of the Acquisition of Conservation,' *Psychological
Review 77* (1970): 302-16; R. Gelman, 'Conservation Acquisition: A Problem of
Learning to Attend to Relevant Attributes,' *Journal of Experimental Child
Psychology 8* (1969): 314-27.

17. J.S. Chall, *Learning to Read: The Great Debate* (New York: Carnegie Corp.,
1965).

18. Bruner *et al.*, op. cit.

19. R. Glaser, *The Nature of Reinforcement* (New York: Academic Press,
1971).

20. E.R. Guthrie, 'Conditioning: A Theory of Learning in Terms of Stimulus,
Response and Association,' in *The Psychology of Learning*, Forty-first Yearbook of
the National Society for the Study of Education, Part II, pp. 17-60 (Chicago:
Distributed by the University of Chicago Press, 1942).

21. N.S. Sutherland, 'Visual Discrimination in Animals,' *British Medical
Bulletin 20* (1964): 54-59; N.J. Mackintosh, 'Selective Attention in Animal
Discrimination Learning,' *Psychological Bulletin 64* (1965): 64, 124-50.

22. Glaser, op. cit.; M. Levine, 'Hypothesis Theory and Nonlearning Despite
Ideal S-R Reinforcement Contingencies,' *Psychological Review 78* (1971): 130-40.

23. W.R. Garner, 'To Perceive Is to Know', *American Psychologist 21* (1966):
11-19; P.E. Bryant and T. Trabasso, 'Transitive Inferences and Memory in Young
Children,' *Nature 232* (1971): 456-58.

24. D.R. Olson, *Cognitive Development: The Child's Acquisition of Diagonality*
(New York: Academic Press, 1970).

25. Herbert and Harsh, op. cit.

26. I.A. Richards, *Design for Escape: World Education through Modern Media*
(New York: Harcourt, Brace & World, 1968).

27. D.J. Wood, J.S. Bruner, and Gail Ross, 'A Study of Tutorial Modeling,' in
preparation.

28. D.R. Olson, 'Language and Thought: Aspects of a Cognitive Theory of
Semantics,' *Psychological Review 77* (1970): 257-73.

29. J.C. Masters and M.N. Branch, 'A Comparison of the Relative Effectiveness
of Instructions, Modeling, and Reinforcement Procedures for Inducing Behavior
Change,' *Journal of Experimental Psychology 80* (1969): 364-68.

30. R. Glaser and L.B. Resnick, 'Instructional Psychology,' *Annual Review of
Psychology 23* (1972): 207-76.

31. S. Jones, 'The Effect of a Negative Qualifier in an Instruction,' *Journal of*

Verbal Learning and Verbal Behavior 5 (1966): 495-501.

32. J. Carroll, 'Words, Meaning and Concepts,' *Harvard Educational Review* 34 (1964): 178-202; Olson, *Language and Thought*, op. cit.

33. N. Goodman, *Languages of Art* (Indianapolis: Bobbs Merrill Co., 1968).

34. P. Goodman, *Speaking and Language: A Defense of Poetry* (New York: Random House, 1971).

35. McLuhan, op. cit.

36. N.R. Hansen, *Patterns of Discovery* (Cambridge, Eng.: Cambridge University Press, 1958).

37. Dewey, op. cit.

38. M. Merleau-Ponty, *Phenomenology of Perception* (London: Routledge & Kegan Paul, 1962).

39. C.H. Judd, 'Practice and Its Effects on the Perception of Illusions,' *Psychological Review* 9 (1902): 27-39.

40. N. Frye, *The Critical Path* (Bloomington: Indiana University Press, 1971).

3.3 The Use of Visual Media in the Service of Enriching Mental Thought Processes

INTRODUCTION

Many of us desire to employ the visual media in the teaching of psychology (we, as teachers who are audio-visually perceived by our students anyway, not included ...). The typical reasoning behind this desire, which is more frequently expressed than practiced, is, however, not well thought out. Is it indeed the case that a picture is worth a thousand words? Is a graph necessarily better comprehended than a verbal description? Why is *Clockwork Orange* more revealing than, say, a scientific analysis of brutality? Why bother to teach group processes through *Twelve Angry Men* rather than read the transcript? Why view *Equus* in film or the play on stage? Why not just read the play at home?

It appears to me that we should attempt to answer such and similar questions in the same way we teach our students to do it. Namely, to begin with a *theory*. Specifically, we need a theory that sorts out the relevant elements, that differentiates between fact and fiction, and which is sufficiently general to guide future questions. This article is devoted to such an attempt.

The rather common answer to the kinds of questions that I have raised is frequently as follows: (a) A-V materials can reveal unique and helpful contents, and (b) they offer that content through concrete, vivid experiences which are (for some unclear reason) superior to texts, lectures or discussions. Similar potentialities are often attributed to the technology associated with certain media (e.g. the ease of transmission through CCTV) or to the didactics

*Source: Paper presented at the IWAPP Festival 1980, Amsterdam, The Netherlands, January 1980, *Instructional Science* 9 (Elsevier Scientific Publishing Company, Amsterdam, 1980), 327-39.

associated with them (e.g. immediate feedback or better structuring of the materials).

Such answers confuse quite a number of issues. For example, contents are by and large transferable: You do not have to watch *Equus* in a film, you can read it: you do not have to observe an interview with Karl Jung on videotape as one can read its content to you aloud. Thus, we confuse some unique attributes of visual media with non-unique ones. Similarly, we implicitly assume that different media offer different experiences, and yet we see them as alternative means to the *same* ends, particularly the acquisition of factual knowledge (Olson, 1976).

UNIQUENESS IN MEDIA

First, then, let me raise the question of what is unique to each medium and what is the *essential* difference, i.e. neither trivial nor accidental correlate, between them? Once I have dealt with this, I will turn to my second question, namely — in what ways do such essential differences make a difference in learning?

To make a very long story short — (more on this issue can be found in Gordon (1969), Olson (1974) and Salomon (1979a)) — we have reason to argue that the essential difference between media is neither their contents (which itself is an outcome of a more fundamental difference), nor the available didactics, but rather *their modes of gathering, packaging and presenting information, that is: their symbol systems* (Goodman, 1968: Gardner *et al.*, 1974; Salomon, 1979a). To presently avoid unnecessary philosophical debate and in the service of brevity, let us speak of media's 'modes of presentation' and symbol system as equivalent. Indeed, remove cartography from maps, language from texts, pictoriality from film, movement from ballet, what are you left with? Not much.

Quite clearly media's symbol systems, or modes of presentation, owe much of their development to technological innovations. More detail and finer depth presentation became available through copper engravings, new 'statements' could be made once the zoom lens was developed, and a new 'language' becomes possible now with the development of holographs. Yet, let me remind you that it is not any technology *per se* that affects learning (e.g. Mielke, 1968; Schramm, 1977). Rather, the new symbol systems and the new combinations of old ones that become possible with new technological inventions, enable us to gather, package and present new aspects of knowledge. Thus, media's unique symbol systems and the unique combinations thereof are the very essence of media: they develop with the advent of new technologies and make new kinds of content available.

If media's symbol systems would be only mediators between technology and presentable content, then we would not have to dwell on their psychological import at all. We would concentrate on what media's contents could do for us. However, following Olson and Bruner (1974), Olson (1976) and my own work (Salomon, 1974, 1976, 1977, 1979b), I want to argue that *media's symbol systems have their own important effects on people's minds*. And it is these effects that, once understood, can lead us to develop novel ways of using the visual media to serve new educational functions.

THE DIFFERENTIAL EMPLOYMENT OF SKILLS

Let me begin with the assumption that while the contents of messages address our structures of knowledge, the means of conveying the knowledge, the symbol systems, address our mental skills (Olson and Bruner, 1974). Thus, one can speak of intelligence as skill in a medium. When you read a book, see a play, watch a film or examine a painting, you may gain knowledge. However, the very *activity* of reading, film-viewing, map-reading or listening, *taps different kinds of mental skills*. As Olson (1978) writes: 'Skills are frequently rendered invisible by our habitual focus on the knowledge specified through the activity' (p. 6). And as Gombrich (1974) shows, numerous skills, often 'automatic' ones (LaBerge and Samuels, 1974) are involved even in reading a regular black and white photograph. We do not read it as representing a gray, flat and framed world.

Salomon and Cohen (1977) have shown that different coding elements within the filmic symbol systems, such as spatial editing, zooms, logical gaps and close-up-long shots, call upon different kinds of mental skills. Hence, film-viewing is a skilled activity, and the specific kinds of coding elements it uses tap differential abilities. Spatially able students extract more knowledge from elements that distort known conceptions of space, while students with better mastery of temporal abilities extract more knowledge when time is being distorted. As Snow *et al.* (1965) have shown long ago, there are more general aptitudes which are called upon when all kinds of film are shown, and these aptitudes are less relevant when face-to-face instruction takes place.

Meringoff (1978) has shown that aside from the above, tele-viewing leads small children to extract different kinds of knowledge than listening to the same story when read aloud. Listening also calls for the generation of more personal inferences than tele-viewing.

Two implications seem to follow. First, as different coding elements within a symbol system call upon different skills, so do whole symbol systems, only on a larger scale. We would expect students with different clusters of aptitudes to benefit differentially from different symbol systems (provided our media presentations employ their unique symbolic potentialities). This, of course, is much in line with the known conceptions of aptitude — treatment interactions (ATI), as formulated by Cronbach (1957), Salomon (1971) and Cronbach and Snow (1977). I will relate to this as a *first order interaction* between symbol systems and learners' aptitudes.

The second implication is somewhat more complex. Traditionally, we attribute to some symbol systems characteristics of 'concreteness' and 'iconicity,' and to others 'abstractness' and 'arbitrariness'. However, following the philosophical works of Goodman (1968, 1978) and my own analyses (Salomon, 1979a), it appears that symbol systems are 'iconic' or not relative to the way one represents the depicted or described entity *mentally.*

I argue this on the basis of the assumption that we use different kinds of symbol systems *mentally* to represent the world to ourselves and to manipulate it in thought (Paivio, 1971: Kosslyn and Pomerantz, 1977). External modes of representation can thus be closer or farther away from the internally used ones.

A verbal description of an activity or process which you, for many cultural, developmental, situational and personal reasons, represent to yourself as visual images, is remote from its cognitive counterpart. Similarly, if I should try to present the ideas of this article through, say, a pictorial symbol system, I would be using a rather remote (i.e. non-iconic) 'language', because many people prefer to think about such issues in terms of internal propositions.

It follows, then, that 'iconicity' is *not* an inherent attribute of a symbol system but a function of the 'distance' between it and one's internal mode of representation. And as such modes differ with content, maturation, preference, etc., also 'iconicity' or 'abstractness' are flexible, relative, quantities. Statistical formulae are neither 'abstract' nor 'arbitrary' for one who thinks in terms of statistical formulae.

When the 'distance' between external and internal modes of representation is large one needs to activate processes of *recoding*, that is, invest mental effort in translating the external symbolic mode into the internal, preferred one. When, then, the information is new, its quantity large, and the recoder not well skilled, much of the information gets lost. But, barring extreme cases, the more one needs to recode (and is capable in doing so), not only does he/she learn more, but he/she also draws more heavily on his/her own mental schemata (e.g. Kane and Anderson, 1978; Gallagher, 1979).

This brings me back to my second implication. Television and film may often be easier for processing (not only for children) because one often represents certain entities through imagery. Pictorial symbol systems thus save much of the recoding effort required by, say, language. But if pictorial systems require (or rather, *allow*) less recoding, then they may lead to less learning. They also often allow us to draw less upon our own mental schemata, as Meringoff's (1978) study shows.

Such would not be the results for learners who think of the same entities in terms of internal propositions. For them, pictorial systems may address a less preferred internal symbol system, require more recoding, and thus lead to more learning.

I would label this implication — *a second order interaction.* That is, an interaction between external and internal modes of representation which results in more or in less skilled recoding, in more or in less learning, and in heavier or lighter reliance on one's own mental schemata. Unlike the first order one, the second order interaction is highly variable, depending on the content presented, the task to be performed, one's preferred cognitive systems, etc.

THE CULTIVATION OF SKILLS

Thus far I have dealt with the different kinds of mental skills that symbol systems call upon and the different amounts of mental recoding they seem to require. But media's symbol systems appear to have other, far more pervasive effects on learners. I will mention here two such effects: the cultivation of mental skills and the cultivation of new internal modes of representation.

If mental skills are involved in extracting knowledge from symbolically coded messages then such skills can and do develop as a result of media's requirements. From watching the film *The Phoenix* you not only acquire knowledge about the emergence of leadership, but also exercise certain film-related mental skills.

The fact that we are often unaware that skills are needed only suggests that they are already well developed and can be used 'automatically'. Yet, as Kintsch (1977) points out: 'Novels or movies are easier when the natural order of events is maintained than when they are full of flash-backs and reversals, but since the latter invite deeper processing, they are more interesting to read or watch' (p. 315). They are indeed more interesting, and may render also more unique information because they call upon not yet 'automatic' skills.

In a series of experiments and field studies (Salomon, 1979b) we could show that when specific coding elements of film — such as close-up — long-shot, varying spatial positions or changing points-of-view — are used under common learning conditions, they lead to improved mastery of relevant skills. Quite clearly, when coding elements call upon certain skills, they can cultivate those best in learners with a modest initial mastery of the skills. Skill-cultivation by activation cannot benefit a learner with no, or very poor, initial mastery of the skills.

When skills such as relating-parts-to-wholes, spatial imagery, changing-points-of-view and possibly others, show improvement through activation, they may also transfer as *mental tools* to new instances. We do not know as yet which skills transfer more widely and which ones begin as, say, film-literacy and stay untransferable to other symbol systems. The well-known rules of transfer-of-learning seem to apply here, as elsewhere. Transferability would depend not only on the nature of the skill but also on the nature and availability of other instances to which the skill can be transferred, and on one's awareness that a skill — such as changing spatial perspectives — is applicable to totally new instances. While we know that the filmic symbol system can be made to cultivate skills, we do not as yet know their potential transferability.

CULTIVATING INTERNAL MODES OF REPRESENTATION

Let us turn now to the effects of symbol systems on the development of internal modes of representation. If we are willing to accept the assumption that people represent the world to themselves and manipulate it mentally through a number of internal symbol systems, we cannot avoid the possibility of interdependence between external-communicational and internal-cognitive symbol systems (see a detailed discussion by, e.g., Huttenlocher and Higgins, 1979).

Numerous psychologists, aestheticians and philosophers (e.g. Bruner, 1964; Brown, 1965; Von Bertalanffy, 1965; Perkins and Leondar, 1977; Vygotsky, 1978; Eisner, 1978) have argued time and again that internal symbolism develops, in part at least, as a counterpart of external-communicational symbol systems. There is little disagreement that language serves prominently in thought.

Even without going as far as Whorf or even Vygotsky (1978), one could agree with Schlesinger (1977) that thinking emerges from interactions with a language community. Ultimately, although not initially, one learns to 'compute' thoughts in those linguistic structures which serve in the production and comprehension of speech.

In short, the linguistic symbol system serves as a system of mental tools which operates in internal manipulations of the world. And it does this apparently in two ways. It summarizes, labels and internally represents already acquired knowledge, thus it serves a *representational function* (Olson, 1978). For example, acquiring new concepts such as 'intrinsic' and 'extrinsic' motivation allows the student to go over, so to speak, his or her past experiences and subsume them under these concepts. The concepts come now to represent in the student's mind a vast array of past experiences, observations and bits of knowledge.

But a symbol system such as the linguistic one serves also to guide and direct our exploratory and data-gathering behavior, thus — to accomplish an exploratory function as *epistemological devices* (Olson, 1978). Once the student in the above example has learned about the two sources of motivation he or she can now start noticing events and behaviors to which he/she attributes hidden causes he/she would not have attributed before. Furthermore, he/she begins to notice things which he/she did not notice before.

Let me embed these arguments into Neisser's (1976) spiral model of perception and cognition. According to this model, one's mental schemata — including different kinds of symbolic representations — direct our perceptual exploration. Exploration, in turn, samples, constructs and provides meaning to external stimuli which are then incorporated into the schemata and change them accordingly.

Note that the acquisition of externally-provided concepts, labels, and other symbolic representations (e.g., a graph, a picture) changes one's relevant schemata. In this sense they serve in what we called a representational capacity of knowledge already stored in the schemata. But, once acquired, such symbolic representations begin to guide perception, information-gathering and comprehension, thus to serve in an epistemological capacity.

Language that figures in thought comes from the outside world of communication. How then is it transformed from a communicational symbol system into an internal, mediational one? Vygotsky (1962) and later Luria (1976), working within a Marxian interactionist framework, suggest that language is interiorized, or internalized, by the child. Luria writes: 'Children assimilate language — a ready-made product of socio-historical development — and use it to analyze, generalize and encode experience' (p. 9). Not only words but also grammatical structures are interiorized: thus, 'Humans have at their disposal a powerful objective tool that permits them not only to reflect individual objects or situations but to create objective logical codes' (p. 10).

Vygotsky does not claim that thought is *created* by language, as Whorf would have it. The internalization of language results in a *reorganization* of thinking into higher order functional systems. Still, *internalization* serves as the key process. Even Fodor (1975, p. 83), the opponent of such views, finds it necessary to qualify his general argument by stating that

> though it might be admitted that the initial computations involved in first language learning cannot themselves be run in the language being learned, it could nevertheless still be claimed that a foothold in the language having once been gained, the child then proceeds by extrapolating his boot straps: the fragment of the language first internalized is itself somehow essentially employed to learn the part that's left. This process eventually leads to the construction of a representational system

more elaborate than the one the child started with and this richer system mediates the having of thoughts the child could not otherwise have entertained.

But language is not the *only* symbol system that participates in thinking. Miller *et al.* (1970) have tried to replicate one of Luria's studies concerning the use of externally provided verbal instructions for self-regulation by three- and four-year-olds. Although they failed to replicate Luria's findings, Flavell (1977) did not reject the internalization conception. Rather, he interpreted the failure as resulting from the assumption that only internalized *language* can serve for self-regulation. Other, non-linguistic modes could serve equally well, or even better, for some children. Shepard (for example, 1978) has shown how important non-linguistic internal codes are in solving spatial problems. The work of Furth (1966) with deaf children shows that, even in the absence of a well-mastered language, thinking can be relatively well developed, suggesting that language is only one of many ways whereby thought is carried out.

Could other, non-linguistic symbol systems become part of our cognitive apparatus in a way that resembles that of language? Could a child learn to think in, say, *graphical codes* as he does with language? Hatano *et al.* (1977) have shown that expert abacus users seem to have internalized the operations of the abacus. This is suggested by the observation that users at intermediate levels still need to use visible finger movements to accompany mental computations. When prevented from using their fingers, such users perform significantly less well. Experimental intervention of this kind has no appreciable effect on expert users. The finger movements of intermediate users of the abacus appear to be very much like egocentric speech, which, according to Vygotsky, is 'overt thought preceding inner speech'. Both are overt activities in the process of becoming totally internalized and covert.

Here, however, we face a possible pitfall. The analogy between the internalization of language and non-linguistic systems may be misleading inasmuch as language is acquired through active *interaction* while most non-linguistic systems are only *observed.* Only a few people interact through pictures, filmic-codes or cartography. Could the latter be acquired through observational learning?

Observational learning of modeled behaviors is a learning procedure that 'enables people to acquire large, integrated patterns of behavior without having to form them gradually by tedious trial and error' (Bandura, 1977, p. 12). However, modeling is not limited to overt physical acts. Observational learning also occurs with linguistic skills (for example, see Bloom *et al.*, 1974), conservation of liquids, attitudes, and emotional responses (Bandura, 1977). Underlying *all* these, according to Bandura, are common processes of attention, internal coding, rehearsal, and reinforcement by self or others.

The teaching potential of modeling need not be limited to observational learning of behaviors of humans nor to the informative contents of 'symbolic modeling'. *One should be able to learn by observing the symbolic code itself as well.* Indeed, this is very much in line with Bandura's explanation of the role of observational learning in language acquisition.

However, lest we oversimplify the case by arguing that all symbol systems encountered in the media can be internalized and used as coding elements in thought, we must at least show *why* they are learned. The internalizability of codes must surely depend on their function. Once we have a plausible (if speculative) explanation, we should be able to generate specific hypotheses pertaining to the conditions in which specific coding elements are internalized.

A verbal construction or spatial depiction, to be learned and used in perception and thought, needs to accomplish some useful function for the learner. It must promise a solution for a perceived difficulty. As Cole and Scribner (1974) theorize with respect to cognition and cultural differences, a skill is evoked and potentially cultivated within the context of functional demands. Thus, for a coding element to become a tool of thought, it must accomplish some useful cognitive function. It needs to accomplish for the learner something that the learner cannot perform on his own yet needs to perform.

Indeed, this is precisely what we have found in our experiments (Salomon, 1974, 1979b). When subjects are shown a filmic operation which *overtly models* an operation — such as rotations in space, changing points of view, zooming, or laying-out objects — the ones with poorer mastery of such operations seem to imitate and internalize the operations. Thus, the overt model seems to *supplant* a mental activity which can then be internalized, provided it has not been well-mastered beforehand. The modeled operation seems to accomplish for the students an operation they cannot yet perform themselves and which does not easily translate into another, say, linguistic code. Our students have learned to use these new symbolic operations in their cognitive representational system and to transfer them to new instances. They have learned to think in terms of filmic codes. (Note that while better skilled students showed improved skill mastery when specific filmic codes *activated* skills, those with poorer initial mastery showed evidence of code-internalization when the latter overtly *supplanted* the skill: a perfect ATI, or first order interaction.)

As we have found similar evidence also in field and cross-cultural studies *outside* the laboratory (Salomon, 1976; Salomon, 1979a), we feel quite confident in arguing that the symbol system of a medium such as film can serve as a cultivator of mental abilities and internal modes of representation. Quite clearly, though, media's symbol systems can cultivate mental skill only if (1) they are sufficiently unique, i.e. do not easily map upon alternative systems (as does the Morse Code with respect to language), and (2) they provide an organization of knowledge not provided by an alternative system (note the uniqueness of a flow-chart).

A THIRD ORDER INTERACTION

Equipped with these theoretical arguments and empirical evidence I can suggest that audio-visual media, when examined through their symbol systems, serve as good or poor conveyors of information in interactions with learners' aptitudes and specific modes of internal representation. But it is also warranted to argue that, apart from the above, media's symbol systems, which can cultivate cognition, enter into another far more pervasive interaction with learners.

We tend often to speak of learners as rather passive recipients of knowledge and as clay-like subjects whose skills are being molded. But once we entertain the possibility that they do something *active* with the skills they acquire and particularly with the symbolic codes they internalize from the media, we will have to look at them as individuals who actively gather information and structure it in terms of what they have acquired. Thus, to quote Bowers (1973): 'The situation is a function of the observer in the sense that the observer's cognitive schemes filter and organize the environment in a fashion that makes it impossible ever to

completely separate the environment from the person observing it'
(pp. 328-329).

The learner who has internalized the filmic code of, say, changing spatial points of view into his/her imagery can now turn to his/
her world of experience and represent it in ways that he/she was
less able to do before. Here is the testimony of a student of mine:

> I am fascinated by how my daydreaming is influenced by
> movies. Processes and techniques of presenting events by this
> Hollywood symbol system are powerfully implanted within my
> cognitive system. I have observed third person narration, flash-
> backs, zooms, slow-motion emphasis of action, audience
> viewing, re-takes, 'voice of conscience', multipersonality
> dialogue, background music, and many other movie means of
> expression in my head. I fear that there is very little original
> style to my daydreaming. It is all influenced by celluloid ...
> There are scenes where I am climbing steps to address a large
> audience, and television shots in slow motion symbolize the
> slow and hard road to significant others and flashbacks to signi-
> ficant moments.

While that student seems to be using filmic structures, in a
representational capacity, it would make sense to hypothesize that
he also examines other people's behavior in similar terms. His
mental, film-like schemata guide his perception and understanding
of the world. This I call a *third order interaction*. It can be
imagined as a spiral in which one's mental apparatus guides
perception and interpretation, which in turn establishes contact
with new symbolic forms. The latter can be internalized, and when
they are — they enrich the mental apparatus.

I think that this third order interaction should serve as our
major justification for using audio-visual materials. It is a justification for audio-visual usage because we want our students to use
rich and alternative modes of internal representations, not just the
verbal one, and we want them to examine the world through more
than one symbol system. After all, insights of many scientists did
not start with propositions. On the contrary, it was imagery —
often adapted from the world of art — which served as the initial
key hole through which phenomena were examined (see Shepard,
1978, for a compendium of such instances in the history of
science).

But such third order interactions, whose nature we know only in skeletal form, need also to serve as a focus for research. We know too little which symbol systems are, or can be internalized, how they guide thinking and perception and how the latter are externalized for communication purposes.

REFERENCES

Bandura, A. (1977). *Social Learning Theory*, Englewood Cliffs, N.J.: Prentice Hall.

Bloom, L., Hood, L. and Lightbown, P. (1974). 'Imitation in language development; if, when and why,' *Cognitive Psychology* 6: 380-420.

Bowers, K.S. (1973). 'Situationism in psychology: an analysis and a critique,' *Psychological Review* 80: 307-336.

Brown, R. (1965). *Social Psychology*, New York: Free Press.

Bruner, J.S. (1964). 'The course of cognitive growth,' *American Psychologist* 19: 1-15.

Cole, M. and Scribner, S. (1974). *Culture and Thought*, New York: Wiley.

Cronbach, L.J. (1957). 'The two disciplines of scientific psychology,' *American Psychologist* 12: 671-684.

Cronbach, L.J. and Snow, R.E. (1977). *Aptitudes and Instructional Methods: A Handbook of Research on Interactions*. New York: Irvington.

Eisner, E.W. (1978). 'The impoverished mind,' *Educational Leadership* 35: 615-623.

Flavell, J.H. (1977). *Cognitive Development*. Englewood Cliffs, N.J.: Prentice Hall.

Fodor, J.A. (1975). *The Language of Thought*, New York: Crowell.

Furth, (1966). *Thinking Without Language: Psychological Implications of Deafness*. New York: Free Press.

Gallagher, J.P. (1979). 'Cognitive information processing psychology and instruction: reviewing recent theory and practice,' *Instructional Science* 8: 393-414.

Gardner, H., Howard, V.A. and Perkins, D. (1974). 'Symbol systems: a philosophical, psychological, and educational investigation,' in D.R. Olson (ed.), *Media and Symbols: The Forms of Expression, Communication, and Education. 73rd Yearbook of the National Society for the Study of Education*. Chicago: University of Chicago Press.

Gombrich, E.H. (1974). 'The visual image,' in D.R. Olson (ed.), *Media and Symbols: The Forms of Expression, Communication, and Education. 73rd Yearbook of the National Society for the Study of Education*. Chicago: University of Chicago Press.

Goodman, N. (1968). *The Languages of Art*. Indianapolis: Hackett.

Goodman, N. (1978). *Ways of Worldmaking*. Indianapolis, Ind.: Hackett.

Gordon, G.N. (1969). *The Languages of Communication*, New York: Hastings House.

Hatano, G., Miyake, Y. and Binks, M.G. (1977). 'Performance of expert abacus operators,' *Cognition* 5: 57-71.

Huttenlocher, J. and Higgins, E.T. (1979). 'Issues in the study of symbolic development,' in A. Collins (ed.), *Minnesota Symposia on Child Psychology*. Vol. 10. New York: Crowell.

Kane, J.M. and Anderson, R.C. (1978). 'Depth of processing and interference effects in the learning and remembering of sentences,' *Journal of Educational Psychology* 70: 626-635.

Kintsch, W. (1977). *Memory and Cognition.* New York: Wiley.
Kosslyn, S. and Pomerantz, J. (1977) 'Imagery, propositions and the form of internal representations,' *Cognitive Psychology* 9: 52-76.
LaBerge, D. and Samuels, S.J. (1974). 'Toward a theory of automatic information processing in reading,' *Cognitive Psychology* 6: 293-323.
Luria, A.R. (1976). *Cognitive Development: Its Cultural and Social Foundations.* Cambridge, Mass.: Harvard University Press.
Meringoff, L. (1978). 'A story, a story: the influence of the medium on children's apprehension of stories.' Unpublished doctoral dissertation, Harvard University.
Mielke, K.W. (1968). 'Questioning the questions of ETV research,' *Educational Broadcasting Review* 2: 6-15.
Miller, S.H., Shelton, J. and Flavall, J.H. (1970). 'A test of Luria's hypothesis concerning the development of verbal self-regulation,' *Child Development* 41: 651-665.
Neisser, U. (1976). *Cognition and Reality.* San Francisco: Freeman.
Olson, D.R. (1974). 'Introduction,' in D.R. Olson (ed.), *Media and Symbols: The Forms of Expression, Communication, and Education. 73rd Yearbook of the National Society for the Study of Education.* Chicago: University of Chicago Press.
Olson, D.R. (1976). 'Towards a theory of instructional means,' *Educational Psychologist* 12: 14-35.
Olson, D.R. (1978). 'Three cognitive functions of symbols.' Paper presented at the Terman Memorial Conference, Stanford University, Stanford, Calif., (October).
Olson, D.R. and Bruner, J.S. (1974). 'Learning through experience and learning through media,' in D.R. Olson (ed.), *Media and Symbols: The Forms of Expression, Communication, and Education. 73rd Yearbook of the National Society for the Study of Education.* Chicago: University of Chicago Press.
Paivio, A. (1971). *Imagery and Verbal Processes.* New York: Holt, Rinehart and Winston.
Perkins, D. and Leondar, B. (eds.) (1977). *The Arts and Cognition.* Baltimore: Johns Hopkins University Press.
Salomon, G. (1971). 'Heuristic models for the generation of aptitude-treatment interaction hypotheses,' *Review of Educational Research* 42: 327-343.
Salomon, F. (1974). 'Internalization of filmic schematic operations in interaction with learners' aptitudes,' *Journal of Educational Psychology* 66: 499-511.
Salomon, G. (1976). 'Cognitive skill learning across cultures,' *Journal of Communication* 26: 138-145.
Salomon, G. (1977). 'Effects of encouraging Israeli mothers to co-observe "Sesame Street" with their five-year-olds,' *Child Development* 48: 1146-1151.
Salomon, G. (1979a). *Interaction of Media, Cognition and Learning.* San Francisco, Calif.: Jossey-Bass.
Salomon, G. (1979b). 'Media and symbol systems as related to cognition and learning,' *Journal of Educational Psychology* 71: 131-148.
Salomon, G. and Cohen, A.A. (1977). 'Television formats, mastery of mental skills, and the acquisition of knowledge,' *Journal of Educational Psychology* 69: 612-619.
Schlesinger, I.M. (1977). 'The role of cognitive development and linguistic input in language acquisition,' *Journal of Child Language* 4: 153-169.
Schramm, W. (1977). *Big Media, Little Media,* Beverly Hills, Calif.: Sage.
Shepard, R.N. (1978). 'Externalization of mental images and the act of creation,' in B.S. Randhava and W.E. Coffman (eds.), *Visual Learning. Thinking, and Communication.* New York: Academic Press.
Snow, R.E., Tiffin, J. and Seibert, W.F. (1965). 'Individual differences and instructional film effects,' *Journal of Educational Psychology* 56: 315-326.
Von Bertalanffy, L. (1965). 'On the definition of the symbol,' in J.R. Royce (ed.),

Psychology and the Symbol. New York: Random House.

Vygotsky, L.S. (1962). *Thought and Language*. Cambridge, Mass.: MIT Press.

Vygotsky, L.S. (1978). 'Tool and symbol in child development' in *Mind in Society: The Development of Higher Psychological Processes* (M. Cole *et al.*, eds.). Cambridge, Mass.: Harvard University Press.

3.4 The Forms of Television: Effects on Children's Attention, Comprehension and Social Behavior

MABEL RICE, ALETHA HUSTON and JOHN WRIGHT*

REPRESENTATIONAL CODES OF TELEVISION

Verbal and nonverbal forms are the representational codes of television. Because children view television at a very early age, it is tempting to assume that these representational codes are simple and of little interest. However, television is a medium that can be processed at differing levels of complexity. There is a difference between superficial consumption of interesting audiovisual events and mental extraction of information from coded messages, a distinction formulated by *Salomon* (1979). He used the term 'literate viewing' to refer to 'a process of information extraction by the active negotiation of the coding elements of the message' (p. 189). The notion of 'literate viewing' is closely related to the more informal term 'media literacy.' With age and viewing experience, children's attention to, and comprehension of, television programs change (e.g., *Collins*, 1979; *Krull* and *Husson*, 1979; *Calvert, Huston, Watkins*, and *Wright*, 1982). It is presumed that these developmental changes reflect increasing facility with television's conventions and content, i.e., the beginning television viewer is not 'media literate' but instead gradually acquires such competence as a function of experience with the medium and the attainment of certain minimal cognitive abilities.

Just because one can become a literate viewer at an early age and without conscious effort does not demonstrate that the task is simple. The representational codes of television range in complexity from literal visual depiction to the most abstract and

*Source: Manfred Mayer (ed.), *Children and the Formal Features of Television*, (Communication Research and Broadcasting No. 6) (K.A. Saur, Munich, 1983), pp. 21-44.

arbitrary symbols, including verbal language and audiovisual metaphor. The child's task is not an easy one. The change from infants' sensory-motor awareness of alternations in patterns of visual and verbal stimuli (*Hollenbeck* and *Slaby*, 1979) to the literate viewing skills of elementary school-age children involves a major qualitative advance, accompanied by developmental growth in related perceptual and cognitive skills.

Levels of Representation

The simplest level of representation is literal visual and/or auditory portrayal of real-world information, e.g., a shot of a car moving on the highway. A child's ability to process this level is presumably dependent primarily on perceptual and cognitive skills used in interpreting real-world stimuli. But even at this literal level, object recognition at unusual angles of viewing, lighting, and distance requires perceptual generalization and constancies not yet fully developed in the youngest viewers.

On the second level of representation are media forms and conventions that do not have an exact real-world counterpart, some of these, such as cuts and zooms, are analogs of perceptual experience. For example, a zoom-in is a perceptual analog of moving close to an object. Other media conventions are more distinct from real-world experience. Dissolves, slow motion, musical accompaniments, sound effects, and electronically generated visual special effects are relatively specific to film and television. These features provide a structure for the presentation of content in a manner analogous to syntax in language. A literate viewer must be able to decode the structural meanings of formal features. For example, fades and dissolves often indicate major transitions in time, place, or content; cuts are more often used for minor shifts from one character or viewing angle to another (*Huston, Wright, Wartella, Rice, Watkins, Campbell,* and *Potts,* 1981). In American children's programs, distinctive visual 'markers' are used to separate programs from commercials; the literate viewer must understand their function. This understanding is not automatic. For example, 5- and 6-year-olds did not understand the meaning of separators between programs and commercials in one recent study (*Palmer* and *McDowell,* 1979).

Media codes can also serve as models for mental representation or mental skills. That is, the child can adopt the media forms as modes of representations in her own thinking. *Salomon* (1979) has demonstrated, for example, that children can learn to analyze a complex stimulus into small parts by observing camera zooms in and out. Apparently, the camera provided a model of the mental process of focusing on specific parts of the stimulus. Media codes can be internalized as forms of mental representation, as suggested by *McLuhan* (1964), so that people can think in moving pictures with flashbacks, fast and slow motion, changes from color to black and white, and other media conventions (*Salomon,* 1979).

The forms of television can also take on connotative meaning, either because of their repeated association with certain content themes or because of their metaphorical similarity to real-world objects and symbols. For example, rapid action, loud music, and sound effects are often associated with violence in children's programs (*Huston* et al., 1981). Commercials for masculine sex-typed toys are made with high action, rapid cuts, and loud noise, whereas feminine sex-typed toys are advertised with fades, dissolves, and soft music (*Welch, Huston-Stein, Wright,* and *Plehals,* 1979). The forms themselves may come to signal violence or sex typing to children, even when the content cues are minimal or nonexistent. Two studies demonstrated that children as young as five or six understand that productions using loud noise, fast pace, and high action have masculine connotations while soft music, frequent fades and dissolves connote femininity. This is evident for content-reduced synthetic ads (*Greer, Huston, Welch, Wright,* and *Ross,* 1981) and for professionally produced naturalistic ads (*Leary* and *Huston,* 1983).

The third level of representation consists of symbolic forms not unique to the medium. Such forms may be nonlinguistic (e.g., a red stoplight) or linguistic. It is also possible for verbal language to encode forms at the other two levels. For example, dialog can encode the literal representation of reality (the first level), as when a speaker describes on-screen objects or events, or dialog can encode the conventional significance of a production feature (the second level), as when a fade is accompanied by the line 'Once upon a time, long, long ago. ...' In this sense of double encoding, it is possible for the first two levels to be nested in the linguistic codes. Such piggybacking of representational means could aid children in understanding the message and also, by association, facilitate their mastery of the codes themselves (cf. *Rice* and *Wartella,* 1981).

It is apparent that the second and third levels of representational codes found in children's television programs not only have different surface characteristics but also are derived from different sources or experiences. The second level of representation, specific knowledge, is probably acquired largely as a function of experience with the medium. That is not the case with the third level, where symbols are shared by the wider culture. By definition, these codes have currency outside the medium of television and can be learned without viewing television. They also have a different utility in the world, leading to slightly different reasons for investigating them. The media-specific codes are important insofar as they reveal what is involved in a child's processing of televised information. The verbal language of television is of special interest insofar as it contributes to a child's processing of televised messages and other media codes and also, perhaps more importantly, as it serves to facilitate a child's mastery of the general linguistic code (cf. *Rice*, in press, a; in press, b).

While the representational functions of the linguistic system have been described by linguists in a long research tradition, the production conventions, or codes, of television have only recently come to the attention of behavioral scientists. The first step in understanding these codes and their functions is to develop descriptive taxonomies for formal features and to describe the ways in which they are used in television productions.

Most descriptions of formal features have been developed for the purpose of studying television's influence on children. This is not to imply that formal features are without relevance for adults or that studies conducted with adult subjects are without implications for understanding children's television viewing experiences. A general discussion of how formal features may influence adult viewers is, however, beyond the scope of this review; only those studies immediately pertinent to child-directed issues and investigations are presented. Readers interested in the effects of television forms on adult audiences may wish to refer to television and film broadcasting and production publications, where issues of form are often discussed in regard to editing techniques. For example, *Messaris* et. al. (1979) argue that editing techniques (the sequence and composition of visual shots) influenced how adult audiences perceived the nature of the interchanges between Carter and Ford during the televised 1976 presidential debates.

Descriptive Analyses of Television Forms

[...] Formal features of children's television programs have been analyzed in our work (*Huston* et al., 1981) to determine what features co-occur, what features characterize animated and live programs, and how formal features differ as a function of target audience or production goals. In two samples of children's programs selected from Saturday morning, prime time, and daytime educational programming (primarily PBS), action (physical activity of characters), variability of scenes (number of different scenes), and tempo (rate of scene and character change) were grouped with visual special effects, rapid cuts, loud music, and sound effects. This package of features was labeled 'perceptually salient' because it was characterized by high intensity, rapid change, and rapid motion.

Commercial programs for young children are packed with these perceptually salient forms. Although such formal features are more frequent in animated than in live shows, Saturday morning live programs have higher rates of perceptually salient features than prime time or educational programs. This pattern of heavy reliance on perceptual salience suggests an image of the child in the minds of producers as a being whose attention must be captured and held by constant action, change, noise, and visual onslaught. Although much of what children watch is family adult programming, these children's programs may be particularly important developmentally because they constitute the child's earliest experience with the medium. They may set the standard for what the child expects from television. In addition, they are less likely than adult programs to be mediated or buffered by parents' or adults' viewing with the child. We do not know what effects early experience with heavily saturated television 'hype' and violence has on later development, later viewing patterns or on taste and preferences in the medium, but these questions are critically important for future research.

Educational programs for young children use some perceptually salient visual features that characterize Saturday morning programs, though at more moderate levels. They combine these features, however, with other forms that have considerable potential for helping children to understand, rehearse, and remember a message. These include child dialog — probably the best form of speech to gain and hold children's attention — as well as songs, long zooms, and moderate levels of physical activity. All of these features provide opportunities for reflection, rehearsal, and review of content. Songs are frequently used to repeat themes and as a device for helping children to rehearse. Long zooms involve slow presentation and/or emphasis of important content. Because young children often understand content that is demonstrated in action, the moderate levels of action may be a particularly important means of conveying information in a form that is interesting and comprehensible to a young child. Educational programs package their content in a set of forms that is quite different from commercial programming for children, and they appear to be designing programs that have good potential to hold attention *and* to communicate a message effectively.

The findings concerning forms in children's programs can also be seen from the perspective of media literacy and its antecedents (*Wright* and *Huston*, 1981). Recall that Saturday morning cartoons were characterized by high levels of action, variability, and tempo. These clusters consist of perceptually salient events, such as physical activity, music, sound effects, scene changes, and visual special effects. The conspicuous nature of these features may allow the forms themselves to become the message. That is, the child may pay more attention to *how* the information is conveyed then to *what* the message is, especially when the plot lines are thin to begin with. Unnoticed in the entertainment value of the features is the tutorial nature of the experience. The child is receiving explicit cues about how messages are communicated on television. In this case, the relationship between form and content is the opposite of the usual assumption. That is, the forms overpower the content (from the young viewer's perspective), whereas the problem is usually regarded as a matter of the content controlling the form (from the producer's perspective).

Linguistic Codes

The coding systems inherent in verbal language constitute another component of the forms of television. In television programs, verbal language is a code within a code. Descriptive studies of the language of children's television can provide information for two purposes: (1) Knowing the nature of television's linguistic conventions or codes and how they interact with other forms of communication in children's programs is a critical part of any attempt to understand how children process televised information; and (2) analysis of television's linguistic codes may show how they are adjusted in different programs to different levels of linguistic competence in the viewer and therefore how they may, under certain conditions, play an important role in furthering language acquisition itself.

In a pilot study of the linguistic structure of children's programming in relation to formal feature use, *Rice* (1979) analyzed 25 categories of linguistic coding in six programs. The programs represented animated stories with high, low, and no dialog; a live program representing situation comedy; and educational programs differing in age of intended audience and format (*Mister Rogers' Neighborhood* and *The Electric Company*). Three sets of linguistic descriptors were scored: (1) 'Communication flow' consisted of measures of length, variability, rate, and repetition of utterances; (2) 'language structure' contained measures of grammatical completeness, descriptive qualifiers, and stressed single words; (3) 'meaning/content' variables included focusing (i.e., giving selective prominence to a particular linguistic constituent), nonliteral meanings, explicit instructions, novel words, and immediacy of reference.

Distinctive patterns of language usage were evident in the two educational programs. *Mister Rogers' Neighborhood*, the educational program for preschoolers, presented a moderate pattern of verbal communication: a moderate amount of dialog, without the use of nonliteral meanings or novel words, combined with moderate amounts of focusing and some use of stressed single words. *The Electric Company*, an educational program designed for early school-age children, used the most dialog of all the shows sampled and incorporated techniques for drawing attention and interest to dialog (e.g., focusing, stressed single words, novel words, nonliteral meanings) while at the same time adjusting for easier comprehension of grammatical forms (e.g., short comments, partial grammatical units, low variability in length) and content (e.g., reference to immediately present events). While it is widely recognized that the purpose of *The Electric Company* is to enhance children's reading skills, the fact that it does so by means of intensive verbal presentation is generally overlooked. Both *Mister Rogers' Neighborhood* and *The Electric Company* used techniques that are likely to facilitate children's comprehension of language (stressed single words, focusing), but the latter also used a more complex pattern of verbal presentation designed to challenge the more linguistically competent school-age viewer.

Unlike the educational programs, the commercial programs containing dialog showed little evidence that language codes were adjusted to the level of the child viewer. Some contained frequent nonliteral meanings and little focusing. The situation comedy was particularly high in descriptive qualifiers and nonreferential content, and it did not share any distinctive language features with the other shows.

Comparison of the linguistic features with the formal production features of the six programs revealed that the shows with low amounts of dialog were high in action, pace, cuts, fades, zooms, visual special effects, vocalizations, sound effects, and music. All of these production features are perceptually salient ones that attract and hold visual attention in young viewers. The two verbally complex shows contained some distinctive uses of salient formal features: one had very high pace, frequent cuts, pans, and background music; the other had a high number of vocalizations.

Such findings suggest a continuum of difficulty of representational coding in this range of children's programs. We would expect linguistic coding to be more difficult for young viewers than the perceptually salient visual and auditory nonverbal codes. The packaging of American cartoons seems well suited to young children of limited media or linguistic competence. Similarly, the simple, comprehensible speech in *Mister Rogers' Neighborhood* is well suited to a preschool audience. More complex packaging in shows aimed at an older audience requires considerable linguistic sophistication and comprehension of distinctive uses of formal features. In some cases, the codes are judiciously mixed in packages of information presentation well suited to the communicative competencies of the intended audience. A moderate level of complexity may be important to maintain interest among older relatively sophisticated viewers.

Just as the conventional meanings of production features can be suggested by exaggerated, perceptually salient presentations used to convey redundant content, so there is evidence of adjustments of the linguistic and production codes that are designed to draw attention to and clarify language forms themselves. For example, the frequent focusing operations and stressed single words on *Mister Rogers' Neighborhood* and *The Electric Company* serve to draw attention to the language codes. Furthermore, in these two programs, the meanings of the linguistic forms are often explicitly depicted. Frequently, the content is a visual representation of the verbal meaning, sometimes highlighted by attention-maintaining visual production techniques, such as cuts to a closer focus or different perspective. At least some children's programs appear to combine language adjustments with selective and supportive use of nonlinguistic salient features, at first to supplement and later to challenge the emerging cognitive competencies of the child viewer.

The language of commercials aimed at children warrants explicit attention from research insofar as the intent goes beyond the communication of messages to the selling of products. Presumably, the effectiveness of commercials is dependent upon the nature of the linguistic codes presented (i.e., their basic understandability), their referential accuracy, and their use within the social context. *Bloome* and *Ripich* (1979) analyzed the social message units of commercials and how the messages related to plot or social context and/or the product. They found that many of the product-tied references were ambiguous in regard to certain features of products, such as the use of flavorings. Also, there was a subtle shift within commercials from using language in a social context to using language to promote products. Language served to establish the social occasion and then to lead the child to a product and its role in enhancing the social occasion.

THE INFLUENCE OF TELEVISION FORMS ON CHILDREN'S MENTAL PROCESSES

When children watch television, they can just sit passively and stare at the set if they choose, but a growing body of empirical evidence suggests that this is not the usual level of response. Instead, children are more likely to become involved in the viewing experience, to work at extracting information from coded messages, to respond cognitively, affectively, and socially to program content. They are mentally and socially active viewers (*Wright* et. al., 1978; *Singer*, 1980). At least some (if not most) of their mental responses are influenced by how the information is packaged, i.e., the media-specific and general representational codes employed (*Rice* and *Wartella*, 1981). The ones for which there is empirical evidence are discussed here: children's visual attention while viewing, and their understanding of television forms, program events, and relationships among characters.

Formal Features and Attention

Visual Attention to Television Forms.   Studies using different types of programs found that certain production features or program attributes attract and hold children's visual attention while viewing television (*Anderson* et. al., 1979; *Anderson* and *Levin*, 1976; *Anderson* et. al., 1977; *Bernstein*, 1978; *Susman*, 1978; *Wartella* and *Ettema*, 1974; *Wright* et al., 1980; *Rubinstein* et al., 1974). Even though different systems of scoring production features have been used, there is consistency in the findings:

1. Auditory features, such as lively music, sound effects, children's voices (but not adult dialog), peculiar voices, nonspeech vocalizations, and frequent changes of speaker attract and hold children's attention.
2. Conventional visual features, such as cuts, zooms, and pans have less influence, but visual special effects do attract children's attention.
3. In most studies, high levels of physical activity or action elicit and maintain children's attention.
4. Changes in scene, characters, themes, or auditory events are especially effective in eliciting attention, though they are less important for maintaining it once the child is looking.
5. Features that lose children's attention include long complex speeches, long zooms, song and dance, men's voices, and live animals.

Auditory Attention.   The finding that auditory events, action, and change elicit and hold children's visual attention, while visual features have less influence, serves to remind us that audition and vision interact in a complex manner during information processing. While there is considerable evidence describing visual attention, little information is available describing auditory attention (or the interaction of the two modalities) while viewing television. Any general conceptual model of how children attend to television (including the factors that are proposed as controlling attention) must take into account both visual and auditory attention. The measurement of auditory attention while maintaining a naturalistic viewing situation has been a challenging experimental problem. Looking behavior can be recorded directly in a reliable and unobstrusive manner; listening is a private mental event without easily observable indicators. We have devised a promising method for measuring auditory attention independently of visual attention. The procedure involves an intermittent degrade of the television picture or sound. As the child views, she can press a lever to restore the picture or sound track when it degrades. The child's responses are automatically recorded and time-referenced to the program. Initial findings with preschool children suggest a close relationship between looking and listening (*Rolandelli, Wright,* and *Huston,* 1982).

In addition to direct measures, auditory attention can be inferred by testing comprehension of material presented in the auditory modality or material presented when the child is not looking at television. Repeated findings that children receive and understand fairly complex messages from exposure to *Mister Rogers' Neighborhood,* despite low rates of visual attention, have led to speculation that children were often listening even when they were not looking (*Tower* et al., 1979). Obviously, auditory attention can facilitate comprehension only for material that is presented in an auditory modality, usually speech. Studies in our laboratory, involving microanalysis of short time intervals within a program, indicate close connections among visual presentation of content, visual attending, and recall (*Calvert* et al., 1982). Similar precision in specifying the mode through which content is presented would be required to infer that auditory attention mediated comprehension.

Auditory attention can also be inferred by observing visual attention to the screen (or lack thereof) and by observing what children talk about while viewing. If they are talking about things unrelated to the television content, they are probably not listening. Even if they are looking at the set, their attention may be only at the level of monitoring instead of active processing. On the other hand, auditory features, such as foreground music and children's speech, recruit visual attention for children who are looking away from the screen — evidence that some form of auditory processing is taking place.

Form and Content Interactions.   One of the original reasons for our interest in television form was the hypothesis that formal features in children's television were more important determinants of attention than violent content. The relative contributions of form and violent content are difficult to disentangle because conventions of production lead to correlations of certain forms with violence. Violence in children's programs is usually portrayed with high levels of action and salient auditory and visual features (*Huston* et al., 1981). Yet, formal features can be separated conceptually and operationally from violent content. In two studies of preschoolers, we selected programs that were high in both action and violence, or high in action and low in violence, low in action and high in violence, or low in both action and violence. Children's total attention differed as a function of action, not of violence. That is, they were as attentive to high action without violence as they were when it accompanied violence, and less attentive to low action (*Huston-Stein, Fox, Greer, Watkins*, and *Whitaker*, 1981; *Huston, Wright*, and *Potts*, 1982).

A more molecular analysis was performed for these three programs and for four other cartoons by dividing each program into 15-second intervals and correlating attention with formal features and violent content. Multiple regressions were performed to determine which features were the best predictors of attention in each program. Violence did not enter any of the seven multiple regressions as a predictor that contributed significant variance independently of formal features, but considerably more data on different programs and different age groups are needed to establish the generality of this null conclusion (*Huston-Stein*, 1977).

Form, Content and Viewership Ratings.   The relation of form and content to children's interest in television programs has also been studied by analyzing feature occurrence rates in nationally broadcast television programs in relation to national audience ratings for different ages, sexes, and regions of the country. For a sample of 34 Saturday morning programs, high action and violent content were predictors of viewership for preschool children. Each made an independent contribution. Among children from age 6 to 11, variability and tempo were the best predictors of viewership (*Wright* et al., 1980). In a similar analysis of general adult audience ratings in relation to violent content of prime time adventure programs, violence accounted for a minuscule and nonsignificant portion of the variance in viewership (*Diener* and *DeFour*, 1978).

How Formal Features Influence Attention

Salience and Informativeness.   Basic research on young children's attention indicates that perceptual salience of the stimulus environment is one determinant of attention. The attributes of a stimulus that make it salient include intensity, movement, contrast, change, novelty, unexpectedness, and incongruity (*Berlyne,* 1960). Many of the production features that attract and hold young children's attention fit these criteria defining perceptual salience. We have proposed a developmental model hypothesizing that perceptual salience is a particularly important determinant of attention for very young viewers and/or for viewers with little media experience (*Huston-Stein* and *Wright,* 1977; 1979).

The theory guiding our work was derived from the more general theoretical work of *Wright* and *Vlietstra* (1975) concerning developmental change from 'exploration' to 'search' in children's modes of information getting. Exploration as a mode of response is governed by the most salient features of the stimulus environment. It involves short duration, discontinuous, and impulsive responding to whatever features of the environment are perceptually dominant from moment to moment. Habituation to the salient features of a particular stimulus environment occurs as one becomes more familiar with it. Application of this model to television experience leads to the hypothesis that, among the youngest and least experienced viewers, the viewing experience consists of the consumption of perceptually salient events as entertainment in their own right. The child's attention is controlled primarily by feature salience. Until the powerful effects of salience have partially habituated, the child is essentially a passive consumer of audiovisual thrills and does not engage in deeper levels of processing (*Wright* and *Huston,* 1981).

Consummatory stimulus-controlled exploration gives way in familiar contexts to perceptual search, a kind of information getting in which the activity is instrumental, rather than consummatory, active rather than passive, and guided by the child's desire to abstract information, rather than by just entertainment, from perceived events. The child's progress from perceptual exploration to perceptual search is believed to be as much or more a function of familiarization through experience and habituation as it is a consequence of cognitive maturation, though, of course, the two are usually confounded. Thus, the older and more experienced viewers are more interested in the content of program and its meaning and less responsive to salient formal features. When older children do attend to formal features, they may use them as syntactic markers to develop a structural framework in which to organize and integrate their comprehension of content meaning (*Huston* and *Wright*, 1983).

Singer (1980) also proposed that high rates of salient audiovisual events on television absorb children's attention, not only because they are perceptually interesting, but because they are affectively involving. His theory does not, however, contain the proposition that developmental shifts will occur as consequences of cognitive development and familiarity with the medium. Instead, he seems to imply that extensive exposure to salient features in the medium will inhibit other forms of interest (e.g., books and verbal media) and will leave the child focused on the absorbing stimulus features of the moving picture on the screen.

Studies comparing attention patterns of preschool children (age 4–6) with those of children in middle childhood (age 8–10) have provided minimal support for the hypothesis that younger children are more attentive to salient formal features than are older children (*Calvert* et al., 1982; *Wartella* and *Ettema*, 1974; *Wright* et al., in press). Both age groups attend to high levels of action and audiovisual 'tricks' (visual special effects, sound effects, and unfamiliar scenes). Although these studies are consistent with the notion that younger children's attention is affected by the perceptual salience of television's formal features, they suggest that many of these features serve other functions as well in the child's processing of televised information.

The complementary hypothesis is that older children's attention is guided more by the informativeness of features. Informativeness depends on the program context and the child's level of processing. For example, in a study comparing high and low pace programs, 8 to 10-year-old children patterned their attention according to the length of scenes so that their average duration per look at the screen was longer in low pace programs (with long scenes) than during high paced programs (with short scenes). Younger children (5- to 7-year-olds) did not show this pattern (*Wright, Huston, Ross, Calvert, Rolandelli, Weeks, Raeissi,* and *Potts*, in press). These findings suggested that the older children used the formal cues in the program to determine natural breaks between scenes with more skill than the younger children did.

When children try to follow a plot or engage in a logical search for meaning, they probably attend to features that provide cues about time sequences, locations, characters, and events in the program. Studies by *Krull* and *Husson* (1979), in fact, suggest that older children may attend to form cues that signal content and form changes during the upcoming 1 or 2 minutes. Preschool children did not show these anticipatory patterns of attention to formal cues. Media literate children may learn temporal associations so they can anticipate what will occur in a program. Older children also attend differentially to informative action and signals associated with scene changes, bit changes, and changes to and from commercials.

Comprehensibility

A somewhat different perspective on the relationship between attention and formal features is proposed by Anderson and his associates, who link attention with the comprehensibility of program content (e.g., *Anderson* and *Lorch*, 1983). They suggest that features such as animation or children's voices may serve as signals that the content is designed for children and is therefore likely to be comprehensible. Children may attend to such features, not because of the inherent qualities of the features, but because their media experience leads them to expect meaningful and understandable program content. The fundamental determinant of attention, according to this formulation, is the comprehensibility of the content. Two sets of data have been used to support this hypothesis. In one study (*Lorch* et al., 1979), children's attention to *Sesame Street* was manipulated experimentally by varying the availability of toys and distractions during viewing. Despite the fact that the nondistraction treatment produced very high levels of attention, it did not produce improved comprehension. Within the distracted group, however, the children who attended more comprehended more of the content. This finding was interpreted as demonstrating that comprehensibility guided attention rather than attention determining comprehension. In a subsequent study (*Anderson, Lorch, Field,* and *Sanders*, 1981), children attended less to a television program in which the speech was incomprehensible because it was backwards or in a foreign language than to a program with understandable speech. Although the influence of comprehensibility on attention has been tested thus far only by varying language features of programs, the hypothesis suggests that the comprehensibility of nonlinguistic formal features should affect attention through a similar mechanism.

This line of research provides important evidence that very

young children are actively processing content when they watch television rather than merely passively consuming audiovideo thrills. It does not, however, establish that feature salience and other noncontent aspects of television programs are unimportant influences on children's attention. In the studies varying comprehensibility, feature salience has been held constant (and fairly high). If salience were low, would comprehensibility alone hold children's attention? Again, the relatively low rates of attention usually found for *Mister Rogers' Neighborhood* suggest not, despite its outstanding comprehensibility. Second, the full range of comprehensibility has not been systematically explored. In a study recently completed in our Center, these issues were addressed. Form and comprehensibility were varied independently. Short educational bits were constructed with identical content in animated, child-format versions and live, adult-format versions. Each format was used to produce bits varying in difficulty or comprehensibility but all were within the range of children's ability to understand. Children attended to the child-format versions more than to the adult-format versions, but they did not attend differently to the bits that were easy or difficult to understand (*Campbell*, 1982). It appears that there are many reasons why animated child formats may be attractive to children. Further, although complex, incomprehensible material loses children's attention in comparison to moderately easy, comprehensible material, one cannot extrapolate that finding to conclude that very easy material would produce more attention than moderately difficult but still comprehensible content. In fact, the model to be proposed here suggests that both extremes of comprehensibility will be less likely to maintain attention than material in the middle range. Moreover, the model explicitly cautions against trying to define moderate comprehensibility as a stimulus feature without taking into account both the cognitive level and the viewing experience of the child.

An Integrative Model of Attention and Development.   These seemingly divergent explanations of the determinants of attention can be integrated in the framework of one established model for attention and interest as a function of familiarity and complexity (*Hunt*, 1961).

That model is illustrated in *Figure 1*. The abscissa is a compound of familiarity and complexity of both form and content.

On the left end are highly familiar and oft-repeated bits, like the standard introductions and closings of familiar program series, whose informative content is minimal, and whose formal features have become habituated and no longer elicit attention among habitual viewers. The joint processes of habituation and familiarization (*Wright*, 1977) serve continually to depress attention on the left side of the inverted U-shaped function. By contrast, the forms and content at the high end of the abscissa are unfamiliar, complex, and incomprehensible to the child viewer. They, too, elicit little interest and attention because the child is incapable of understanding their meaning and their relation to other parts of the program. Their decoding requires comprehension of standards the child has not yet acquired and logical integration for which the child is not yet cognitively ready. They also often make reference to outside information and contextual knowledge that only adult viewers possess. Thus, attention on the right side of the curve is also low, owing to incomprehensibility. But cognitive development and the child's growing store of background information will, over time, tend to raise attention on the right, just as familiarization and habituation tend to reduce it on the left. The result is a developmental migration of the curve describing a child's attention from left to right as a function of cognitive development and viewing experience. What was interesting for its perceptual salience or simple content becomes boring by its redundancy, and what was incomprehensible or formally complex, and therefore ignored, gradually becomes meaningful and informative in the decoding process and, therefore, of greater interest. If the abscissa is defined in terms of the form and content of a televised stimulus, the location of the curve for a particular child along that gradient is a function of cognitive level (on the right) and viewing history (on the left).

How Formal Features Influence Comprehension

As children attend to television, their immediate task is how to interpret the information they receive, what to make of the messages. The medium's representational codes influence this process of comprehension in a number of ways. The media-specific codes themselves require some interpretation, as do the general representational codes, such as language. The coding systems also interact with content in ways that can enhance or interfere with how easily the content can be understood.

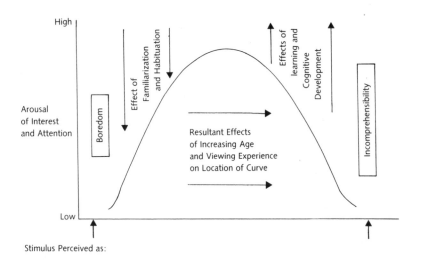

Stimulus Perceived as:

Familiar	Moderately Novel	Novel
Simple	of Intermediate Complexity	Complex
Wholistic	Integratable	Incongruous
Redundant	Somewhat Regular	Inconsistent
Repetitive	Partially Ordered	Unpredictable
Expected	Recognizable	Surprising

Figure 1: Theoretical model

Media-Specific Codes and Mental Skills.   Recall our opening remarks about how television does not literally present events as we perceive them in the real world. Instead, the representational codes package messages in a manner that requires mental transformations in order to interpret them. The linkage between forms and mental processes can be quite specific and intimate. *Salomon* (1979) proposed that some production features may be viewed as representing certain mental skills or mental operations. For example, zooming in and out literally portrays the mental operation of relating parts to a whole. Camera cuts that make the image jump from one part of a physical space to another, or from one view of an object to another, correspond to the mental operations of coordinating spaces and taking different perspectives.

Salomon (1979) distinguishes two different ways in which production features can function in relationships to mental processes, at two different levels of interpretative difficulty. One is the function of 'supplanting' the skill. That is, the camera essentially performs the operation for the viewer; presumably, the viewer can learn the skill from watching through the eye of the camera. A zoom-in is an example of a camera operation that supplants the skill of analyzing a complex array into subparts or isolating one small part at a time. The second function of media codes is to 'call upon' an already existing skill in the viewer. For example, a cut to close-up shot presumes that the viewer can already relate small parts to a larger whole; it does not perform the operation as a zoom does.

Data on both Israeli and American children support the hypothesis that the understanding of and ability to use common media codes increase with age and, in some cases, with media experience. Younger and less experienced viewers benefit more from media formats or formal features that supplant the intellectual skills to which they relate. Older and more experienced viewers understand recurring formats that call upon related mental skills better than do younger and less experienced viewers (*Salomon*, 1979; *Palmer*, 1978). For example, children who were skilled at visual analysis performed better when shown a 'cut to close up' format than when shown zooms (*Salomon*, 1974).

Salomon (1979) argues that the relationship between media codes and children's mental processing is not just a one-way process of using mental skills to interpret media codes. Instead, the influence is reciprocal: Experience with media codes actually cultivates the existing mental skills to which they relate; the media codes can become part of children's mental schemata, resulting in their ability to think in terms of such codes as zooms and camera cuts. *Salomon* cautions, however, that the media-specific codes are not the only messages to affect cognition, and not all of television's codes function in this capacity. He suggests that those codes that are unique to television and have a wide potential field of reference are those most likely to contribute to viewers' mental schemata.

The supplanting function of media form was tested in our laboratory in two studies designed to teach conservation of number by showing children animated television sequences demonstrating that the number of objects was independent of their spatial configuration. Pairs of white and black squares separated into designs, danced around one another, and played games; then they returned to their original arrangement with a narrator's reminder that there were still the same number of blacks and whites. Training improved conservation on a televised post-test of number conservation, but did not generalize to a live test, in the first study. In the second, training influenced performance on both televised and live post-tests (*Butt* and *Wright*, 1979; *Raeissi* and *Wright*, 1983).

Children's understanding of how media-specific forms mark temporal relationships was investigated in two studes of instant replays. Two factors were varied: The content of the replay and the presence or absence of an accompanying special effect (opening and closing geometric shape). We were interested in when children noticed that a replay had been inserted and how they interpreted what it depicted. It was not until around age seven years that children noticed a majority of the replays. The most likely context for noticing the replay was that of simple, everyday events (such as phone calls). Younger children (ages four to seven) interpreted replays as repetitions, as if there had been no cut back to the start of the sequence and the actor had simply repeated their actions or another actor had duplicated the actions of the first. Older children gave media-related explanations that were most likely for sports contexts, i.e. baseball games (*Rice, Wright,* and *Huston*, in progress; *Weeks* and *Rice*, 1982).

Language Codes.   There are several aspects of verbal language that have relevance for how children comprehend the messages of television. The first is how children comprehend the verbal dialog itself. This question has yet to be the subject of explicit empirical investigation (beyond a few observations of how children interpret disclaimer phrases in commercials). We can presume however, that children interpret televised verbal information according to the same linguistic processing strategies and constraints that they draw upon in the presence of live speakers. In other words, insofar as the general representational codes of television are like their real-world counterparts, children probably interpret them in much the same way as they do in other social contexts. The second aspect of verbal language with relevance for comprehension is the fact that, unlike the media-specific representational codes, viewers can produce the general codes themselves to communicate their reactions to and understandings of television. Viewers can process the messages of television and then respond in some of the same codes; indeed, they can literally imitate and rehearse the verbal messages, if they choose to do so.

In one study, we explored what children talk about when they watch television as a function of the amount of dialog present in the programs. Preschool and third-grade children watched four shows that differed in the amount of dialog (one show with none, two with moderate amounts, and one with a high frequency of dialog). The children watched in pairs, and they were free to pursue other play activities. Their comments while viewing were transcribed and coded for content categories. The children made the most comments about the television program when viewing the program with no dialog. This trend was more pronounced among the third-graders than the preschoolers. Furthermore, the television-related comments fell in a distinctive pattern: more descriptions of actions and events, more emotional and self-referenced comments (e.g., 'I like this part'), more questions about program content, and more statements of knowledge of recurrent program themes for the no-dialog program than for any of the other three. There were very few directly imitative responses (*Rice*, 1980).

The most obvious interpretation of these findings — that children listen when there is dialog and talk when there is no dialog — does not completely account for the results. The total amount of talking was highest in the no-dialog show, but second highest in the high-dialog show. Children talked to one another extensively during a program with frequent dialog, but they more often talked about topics that were irrelevant to the program. In the program without dialog, the absence of dialog, as well as the fact that the program was familiar and repetitive, appeared to stimulate children to talk about the program. Whether or not similar effects would occur for programs that were less repetitive or familiar is not yet clear, but in a program that is interesting, familiar, and simple to understand, it appears that the absence of dialog may elicit comments about aspects of a program that are of interest to children.

Verbal Mediation of Content.　Another aspect of verbal language with relevance for television viewing is that it can be used to mediate and direct more general mental processes, such as attention, comprehension, and recall. Verbal labels and explanations have been used in a number of experiments to clarify children's understanding of program content. In one study, preschool children imitated sharing from a television program more when the program included verbal labeling of the characters' behavior than when the behavior was not labeled (*Susman*, 1976). In another investigation, verbal explanations of program themes inserted in a cartoon with a moderately complex plot were relatively ineffective in improving comprehension, but the same explanations provided by an adult viewing with the child aided comprehension considerably. In particular, children who received the adult explanations recalled the temporal order of events in the program and were able to make inferences about implicit content better than controls. They also attended more to the program. Temporal integration and inferential processing of televised information are skills that are difficult for third-graders, yet even 4- to 6-year-olds were able to do them better than chance after the adult explanations (*Watkins* et al., 1980). Other studies have demonstrated similar benefits for kindergarten-age children from verbal labeling of central program themes (*Friedrich* and *Stein*, 1975).

Television Form and Plot-relevant Content.   Many television programs are narratives; that is, they tell a story consisting of interrelated events. The content of such stories can be distinguished as plot-relevant (central content) or irrelevant to the plot (incidental content). Developmental changes in comprehension of such content have been explored in some detail (*Collins*, 1979). Through second grade, children have limited and fragmented comprehension of story material, fifth-graders do better, and eighth-graders comprehend most of the story. In particular, younger children tend to recall material that is incidental and irrelevant to the plot, whereas older children appear better able to select central content messages. Younger children also have difficulty in integrating facts of the story that are separated in time (e.g., connecting an action with its motives and consequences), and they have difficulty inferring content that is implicit in the story but is not explicitly shown. All of these findings are based on children's responses to adult prime time dramas (*Collins*, 1979; 1982). The specific ages at which changes in comprehension occur may be slightly different for other types of programs, such as those made for children, but the direction of developmental trends is probably the same.

While developmental differences in children's understanding of television content undoubtedly reflect cognitive developmental changes, they may also vary, depending on the form in which content is communicated. In general, children understand information presented visually, so that character actions can be observed, better than they understand information presented in verbal form without accompanying visual cues. In addition, high action and other perceptually salient features maintain children's attention better than dialog and narration, so children may retain the content presented with salient features better than content conveyed primarily through dialog. Obviously, the combination of visual and verbal cues is likely to be most effective (*Friedlander* et al., 1974).

In one study (*Calvert* et al., 1982), children's recall of a televised story was measured for four types of content: central or incidental content was presented with formal features that were either high or low in perceptual salience. High salience features included visual features and moderately high action; low salience features included adult and child dialog. Central content questions often involved inferences; incidental content usually consisted of isolated factual events. Children remembered central, theme-relevant content better when it was presented with highly salient formal features than when it was presented with low salience techniques.

Some parallels appear in a study of commercials in which visual cues and words in the form of slogans or labels actually conflicted with the more abstract verbal message. Visual cues and word slogans suggested that the advertised products contained fruit, although the 'higher level' abstract verbal message indicated no fruit content. Children from kindergarten through sixth grade accepted the false message conveyed by the visual and associative word cues. Apparently they did not understand the abstract implied message that there was no real fruit in the products (*Ross* et al., 1981).

Salomon's work (1979) also indicates that children understand content messages better when they understand the formats used to present the content. For instance, children who were good at relating parts to a whole, and who could, therefore, understand a close-up format, learned more content from a film using cuts to close-ups than did children who were less skilled in understanding that format.

This prediction is upheld in an investigation of the effect of media-specific forms on children's comprehension of nutritional announcements. Nutritional messages containing identical visual and verbal content were produced with two types of formal features selected to represent the forms typically used in adult and child programming respectively. The adult versions were made from live footage with an adult male narrator and sedate background music, while the child versions were animated with peculiar 'character' voices, and sprightly, whimsical music. Children comprehended nutritional messages better in the child-format presentation than in the adult format (*Campbell*, 1982).

These findings suggest that associating content with certain media codes may increase comprehension of the content, if the production feature is familiar and understood by the child and if it focuses attention on central rather than incidental content. If the child does not understand the code represented by the feature or if the feature focuses attention away from the central content, it may interfere with comprehension. These conclusions may apply to the verbal codes of television as well as to the media-specific production features.

To conclude this section on how children's comprehension of television is influenced by the representational codes, we can offer some general observations. The child viewer has the job of making sense of the medium at several different levels: the codes themselves, the immediate content, and more abstract interrelations relevant to story lines. The representational codes are implicated at each of these levels. Children learn to interpret the media-specific codes as a function of age and viewing experience. Furthermore, certain media codes may come to be incorporated in children's general mental schemata. The general representational code of verbal language has a twofold relevance for increasing our understanding of how children comprehend television: (1) We need to be aware of the particular interpretative demands presented by the verbal dialog as a linguistic code; and (2) children's own verbal comments while viewing can provide further clues about how they comprehend television's messages (cf. *Rice* and *Wartella*, 1981). The psychological dimensions of television codes can be used to enhance children's comprehension of plot-relevant content: the association of attention-getting features or codes that are readily understood with content central to the story should contribute positively to children's ability to understand the plot.

REFERENCES

Anderson, D.R., Alwitt, L.F., Lorch, E.P., and Levin, S.R. Watching children watch television. In G. Hale and M. Lewis (Eds.), *Attention and the development of cognitive skills.* New York: Plenum, 1979.

Anderson, D.R., and Levin, S.R. Young children's attention to *Sesame Street. Child Development.* 1976, *47,* 806-811.

Anderson, D.R., Levin, S.R., and Lorch, E.P. The effects of TV program pacing on the behavior of preschool children. *AV Communication Review,* 1977, *25,* 154-166.

Anderson, D.R., Lorch, E.P., Field, D.E., and Sanders, J. The effects of TV program comprehensibility on preschool children's visual attention to television. *Child Development,* 1981, *52,* 151-157.

Anderson, D.R., and Lorch, E.P. Looking at television: Action or reaction? In J. Bryant and D.R. Anderson (Eds.), *Children's understanding of television: Research on attention and comprehension.* New York: Academic Press, 1983.

Berlyne, D.E. *Conflict, arousal, and curiosity.* New York: McGraw Hill, 1960.

Bernstein, L.J. *Design attributes of Sesame Street and the visual attention of preschool children.* Unpublished doctoral dissertation, Columbia University, 1978.

Bloome, D., and Ripich, D. Language in children's television commercials: A sociolinguistic perspective. *Theory into Practice,* 1979, *18,* 220-225.

Butt, Y., and Wright, J.C. *Televised training of preschoolers in number conservation.* CRITC Report 24a. Center for Research on the Influences of Television on Children, University of Kansas, Lawrence, Kansas, 1979.

Calvert, S.L., Huston, A.C., Watkins, B.A., and Wright, J.C. The effects of selective attention to television forms on children's comprehension of content. *Child Development,* 1982, *53,* 601-610.

Campbell, T.A. *Format cues and content difficulty as determinants of children's cognitive processing of televised educational messages.* Unpublished doctoral dissertation. University of Kansas, 1982.

Collins, W.A. Children's comprehension of television content. In E. Wartella (Ed.), *Children communicating: Media and development of thought, speech, understanding.* Beverly Hills: Sage, 1979.

Collins, W.A. Cognitive processing in television viewing. In D. Pearl, L. Bouthilet, and J. Lazar (Eds.), *Television and behavior: Ten years of scientific progress and implications for the eighties.* (Vol. 2). Rockville, Md.: National Institute of Mental Health, 1982.

Diener, E., and DeFour, D. Does television violence enhance program popularity? *Journal of Personality and Social Psychology,* 1978, *36,* 333-341.

Friedlander, B.Z., Westone, H.S., and Scott, C.S. Suburban preschool children's comprehension of an age-appropriate information television program. *Child Development,* 1974, *45,* 561-565.

Greer, D., Huston, A.C., Welch, R.L., Wright, J.C., and Ross, R.P. *Children's comprehension of television forms with masculine and feminine connotations.* Paper presented at biennial meeting, Society for Research in Child Development, Boston, April, 1981.

Hollenbeck, A.R., and Slaby, R.G. Infant visual and vocal responses to television. *Child Development,* 1979, *50,* 41-45.

Hunt, J. McV. *Intelligence and experience.* New York: Wiley, 1961.

Huston, A.C., Wright, J.C., Wartella, E., Rice, M.L., Watkins, B.A., Campbell, T., and Potts, R. Communicating more than content: Formal features of children's television programs. *Journal of Communication,* 1981, *31* (3), 32-48.

Huston, A.C., Wright, J.C., and Potts, R.P. Fernsehspezifische Formen und kindliches Sozialverhalten. (Television forms and children's social behavior.) *Fernsehen und Bildung*, 1982, *16*, 128-138.

Huston, A.C., and Wright, J.C. Children's processing of television: The informative functions of formal features. In J. Bryant and D.R. Anderson (Eds.), *Children's understanding of television: Research on attention and comprehension.* New York: Academic Press, 1983.

Huston-Stein, A. *Television and growing up: The medium gets equal time.* Invited address to Divisions 15 and 7 at the meeting of the American Psychological Association, San Francisco, 1977.

Huston-Stein, A.C., and Wright, J.C. Children and television: Effects of the medium, its content, and its form. *Journal of Research and Development in Education*, 1979, *13*, 20-31.

Huston-Stein, A., Fox, S., Greer, D., Watkins, B.A., and Whitaker, J. The effects of action and violence in television programs on the social behavior and imaginative play of preschool children. *Journal of Genetic Psychology*, 1981, *138*, 183-191.

Krull, R., and Husson, W. Children's attention: The case of TV viewing. In E. Wartella (Ed.), *Children communicating: Media and development of thought, speech, understanding.* Beverly Hills: Sage, 1979.

Leary, A., and Huston, A.C. *The influence of television production features with masculine and feminine connotations on children's comprehension and play behavior.* Paper presented at biennial meeting, Society for Research in Child Development, Detroit, April, 1983.

Lorch, E.P., Anderson, D.R., and Levin, S.R. The relationship of visual attention to children's comprehension of television. *Child Development*, 1979, *50*, 722-727.

McLuhan, M. *Understanding media: The extensions of man.* New York: McGraw-Hill, 1964.

Messaris, P., Eckman, B. and Gumpert, G. Editing structure in the televised versions of the 1976 presidential debates. *Journal of Broadcasting*, 1979, *23*, 359-369.

Palmer, E.L. *A pedagogical analysis of recurrent formats on Sesame Street and The Electric Company.* Paper presented at the International Conferences on Children's Educational Television, Amsterdam, 1978.

Palmer, E.L., and McDowell, C.N. Program/commercial separators in children's television programming. *Journal of Communication*, 1979, *29*(3), 197-201.

Raeissi, P. and Wright, J.C. *Training and generalization of number conservation by television for preschoolers.* Paper presented at biennial meeting, Society for Research in Child Development, Detroit, April, 1983.

Rice, M.L. *Television as a medium of verbal communication.* Paper presented at the meeting of the American Psychological Association, New York, 1979.

Rice, M.L. *What children talk about while they watch TV.* Paper presented at the meeting of the Southwestern Society for Research in Human Development, Lawrence, Kansas, 1980.

Rice, M.L., and Wartella, E. Television as a medium of communication: Implications for how to regard the child viewer. *Journal of Broadcasting*, 1981, *25*(4), 365-372.

Rice, M.L. The role of television in children's language acquisition. *Developmental Review*, in press.

Rice, M.L., Wright, J.C., and Huston, A.C. Children's comprehension of instant replays. (In progress.)

Rolandelli, D.R., Wright, J.C., and Huston, A.C. *Auditory attention to television: A new methodology.* Paper presented at biennial meeting, Southwestern Society for Research in Human Development. Galveston, April, 1982.

Ross, R., Campbell, T., Huston-Stein, A., and Wright, J.C. Nutritional misinformation of children: A developmental and experimental analysis of the effects of televised food commercials. *Journal of Applied Developmental*

Psychology, 1981, *1*, 329-345.

Rubinstein, E.A., Liebert, R.M., Neale, J.M., and Poulos, R.W. *Assessing television's influence on children's prosocial behavior.* Occasional paper 74-11. Stony Brook, New York: Brookdale International Institute, 1974.

Salomon, G. *Interaction of media, cognition, and learning.* San Francisco, Jossey-Bass, 1979.

Singer, J.L. The power and limitations of television: A cognitive-affective analysis. In P. Tannenbaum (Ed.), *The entertainment functions of television.* Hillsdale, N.J.: Erlbaum, 1980.

Susman, E.J. Visual and verbal attributes of television and selective attention in preschool children. *Developmental Psychology*, 1978, *14*, 565-566.

Tower, R.B., Singer, D.G., Singer, J.L., and Biggs, H. Differential effects of television programming on preschoolers' cognition, imagination, and social play. *American Journal of Orthopsychiatry*, 1979, *49*, 265-281.

Wartella, E., and Ettema, J.S. A cognitive developmental study of children's attention to television commercials. *Communication Research*, 1974, *1*, 69-88.

Watkins, B.A., Calvert, S., Huston-Stein, A., and Wright, J.C. Children's recall of television material: Effects of presentation mode and adult labeling. *Developmental Psychology*, 1980, *16*, 672-679.

Weeks, L.A., and Rice, M. *Replays and repetitions: How children interpret television.* Paper presented at biennial meeting, Southwestern Society for Research in Human Development, Galveston, April, 1982.

Welch, R.H., Huston-Stein, A., Wright, J.C., and Plehals, R. Subtle sex-role cues in children's commercials. *Journal of Communication*, 1979, *29*(3), 202-209.

Wright, J.C. *On familiarity and habituation: The situational microgenetics of information getting.* Paper presented at the meeting of the Society for Research in Child Development, New Orleans, 1977.

Wright, J.C., Calvert, S., Huston-Stein, A., and Watkins, B.A. *Children's selective attention to television forms: Effects of salient and informative production features as functions of age and viewing experience.* Paper presented at the meeting of the International Communication Association, Acapulco, Mexico, 1980.

Wright, J.C., and Huston, A.C. The forms of television: Nature and development of television literacy in children. In H. Kelly and H. Gardner (Eds.), *Viewing children through television.* San Francisco: Jossey-Bass, 1981.

Wright, J.C., Huston, A.C., Ross, R.P., Calvert, S.L., Rolandelli, D.R., Weeks, L.A., Raeissi, P., and Potts, R. Pace and continuity of television programs: Effects on children's attention and comprehension. *Developmental Psychology*, in press.

Wright, J.C., Huston-Stein, A., Potts, R., Rice, M., Calvert, S., Greer, D., Watkins, B.A., Thissen, D., and Zapata, L. *The relation of formal features of children's television programs to viewership by children of different ages: A tale of three cities.* Paper presented at the meeting of the Southwestern Society for Research in Human Development, Lawrence, Kansas, 1980.

Wright, J.C., Watkins, B.A., and Huston-Stein, A. *Active vs. passive television viewing: A model of the development of TV information processing in children.* Paper presented at the meeting of the American Psychological Association, Toronto, 1978.

SECTION 4

MEDIA EDUCATION

INTRODUCTION

Contributions to section 3 looked at the significance of media forms in relation to general theories of learning. This section moves closer to the world of formal education. The volume introduction outlined four major ways in which the worlds of media and education can be said to interface. In specific relation to formal education it is useful to think in terms of there being four major areas of concern. Arising from the first of these is concern about how exposure to the typical range of content in general audience media may influence the scholastic achievements of children, or their attitudes to schooling and education. Secondly, there is the question of how the media, whether labelled 'educational' or otherwise, are put to use by teachers and students in educational contexts. Thirdly, is the question of how media programming for education actually frames its subject matter. This would include considerations of how educational television might represent and influence conceptions of any given subject discipline or even conceptions of what counts, say, as scientific knowledge. Finally, there is the issue of how knowledge about the media, appreciation of media products, and practice in self-expression through the use of media should be taught.

Some of the contributions in this section address issues from more than one of these four major areas of concern. Fishbein's review of research into the role of television in the socialization of children considers the consquences of exposure to both general entertainment programming and more specific educationally-oriented programming. His opening sections on attention and comprehension cover ground similar to that of Rice *et al.* in the previous section, but the review also deals with research into the influence of specific kinds of content. In studying this review, readers may find it helpful to try and distinguish between studies whose findings are limited to establishing correlations between variables and those which go some further way towards demonstrating cause-effect relationships, the latter perhaps offering more scope for long-term understanding and for theory-building. It may be useful also to distinguish between studies which are concerned with the impact of given quantities of viewing (e.g. 'heavy' versus 'light'), an approach which is perhaps less easily justified now that video and cable offer so much opportunity for viewers to choose for themselves what they will see, and those which look at the impact of specific programmes or types of content. Among the latter, however, one must distinguish between those which rely on relatively crude categories of content, and those which grapple with the more difficult task of defining the 'meaning' of particular dramatic events in terms of how those events are structured into the overall dramatic content. The general thrust of Fishbein's survey argues in favour of the view that the media can and do have important influences on behaviour and attitude. Based on the kind of studies which, like those in the previous section, tend to go unremarked in 'media studies' theorizing (with the exception of studies of television violence), the review suggests there may be scope for more cross-fertilization between the traditions of media sociology and developmental psychology.

Published for the first time in this volume, the Bates and Gallagher chapter examines the use of television case-study programmes as components of Open University courses. It illustrates an approach to the evaluation of effectiveness of educational television. The authors pose key questions: what teaching functions are intended through the use of case-studies, what kind of programmes are most likely to achieve these objectives, and what help or guidance will students need? They identify a number of educationally-relevant dimensions for the analysis of case-study programmes: the extent to which they are didactic or open-ended; whether they encourage passive or active involvement of students; complexity of structure and format; degree of integration with other parts of the course; whether they are polemical or neutral with respect to particular issues and policies.

Three subsequent contributions focus on the role of information technology and these relate to the broad area of concern about the uses of media in education, their implications for teacher-student relationships as well as for approaches to the teaching of particular subjects. They are each written by practising teachers and in various ways pose the problem of how far individual reports of good practice can be generalized to other contexts. This is inevitably a tricky issue in such a richly variegated and rapidly changing field of technology where systematic research can only hope to cover a tiny fraction of the range of actual cases. Robinson examines the potential of microprocessors for the teaching of writing, showing how microprocessors not only aid the teaching of traditional skills which have played a central part in the development of education but simultaneously revolutionize the nature of those very same skills. Hewitson examines the use of microprocessors for the simulation of complex processes through modelling in the context of biology teaching. John Arnott's chapter on the use, in his school, of Prestel for educational software is taken from a wider survey by the Council for Educational Technology, and argues that teachers should take greater responsibility for finding effective ways of reporting to each other on their experiences with and uses of information technology.

The final contribution in this section concerns the teaching about media in schools, and is taken from a book that has been very influential among media studies teachers. However it is not Masterman's advocacy of a central place for television in teaching about media which accounts for the inclusion of the chapter here — Masterman himself has retreated from that position in a subsequent publication. In this context its interest lies in its identification of some of the difficulties encountered by media studies teachers, and its pinpointing of some of the essential questions which need to be asked in the formulation of a discipline of study. In common with the chapters on information technology, an implied requisite for improvement in teaching practice is the existence of effective opportunities and channels for communication among professionals, a topic to which this volume will move in its final section.

4.1 Socialization and Television

HAROLD FISHBEIN*

Between 3 and 12 years of age the average North American, British, and Australian child increases his television viewing from 1.5 to 4 hours a day. Younger children watch less often. These patterns are observed in other European and in Japanese cultures as well (Murray, 1980). However, in all societies, teenagers and young adults decrease their daily viewing time to about 3 hours. When children watch television they are choosing it rather than other activities. The activities that suffer most are listening to the radio, going to the movies, reading comic books, and 'hanging out' or in Murray's words 'unstructured outdoor activities.' The data on book reading are inconsistent, but it is clear that spending time with friends and participating in sports, hobbies, and pursuing personal interests are unaffected. [...]

As will become clear, psychologists have learned a lot about the effects of television on children. However, there is a great deal we don't know. For example, some studies found heavy viewing associated with extensive book reading, others with limited reading and some with no effect (Murray, 1980). The topics we'll discuss are those that have been highly researched and for which at least tentative conclusions can be reached.

CHILDREN'S ATTENTION TO AND COMPREHENSION OF TELEVISION

Some people refer to television as the 'boob tube' or 'idiot box.' One implication is that when you watch it, you put aside all judgment and reasoning and react to whatever is presented in a passive way. The opposite position is that children and adults bring to the situation active thought processes oriented toward uncovering the meaning of their experiences. In this view, if television is idiotic,

---

*Source: Harold Fishbein, *The Psychology of Infancy and Childhood* (Lawrence Erlbaum Associates, Hillsdale, New Jersey and London, 1984), pp. 348-67.

it's the content of the programs and not the persons watching it. Yet, television is designed to grab and hold our attention. When this happens, we may put aside higher level thinking and stay plugged in. Which view is correct?

Wright and Huston (1983) have evaluated the attention-getting (*perceptually salient*) properties of television and measured their impact on different-aged children. Some of these are animation, rapid movement of characters, fast scene changes, rapid cuts as opposed to slower zooms, loud music, laugh tracks, special effects, and peculiar sounding voices. Saturday morning commercially produced programs are generally highly salient, much more so than afternoon educational programs and prime-time shows. The educational programs such as *Sesame Street* tend to emphasize long zooms, moderate character movement, and singing. Less use is made of animation and special effects. Prime-time shows rely much more than others on adult dialogue. Unlike programs designed for children, this dialogue is often oriented to the future or the past.

Wright and Huston summarize research concerning age changes in sensitivity to perceptual salience. Between 1 and 4, children become increasingly attentive to these features. This probably accounts for the dramatic increase in television viewing during these years. However, there are essentially no differences in attentiveness between ages 4 and 10. Highly salient properties grab and hold children's attention. From about 8 onwards, people become increasingly interested in human dialogue, a nonsalient feature. This finding indicates that after 8 years story and content become a very strong focus for attention.

Anderson and Lorch (1983) have closely examined pre-schoolers' television behavior, focusing primarily on programs such as *Sesame Street*. In their work, 2- to 5-year-old children are brought into a comfortably furnished room containing a variety of interesting toys and a television set. In all experiments, their mother is present, and in some cases, other children, too. The television is turned on to *Sesame Street*, and the children are observed. One of the most striking findings is that preschoolers are not glued to the television. Rather, on the average, they look at and away from it about 150 times an hour. During this time they play with toys and talk with their mother or peers. When the program ends, they devote most of their time to play. The quality of this play is equivalent to that which occurs after listening to a parent reading a story. It seems clear that young children integrate their viewing with other available attractive activities. When the television is turned off, they merely shift attention to those activities without any impairment in functioning.

Anderson and Lorch believe that children's television viewing is an active process guided by their comprehension of what they are attending to. When children look away from the television they are often still listening to what is going on, but dividing their attention with other activities. Importantly, these shifts do not appreciably affect their understanding of the program. Anderson and Lorch verified this idea by comparing two groups of 5-year-olds watching *Sesame Street.* One group was allowed to play with attractive toys, whereas no toys were available for the others. The latter group spent twice as much time looking at the program as those with toys. When tested for comprehension after the program ended, however, there were no differences between the groups. Other research using different techniques confirmed the position that children's attention to television is usually guided by their under-standing, and not by its perceptual saliency.

There is another side to the story, which Anderson and Lorch refer to as 'attentional inertia.' This refers to the observation that the longer a person has been looking at a program, the longer he will continue to keep on looking, without turning away for 1 or 2 minutes. Attentional inertia has been observed in 1-year-olds, children, adolescents, and adults. The critical looking duration is about 15 seconds. If you've not turned away by then you'll keep on looking for a relatively long while thereafter. Research with preschoolers shows that this inertia is not linked with attempts to understand specific content. For example, when content shifts in *Sesame Street,* which it does up to 40 times an hour, children in a state of attentional inertia keep on watching. These data strongly suggest that states of inertia are passive responses to television, not guided by comprehension.

The above research indicates that television viewing by pre-school and grade school children is generally guided by higher level thought processes. These processes guide their attention to and away from it. Although perceptually salient features can grab their attention, they can't hold it. Occasionally, children and adults enter a passive viewing state in which their attention seems to get locked in. These states comprise a minority of viewing time.

We conclude the present section by discussing Collins' research

(1983) concerning developmental trends in understanding program content. A typical dramatic program has a basic story plot, but presents a number of cognitive challenges to its young viewers. For example, material irrelevant to understanding the plot is shown; some of the relevant information is implied by the action as contrasted with being explicit; and material presented early in the program may be crucial for understanding scenes occurring later. These and other factors require the viewer to remember a lot of information and to make a number of inferences about the content. Young children often get hopelessly lost in the process.

In one set of experiments Collins showed television dramas and then asked children and adolescents questions testing recall of two important specific incidents and an inference based upon the two. For example, John saw Bill steal money (Incident 1). Bill subsequently shot John (Incident 2). Why did Bill shoot John (Inference)? Regarding recall, second graders remembered far less than either fifth or eighth graders, who performed near adult levels. The inference questions were scored if the children had answered both recall questions correctly. The second graders were correct about half the time, fifth graders about two thirds, and eighth graders, three fourths of the time. Thus not only do 8-year-olds forget crucial story information, but even when they remember it, incorrect inferences are frequently made.

In other studies Collins showed second and fifth graders one of two versions of an adventure drama in which most of the irrelevant-to-plot information was edited out. In the first version, the scenes containing the chief character's motives and attempts to kill his wife were shown 4 minutes apart. In the second, the scenes were shown with no time separation. At the end of the program children were asked why the man tried to kill his wife. The fifth-grade children were correct about three fourths of the time for both versions. The second graders responded at a chance level in the 4 minutes, and about 50% correctly in the no-separation version. These results indicate that the memory capacities of 8-year-olds place severe limitations on their understanding. They do not accurately recall or infer motives if the motive and action are separated by only 4 minutes. Moreover, when there is no separation, they still make many comprehension errors. These and the above results strongly imply that children under 8 years have a very incomplete understanding of television drama.

TELEVISION VIEWING AND ACADEMIC SKILLS

In this section we describe research concerning the impact of television viewing on the development of school-related skills. The first studies by Ball and Bogatz (1970) and Bogatz and Ball (1971), evaluate *Sesame Street*, a program explicitly designed to teach 3- to 5-year-olds numbers, letters, geometric forms, and various problem-solving skills. In the research dealing with the first season of the program, a large group of low- and middle-SES children were initially given a battery of tests. These were designed to assess the above cognitive skills targeted by the program. At the end of the television season the children were retested. The researchers compared gains in cognitive skills as a function of how frequently, the children watched the program.

The results were clear and consistent. Children who watched *Sesame Street* three to five times a week showed greater cognitive gains than those who watched two or fewer times. Three-year-olds gained more than 5-year-olds, and low-SES children as much as middle-SES if they watched often. However, for the infrequent viewers, middle-SES children gained more than the low-SES children. The latter findings suggest that middle-relative to low-SES families provide greater opportunities for development of cognitive skills, but that frequent watching of *Sesame Street* can overcome these differences.

In the study focused on the second season, two low-SES groups were selected from a city in which *Sesame Street* was only available through cable. One of the groups was given cable and encouraged to have its preschoolers watch the program. The children were tested before and after the television season. Those given cable television showed cognitive gains almost twice as great as those without cable, confirming the direction of the first-year result. Thus, *Sesame Street* has powerful effects on the development of the cognitive skills toward which it is targeted.

A second set of experiments are concerned with the impact of the introduction of television into a community. We rely on Murray's (1980) summary of Corteen's (1977) and Harrison and Williams' (1977) papers, which were orally presented at the 1977 meetings of the Canadian Psychological Association. Corteen studied second, third, and eighth graders, and Harrison and Williams, second and third graders in three Canadian towns that differed in television access. In the first part of the study, Notel (the names are fictitious) had no television, Unitel had access to only one public television channel, and Multitel had access to several public and commercial television channels. The children in Corteen's research were tested in reading skills, and those in Harrison and Williams's research were tested in vocabulary, visual-spatial ability, and creative language use. For reading skills, second- and third-grade children in Notel scored higher than those in Unitel, who in turn scored higher than those in Multitel. There were no differences among the eighth graders. For creative language use, Notel children performed better than those in the other two towns, but there were no effects in either vocabulary or visual-spatial ability.

The second part of the study compared second- and third-grade children in these towns 2 years after television came to Notel. The children from the first part were retested, as well as a new group of second and third graders. No performance differences were found at this time. Children from Notel, previously superior in reading ability and creative language use, experienced relative performance decreases. And the new groups of second and third graders all tested at about the same level, comparable to that of the first part. These findings show that the introduction of television into community has a negative impact on reading skills and some language ability of primary grade school children. Corteen's data indicate, however, that the early depressed reading skills are over-come by eighth grade. It is likely that other cognitive skills, on the average, also catch up by this age.

A third group of studies deals with the relationship between amount of daily television viewing and both IQ and academic achievement. The findings fit nicely with those described above. We follow Morgan and Gross' (1982) review of the available research. Regarding IQ, a consistent result is that prior to about age 13, children with high IQs (greater than 115) watch more tele-vision than those with low IQs (less than 100). After age 13, the reverse holds. Morgan and Gross (1980), for a large sample of sixth through tenth graders found the correlation between IQ and self-reported daily television viewing to be $-.27$. Close examina-tion of their data further showed that heavy viewers infrequently had high IQs, whereas light viewers had a wide range of IQs. Although correlation is not the same as cause and effect, this suggests that heavy viewing indirectly leads to a relative lowering of IQ. We know that children's IQs can change tremendously prior to adulthood. Early in development, television viewing may positively accelerate IQ. Later in development, too heavy viewing may exclude intellectually stimulating activities, and thus reduce the potential for further growth.

The results concerning academic achievements are more complicated. A number of studies have found for children up to about age 13 that those who watch from 1 to 2 hours daily score higher in reading and mathematics than those who watch *less* or *more*. After age 13, however, these scores are negatively correlated with amount of daily viewing, paralleling the IQ result.

Finally, Morgan and Gross (1980) report seven separate achievement-television viewing correlations for boys and girls of low, medium, and high IQ. For low-IQ boys, reading, vocabulary and mathematics, and for high-IQ boys, reading, spelling, and mathematics were negatively correlated with amount of viewing. For low-IQ girls, reading and vocabulary were *positively* correlated, but for high-IQ girls, *negatively* correlated with amount of viewing. For middle-IQ boys and girls, no systematic positive or negative correlations were found. Does heavy television viewing interfere with academic achievement? It depends on gender, IQ, and area of achievement.

The fourth set of results is a longitudinal study by Singer and Singer (1983) concerning the combined effects of family characteristics and television viewing on several cognitive abilities. The importance of this research stems from the fact that children's television viewing occurs within a family context. The impact of television is probably influenced by parental values and beliefs as well as their own involvement with viewing.

The Singers extensively studied a group of 4-year-old nursery school children and their parents in 1977, and again observed and interviewed them in 1980, 1981, and 1982. The parental interviews covered such aspects as their own, self-described values, child-rearing techniques, beliefs about the world, and daily lifestyle. They were also asked about their own and their children's television viewing behaviors. When the children were in second and third grade, their comprehension of television drama, reading ability, language use, and imaginativeness were evaluated. As might be expected the results were complex.

For comprehension of dramas and reading ability, children perform poorly if they come from families who frequently watch and highly value television, whose mothers are self-reportedly not imaginative, and who use force rather than reason in their discipline. For language usage, highly effective children come from families who watch relatively little television who are flexible in house routines, and whose fathers are self-reportedly imaginative. For imagination, those who score high watched relatively little television as preschoolers, currently watch little realistic action-adventure programming, have parents who self-describe themselves as imaginative, and who use reason rather than force in discipline. As can be seen, the development of these cognitive abilities in 8- and 9-year-olds jointly depends on characteristics of the parents and the nature and frequency of children's television viewing. The two, of course, are intimately related; e.g., parents who frequently watch television also encourage their children (by role modeling) to do the same.

In looking at this section as a whole, we can conclude that television programs directed toward enhancing the cognitive skills of preschoolers can be successful. But television viewing by young children in general seems to have a positive effect on their cognitive growth, provided that they live in communities with established programming. For teenagers, extensive viewing is usually associated with lower IQs and poorer academic achievement. Within this set of results, parental attitudes and values play an important role.

SOCIAL BELIEFS AND SOCIAL BEHAVIOR

In this section we closely follow the reviews of Greenberg (1982) concerning the impact of television on social beliefs, and of Rushton (1982) dealing with positive social behaviors. The next section considers aggression and violence.

Greenberg selected for analysis five social roles — family, sex, race, job, and age — and presented a content analysis of how these roles are portrayed during prime time and Saturday mornings. He then evaluated research relating amount of children's viewing to their beliefs about these roles. In only a few cases did the research connect viewing a specific program to a shift in social beliefs. Thus the assumption is made that children who watch a great deal of television will likely be exposed to and influenced by the typical social portrayals. Owing to the fact that there are few studies dealing with the impact of the effects of job and age role portrayals on children's beliefs, we will not consider these further.

Family

The research about beliefs emphasizes how children perceive family interactions. Television families are typically portrayed very positively, with about 90% of their interactions being helpful, mutually supportive, and cooperative. Conflict occurs only about 10% of the time, but is higher in broken families than intact ones, and with teenagers than with younger children. In one major study, fourth, sixth, and eighth graders filled out questionnaires that assessed their viewing habits and beliefs about both television and real-life families. It was found that (a) frequency of watching dramas and/or shows featuring small children was correlated with the belief that real-life families typically had positive interactions; (b) frequency of watching dramas featuring teenagers and/or broken families was correlated with the belief that real-life families are typically conflictual; (c) children's perceptions of how television families interacted were correlated with perceptions of real-family interactions; and (d) when parents watched and favorably commented to their children about the portrayals, this increased the correlation between viewing and beliefs.

Sex Roles

In general, sex roles are heavily stereotyped on television. During the 1970s males in major roles outnumbered females by at least two to one. Women are typically married and are parents, whereas with about one half the men, marital and parental status are uncertain. Men nearly always have jobs, but about two thirds of the women are not employed outside the home. About 90% of doctors, lawyers, ministers, and business owners are men, whereas women are typically secretaries, teachers, nurses, journalists, and entertainers. About 90% of supervisors are men — thus women nearly always report to them. Men overwhelmingly have the prestigious jobs.

Not surprisingly, these consistent male-oriented messages influence children's beliefs and attitudes. When grade school children were asked which 'characters they would like to be like when they grow up' boys chose many more characters than girls, and almost never chose women. About one fourth of the girls chose at least one man. Further, preschool and primary grade school children who were heavy watchers, had stronger sex stereotypes than light watchers. However, girls who watched programs in which women portrayed counter-stereotype sex roles, e.g., police officer, school principal, accepted these occupations as appropriate for women.

Race

During the 1970s, between 10% and 15% of all prime-time characters were blacks. They were the only minority portrayed in significant numbers on television. Blacks typically appear in situation comedies and Saturday morning programs often with no white characters. Blacks under 23 are the most frequent characters portrayed, whereas the majority of whites are older. Blacks are usually unemployed or have lower prestige jobs than whites. In situation comedies blacks are dominant over whites, but in crime shows the reverse holds.

In general, the portrayal of blacks on television has had positive effects on both white and black children. For black children, there is a correlation between frequency of watching shows featuring black characters and cultural pride and self-confidence. Further, black children have more positive perceptions about the black characters than the white characters depicted, despite the opposite bias in television content. White children who have little contact with blacks state that their basic knowledge about blacks comes from television. In addition, they display very positive racial attitudes. Other research shows that white children who watched *Sesame Street* for 2 years developed more positive racial attitudes than those who watched for a shorter time span. Interestingly, *All in the Family* had no consistent impact on the racial views of white primary grade school children.

We can conclude from the above that television can and does help to shape the social beliefs of children. In nearly all cases the correlations between extent of viewing and beliefs were about .25, not strong, but consistent. We saw in the case of sex and race beliefs that these effects were often socially desirable. Some were not. One of the most important findings is that when parents watch and favorably comment about the portrayals, beliefs are strengthened. Other research, summarized by Huston and Wright (1982) has shown that parents' unfavorable comments can also counteract the effects of these portrayals. The implication is that parents should watch television with their children and discuss content with them.

Rushton's (1982) analysis includes laboratory studies and

naturalistic observations concerning the behavioral effects of show-ing altruistic, friendly, self-controlled, or fear-coping behaviors on television. Nearly all these studies were carried out since 1970. Most used materials from public and commercial television, and some developed special videotapes designed to produce given effects. The results with all procedures and situations were highly consistent with each other.

Altruism

In a typical laboratory study of altruism 5- to 10-year-old children watched a short videotape of a child playing a game and winning gift certificates. In one condition the child donated some of the certificates to charity, and in the other condition, acted selfishly. The viewers then played the same game themselves and won gift certificates, which they could donate to charity. The children who had watched the generous child donated more than those who watched the selfish child. Parallel results were found in other research for selected commercial television programs.

The majority of naturalistic studies of altruism were situated in pre-school and kindergarten classrooms. Children were shown anywhere from 4 to 20 half-hour segments of programs showing an abundance of positive social interactions, e.g., *Mister Rogers' Neighborhood*, neutral content, or aggressive interactions. In some studies, teachers and children also role-played the positive inter-actions. The children's classroom behavior was then observed for several weeks thereafter, and compared with their pre-watching experience. Generally, for 1 to 2 weeks after viewing, children who saw the positive interaction programs were more cooperative and helpful during free play than those who saw the other programs. These effects were more dramatic if role playing had occurred. However, by 4 weeks post-viewing, virtually all group differences had disappeared. This implies that consistent altruistic effects require persistent viewing of altruistic-oriented programs.

Friendliness

Rushton reports two laboratory experiments dealing with friendly behaviors. In the first, nursery school children watched either a brief segment showing an adult demonstrating affectionate be-havior toward a toy clown, or a neutral segment. When given an opportunity to play with a group of toys, including the clown, those who saw the affectionate behavior acted more affectionately toward the clown than the other group. In the second, nursery school children watched either segments of *Sesame Street* containing nonwhite children, or neutral segments. Subsequently, the first group showed a stronger preference than the 'neutral' group to play with nonwhites.

Several of the naturalistic studies dealt with the use of television to help socially isolated nursery school children to interact positively with their peers. In these experiments, special videotape segments were created that graphically showed similar-age children successfully interacting in a nursery school setting. Children watched either these brief segments or nature films over a period of 1 to 8 days. Those who watched the successful interactions markedly improved their social behavior, and these changes lasted throughout the school year. Those who saw the nature films evidenced no changes. Thus, unlike altruistic behaviors, which apparently have little payoff for young children, changes in friendly behavior are sustained for long time periods. These are important results that should be further evaluated in a variety of settings.

Self-control

Several laboratory studies have dealt with the effects of televised self-control. In the typical experiment children between 5 and 8 years old are presented with a collection of toys to play with, but forbidden to touch them. They are then shown a videotape of a child with a similar collection of toys. The child either plays with the forbidden toys or does not touch them. The experimenter then leaves the room and through a one-way mirror observes the child with the toys. Children who saw the obedient child, relative to those who watched the transgressor, showed more self-control. They waited longer before touching the forbidden toys and played with them for a shorter time period. However, when tested one month later, without any intervening television experience, these differences washed out. Thus, like altruism, self-control requires frequent exposure.

Friedrich and Stein (1973) showed nursery school children three segments a week for 4 weeks of *Mister Rogers' Neighborhood*, aggressive programs such as *Batman* and *Superman*, or neutral nature-type programs. During this time and 2 weeks postviewing, three categories of self-control behavior were noted during free play: tolerance of delay, obedience to rules, and task persistence. Although there was some variation across categories, the children who watched *Mister Rogers* showed the most self-control and those who watched the aggressive programs, the least.

Fear coping

In three laboratory studies dealing with fear coping, subjects were 3- to 9-year-old children afraid of either dogs or snakes. Over a 2- to 8-day period they were shown either brief videotapes of children enjoyably interacting with the dreaded animal, or neutral films. Those who saw the successful children were much more likely than those who saw the neutral films to approach and interact with the animal they feared, e.g., a 4-foot-long boa constrictor. These positive effects lasted between 2 and 4 weeks post-viewing.

The naturalistic studies have used videotapes to help children overcome fear in either dental or hospital settings. In one of these experiments, by Melamed and Siegel (1975), 4- to 12-year-old children about to receive elective surgery were shown a short videotape of a child undergoing surgery or a neutral film. The group who saw the surgery videotape experienced less fear both preoperatively and postoperatively than the other group. Moreover, these effects lasted at least 4 weeks after surgery.

On the whole, the experiments dealing with the behavioral effects of television indicate that children can be positively influenced by their viewing experiences. If the social environment does not provide rewards for these behavioral changes, they quickly trail off to pre-viewing levels. If the environment does reward the changes, then they are maintained for long time periods. These results are consistent with the theories of Albert Bandura (1973, 1977) whose thinking has been of major importance in laying the groundwork for much of this research.

VIOLENCE AND CHILDREN'S AGGRESSION

North American television, especially during prime time and Saturday mornings, is filled with portrayals of violence. More than 80% of all programs show at least one violent encounter, with the average being 7.5 acts per hour. Most characters are either on the giving or receiving end of violence. Importantly, Saturday morning commercial programs portray the highest levels of all (Gerbner, *et al.*, 1980).

A distinction is made between 'aggression' and 'assertiveness.' Violence is an extreme form of aggression. Aggression involves the intentional physical or psychological harm to others. Assertiveness involves personal striving, achievement, or self-confidence. Assertiveness may be directed in relation to others as in sports competition, or in relation to noninterpersonal activities as in making art. In the popular literature, aggressiveness and assertiveness are often confused, e.g., 'Irving is not an aggressive salesman.' The present discussion is restricted to aggression, as defined above.

Most researchers and reviewers of the literature dealing with the effects of television on children and adolescents have concluded that viewing violence does increase aggression, e.g., Huston and Wright (1982); Pearl, Bouthilet, and Lazar (1982); Singer and Singer (1981). However, the ABC television network, in their own analysis of the data, has challenged that conclusion (ABC Social Research Unit/Broadcast Standards and Practices Department, 1983), as have the authors of a recent large-scale study (Milavsky *et al.*, 1983).

The key issue in this disagreement hinges on the concept of *causation*. To show that watching violence and acting aggressively are *correlated* does not prove that watching *caused* the aggression. It's possible that aggression caused the watching; e.g., highly aggressive people seek out violent programs, or that a third factor caused preference for both violent programs and aggressiveness. Laboratory studies similar to those discussed by Rushton (1982) overcome the causal problem. We will summarize this research. However, to show that watching *Batman* and *Superman* in nursery school increases short-term aggressiveness in that setting does not prove that long-term preferences for violent programs cause long-term aggression.

In a dilemma like this, most researchers adopt the strategy of examining findings from various settings with a variety of procedures and looking for converging or compatible results. If a consistent pattern is found, then one is in a strong position to infer causation. Fortunately, such a variety of settings and procedures exists. We presently describe four different types: laboratory findings, naturalistic field studies, short-term and long-term correlational research.

Laboratory Studies

Dozens of laboratory investigations have been carried out relating exposure to violent programs with children's and adolescents' immediate aggressiveness. Three of the major researchers have been Bandura (1973), Berkowitz (1973), and Liebert (1974). In a typical experiment, preschoolers through adolescents were shown a videotape depicting aggression on a commercial television program containing a large number of violent acts, e.g, *The Untouchables*, or a neutral program. Immediately thereafter, they were given opportunities to interact with toys or peers. In the overwhelming majority of experiments, children who viewed the violent program acted more aggressively than those who watched neutral programs (Murray, 1980). For example, in Liebert and Baron's (1972) study, children who watched violent segments of *The Untouchables* were more likely to hurtfully interfere with the play of another child than those who watched a track race.

Naturalistic Field Studies

Large numbers of these studies have been carried out with preschool and young grade school children. In the typical experiment children are shown either 1 to 12 violent or neutral programs while at school, and their peer behavior observed thereafter. As an example, in the Friedrich and Stein (1973) experiment, preschoolers' behavior was first observed for 3 weeks. They were then shown 12 violent, neutral or positive social programs over a 4-week period, and observed for an additional 3 weeks. Children who were initially highly aggressive were most affected by viewing violent television. Their peer aggressiveness increased substantially during the 4-week viewing period and stayed high for the following 2 weeks. The behavior of children initially low in aggression was unaffected by viewing the violent programs. As with the laboratory work, the overwhelming majority of field studies have found that in-school exposure to violent programs increases subsequent interpersonal aggressiveness.

Short-term Correlational Studies

This category includes all the experiments in which current television viewing habits and preferences were related to current levels of interpersonal aggression. For preschoolers and kindergartners, television viewing was typically observed by the parents. The older children reported on their own viewing. Current levels of aggression were assessed in one of three ways, depending upon the study: self-reports, reports by peers and teachers, observations by experimenters. In addition to older studies, several relatively large-scale experiments have recently been published, i.e., Belson (1978) with English 12- to 17-year-old boys; Singer and Singer (1981) with North American preschoolers; Huesmann (1982) briefly summarizing results with first- through fourth-grade Finnish and Polish children; and Eron et al., (1983) with first- through fifth-grade children from the United States. There is striking agreement across all these studies despite substantial differences in how television viewing and aggression were observed. For the boys, amount of violent television watched correlated about .20 with aggressiveness. For girls from the United States, the correlations were about the same, but for Finnish and Polish girls, the correlations were generally at a chance level. Thus, viewing of violence on television is consistently associated with levels of aggressive activity, especially among American children.

Long-term Correlational Studies

Three large-scale experiments with North Americans fall into this category. Eron et al. (1972); Huesmann (1982); and Milavsky et al. (1983). In these experiments children's previous levels of watching violent television were evaluated with subsequent levels of interpersonal aggression. In two cases television viewing was measured by self-report, and in one case by the child's parents. In all three, aggression was measured by the reports of their peers. In the Eron et al. (1972) study, television viewing preferences at ages 8 and 9 were correlated with reported aggression at ages 18 and 19, a 10-year lag. In the Huesmann (1982) study, television viewing at ages 7 and 9 years and in the Milavsky et al. study, television viewing at ages 7 to 16 were correlated with aggression during each of the next 3 years. Finally, Eron et al. and Huesmann analyzed their data with cross-lagged correlations and Milavsky et al. with regression coefficients.

In all three studies, present levels of viewing violent television were found to be correlated with current levels of aggressive behavior. In the Eron et al. and Huesmann experiments previous viewing was also found to be correlated with subsequent aggression levels, but in the Milavsky et al. experiment they correlated at a chance level. It's not clear whether the various statistical techniques used by these researchers produced their different findings.

In the cross-lagged technique, television viewing of violence at Time 1, e.g., 1977, is correlated with aggression at Time 2, e.g.,

1978, and compared with the correlation between aggression at Time 1 with viewing at Time 2. If viewing violence causes subsequent aggression then the first correlation should be higher than the second. If aggression causes subsequent viewing of violence then the second correlation should be higher than the first. In both the Eron *et al.* and Huesmann studies, the cross-lagged correlations were consistent with the conclusion that viewing television violence causes subsequent aggression. The results of the Huesmann study are shown in Fig. 1. However, as we noted earlier, it's possible that a third unknown factor produced the pattern of correlations.

Where do we stand on this issue? The data linking television violence to aggression are stronger than those relating viewing positive programs to social behaviors. All four types of studies converge on one conclusion — heavy viewing of televised violence increases the likelihood of acting aggressively toward others. Although the correlations are not large, owing to the fact that millions of children and adolescents are involved, even a very small increment in aggressiveness can have striking negative effects. Additionally, there is no convincing evidence that watching violence has any positive effects, such as reducing subsequent aggression (the catharsis hypothesis).

Huesmann (1982) has analyzed the research from the perspective of understanding the psychological processes that underlie the relationship between television violence and aggression. He concludes that two of the major processes are observational learning

Figure 1: Cross-lagged correlations between peer-nominated aggression and television violence viewing obtained in the current US data. (Source: Huesmann, L.R. 'Television violence and aggressive behavior'. In D. Pearl, L. Bouthilet, and J. Lazar (eds.), *Television and Behavior* (Vols. 1 & 2). Washington, DC: US Government Printing Office, 1982.)

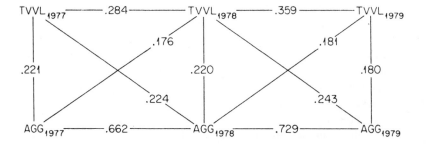

and attitude change. Through observing television characters engage in violent acts, especially those that bring rewards, children develop a model for aggressive behavior. When they find themselves in situations even minimally similar to those depicted on television, aggression gets activated. Further, persistent viewing of violence shapes their attitudes toward aggression, making it a more acceptable mode of behavior.

Given the above conclusion that heavy viewing of television violence at least partially causes increased aggressiveness, our view is (others may disagree) that parents have a strong responsibility to take action. At a minimum they should closely monitor their children's viewing choices and prevent extensive viewing of violence. With slight effort they can urge commercial networks to decrease the amount of violence shown. Also, they can attempt to influence members of government to place severe restrictions on programs aimed toward children. We live in violent times that require positive, not negative, social messages.

[...]

Research has shown that television produces both positive and negative effects on the socialization of children. However, these effects were often complexly related to children's age, as well as to parental behaviors and values. The research dealing with children's attention to and comprehension of television found vast age-related effects. Children under age 8, for example, apparently are very limited in their ability to comprehend story lines that extend longer than 4 minutes. Children's cognitive and academic performance have usually benefited from television viewing. Programs specifically designed to stimulate cognitive growth in preschoolers have been found to do so successfully. These effects are usually greater for low- than for middle-SES children. It has been found that IQ development in grade school children is positively correlated with the amount of viewing they do. However, after children reach the age of 13, their IQs are negatively correlated with the amount of television viewing in which they engage. The relationships between the amount of children's viewing and various academic performances are influenced by age, sex, parental involvement, as well as when television was introduced into the community.

Television viewing has also been found to have positive effects on children's social and emotional behavior, as reflected in their attitudes toward women and minority groups. Family life, however, is usually portrayed in unrealistically positive ways, such as the absence of conflict, which may be inconsistent with the actual daily experiences most children have. The selective viewing of programs having positive social content like *Mr. Rogers' Neighborhood* generally produces positive social behaviors in children, such as altruism and friendliness. However, if the home or school environments don't support these positive social behaviors, children stop engaging in them. On the negative side of the picture is the finding that extensive watching of televised violence leads to increased aggressiveness in children of all ages. Another negative effect is that commercials aimed at children encourage them to eat sugared foods and fast foods at the expense of good nutrition. Our view is that parents should take a more active role in combating these negative influences.

REFERENCES

Anderson, D.R., and Lorch, E.P. 'Looking at television: Action or reaction?' In J. Bryant & D.R. Anderson (eds.), *Children's Understanding of Television: research on attention and comprehension.* New York: Academic Press, 1983.

Ball, S., and Bogatz, G.A. *The First Year of Sesame Street: an evaluation.* Princeton, NJ: Educational Testing Service, 1970.

Bandura, A. *Aggression: social learning analysis.* Englewood Cliffs, NJ: Prentice Hall, 1973.

Bandura, A. 'Behavior theory and the models of man.' In A. Wandersman, P. Poppen and D.F. Ricks (eds.), *Humanism and Behaviorism: dialogue and growth.* New York: Pergamon Press, 1976.

Berkowitz, L. 'The control of aggression.' In B. Caldwell and H. Ricciuti (eds.), *Review of Child Development Research* (Vol. 3), Chicago: University of Chicago Press, 1973.

Belson, W.A. *Television Violence and the Adolescent Boy.* Westmead, England: Saxon House, 1978.

Bogatz, G.A., and Ball, S. *The Second Year of Sesame Street: continuing evaluation.* Princeton, NJ: Educational Testing Service, 1971.

Bryant, J., and Anderson, D.R. (eds.) *Children's Understanding of Television: research on attention and comprehension.* New York: Academic Press, 1983.

Collins, W.A. 'Interpretation and inference in children's television viewing.' In J. Bryant and D.R. Anderson (eds.), *Children's Understanding of Television: research on attention and comprehension.* New York: Academic Press, 1983.

Corteen, R.S. 'Television and reading skills.' Paper presented at the annual meeting of the Canadian Psychological Association. Vancouver, BC, June, 1977.

Eron, L.D., Huesmann, L.R., Brice, P., Fischer, P. and Mermelstein, R. 'Age trends in the development of aggression, sex typing, and related television habits. *Developmental Psychology,* 1983, 19, 71-77.

Eron, L.D., Huesmann, L.R., Lefkowitz, M.M., and Walder, L.O. 'Does television violence cause aggression?' *American Psychologist*, 1972, 27, 253-263.

Friedrich, L.K., and Stein, A.H. 'Aggressive and pro-social television programs and the natural behavior of preschool children.' *Monographs of the Society for Research in Child Development*, 1973, 38, No. 151.

Gerbner, G., Gross, L., Morgan, M., and Signorelli, N. 'The "mainstreaming" of America: Violence profile No. 11,' *Journal of Communication*, 1980, 30, 10-29.

Greenberg, B.S. 'Television and role socialization: an overview' In D. Pearl, L. Bouthilet, and J. Lazar (eds.), *Television and Behavior* (Vols. 1 & 2). Washington, DC: US Government Printing Office, 1982.

Harrison, L.F., and Williams, T.M. 'Television and cognitive development.' Paper presented at the annual meeting of the Canadian Psychological Association. Vancouver, BC, June, 1977.

Huesmann, L.R. 'Television violence and aggressive behavior.' In D. Pear, L. Bouthilet, and J. Lazar (eds.), *Television and Behavior* (Vols. 1 & 2). Washington, DC: US Government Printing Office, 1982.

Huston, A.C., and Wright, J.C. 'Effects of communication media on children.' In C.B. Kopp and J.B. Krakow (eds.), *The Child: development in a social context*. Boston: Addison-Wesley, 1982.

Liebert, R.M. 'Television violence and children's aggression: the weight of the evidence'. In J. DeWit and W.W. Hartup (eds.), *Determinants and Origins of Aggressive Behavior*. The Hague: Mouton, 1974.

Liebert, R.M. and Baron, R.A. 'Some immediate effects of televised violence on children's behavior.' *Developmental Psychology*, 1972, 6, 469-475.

Melamed, B.G., and Siegel, L.J. 'Reduction of anxiety in children facing hospitalization and surgery by use of filmed modeling.' *Journal of Consulting and Clinical Psychology*, 1975, 43, 511-521.

Milavsky, J.R., Kessler, R.C., Stipp, H.H., and Rubens, W.S. *Television and Aggression*. New York: Academic Press, 1983.

Morgan, M., and Gross, L. 'Television viewing, IQ, and academic achievement.' *Journal of Broadcasting, 1980*, 24, 117-133.

Morgan, M., and Gross, L. 'Television and educational achievement and aspiration.' In D. Pearl, L. Bouthilet, and J. Lazar (eds.) *Television and Behavior* (Vols. 1 & 2). Washington, DC: U.S. Government Printing Office, 1982.

Murray, J.P. *Television and Youth*. Boys Town, Nebraska: The Boys Town Center for the study of youth development, 1980.

Pearl, D., Bouthilet, L., and Lazar, J. (eds.) *Television and Behavior* (Vols. 1 & 2). Washington, DC: US Government Printing Office, 1982.

Rushton, J.P. 'Television and prosocial behavior.' In D. Pearl, L. Bouthilet, and J. Lazar (eds.) *Television and Behavior* (Vols. 1 & 2). Washington, DC: US Government Printing Office, 1982.

Singer, J.L., and Singer, D.G. *Television, Imagination and Aggression*. Hillsdale, NJ: Lawrence Erlbaum Associates, 1981.

Singer, J.L., and Singer, D.G. 'Psychologists look at television: cognitive, developmental, personality, and social policy implications.' *American Psychologist, 1983*, 38, 826-834.

Wright, J.C., and Huston, A.C. 'A matter of form: potentials of television for young viewers.' *American Psychologist*, 1983, 38, 835-843.

4.2 Improving the Educational Effectiveness of Television Case-Studies and Documentaries

ANTHONY BATES AND MARGARET GALLAGHER*

THE PROBLEM OF DEFINITION

At the Open University, most of the programmes we examined in this study were termed 'case-study'. This term has been used very loosely to cover a wide range of programme styles, course designs and teaching functions. It is often used instead of the more accurate term, 'documentary'.

The programmes we examined tended to present concrete examples of behaviour operating in a 'normal' context. Whereas other kinds of programmes, and other components of the courses, tended to be analytic, abstract and presented sequentially, breaking down the subject into 'chunks' and into general principles, case-study/documentary programmes tended to be concrete and synthetic, anchored in or drawn from the 'real' world, reflecting the interrelatedness between various concepts and the complexity of real-world situations.

THE RESEARCH

This paper is based on six in-depth evaluations of Open University case-study/documentary programmes, using student questionnaires, based on proper samples and high response rates, content analysis of the programmes, and recorded student discussions. The findings from these six studies are also supplemented by quantitative data collected on a further seven case-study/documentary programmes, and observation of the design of such programmes as

---

*Source: Anthony Bates and Margaret Gallagher, 'Improving the Effectiveness of Open University Television Case-studies and Documentaries', IET papers on broadcasting, no. 77 (Open University, 1977) (Reduced from the original.)

course authors on a further four courses.

These studies are written up and available on request.[1,2,3,4,5,6]

The main empirical findings from these studies can be summarised as follows:

1. Case-study/documentary programmes provide Open University students with material which is not available to them elsewhere on the course, and which it would be extremely difficult to provide in any other way.
2. In general, the course team or producer intention was that students would apply what they had learned in the texts to an analysis of the programme material, or would find in the programme material illustrations of abstract ideas dealt with in the text, or would use the programme material to test out or evaluate what they had learned in the texts.
3. Many students — even on third level courses — did not know how to handle this material. We discovered a 'one-third' rule: one-third of the students on a course (at a maximum) knew what they were supposed to do with case-study material and were able to do it; one-third knew that they were meant to apply what they were studying in the texts to the programme material, but were unable to do this satisfactorily (as measured by tests and content questions, as well as self-rating); at least one-third not only were unable to analyse documentary-style programmes, but misunderstood completely their purpose.
4. There was a strong correlation between general ability (as measured by end-of-year grades) and facility to use case-study/documentary materials in the way intended.
5. There was a strong relationship between preferred learning styles and ability to handle case-study material. 'Structured' learners, i.e. those seeking guidance and direct teaching, were unable to handle case-study programmes, compared with students with more open attitudes to learning.
6. The majority of students acknowledged the potential value of these kinds of programmes, but 86% wanted more guidance and help on how to use them.

DIMENSIONS OF CASE-STUDY PROGRAMMES

Didactic: Open-ended

Perhaps the most important dimension is one we would describe as 'didactic: open-ended'. This describes the extent to which the programme material is overtly *analysed* and/or *explained* for the student by the academic, or is simply *presented* to the student, for him to interpret as best he can. For instance, three Open University documentary programmes we evaluated could be placed along the dimension as follows:

	Course Codes	
D282	E221	D302
TV4	TV3	TV1

←———→
DIDACTIC   OPEN-ENDED

D282, TV4 provided students with considerable guidance to the analysis of the interview material through the programme commentary. Nevertheless, the students had to listen carefully to what those being interviewed were saying. One could imagine a much more didactic case-study, in engineering perhaps, where a 'real' engineering problem or 'case' had been examined, and the solution worked through for the student by those who actually solved it, e.g. the design of milk bottles in TS252. E221, TV3, was less didactic than D282, for although pointers were given during the programme to what were considered to be important or significant statements or interactions, the student had to observe what was going on for much of the time and form his or her own conclusions about the 'meaning' of what was observed. D302, TV1, gave virtually no guidance to the student in the programme itself, but considerable help was given through the broadcast notes.

The decision on whether case-studies should be didactic or open-ended should to some extent depend on empirical information. For instance, do students have general analytic skills, or do students have to be taught how to analyse case-study materials? These questions still need to be resolved to some extent, but our research suggests that, even though some of the skills involved may be related to general academic ability, these can certainly be developed by training, as was shown by the better performance of experienced students on D282 TV4 and by the improvement in students' understanding of D302, TV1, after a second programme showed them how to handle such material.

If students do need to *develop* skills in handling such programmes, it would seem sensible, in the absence of any other
information, to assume the need for a steady progression in programmes, from showing students how to organise and analyse
case-study material, to gradually withdrawing guidance until the
student can handle such material on his own.

It should not be assumed though that one 'exposure' to showing
how open-ended programme material should be analysed will be
sufficient. D302, TV2 failed to help most students to link the programme material of TV1 to the concept of ideology. It may take
several programmes where analysis is carried out for the students
by the academic before the students really understand how the
material is to be approached, and it may take several more
exposures to open-ended presentations before the students are
able to carry out the analysis for themselves. [...]

There are several possible teaching functions for open-ended
case-studies. The most obvious is to get students to analyse and
interpret what they are seeing in terms of concepts and principles
learned elsewhere in the course. Another is to present material in
terms of a problem, which the student is then asked to solve, also
using analytic techniques developed elsewhere in the course. [...]
Case-studies are often used because they synthesise or bring
together concepts treated separately in the correspondence texts.
In such cases, the timing of the broadcasts in relationship to the
study of the correspondence texts is crucial. One reason why
D302, TV1 was not as successful as it might have been was that
the students had not really got started on the course, and therefore
were not really familiar with the concepts of ideology and class,
which were necessary for them to interpret what they were seeing.
In the early part of a course, case-study material needs either a
large amount of academic analysis in the programme itself — and
even then needs to build on familiar concepts — or the material
should be capable of student analysis solely in terms of the few
concepts already mastered.

Passive: Active

A second important dimension in case-studies is what we would
term the 'passive: active' dimension. In other words, to what
extent, and in what ways, is the student expected to respond to
case-study programmes? Activity can take a number of forms.
Overt activity might include pre-reading of notes before the broad-

cast, taking notes during the broadcast, or post-broadcast activities. These latter might include further reading, writing self-assessment answers, the written solution of a problem set up in the programme, or even formally assessed assignments which can only be answered by viewing the programme. A more subtle overt activity might be the writing of a TMA answer which enables or encourages the student to draw on material presented in a programme, but which could be answered in other ways, as well. Covert activity would include analysis or interpretation of the programme material while watching, or thinking through the relationship between the programme and other parts of the course after watching.

There is overwhelmingly conclusive research evidence, from many studies, that learning takes place more effectively when students make an active response to a programme. Unfortunately, the times at which OU programmes are broadcast, and the similarity in format between OU case-study programmes and general service documentaries, combine to encourage students to take a passive attitude to the broadcasts. For instance, in the case of D302, TV1 the majority of students saw the programme as a source of *information* rather than — as was intended — as a *resource* for the development of course skills. This is a particular danger with 'open-ended' case-study programmes, which do not provide explicit cues or sign-posts in the programme itself to how the broadcast material relates to the general aims of a course. We believe that it is a mistake to assume that open-ended programmes will automatically lead to a more active response on the part of the student, than didactic programmes. In fact, the reverse is more likely to be true. [...]

Getting students to respond actively then to such programmes is not an easy task, and the procedures we have adopted so far to get students to 'distance' themselves from the material have been exceedingly weak. Most students find it difficult or impractical to take notes during the programmes. The D302 TV1 evaluation showed that while many students did do the extra reading, very few attempted those study activities which required thinking and writing. In particular, students were unable — rather than unwilling — to integrate the programme's empirical content with the related theory and this applied especially to those students — in this case, women — who were *most* interested and involved in the material dealt with in the broadcast.

Traditionally, case-studies, either directly or on film, have been used in teaching to stimulate discussion, with a teacher present to guide the discussion, and to assist students in their interpretation of case-study material.[7] Our students however are in a totally different situation, and much more thought needs to be given to how students are to be active in response to case-study material. We will return to this point later.

Structure and Format

The internal structure of case-study programmes can vary widely. D282, TV4 had a very simple structure. It had six segments, beginning with a brief description of full and overfull employment and the three types of unemployment, given by the presenter in the studio. This was followed by brief background information about Corby, using location film. Evidence for each of the three types of unemployment in Corby was then illustrated, in sequence, by using extracts from interviews with key people in Corby, ending with a summary by the presenter in the studio.

D302, TV2, however had a much more complex structure. The first five minutes contained 'vox pop' statements, films, and advertisements to introduce conventional views about women's role at home. The second section, lasting 17 minutes, contained a collage of film material exploring various aspects of the working situation for women at the Raleigh cycle factory, illustrating the special problems of women part-time workers, the possibility of change through women participating more in union activities, and the question of male domination in the supervisory positions, management and union executives. The third section, lasting 20 minutes, related to women working in the film and television industry. This section drew on a research study carried out for the industry's union on sexual discrimination in the industry. Using film material and a commentary by the woman who carried out the research, the programme focused on factors such as education, job and career structures, training, social conditioning, role perceptions and general economic structure, as reasons for women's work status and position. The final section of the programme, lasting 7 minutes, and still using film material, briefly mentioned various attempts at reform, such as success and failure in union support, legislation, and job evaluation.

One would obviously expect a broader range of topics to be covered in a 50-minute programme, but we have provided this detailed analysis to show how complex the structure of a programme can be. Although there were four main sections, within each section the number of topics dealt with was very large. The topics were dealt with sequentially, but there were no clear conceptual links between one topic and another, except that they were related to the overall topic of sexual inequality. At the same time, each topic illustrated simultaneously a number of the major concepts, such as ideology and class, without this relationship ever being pointed out in the programme commentary, although the broadcast notes did provide guidance.

The structure of case-study programmes can vary enormously, from a simply story, with a continuous, single, sequential thread, to a collage of unconnected shots, with no underlying rationale for the ordering of these shots apparent to the viewer. Related to this is whether a case-study deals with single or multiple cases: D302, TV1 for instance dealt with two cases, a manufacturing setting (Raleigh) and the film and television industry, whereas E221, TV3 dealt with a single committee meeting.

Another aspect of the structure of a programme — and also related very closely with the 'didactic: open-ended' dimension — is the role of commentary and the relationship of commentary to visuals. Very often the structural links are provided by the 'academic' commentary, either direct to camera, or, more often, by voice over film. Commentary is not necessarily needed to provide structure, however. DT201, TV7, 'Chicago: A Day in the Central Business District', used no academic commentary, the structure being provided by the ordering of the shots, following both a chronological pattern (beginning in the morning, and showing the 'use' of the central business sector at various times of the day, ending with a late-night shot) and a geographical ordering (moving in from the outer suburbs, by various transport means, to the central business sector).

Whether or not a simple structure is required, and whether or not a commentary should provide that structure, ought to depend once again on pedagogic issues, as well as production considerations. It may be the intention of a course team to provide students with a programme whose structure is complex, because the students are required to try and sort out the issues, and themselves to impose some sort of structure on what they are seeing. However, we are frankly sceptical that this is the real — or at least the original — intention in many case-studies with complex structures (and if it is, it is a very ambitious one). A complex structure is more likely to derive, in our experience, from uncertainty on the academic's part as to what material is required or will be collected during the process of filming in order to fulfill the programme's teaching function, or to derive from the artistic and technical considerations of the producer and film editor.

If we consider the context in which our students view — often at very difficult times, seeing the programme once only, over a 25 minute period, as a small part of their overall learning package — it would seem obvious that the structure and format of a case-study programme should as far as possible reinforce rather than detract from the educational aims of the programme. [...]

It seems to us then that learning will be aided, if, when making case-study programmes, the structure of the programme is kept as simple as possible, if strong story lines are chosen, rather than a collage of unrelated events, if single cases are chosen rather than multiple cases, and if one theme is pursued in depth, rather than a number of themes superficially.

Integration

Integration is another word much used in the Open University, but one which has never been clearly defined or understood. The question of integration appears very early in course design. Should programmes be linked to one another? Should we carve out a special area for broadcasting, in parallel to the texts? Should we have a set of media booklets, as well as the texts? Much of the discussion about integration centres on these organisational questions. In what order should students work through the different media? Should broadcasting be a 'free-standing' component or not? How can we *organise* the teaching material so that integration is helped?

Integration can vary along the organisational dimension, from tightly integrated — with text, broadcasts and notes all directly related to one another, and to be worked through in a certain order for fullest understanding — to an almost free-standing component, with very tenuous links between broadcasts and texts in any one week's work. E221 TV3, ('Cumbria Case-study') is a good example of tight organisational integration. Here the relationship between the text, programme and programme notes had been carefully thought out, and students were recommended to work through the media in a particular order (read text, read broadcast notes, see TV, listen to radio, read notes again). Unfortunately, students found it difficult to work through the materials in the recommended order. Because of marked differences in individual work-patterns, and because of a general difficulty for most students in working to a tightly preordained pattern, close organisational integration is in practice very difficult to achieve.

For this and other reasons — for instance, because there are fewer broadcasts than units — it has become more typical for course teams to opt for relatively free-standing media components, with the linking or integration assisted by specially written media handbooks. In some cases, the media booklet and three or four programmes relate primarily to certain texts being studied more or less at the same time (e.g. E283, TV6, 7 and 8, and texts 14-17). In most cases however — DT201, DT352, DT353 — there may be little or no direct connection at all between the programmes and the units being studied at the time of viewing. Thus, students' perceptions sometimes may be that they are in effect studying two mini-courses in parallel — the media component and the correspondence texts. For instance, in DE353 there are three distinct broadcasting case-studies — dealing with television and politics, the making of a feature film, and black music. Each of these relates in a general conceptual sense to the issues of the course as a whole, but not in terms of any chronology imposed by the themes of the correspondence texts being studied at the time of programme transmissions. So while the early broadcasts are dealing with television coverage of political conventions and conferences in the USA and in Britain, the first written units are concerned with the history of the mass media, theories of mass society and of culture, and the role of the media in the developing world. When this sort of model is used, it is likely to be only towards the end of the course that the various conceptual strands can be pulled together by students.

Does this matter? It may not, if the case-study materials are in themselves considered to be as important as the theoretical or analytical concepts being covered in the texts. McCormick[8] makes the point that for many technologists, case-studies are what technology is all about, implying that the importance of the 'case' itself is the determining factor for what to teach, and how to approach it. For instance, it can be argued that in a course about 'Mass Communication and Society' it is as important for students to observe and be aware of the simple technical and logistic constraints on programme production (clearly illustrated by the 'politics' case-study *in its own right*), as it is that they should examine 'evidence' of the role of ideology and the 'filtering' processes used by media professionals in structuring programme content (an aspect of the 'politics' material which would only become fully clear in relation to study of later correspondence texts). The first approach emphasises observation of the event itself and its phenomenological characteristics, the second stresses analysis of the event and its underlying structure.

We are not arguing that one or other approach is right or best. It may be possible for both approaches to exist side by side. [...] In any case, it should not normally be difficult for case-study programmes to be filmed and edited so that they not only tell a story — 'this is what happens' — but also be structured in such a way that the analysis of *why* it is happening can also be carried out by the student. *Undue* emphasis however on the 'event' can make it very difficult for students to know how they should approach the television material other than to recall it in their own words at a later date. [...]

Once again, we wish to stress that we are *not* arguing that one should *never* have a free-standing broadcast component, or separate media handbooks, and so on. If, however, the aims are an *integrated* course, and the development of intellectual skills in analysing case-study programmes and applying academic concepts to such programmes, then texts and broadcasts ought to be developed together, rather than separately.

Ideology, Neutrality and Truth

The fifth dimension we wish to discuss is one we would term as 'polemical: neutral'. Should a case-study programme take a stance, should it be committed towards a particular argument or viewpoint, or should it be neutral, objective, balanced, present all sides of an argument, etc.? This of course is a very contentious issue, and one which is central to the role of both broadcasting and education. We realise that this involves more than just educational arguments, especially for the BBC, and it is an issue which has been discussed in its broader aspects by a number of commentators.[9, 10] We wish here though to deal specifically with the educational problems involved.

Our basic standpoint is that it is impossible to portray, through a 25 minute television case-study programme, a truly objective view of the world. It must be a selective and edited view of reality, and hence represent the ideology or viewpoints of those responsible for making the programme. We believe this statement to be true, even for scientific or technological case-studies, since at most they represent only a set of 'best' solutions to particular problems, in the light of current knowledge. (The fact that a certain viewpoint or ideology has widespread public or academic acceptance does not alter the fact that it is still a viewpoint.)

Secondly, teachers are generally as concerned with establishing ways of thinking, as with presenting just 'facts' or 'theories'. Thus, a teacher is often as concerned with what establishes the *validity* of an argument, or viewpoint, as with the argument itself. To give an example, one of the major aims of D302, TV1 was not to prove that women are unequally treated at work — this was almost taken for granted — but to point towards explanations and an understanding of this phenomenon. A case-study programme therefore often plays a dual role: it sets out to help students to analyse or explain phenomena or solve problems; and it provides evidence itself in support of arguments or theories. D302, TV1 is an interesting example of this, since by making no real attempt to examine or destroy the argument that women are *not* treated unequally, it acted as evidence for the fact that women *are* treated unequally.

Much of the teaching in conventional universities is concerned with developing in students a critical approach to reading. Television though is just as susceptible as print to bias, to the use of illogical arguments, to the presentation of unreliable information, or to the power of emotional persuasion. It can be argued that because of its public nature, television is a good deal *more* susceptible to social and cultural influences. Despite the BBC's code of ethics and guidelines regarding objectivity and lack of bias in programmes, and no matter what safeguards are built into monitoring them, programmes will inevitably reflect the standards and value-systems of those responsible for their production. We believe, therefore, that it is the responsibility of the university to develop in students a critical approach to television, when this is used as a major source of academic evidence and argument, as it is with case-study material.

However, the skills that one hopes the university is developing in students for critical reading are not in all cases directly applicable to the critical viewing of educational television programmes. Television has its own unique ways of supporting or attacking arguments or viewpoints, of choosing and presenting evidence, of manipulating the feelings and emotions of viewers. Although television is no less valid than print as a teaching medium, its techniques and characteristics are different. Students need to be aware of these techniques and characteristics, and be taught specifically to deal with them.

Some of the features unique to television (or film) that can be — and are — used to influence the viewer's acceptance of an argument are purely presentational, and spring from the formal conventions of film or television production. As Dai Vaughan, an editor of television documentary films, puts it:

> If we switch on our sets and see someone addressing us directly, we know he is a narrator or presenter. If his gaze is directed slightly off-camera, we know he is an interviewee, a talking head. If he is turned away from us by an angle of more than about 15°, he is part of an action sequence. It is clear that there is a hierarchy of authority implicit in this code. The talking head [interviewee] is permitted to gaze into the sacred sector only through the priest-like intercession of the interviewer ... Thus the function of a presenter introducing a documentary ... is to diminish the authority of the people filmed and to posit the film itself, in contrast to the pro-filmic reality, as the object of scrutiny.[11]

Baggaley and Duck[12] have shown empirically that viewers' perceptions of the reliability and credibility of television presenters are influenced by a whole range of presentation factors. We believe students need to be aware of how these conventions might influence their perception, when case-study programmes are being used to present a view of reality.

We believe that it is relatively easy to raise students' level of sophistication regarding the influence of presentation factors. It would seem to be much more difficult to develop an awareness in students of the influence of several more fundamental factors that arise when television is being used to provide evidence of the 'real' world. We will choose just four aspects, as examples.

First of all, there is the editorial process. Reducing an 'event' or information about a topic to less than 25 minutes inevitably leads to a process of selection and condensation. The problem for the student is that he is not a party to this process, but merely sees the end result. For instance, we have quoted an extract from Vaughan's pamphlet. If readers feel we have misquoted him, they can go to the pamphlet and check that we have not quoted him out of context. This process of validating evidence is not open to the television viewer, for not only is the information transient, but the source of the information is inaccessible. The standard defence against misrepresentation is accuracy in the editing process, but even the most careful producer will interpret events as he sees them, and even the most careful juxtaposition of film sequences can have unforeseen and unintended consequences. To quote Vaughan again:

> Even the talking head is not immune from the use of techniques which will rob it of its proper significance ... First of all, the exclusion of hesitancies and qualifications diminishes the personality of the speaker in favour of the abstract content of his words. These will then be organised into a structure which was not the structure of his discourse; and the steps of his argument will be used to lead, not to his own conclusion, but to a conclusion with which he may not even agree. Early in my career I was told, 'You'll have to put this man in, to ensure a fair balance of opinion. If you don't like what he says, you can always cut to a wall being knocked down.' What we see here, both with the talking head and with the wall, is their reduction towards the symbolic through submission to a syntax not of their own generation. ... I was recently shown a rough cut of a film in which someone saying 'The man's a fascist' led directly into a talking head of a government minister. When I commented that this seemed a disagreeably snide way of suggesting the minister was a fascist, the director replied that he had not noticed, still less intended, the implication. The implication could, nonetheless, be construed upon the cut ...[13]

These comments were made, not in the context of Open University programmes, but of general service documentaries. Yet the BBC guidelines for general documentaries are firm and clearcut. To quote from Cawston *et al.*:

> The BBC is formally required to refrain from expressing its own opinion on current affairs or matters of public policy. Also, its own code of practice developed over the years — in recognition

of the powerful position it occupies — demands that its programmes should be fair and without bias, and that those who
produce programmes should never abuse their position for purposes of propaganda or the expression of personal
commitment.[9]

Yet as we have seen, 'reality' *can* be seriously distorted. The
BBC itself recognises that this is unavoidable, for, quoting
Cawston *et al.* again:

It has often been claimed that there is no such thing as an
objective documentary. Because it is the work of human beings,
the argument goes, it must be subjective. The answer is that it is
the production *intention* that is important. One cannot ask more
than that the intention should be correct, and that its execution
should be carried out with the maximum of skill and with a
proper application of the various responsibilities outlined
[earlier].[9]

In an academic context, however, intention is not enough. It
would be absurd to judge the 'truth' of a scientific paper solely by
the intentions of its author. As Thompson[14] puts it:

Any ideological framework is represented in the structure of the
programme itself, in its various narratives and their combination. This may actually be entirely different to what was
intended or even what was thought was being done by the
author. It seems to me that this is the only way in which any text
can be read, to try and discern what is actually 'foregrounded'
and not what is 'backgrounded', what is actually present and its
articulation and not what its 'origins' were.

When Open University programmes are using television
material as 'evidence' of the real world, the student must be
equipped to judge the context in which the evidence has been
chosen and put together, even taking for granted the good intentions of the producer and academic. This means revealing much
more about how the programme is assembled. For instance, it is
common practice to edit out an interviewer's questions, but to
include the interviewee's responses, as if these were spontaneous
statements. Yet questions structure the nature of the response, and

can completely alter the emphasis an interviewee might give to a point. In D302, TV1, for instance, the women at the bicycle factory were asked by the interviewer (who was never shown) about the need for a women's union. The question was not included in the programme. The response to the suggestion was enthusiastic — 'A good idea' — until someone said, 'Well, why don't we do something about it?' At this point, another of the women said, 'Well, we've only just thought about it, haven't we?' Students however are not usually given such clues as to the influence of an unseen interviewer in evoking such a response.

A second factor which constitutes a problem in using television to provide evidence of 'reality' is the difficulty of getting case-study material which illustrates the points the academic wants to make. The 'real' world is usually not so tidy as the academic world. Practical difficulties — like the intrusive presence of a camera crew on mother-child relationships — may frustrate the most carefully prepared plans. The evidence which the academic 'knows' exists may not be captured by the cameras, because the circumstances are just not right at the time of filming. To be frank, there are also occasions — particularly in social sciences and educational studies — when the academic theories do not hold up well in the real world. We know of at least one case where, after 50 hours of sound recording, in a wide range of school settings, no examples were discovered of a particular form of teacher-pupil interaction described in a correspondence text. The thought did cross our minds that such an interaction just did not occur in 'real' life. On another occasion, a producer was asked by an external consultant to completely change or withdraw a previously made programme — already approved by the course team — because it completely contradicted the theoretical position being taken in the consultant's text. The film was about the events in two people's lives. Both the main participants believed the programme was an accurate account of what had happened to them. Could it have been the theory that was at fault? In such circumstances, should 'evidence' contradictory to such a theory be suppressed? It is interesting to note that in the first case, students were unaware of the problem of finding such evidence of classroom behaviour and that in the second case, the students were asked in the broadcast notes if *they* could perceive or resolve the contradiction between programme and text. [...]

The student is faced with another problem in evaluating television evidence, caused by having to deal simultaneously with two channels of communication: vision and sound. We have noticed for instance that in many case-study programmes, the sound track provides the main source of 'academic' information. This is particularly true when interviews are heavily used. This applies for instance to D282, TV4, where nearly all the conceptual and factual information is conveyed by the sound track. It is therefore important that the visual component reinforces or matches the sound track.

We have noticed though that visuals, although illustrating the *content* area, do not necessarily reinforce the 'argument' on the sound track. For instance, it is common practice to cut from a picture of a person being interviewed to a location film shot, with the interviewee's voice continuing over the shot, as if explaining the shot. However, the same film could often be used to 'illustrate' almost the opposite point, if there was a different commentary provided. For instance, film of the courting behaviour of sticklebacks was used in a *Horizon* programme on the theory of the 'selfish' gene. The main elaboration of the theory was contained in the sound commentary, with filmed examples of animal behaviour being used as illustration. But illustration of what? The use of such film was perfectly justifiable as an illustration of the type of behaviour which the theory was attempting to explain, but the way the programme was constructed was likely to result in most viewers perceiving the visuals as validating the theory. However, compare this with the use of film of stickleback behaviour on SDT286, TV 14. In this programme, the film was used to make the point that certain behaviour patterns in sticklebacks are automatically and invariably triggered by specific stimuli. Students observed these stimuli being varied, and observed the direct effect of this on the creatures. Thus the visuals were being used as 'evidence' in a more restricted, and, we believe, more justifiable way, than on the *Horizon* programme. Thus similar film can be used in entirely different ways, depending on the way the commentary is written, and the student needs to be very sophisticated in his use of television, and already very knowledgeable in the subject area, to be able to differentiate such differences.

Finally, the power of television to influence viewers subjectively, and hence to validate or refute arguments through reference to primarily emotional bases, is a subject of some controversy. However, there was clear evidence from the D302, TV1 evaluation that students can react emotionally to a programme, and that this can have a negative influence on their capacity to deal analytically with the material. For instance, women expressed stronger feelings about the content of D302, TV1 than men, but were less able, on average, than men in recognising the function of the programme, and in analysing it in the way the course team wanted. Course teams need to be clear as to what is more important — an affective or strong emotional reaction to a programme, or a cool intellectual analysis of the material — the two reactions are not necessarily compatible.

We have spelled out in some detail some of the implications of using case-study material as sources of evidence and some of the difficulties students face in dealing with such material. It was very clear from the D302, TV2 evaluation that many students wanted more help and guidance in dealing with case-study material. Students have been brought up by and large to believe in the special claims to impartiality and objectivity in BBC broadcasts. We are not concerned here with whether or not this claim is justi-fied regarding the general broadcasting service. We are arguing that when, in an Open University programme, students are required to analyse case-study material, they will need an approach which is radically different from their 'feet up and watch telly' attitude towards general service documentaries.

We believe then that the first priority in case-study programmes is for the academics to be clear, before the course goes out to students, as to the main educational functions to be played by the case-study material. The second priority is to ensure that students are able to — or are gradually shown how to — analyse the material in the way intended. If the course team can satisfy these conditions, we see no *educational* reason why programmes should not be as polemical as the course team wants. Indeed, as we said earlier, we believe it is impossible to produce an academically 'neutral' case-study, nor does this matter, so long as certain guide-lines or criteria are met. These would include accurate 'labelling' of the programme, so that it is clear that it reflects the viewpoints of its makers, and a method of production which enables the student to assess the reliability and validity of the evidence being presented to him.

We believe in fact that it would often be both more honest and more educationally fruitful for a programme to take a clear stance regarding a subject, one which the student can recognise immediately, than to hide an ideology or viewpoint behind a contrived mask of neutrality. If this view could be accepted, it would enable course teams to consider a much broader range of roles for case-study material. Barnouw,[13] in his history of the non-fiction film, classifies seminal documentary films under a variety of descriptive roles: prophet, explorer, reporter, poet, advocate, prosecutor, promoter, observer, catalyst, guerilla, etc. There will be many occasions when case-studies will be nearer to the observer, reporter, explorer, catalyst end of the dimension. But there may be occasions when a course team wishes to use the advocate, prosecutor, promoter roles as specific teaching devices.

CONCLUSIONS

We have argued that students find it difficult to reap the full potential of case-study programmes, and find it particularly difficult to integrate material from television case-studies with the material contained in correspondence texts. We have tried to explain these difficulties by examining more closely the various dimensions of a 'television case-study'.

We have found that case-studies can vary along each of at least five different dimensions. We have described these as didactic/open-ended; structured/unstructured; active/passive; neutral/polemical; and integrated/free-standing. The choice of a particular style of case-study programme tends in practice to be rather arbitrary, and so we suggest that course teams ought to make a conscious decision about what kind of case-study approach they want for each programme. This decision should be determined by the extent to which students will have developed prior skills in the use of case-study material. The less experience students have in using television case-studies, the more the programmes should begin at the didactic, structured, active, neutral and integrated ends of the various dimensions. We would however like to see students progressively weaned away from this kind of approach, until at the end of a third or fourth level course, they can handle a wide variety of programmes, including those which are open-ended, unstructured, polemical or free-standing.

We have suggested that the main academic justifications for television case-studies could be two-fold. The cases being studied may be of intrinsic value in themselves — they may, in effect, be major content areas, with which students should be familiar. More generally, however, television case-studies will be used to develop learning skills, particularly of a higher order, such as the interpretation and analysis of phenomena, through the application of theoretical and abstract concepts to such phenomena. [...]

We have argued that students need to develop a variety of skills for making full use of television studies, and that the onus for developing such skills should fall on the programmes themselves, rather than on extended supplementary material or structural tinkering with the course. At the same time, carefully designed broadcast notes, special programmes showing students how to analyse case-study material, and appropriate tutorial back-up are nevertheless likely to be invaluable, if not essential.

Our concern at the apparent difficulty of many case-study programmes in achieving academic objectives should not be misunderstood. It is quite likely that we have under-measured the impact of case-study programmes, a difficulty faced by all concerned with measuring learning. Our methods may not be adequate for finding out what students have really learned, or we may have measured only short-term rather than long-term effects. We know for instance that the Examining Board for DE351 ('People and Work') were pleased with the intelligent use made by students of television case-study material in their examination answers. Nevertheless, we are confident that assumptions made by producers and academics about what students will get from case-study programmes will generally be over-optimistic. [...]

This does not mean though that we think the use of television for case-studies is mistaken; quite the opposite. In many of our courses, the television programmes provide students with their *only* opportunity for developing the higher order learning skills of application of theoretical concepts, and the analysis of real-world phenomena, as distinct from reproducing and regurgitating correspondence texts and set reading. Thus television case-studies can play a vital part in developing the abilities one expects to find in university graduates. [...]

NOTES

1. Gallagher, M. Broadcast Evaluation Report No. 2, E221, TV3, Radio 6, *Cumbria Case-Study*.

2. Brahmawong, C. and Bates, A.W., Broadcast Evaluation Report No. 24, D282, TV4, Radio 7, *The Concept of Full Employment.*

3. Gallagher, M., Broadcast Evaluation Report No. 22, D302, TV1, *A Woman's Work.*

4. Gallagher, M., Broadcast Evaluation Report No. 23, D302, TV2, *Looking at Inequality.*

5. Gallagher, M., Broadcast Evaluation Report No. 4, S24-, TV7, Radio 3, *Industrial Chemistry Component.*

6. Gallagher, M., Broadcast Evaluation Report No. 8, E221, Radio 15, *Caught in the Net.*

7. Wittich, W.A., and Schuller, C.F., *Instructional Technology: Its Nature and Use*, London: Harper and Row, 1973, pp. 463-464.

8. McCormick, R., *Teaching Technology by Case-Studies*, IET internal paper, 1974.

9. Cawston, R. *et al.*, *Principles and Practice in Documentary Programmes*, London: BBC, 1972.

10. Glasgow University Media Group, *Bad News*, London: Routledge and Kegan Paul, 1976.

11. Vaughan, D., *Television Documentary Usage*, London: British Film Institute, 1976.

12. Baggaley, J.P. and Duck, S.W., *The Dynamics of Television*, London: Saxon House, 1976.

13. Barnouw, E., *Documentary*, New York: Oxford University Press, 1974.

14. Thompson, G., *Interdisciplinary Case-Study Programmes*, OU internal paper (mimeo.), 1977.

4.3 Computers and Writing

BRENT ROBINSON*

For young language learners, writing commences as an adjunct to other language skills. As part of the phonological aspect of reading, children will have come to recognise symbol-to-sound relationships as they decode the characters. Now they must come to perform the reverse, as they hear sounds, repeat them themselves, identify specific graphical representations of them and encode the sounds in symbols. The process is not confined to early writers. When confronted with a new word to write, adults tend to vocalise it (albeit internally) in order to apply generalisations about graphic representations that they have made from previously acquired data. Punctuation, too, may depend on sound as much as on sense or syntax — witness the use of the comma.

Immediately a problem arises. Computerised speech is not yet at the stage of development where it can easily and widely be utilised in present hardware. This is not to say that it is impossible to use other sound sources in conjunction with a computer. It would be possible to use the 'sound through' system of some computers, which pass recorded sound from cassette to the speaker of a television interfaced with the computer. It is also possible to control a tape or video disk from a computer to provide a speech accompaniment. This sound track might be used as a subsidiary enforcement to other work or it might be integral to the task. Users might be asked to key in letters in response to hearing their names or phonic value, or they might be asked to spell individual words and so on. Some portable devices making use of computer-synthesised sound are now appearing dedicated to letter recognition and spelling drill. The quality of speech is still poor, but the machines demonstrate some of the advantages of solid state technology. They have random access to data, so there is unlimited opportunity for repetition and reinforcement of sound. At the time of writing, we are seeing early versions of voice chips for inserting

---

*Source: Robinson, Brent *Microcomputers and the Language Arts* (Open University Press, Milton Keynes, 1985) (Extracts from chapter 3: 'Computers and Writing'.)

inside computers and peripheral speech synthesis devices for use alongside. Further research is being undertaken into the production of speech from allophones, the constituent parts of speech sounds. Soon it may be possible to utilise speech in software for writing development. This is assumed in some of what follows, though much of the work may be usefully and sometimes advantageously undertaken without any computer speech facility.

LETTER FORMATION

Work might begin with the demonstration of symbols on a visual display unit with their oral representation being heard simultaneously. This could be followed by the learner selecting an appropriate graphic symbol from a range of distractors, which is best conducted using a screen with some peripheral device attached. A light-pen, joystick, paddle or mouse will allow the user to select an appropriate symbol on screen. The use of a touch-sensitive pad with an overlay will permit larger and fewer symbols than appear on a conventional keyboard. This device will also permit a range of graphic character alternatives to those on the keyboard, including representations of handwritten symbols. Initial practice might leave the chosen letter on screen to be matched against itself in a sequence of other letters in another part of the screen. With greater proficiency, users should be able to identify a character after the original has been removed from the screen or simply in response to its sound equivalent. Programs might then limit the time for response as a prompt to greater efficiency.

Using the same type of software, a keyboard might then be introduced. The task now is to correlate a key with the visual display of a character or its sound representation. This activity might begin with the utilisation of only a limited number of keys, and even these might be covered with masks depicting variant letter shapes — lower case, for example, or a closer match between screen and key fount.

From a one-to-one correspondence, users can move on to more complex graphic representations of sounds. This will include the use of different sounds for one symbol and multiple symbols for one sound. When this graphic representation is in the form of words, there is no need for the whole word to be input. A word may be shown with letters missing, so users can concentrate on perhaps one particular phonic structure — such as 'tele*ph*one'/ '*f*eel', '*ch*oose'/'*c*oal'/'*c*eremony', '*y*oung'/'sk*y*'/'mess*y*'. At the same time, however, some of the earlier software strategies might now be presented using whole words for learners to select from a menu, or to key in, themselves.

While such activities are proceeding, there will be a need for practice in letter formation. This will help to reinforce letter shape but also help distinguish between printed and written graphic forms. The ability to perceive that letters and words have the same function and value in different presentational locations is a difficult conceptual skill to acquire. A computer can provide yet another and important location. It can also present letter shapes in a variety of founts including approximations to handwritten characters if its graphics potential is brought into use.

The graphics potential of a computer also means that letter formation can be demonstrated. The advantage of a computer is that the demonstration can be repeated many times — each demonstration being consistent and identical to the last — until a pupil has acquired proficiency. The computer can also provide demonstrations that vary: slow and large to start, becoming quicker and smaller until they replicate the size and speed of fluent writers' work.

Monitoring by Machine

The use of a light-pen here might be advantageous so that users can trace the shapes on screen under machine supervision. A light-pen, however, can go little further than reinforcing letter shape and direction of flow. Its lack of sensitivity normally requires that letters are large. Being operated on a vertical screen, it has little to do with the motor activity associated with handwriting itself. A touch-sensitive video screen could also be used but again it suffers from the same constraints. The use of a graph plotter could more nearly demonstrate the conventional use of a pen or pencil, while a touch pad or graphics tablet could monitor letter formation. With a graphics tablet, the signals are propagated in the surface of the tablet and coded in such a way that a receiver above the surface will pick up the signal indicating where it is located. The receiver is usually contained in the tip of a stylus; and, since the lines are typically ruled at 100 to an inch, the device is suitable for monitoring the precise motor activity associated with users' manipulation of a pen- or pencil-like object.

This monitoring is important. The teaching of writing, like many other language skills, is basically a question of initial demonstration and subsequent practice. A computer not only facilitates this, but can also give more attention than a teacher can afford to each pupil's particular difficulties. This is especially true of the early stages where the problems tend to be mechanical: an inability to perceive small differences in letter shapes; or an inability to form shapes, space them correctly or keep them in a straight line. A computer can monitor minute malformations and errors such as might be missed by a teacher unable to supervise each and every pupil's writing all the time.

The display of letter formation and subsequent practice could begin with the letters themselves categorised according to their use of lines, curves and a mixture of both. It might begin with the writing of whole words. Later, a computer will be important to monitor practice in likely areas of confusion that might arise from either approach: $n/m/h$, $d/p/q$, 'that'/'what', 'these'/'those' and so on. After initial demonstration on screen (or graph plotter), users could copy using a light-pen or graphics pad. Alternatively, they might be asked to trace over the letters of a template spread on top of a graphics or touch-sensitive pad.

Users will need to be encouraged to make 'pen' strokes without hesitation. To facilitate this, the rate of letter formation display could increase in pace as the computer monitors and detects users gaining in competence. The opportunity for response could be similarly determined. It could be defined by teachers before any hands-on experience, or it may vary in run according to user performance. If a screen is being used for display, it would be possible to remove a letter, sequence of letters or word while users attempt to reproduce it. Not only might this develop greater speed: it could also assist spelling. It is likely to give practice in memory recall and encourage mental retention of the visual pattern of letters and words as a complement to the phonological spelling skills applied by competent spellers. With words, writers will need longer to perceive the item to be copied and also to write down. During this time the word might therefore be pronounced to refresh their memory as well as to reinforce graphic and phonic correspondence. Alternatively, or in addition, a related picture to reinforce meaning might replace the blank screen while they write.

These techniques might also be applied in the use of a keyboard. The letters or words might have to be removed from the screen by the depression of a predefined key before users can proceed to key in from memory what they saw on the screen. The program might remove the display automatically after a timed exposure. The technique will reinforce not only letter and word shapes but also letter sequence or spelling. The same techniques could be used for whole sentences to encourage good spelling, correct punctuation, awareness of syntax and, possibly, the appreciation of style.

SPELLING

A computer is well suited both to the manipulation of characters and to their display, so it lends itself well to many spelling and alphabetical activities. Sequences of letters may be stored in a computer memory as character strings. Since this representation is almost identical to the real data itself, it can be used for any basic linguistic processing including that of user input of characters or longer lexical items. String programs can thus be written to look for particular characters or character combinations in any text already within the computer's internal or external memory store or keyed in by the user. A computer can therefore match a displayed character string against one typed in to check spelling; segregate and fragment strings as in the separation of base words from suffixes or verb stems from case endings to show the internal structure of words; re-order characters for alphabetical sequencing or anagram solving and so on.

Spelling Puzzles and Games

There are a number of programs on alphabetical ordering that demonstrate, simply, a computer's facility for such tasks. Some present series of random letters that users must place in correct order. The more difficult versions do not provide any on-screen help in the form of a menu of choices from which to select; instead users are left to key in the next letter from memory. More complex programs take a sequence of words selected at random from an inbuilt database or input by the teacher and hide them in a letter grid on screen, filling unused grid locations with random distractor letters. The words may be printed horizontally, vertically or diagonally, which makes the user's task of finding them more difficult.

Some versions of this program offer the option of a printout of the screen display. This extends the activity beyond direct hands-on experience of a computer, and allows the teacher to use the computer simply for the generation of materials for language work — a facility that is all too rare in current software. A computer used in this way can produce a limitless number of different worksheets simply by organising the raw data in different ways. Considering the number of computers available per class of pupils, printout worksheets can relieve pressure on the use of this resource. Pupils can often start or finish their work away from the computer, simply using it for essential elements of the activity like demonstration or marking.

The computer, then, can only match one string against others that it has been programmed to accept. In this, however, it is very rigorous; so much so that while the attribute is of help in spelling programs, it can be problematic in other software. Too often, a computer fails to recognise user input because it is poorly spelt. In some badly written programs this might still be enough to cause the program to halt or malfunction.

It is easy to assume that the meticulous string processing attributes of a computer allow only for precise and structured software working to predefined rules and data. This would be a misconception. It depends on how the facility is employed. Users could be allowed to make the machine work for them rather than the reverse. Keying in their own words, a computer program could display all the possible letter combinations on screen or hard copy. The computer cannot identify those that constitute recognisable English words, since the vocabulary that would have to be provided for the computer to check every variation against would be too large for any current microcomputer. Textual strings take up a large amount of memory and cannot be stored in sufficiently large quantities without large back-up external storage facilities. The matching would also be a very tedious process. More important is the educational argument: the onus should be on users employing their skills and working with others and/or a dictionary to select only those strings that are legitimate. These strings could then be stored on tape, disk or as hard copy for use in a game or other language activity of the teacher's or pupil's own devising.

An obvious way in which the manipulatory power of computers over language can be used is for the preparation of crossword puzzle games. Most software examples give teachers the option of using a pre-programmed vocabulary set or one keyed in, to generate the word grid. The candidate words are then inserted in the grid by the computer and the final crossword presented on screen. In many cases, the grid can also be printed out for completion away from the computer. Besides the obvious logistic advantage provided here, a printout solves the problem of screen space that most crossword programs encounter. A video display screen cannot hold the grid and all the clues on screen at once. Instead, users must access individual clues to be displayed one at a time alongside the grid. Personally I find this cumbersome and frustrating since I often want to cross-reference or scan a number of clues and the half-completed crossword at the same time.

Much of the software involves considerable mechanical drill. This is not necessarily a bad thing, for writing as an encoding process involves a very mechanical set of skills. The computer's contribution is that it can perform or demonstrate the skills in an efficient and accurate manner, and has at its disposal a dynamic display mechanism that — in terms of speed, animation and colour — surpasses the conventional media available to the teacher. It also provides a degree of privacy and interaction that the teacher cannot achieve under normal circumstances.

This interaction can be capitalised upon so that even drill and practice activities become more inviting to the user. One of the most ubiquitous exemplars of the gaming element in spelling drill is 'Hangman'. In one form or another the game appears with regular monotony on software lists. A word is taken at random from a database and displayed on screen with each character replaced by a symbol of some sort. The player then inputs letters, which are revealed in their correct position if they are present in the word. If they are not present, a penalty is awarded against the player. Typically, a wrong input results in another piece being added to the image of a gallows and felon being built up on screen. The aim is to use knowledge of spelling patterns to complete the word before the image is completed and the felon hanged.

Use of Graphics and Interaction

While some language programs may be based on conventional

games, others are more original. Graphic games are common, often based on arcade games formats and employing the loud noise and lively aggressive action that we have come to associate with this form of entertainment. Too often, however, the addition of sound and graphics serves only to provide some form of extrinsic motivation for pupils. Absurdity can arise when pupils deliberately set out to fail because the special effects are so much more spectacular when they do.

More interesting is the software that uses computer graphics and interaction to highlight salient language features, thus making the game integral to the learning process involved. This can be explicit demonstration but it can also be built into game-type software. One graphics program is set on a building site where users have to build compound words. Another uses a bulldozer to join letter combinations together into words. A third is set in a zoo where users are asked to group words in cages according to meaning sets.

CONTEXT AND MEANING

This software provides novelty and can be a technically revealing utilisation of mechanical skills, but there are important reservations. Primarily, this type of software presents language drills without any form of contextualisation. The words themselves are provided in isolation without any reference to their natural function in language use. One form of contextualisation could be provided immediately. There is no reason why software cannot be designed to allow teachers to key in lexicons specific to individual pupils' needs and interests. These vocabulary sets might be based upon particular terms needed by pupils at any one time for a project or essay. They might also be based upon words they commonly find difficult.

Further contextualisation is also required. Without consideration for the semantic value of words or their syntactic context, the spelling and writing of them can become a mindless activity. It might also become ambiguous, confusing or even erroneous. One example will suffice: many English words are homonymns in need of semantic or syntactic contextualisation before they can be spelt correctly. Without seeing a bottle of perfume or a letter being posted, one cannot determine between the graphic representations 'scent'/'sent'. Alternatively, one needs to see the relationship and function of a word within a grammatical construct — 'you are wearing scent'/'I sent you a letter' — to distinguish correct spelling.

There are a number of ways of providing this contextualisation, beyond reference to a dictionary or referents external to the medium. The graphics potential of the computer on its own or interfaced with a video disk can provide a visual context. Pupils can be asked to spell objects and actions that appear on the screen. These objects can be associated so that a complete picture is built up with a specific vocabulary set. Further software could present other scenes. Some of these might be connected because of semantic affinity or to show transformations. One image could show a cat on the mat with users prompted to supply the preposition. A subsequent image might show the cat beside the mat, and so on. Some images might be shown to highlight specific spelling patterns. To highlight such patterns further, certain letters could be already supplied and users asked to concentrate on selecting the remainder, these being the ones specifically isolated for attention. One successful program I have seen used deletes vowels from sentences of text; here the contextualisation is provided solely by the verbal construct, however, and later software might similarly omit the visual referent. The screen could then present single words within semantic clusters. The words 'bore'/'boar' might be displayed at the top of the screen, and users asked to select the word that suits most appropriately the set 'pig'/'hog'/'sow', which appears at the bottom.

Extended texts rather than individual words will tend to make language activities more meaningful to children. This is particularly so if the texts can be related to children's educational needs or to their other activities, in class or beyond. There is no reason why longer texts cannot be input in the same way as proposed above for use with isolated word sets. With my software, it is possible for whole frames of text to be typed and saved electronically. They might be discrete or sequential, original writing by a particular pupil or a transcription from another book (fiction or reference) used in the classroom. Whatever their source, they will be suited to the child's interests and linguistic needs at that time and matched to his or her ability. These texts can then be loaded into a computer and used with any one of a number of language programs since they are all compatible.

One program will select individual words from the text (chosen according to parameters specified at the start of the program) and present these in a 'Hangman'-type activity. Another will jumble the letters in these words. Another will replace the whole text with asterisks and ask pupils to reconstitute the text letter by letter, wherever they can recognise particular words or spelling patterns. In each program, the activity has a meaningful context. Pupils are working on real sustained texts that have an interest and/or suitability for them. At any time, they can recall that text for reference.

PUNCTUATION

Punctuation and grammar are important to the writing process. Both are susceptible to precise rules and therefore amenable to software application. In addition, a computer can handle punctuation and spaces within character strings with the same facility as letters.

Punctuation Exercises and Games

As a routine exercise for the use of capital letters, lists of nouns can be displayed on screen and users asked to identify those that are proper nouns warranting an upper-case initial letter. While this exercise can be conducted in a number of ways, including with the use of a peripheral device, it is probably best conducted as a string matching exercise in which users are asked to key in the word using upper- and lower-case characters. The multiple keystroke required to produce the upper-case symbol (normally a shift and character key depression) is likely to enforce the use and differentiation of upper and lower case. Subsequent keying in of the remaining lower-case letters will reinforce spelling and word shape. This same process can be applied to sentences. Initially, users might be asked simply to be aware of the initial letters in sentence structures but later practice might involve proper nouns embedded within the constructs.

Similar activities can be used for practice in the use of full stops, commas and other punctuation, users keying in correct versions of incomplete or totally unpunctuated sentences. The use of a light-pen to identify the positions of punctuation might be another way of practising the skill. The layout of a text might be treated in the same way with users identifying appropriate breaks in the text and with the aid of a keyboard or other peripheral device, manipulating the display of direct speech, script, paragraphing, letter headings, subscripts and so on.

Many of these activities can be built into games. The game 'Space Invaders' is well known for its exploitation of computer interaction and makes great use of the machine's graphics and sound potential. There is now a version in which users score points by dropping punctuation marks into their correct positions in sentences. The arcade game 'Pacman' has also been adapted for the microcomputer. A fiendish screen character moves along the text, devouring capital letters and punctuation marks before spewing them forth at the end. Users must manipulate another character to return them to their rightful place. The unique facilities of the computer can be used in more sober ways to practice punctuation skills. One of my programs presents texts in which all the punctuation marks, or all the letters, or both, have been removed. Users must then reconstitute the text using all the reading, spelling, punctuation and typographic clues they can muster. One advantage of this program is that it is content free. I can prepare any electronic text I want pupils to use. It is thus possible to copy or construct texts in which particular punctuation skills can be practised; also, texts can be provided that are well suited to the ability of individual pupils or to their interests. Extremely useful is the fact that texts written by the pupils themselves on a word processor can be loaded into the program. These are then manipulated to remove punctuation so the students can see their own strengths and weaknesses in this area as they struggle to reconstruct the text.

In the same way, my students have also used a version of a sequencing program I developed to help them with their awareness of punctuation. I prepared a number of texts in which complex sentences were split into discrete words, phrases and clauses, which the computer then presented for users to sequence. In so doing, they made considerable use of the punctuation clues left alongside adjacent words in the jumbled sequence. A capital letter at the beginning of an item indicated the start of a sentence (unless it signified a proper noun); a full stop after a word or phrase hinted that this item should be the conclusion of the sentence; dashes and brackets at the beginning and end of two items suggested the order in which these should come in parenthesis; an opening pair of quotation marks provoked the search for another item containing the closing pair. Commas, semi-colons and colons also helped in the eventual sequencing of the sentence. Again, it was possible for students to write and load into the program their own electronic texts before working on them in this way.

Punctuation in Processing and Composition

As well as employing a computer to process text and present it as some form of exercise, it is possible to employ the computer simply as a tool for user processing of text. Advanced software could emulate a word processor and allow the user a number of facilities for the processing of text. Indeed, there is no reason why many activities cannot be provided on a word processor. Texts can be typed in and jumbled by the teacher for later sequencing either back on the word processor or on worksheets printed out from the machine. The teacher could prepare a text that is incomplete in some way, and students could then use the word processor to complete it, inserting punctuation, altering lower case to upper (and vice versa), experimenting with layout until they are satisfied with a final version. This version can then be printed out for marking or circulation and discussion among peers. If a number of students have prepared their own individual versions of the same text, a comparison of these in class can give rise to much worthwhile discussion.

As word processor design becomes more sophisticated, a number of interactive features are being incorporated to help users in composition. The first feature analysis programs can now be loaded into a computer to analyse texts that have been written on the machine. These programs can provide useful stylistic evaluations of sentence length, readability, word frequency and so on. Writers can then act upon these prompts and redraft the text accordingly. It is realistic to foresee a word processor that continually provides a commentary to writers as they compose their text, so that they can revise it immediately. Many users would find invaluable a machine that draws their attention to the fact that the last time they used a full stop was 300 words ago; that the average length of their sentences was 250 words; that they have used only four commas in the whole work; or that the last full stop was not followed by a capital letter. Such prompts could be provided on screen in a small text window separated from the text. The text itself could be highlighted in colour or marked with a flashing cursor to reveal exactly where the problem lies. Eventually, it will be possible for an audio commentary to accompany the writing task on a computer.

GRAMMAR

A range of software can be developed for grammatical skills. School textbooks contain countless examples of mechanical exercises that may be transferred to a computer. Here they gain from novel presentation, structured development and immediate monitoring and reinforcement, though their value might reasonably be questioned even as textbook activities if not treated sparingly and with extreme care.

Syntactic Exercise Programs

There are already a number of sentence analysis programs in which users are asked simply to identify parts of speech or structures within a particular utterance displayed on screen. Substitution and transformation exercises are also feasible. In the first, a user is asked to delete incorrect words in a sense group and to enter the correct words. In transformation exercises, users can be asked to give the plural forms of singular nouns, change adjectives into adverbs, alter present tense to past tense and so on. At the simplest level, users can be prompted to select the correct transformations from a range of distractors. More complex would be the keying in of the transformations without assistance other than, perhaps, from the provision of an incomplete answer for those experiencing difficulty. Sequencing programs, too, should help in the awareness and understanding of syntax. The program mentioned in the last section that split down complex sentences into random sequences for reordering has proved useful for syntax as well as for punctuation. It is also possible to provide higher order sequencing of sentences to construct paragraphs. A more flexible approach would be to allow users to construct as many sentences as possible from a given set of phrases or other syntactic word groups.

At a higher level still, guided composition techniques for the formal control of writing might find a use. A series of sense frames can be presented in specific sequence such that the choice of any item from each frame in turn will form a logical, connected passage of prose. To begin with, any choice from the frames could yield a correct passage of writing; pupils could choose any item from each frame in sequence and still be presented at the end with a satisfactory composition. Later, however, the choice in the frames might depend upon structural criteria. The choice of an initial noun form will dictate the choice of subsequent pronouns; having selected one tense, students must then select the appropriate verb form consistently in the choices that follow.

The graphics potential of microcomputers is not confined simply to the presentation, animation and manipulation of text. One early piece of software from the United States used cartoon-style graphics to reinforce grammatical function and word meaning. Several printed nouns were displayed on screen. One of these was selected by the user with a light-pen. A picture of the selected noun then appeared, closely followed by a list of verbs down the right side of the screen. On touching a verb with the light-pen, the noun acted out the intended meaning of the verb. A subsequent development prompted users to select words from a menu to create a sentence. When all the words had been selected in correct order, an animated sequence demonstrated the meaning of the sentence.

A number of commercial programs now exemplify a similar approach. One shows a randomly drawn face that is then blanked out after sufficient time has been given to study it. Users must then re-create the face by typing in words to identify and describe its salient features. Each feature can be modified through the use of adjectives (including comparative forms). Finally both faces are displayed together with a list of the differences.

Much of the grammar software so far envisaged has been concerned with relatively routine, mechanical activity. Certainly, this would be true of most of the software commercially available. This is not altogether surprising. Microcomputers can only process the quantifiable, and grammar can easily be seen in this way. This is not meant to be an outright condemnation of it: I have given these software examples because I believe there are appropriate educational opportunities for this type of activity. Part of language learning must develop from some form of initial demonstration even if it is not presented as such. This awareness will be followed by competence only if sufficient opportunity is afforded for practice. Remediation of language difficulties is often effected only in this way; but, at the same time, there has been a marked trend away from drill and rote learning — particularly, though not exclusively, among teachers concerned with early language acquisition. Some of this accords well with modern linguistic research in its attempt to present and investigate language within, rather than divorced from, its use in a linguistic context. It also accords well with the current move away from computer-assisted instruction to computer-assisted learning. In other words, learners are released from tightly structured and mechanical teaching to learn more by their own discovery than by instruction. The question is, therefore, can a computer meet the demands of this new situation?

Learning Grammar through Discovery

At the University of Birmingham, John Higgins has devised some simple programs dealing with the problems of inflectional English morphology, which provide an interesting reversal of the usual expectation that computers should set users tasks for them to solve. Instead, this software adopts an exploratory approach in which users set tasks for the machine to solve. One program's offer is to place the correct form of the indefinite article before any noun phrase that a user cares to key in. On the basis of simple pattern recognition techniques, the program enables the computer to distinguish between such minimal pairs as 'an uninformed person' and 'a uniformed person'. But there are situations where the program does make an error. Such programs might be inappropriate for individual use but they can be powerful stimulations of group discussion, the focus being either to 'defeat' the program by inventing tasks that the computer cannot solve (and reasoning why) and/or to discover the principles the program is applying to produce its correct and incorrect versions. Another program offers to accept any word — whether real or invented — and to add an *s* to form the third person of a verb or the plural of a noun. Users can have great fun attempting to confuse the machine and by inventing their own words obeying the grammatical rules of English.

The new programming language Prolog (PROgramming in LOGic) indicates another way forward. 'Balloon' is a variation on the parlour game in which one person adopts the role of a hot-air balloon owner. The other players decide what objects they wish to take on a journey and the owner dictates what may be taken and what must be left behind. The object of the game is for the players to establish the criteria by which the owner makes his decisions. One Prolog version gives the computer the role of owner while the users input their choices to be told in reply what they might take. Each user then tries to establish the inclusion/exclusion rules by which the computer is operating. In the published version, the suggested criteria include a semantic option (for example, all objects must be black) and a spelling option (one rule insists that objects must contain only four letters or begin with a certain letter). The program is easy to modify so that a wide range of other criteria might be included: other spelling patterns or specific grammatical functions of words (abstract nouns, proper nouns and so on).

There are two significant advances in this type of software. The first is that Prolog programs, being databases established and interrogated in a high level language not too dissimilar to English in logical structure, are easy to access and amend or enlarge. Thus the interaction of the program is user-friendly to an extent that BASIC is not, and the changing of data to accept new inclusion/exclusion criteria is more easily executed by pupils themselves. Further, in establishing the database or interrogating it, pupils are forced to classify and categorise. This has many applications across the curriculum — no less in explicit grammar work involving parsing and the grammatical function of words.

Software can be used in many other ways to help users learn about language. One set of unpublished programs I have seen used encourages learners to devise their own language. Users are given a lexicon of invented words grouped according to grammatical function. In the first program they are nouns, adjectives, verbs and adverbs, which users are then invited to construct into 'sentences'. Each program increases in complexity to include further parts of speech and translations from the new language back into English and vice versa. This new language is artificial: it does not have its own structure and rules but borrows these from English. Yet precisely because it does this it is a useful education aid. Users apply their knowledge of English syntax in a novel situation where the emphasis is on grammatical structure rather than on semantics. It is interesting that while this software is still concerned with a very precise and mechanical activity, it is not prescriptive. It would be easy to monitor the user's language constructs for correctness. Instead, the computer is employed to offer the information in a structured way and to provide a printout facility for easy recording of the sentences constructed. The emphasis is upon what users, working as a group, bring to bear and discuss in relation to language as they compose and translate structures or as they later exchange and evaluate hard copy of their work with their teacher or with each other.

WORD PROCESSING

Word processing takes over much of the mechanical operation involved in the writing process and allows writers to concentrate on the thoughts, the semantics, behind the words. When composing text on paper — whether by use of a typewriter or by pen and ink — writers have to concern themselves simultaneously with choosing, editing, formatting and printing the words. The mechanics of production are apt to interfere with the process of creation. Second thoughts about choice of words or the sequence of sentences are discouraged by the logistics of erasers, liquid paper and legibility. The rearrangement of paragraphs is prohibited by the prospect of copious rewriting. By contrast, in word processing the stages of composition and production are distinct and do not distract from each other. The ultimate certainty of effortless production of final copy emancipates thought from the labour of production. Advanced software can even provide facilities to check spelling and punctuation, leaving writers free to concentrate on what they are saying. Such software can also facilitate the search for expression of thought.

Writing requires more consideration than the other language skills. Much material is rewritten several times before it appears in print. It is hard for authors to write down exactly what they want to say without spending time on it. An electronic thesaurus allows writers to move through their text summoning up a lexicon of synonyms to replace individual words. This extends vocabulary, and might also extend thought by providing new images and concepts to the context via the lexicon displayed. Further, the words, sentences and paragraphs may be manipulated, rearranged in new sequences, embedded in other structures, substituted or simply deleted. Writers can experiment with new styles and diverse ways of saying things. Sometimes they can be faced with new meanings and concepts simply by a fortuitous rearrangement of text.

Classroom Applications

In a classroom, word processing can have a liberating effect. Conscious choices of language cannot always be made at the same time as the formalisation and shaping of thoughts. The latter come — or so teachers hope — from a deeper subconscious level. Children need to formalise and write down their thoughts and experiences before preparing them for interpersonal communication. For this reason there is a prevalent desire among teachers of the language arts to separate the writing process from the product. A word processor can encourage this distinction, allowing pupils to draft and redraft their work effortlessly and then to produce a variety of versions in hard copy for circulation and comment. A word processor might be utilised further to give insight into formal editing procedures. It could even be used in a classroom for simulation of business situations and newspaper editing or for the printing of students' own books.

Students' willingness to spend more time on process is likely to arise not only because of the novelty of a word processor, or because of its effortless redrafting potential, but also because of the standard of final product possible. A word processing system can encourage perfectionism in formal presentation. The neatness of a final draft from a printer can be an incentive towards mechanical precision in syntax and spelling to match the professional appearance of copy. It might also encourage a heightened effort in content, aided by the word processor's capabilities in that field, to match the style of presentation.

All pupils might be stimulated to write more and better simply by the novelty of a word processor. For the children with writing problems, the novelty might be more significant: it might indicate to them that this is a medium in which they have not failed; it is also a medium that can assist them to overcome their faults, and aid their confidence in expressing themselves. The keyboard can help develop a rhythm in writing. On a visual display screen, word shapes are always identical and so easier to remember. Some software will help children check spelling and punctuation. (Personally, I prefer to see children use the word processor to search their text for particular spelling patterns that they always confuse, so that they can then correct them themselves.) The final hard copy will not betray their poor handwriting. In presentation, their work will be identical to that of their peers. Only in content might it be dissimilar, and this is not to say necessarily inferior — though even drivel can appear superb. Pupils' low levels of literacy might be confined to handwriting, spelling and punctuation rather than grammar or thought, and it might take a word processor to clear the wheat from the chaff and make teachers or other students realise this fact.

4.4 Computer Models in the Teaching of Biology

JOHN HEWITSON*

INTRODUCTION

Computer models and their software have now been in use in the biology laboratory long enough for us to stand back and try to answer some questions. Amongst these questions are 'What effects does this technology have on our students?', 'What new insights does the technology give us into the biology we are teaching?' and 'What new teaching opportunities does the new technology enable?'

Our students have experienced the new technology outside the classroom as well as inside. What effects has this had on them? How do they approach the new technology when it is presented to them in the classroom? Perhaps the most common application of computers in our students' experience is the electronic game. These games are great fun, almost addictive and often set in a world of fantasy. The user enters the game and becomes totally involved in exploring the universe described there, becoming adept at discovering its properties and learning the new skills required to succeed there. This is our students' background as they encounter a computer program in biology. The games are taken completely on trust, they are not relevant to life outside the computer, they do not need to be verified or applied. Such attitudes are certainly not appropriate when using computer simulations in biology! It is quite irrelevant for the games player to ask 'Is this like the real world?' or 'What is the computer actually doing?' or even 'Can I rely on my discoveries in the game and apply them in the real world?'

In physics and chemistry, the world can be more predictable than in biology; laws are often expressed in mathematical terms and the universe can sometimes be constrained to be 'frictionless' or 'at absolute zero' or 'for a perfect gas' or other unnatural con-

*Source: John Hewitson, 'The Role of Computer Models in the Teaching of Biology' in C.J. Smith (ed.) *Exploring Biology with Microcomputers* (Council for Educational Technology, London, 1985), pp. 63-72.

ditions. Such predictability, mathematical laws or unnatural conditions are not the world of the biologist. The biologist cannot therefore take simulations on trust to the same extent that the other disciplines can. However, we expect our students to learn biology from their use of simulations and then to apply that knowledge to other arenas. As teachers, we are often expected to take simulations on trust with little chance of satisfying ourselves that the model being used is relevant to our application.

This article aims to illustrate, by considering some examples, that the study of (or at least some knowledge of) the model being used in a simulation can be very useful for both teacher and student.

THE USE OF A COMPUTER MODEL AS AN AID TO TEACHING BIOLOGY

Monohybrid is a model of Mendel's 3.1 ratio with tall and short pea plants. One of the more predictable and mathematical areas of our biology syllabuses is the study of genetics. Here the underlying laws can be expressed in mathematical terms of ratios or fractions. As such they are readily reproduced as computer simulations. When presented with these simulations, it is not unusual for students to ask what the computer is actually doing and even to ask to see the program listing. This can be used as a valuable teaching point.

Take, for example, Mendel's simple 3:1 ratio observed in the offspring of heterozygous parents. There are two possible ways of writing a computer program to generate two different categories in the ratio of 3:1. One way is a model of the biological mechanism. the other is quicker, shorter and more economical on computer memory, but bears no relationship to the genetics involved. This is best illustrated by looking at the two flowcharts in Figure 1.

The 'Computer Programmer Flowchart' is probably the quickest way to generate offspring one at a time in the ratio of 3:1. The 'Biologist's Flowchart' will also generate offspring one at a time in the ratio of 3:1, but it is also a model of the biological mechanism concerned.

(1) Each offspring is the product of two gametic nuclei, one from the male and one from the female — the loop (A) in the flowchart models the production of two gametes.

Figure 1.

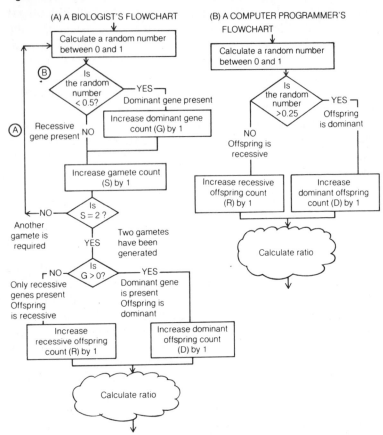

(2) Heterozygous parents produce gametes of two types. Half the gametes carry a dominant gene for the characteristic concerned, and the other half carry a recessive gene. The genes fuse together in pairs, at random. There is a one in two chance of any particular gamete carrying a dominant gene — the conditional step (B) uses the computer's random number function to simulate this chance, rather like tossing a coin.

(3) If either male or female gamete carries a dominant gene, then the offspring will show the dominant characteristic. The program tests at (C) for a dominant gene. If one or more is found, the running total of dominant offspring is increased by one, otherwise the offspring is recessive.

A formal consideration of the flowchart and the program listing can be particularly helpful when discussing the mechanism behind Mendel's 3:1 ratio with a group who are mathematically competent. For those students who find mathematics a foreign language, the exercise is less than beneficial! However, flowcharts and computer programming are becoming commonplace for our students and this is a language they will understand even more readily in the future.

MODELLING AS AN APPLICATION AND VERIFICATION OF THEORY

Natural selection is an example of modelling as an application and verification of theory.

The Hardy-Weinberg equation is a common item of theory in A-level biology which seems to many students to be of very little practical value. Some applications for the Hardy-Weinberg equation at this level seem contrived and trivial. The Hardy-Weinberg equation can be used as part of a model of natural selection using the following outline flowchart (Figure 2).

Figure 2.

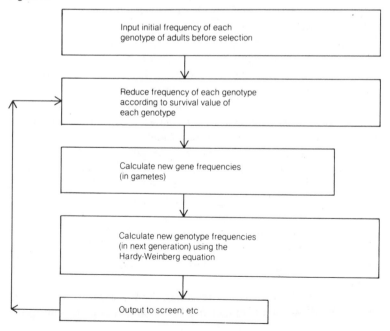

The properties of this model make interesting material for discussion. The Peppered Moth provides sufficient background data to enable the model to be run as a simulation of a well documented example of natural selection. The starting population (in 1848) is known. Some idea of the situation in 1886 is known and the proportions in 1895 are recorded in the literature. These data can be compared with those generated by the computer model using survival rates (different for each different genotype) from the literature. Predictions can be made for the reverse selection that is taking place since the Clean Air Acts and these can be compared with actual published data of the natural moth population which have been gathered from moth traps and by counting the wings of moths collected from under bat roosts.

Such a simulation not only illustrates the effects of natural selection in action, but the way the program works (the model) should be comprehensible to an A-level student and gives a good practical illustration of the use of the Hardy-Weinberg equation.

The fact that the real world and the model are in agreement is confirmation that the theory is valid.

TO APPRECIATE THE VALIDITY OF CONCLUSIONS WHICH ARE BASED ON MODELS

Predator-prey is an example of a program that encourages appreciation of conclusions based on models. Biology is full of models which can be mistaken for the real thing. This can be true in the areas of DNA structure, genetic code, membrane structure and the process of osmosis, for example. These are physical models and it is relatively easy to understand the model and to appreciate that it is only a model which may be an over-simplification of the real-life situation. However, in the case of mathematical models it is less easy to disentangle the model from the natural world.

A case in point is the relationship between predators and their prey which is almost synonymous in the mind of an A-level student with 'predator — prey curves' — it is often assumed that the usual relationship between predators and their prey is one of oscillating numbers, out of phase, with one curve leading the other.

This view of predator — prey interaction has more to do with the work of two mathematicians, Lotka and Volterra (who produced theoretical equations based on a simple model of their own making) rather than the records of animal numbers in the wild.

The Lotka-Volterra equations are tedious to calculate without a computer, but now students have the opportunity to experiment with the model and to appreciate some of the assumptions which are implicit in it. To take the Lotka-Volterra model of predator — prey interaction on trust and to assume that the model can predict the real-life situation is to misunderstand the nature of the model and to turn a blind eye to the complications of the natural world which are not included in their model. For instance, Lotka-Volterra makes the following assumptions.

(1) Predator appetite is limited only by the availability of prey. If prey numbers are very high indeed then predator appetite will also be very high. There is no upper limit to the appetite of a predator.
(2) Predator reproduction rate is only limited by the availability of food. There is no upper limit to the predator rate of reproduction.
(3) Prey numbers are only limited by their rate of reproduction. In the absence of predators, there is no upper limit to the density of the prey population.
(4) There is no immigration or emigration of predators or prey.
(5) Predators feed almost exclusively on this single species of prey.
(6)   Prey are killed almost exclusively by this species of predator — deaths from other causes are a constant rate.

If these assumptions are not valid, then the oscillating numbers conclusion may also be suspect! This is especially interesting when one considers that there are few natural cases of animal numbers oscillating in a regular cycle. What is more, those cases where oscillating cycles have been established in the wild have been shown to be unlikely to be a result of the mutual interaction between predators and their prey (and this includes those cases where predator and prey numbers both oscillate in a regular cycle).

These points arise as a result of the study of one model of predator — prey interaction. Such a model should not be accepted on trust, but should be clearly stated for the user to make up his own mind. Modifications can be made to the simple model to satisfy some of the objections raised above. The computer gives an opportunity to explore the properties of new models based on these modifications. Do some of these modifications damp out or even eliminate the oscillations which many have come to believe are a natural feature of wild predator — prey interactions? It turns out that some seemingly minor modifications to the model completely alter its properties, but a student can discover these with a microcomputer rather than take them on trust from a mathematician.

MODELLING AS A METHOD OF ANALYSIS

Biological control is a program for modelling the population dynamics of a pest and its parasitoid. Anyone who has written a computer program knows the kind of analysis of the problem which must take place before the program is written. There are even more numerous questions which arise as the program is being written and tested. There is no better way of exploring a topic in minute detail than to attempt to write a computer program to model the situation.

Consider, for example, a program to model the population dynamics of glasshouse whitefly, its parasite *Encarsia formosa* and their effects on a commercial tomato crop. *Encarsia* is used commercially as a method of biological control of whitefly. Here are some of the questions that arose as the model was constructed.

(A) For the whitefly
How long do whitefly live?
How many eggs do they lay each day?
How long do the eggs take to hatch?
How long do the various larval and pupal stages take to develop?
How do they harm the crop?
Which stages harm the crop?
Assuming only females lay eggs, what is the sex ratio?
Where does a whitefly infestation come from?

(B) For the 'Encarsia'
How long do *Encarsia* live?
How many whitefly can they parasitize each day?
What stage of the whitefly life cycle do they parasitize?
How long do their eggs take to hatch?
Assuming only females lay eggs, what is the sex ratio?
How long do artificially introduced *Encarsia* take before they become active parasites?

(C) For the tomato crop
When are the plants put into the glasshouse?
When does fruit start to become mature?
What is the cash value of the crop?
At what level of infestation does whitefly cause harm?
What is the cash value of the harm caused by the whitefly?

Not surprisingly, many of these components are affected by temperature, which in turn may be controlled by heating. Therefore, further questions must be answered.

(D) For the glasshouse
What are the normal temperatures throughout the year?
What rise of temperature can be obtained by normal heating?
What are the costs of glasshouse heating?

When comparing biological control with control by spraying with insecticide ...

(E) For the insecticide
What is the effect of the insecticide on each stage of the whitefly life cycle?
What is the effect of the insecticide on *Encarsia*?
How persistent is the insecticide?
What are the costs of the insecticide and its application?

The answers to such questions are not readily available, but they were just the questions which the Glasshouse Crops Research Institute at Littlehampton had been researching to enable them to advise commercial growers who wished to use *Encarsia* for biological control and they had all the answers.

It was particularly exciting to find out how the final model compared with the real world. Whitefly numbers built up and could be controlled by *Encarsia* (in the right conditions) in a way which was not dissimilar to that observed in a glasshouse. However, one major flaw appeared — it was impossible to control whitefly by the use of insecticide unless spraying was carried out every single day! This puzzled even the experts, for clearly something was wrong with the model as growers *can* control whitefly with insecticide without daily spraying. After much thought and searching of the literature, the experts cracked it. Insecticide does not kill the larvae or pupae and in the model, these were allowed to emerge as adults the day after spraying was carried out, to lay their eggs and thereby to reinfect the glasshouse. In the real world however, whitefly do not lay eggs for the first couple of days after they emerge from their pupae and this gives the insecticide a much greater effect on the numbers of eggs being laid.

The building of the computer model brought a great deal of the biology of the situation to light. Students are expected to experiment with the model to find out which questions are important to ask and what are the answers to those questions which enable the biological control to be optimized. Several points can be made from this experience:-

(1) Biological models are often very complex. The final BASIC listing of such a program is impossible to unravel and to understand biologically.

(2) Therefore, the teacher's guide must give *details* of the model used and the ways in which the model is only an approximation (or simplification) of the real world.

(3) The answer to the biological questions which are the basis of the model must be clearly stated (a) because others may disagree with the data used, (b) to alert users who may try to use the model in an inappropriate situation, (c) to enable others to modify the model in the light of new data or new applications and (d) because the questions and answers themselves are valuable teaching material.

(4) The analysis which is required to build such a model has to be very thorough. The writing of the program actually asks the questions. The act of modelling is a very precise way of studying a biological system rigorously.

(5) When a model is being used, the user should be alert to spot (and to explain) any anomalies which arise between the model and the real world.

(6) When a model differs from the real world, new questions are posed and more investigations may be suggested by the divergence.

It may be possible for students to build their own simple models of biological systems if suitable situations can be identified and the necessary information made available. Such systems might be:

(a) the control of cardio-vascular and/or respiratory systems in response to the demands of exercise.

(b) the tactical movement of woodlice in response to humidity (etc): is it possible that this response is the result of (i) turning often in optimal conditions but (ii) travelling in straight lines when in unfavourable conditions?

(c) the effects of light intensity and temperature on the light-dependent and light-independent stages of photosynthesis; the build-up of the intermediates and the effects of flashing the light with different proportions of ON and OFF time.

Even if a complete program does not result, the analysis of the problem will have been a useful exercise in itself. Such an analysis may lead to investigations of the real world which could be conducted to answer some of the outstanding questions posed by the model.

MODELS FOR ALL?

There are many examples in science where what started as a model has now become so firmly established that we have come to accept it as if it is reality. Certainly, as teachers we find ourselves guilty of passing off models as factual reality. In such cases, the model *already exists* and the computer simply enables construction of the model in a form with which we can experiment. The computer can give us the opportunity as teachers and as students to explore models in a quite unique way.

With a model exhibited on a computer there is *less* chance of students mistaking the model for reality. After all, their experience with computer games has preconditioned them to a world of fantasy and make-believe within the computer. This is of real benefit as we explore with our students the correspondence between the model and reality. In order to be able to criticise the model constructively when it diverges from reality, we need to understand the model as well as the real world. This requires the dual skills of the computer programmer and the biologist. The real power of the computer lies in its ability to carry out the arithmetic of a model so quickly that the properties of the model can be investigated painlessly and more easily be compared with the real world. Thus, exploration of a computer model can stimulate a deeper understanding of the natural world itself.

So, there can be benefit for all in the exploration of models on a computer, but is there equal benefit in the construction and analysis of computer models?

There is no doubt that modelling is a high-level exercise. It requires a detailed knowledge of the biology, a willingness to describe it in mathematical terms (this often involves compromise) and a competence of computer programming. These skills are not commonly found together in the present generation of biologists. The situation is bound to change as our present generation of students follows through its training and a new generation joins us from the primary and middle schools where microcomputers are becoming commonplace.

However, the fact remains that we cannot expect our average students to find computer modelling an easy task. Indeed, some of our students enjoy their biology because they cannot appreciate the joys of mathematics and they find biology a different world from that of the mathematics department! To thrust the mathematical details of models before all students is a recipe for classroom boredom. On the other hand, there are some students who really 'switch on' to this area and all should have some concept of what a model is doing.

We should not expect our students to accept the computer as a 'black box' any longer. Computer models should at least be a 'transparent box' even if all do not wish to study the detailed mechanism of the model inside. For some, their enjoyment of biology is increased by being given the opportunity to study the mechanism and thereby to appreciate the details of the biological system more fully than is possible by other means.

NOTE

The computer models used as examples in this article are published by Longman Group Ltd, Longman House, Burnt Mill, Harlow, Essex, as part of the Warwick Science Simulations.

4.5 Software through Prestel: the Case of Inverkeithing High School

JOHN ARNOTT*

AIMS

The way in which Inverkeithing got involved with the project[1] was somewhere above my level in the hierarchy, but I would assume that someone in the region either thought that we were quite 'go ahead' with computers, or, more likely, that we were the closest school to Edinburgh and would therefore incur lowest phone bills! However, like many things, I knew nothing about Prestel, not even what it was, but was very keen to find out more. This aim has certainly been fulfilled, both for myself and for a lot of people in the school, both staff and pupils. We also quite soon realized that this was going to be a fruitful source of software for us, at a time when to a large extent we thought of software as something that we had to write ourselves.

USERS

A lot of different people have used the system so far, some for telesoftware but most for access to Prestel. I would say that about 70 per cent of the overall use has been made either by me or by pupils under my supervision, and about half of that would be the pupils. Downloading of telesoftware has been done exclusively by me, although sometimes with pupils or staff in attendance for demonstration purposes. Teachers using Prestel have included the business studies department looking at financial and company information and also demonstrating Prestel as a modern business

---

*Source: John Arnott, Inverkeithing High School in C. Knowles and P. Bell (eds), *Distribution of Educational Software through Prestel* (Council for Educational Technology, London, 1984), pp. 135-8.

tool; the economics teacher for financial information; the geography department getting information about foreign countries; the home economics department looking up consumer information on such things as washing machines and fridges, and using the MAFF pages on nutritional values and food additives; staff involved in guidance and careers using the COIC pages with small groups of pupils or pupils on their own, in association with other computer-aided activities. Also on a large number of occasions both individual pupils and staff and non-teaching staff have used Prestel to look things up. The main use that I have made of the system, apart from the acquisition of software, has been to demonstrate Prestel as an example of information technology. I would estimate that approximately 800 of our pupils have, so far, had a demonstration, often involving looking up items of information suggested by individual pupils, and the pupils in my O-level computing class have had extended periods of individual use.

ADMINISTRATION

The use of the system was controlled by me. To a large extent of course this meant encouraging others to use it, but it did also mean, at times, resolving conflicts over use. The equipment was sited in a relatively small computer room but could, by suspending the phone wire across a corridor, be used in my classroom opposite. Most other users only had small groups of up to 10 pupils and so used the system on site, but I generally had larger groups of either 20 or 30 and so shifted it about. I produced a small form on which users recorded their use of Prestel, both in terms of costs and content. These were only completed on about half the actual occasions however, and even then would most often be completed at the end of a session with the costs and without giving a picture of the type of pages accessed. As regards telesoftware, I would generally look through the CET's telesoftware section once a week and download any new programs. I usually downloaded everything unless I was sure that no one in school could make a use of it, and then invited teachers from the appropriate departments to come and try out the programs obtained. Since the region was paying centrally for the running costs of the project, this meant that both my and other departments were getting free software. I certainly appreciated this fact, but I think other departments did not, mainly because they had never bought computer software before. In fact, in some ways this has been a bad thing since they now don't expect to have to pay for software. However, this situation may be resolved if a central school budget for the purchase of software is set up.

TELESOFTWARE

The telesoftware system certainly worked extremely well. There were only about four occasions in the whole two-year period when things went wrong during downloading and they were all recoverable. As a means of acquiring software the system is very good, its main advantages being the ability to browse and getting the programs straight away.

PROGRAMS

I actually downloaded almost every program from the CET's telesoftware section over the two years, and many others from Aladdin's Cave and subsequently Micronet 800. The programs were for the BBC computer and for the RML 380Z. A lot of the programs have been very useful, though to different people. Those that spring to mind are the 380Z utilities: COPY, UNERA, TURNKEY; the primary programs for the BBC, used by our remedial department and support unit: TABLES, FRAC, etc. There have also been many programs I have downloaded which I thought were going to be useful that have in fact never been used at all. This is probably a consequence of the fact that it is me who is choosing which programs to download, not the potential user. I think that the constraints imposed by having to budget for the purchase of telesoftware would lead to a different approach, namely consulting potential users, with details of the software, before actual purchase.

USEFULNESS

Prestel has certainly been very useful in school, to me and to several other teachers, as an example of the application of information technology. Its usefulness as a source of information has been limited so far. This is in part due to the quality of information available, and in part due to the fact that schools do not seem to want up-to-date information. But I think that really, as was said at the end-of-project conference, it does take at least two years for something new to be taken on board by teachers and included in their teaching schemes. I am fully expecting Prestel to be used more and more throughout the school and in fact to create problems as regards booking in the near future.

LOCAL VIEWDATA

The local viewdata system is a very impressive piece of software with a great many potential applications. Once non-experts have seen Prestel and an example of a local viewdata system their imagination very often seems to be fired to produce something of their own. The problems of designing a database and of entering the pages are not seen as insuperable but rather as a challenge and a practical way in to computer usage for both teachers and their classes. I would like to see someone produce and maintain a register of local viewdatabases. It would have to include both proposed and actual databases with some indication of their degree of completeness and what their host computer was.

COSTS

Costs are certainly the biggest worry in potential users' eyes, the concern being over how much it would cost for a whole year and how this would be shared by the users. It is a problem which I have not yet tackled but will have to do in the near future. I shall probably propose that a budget of £200 be set aside for Prestel for this coming year and that a careful monitoring of departmental use is done in order to see how it should be paid for in subsequent years. Telesoftware, I shall propose, should be paid for on a departmental basis as and when it is purchased, the debiting of individual departments' budgets being done in the school office in much the same way as it is done in the case of other materials purchased.

CONCLUSIONS

In order to make Prestel more useful within schools it would be good to have descriptions of use made of Prestel by individual teachers. For example, a set of guides on the lines of 'How to use Prestel in the geography department' or 'How I use Prestel in my English teaching' would be extremely useful, if only the teachers could be found to write them. (I think I could write one called 'How I use Prestel in computer studies and computer awareness courses'!). As regards improving the usefulness of telesoftware, I think there are two main things. The first is to have *all* educational software published on Prestel — if not the actual software then at least a description of all published software including information on where it can be bought. This exhaustive approach would certainly be an enormous task but would be very useful to all potential purchasers of educational software, and would make Prestel essential reading. Secondly, there has to be a better way of finding out about the purpose and content of a piece of software before buying it. It seems the best way would be to have sampler programs available free, but alternatives would be to have response frames available to request more detail about the program by post or simply much more descriptive text about each program.

I do intend that Inverkeithing High School should continue to use Prestel and telesoftware in the future, but I don't as yet know how it's going to be financed. I also hope that within Scotland we shall be able to continue to access the SCET's viewdatabase in Glasgow and to perhaps be able to download all the software available from SMDP.

NOTE

1. A reference to the CET Telesoftware Project, on which the Knowles and Bell (op. cit.) volume is based.

4.6 Television, Film and Media Education

LEN MASTERMAN*

Precisely how is television studied in schools and colleges at the present time? How should the study of television relate to already established courses in film studies, and the growing development of general mass-media courses in secondary schools and colleges? What problems surround the independent study of television as a viable intellectual discipline? And on what basis has the study of television and the mass media been urged by educational reports and media experts? This chapter attempts to answer these questions, and to clarify some of the theoretical problems underlying the study of the mass media. It ends with a critical survey of discriminatory approaches to mass-media teaching.

1. THE PRESENT SITUATION

At the present time there are two major trends apparent in the development of media education. First of all, more than a decade after the Newsom Report, the problems and difficulties of establishing film as an autonomous study within the secondary school curriculum are now becoming quite apparent. Secondly, a general movement has already taken place within schools towards the umbrella discipline of media studies. The situation was nicely summarised in a report by the Television Commission of a recent conference of film and television educators at York University:

> The most positive and perhaps, in terms of its importance for the future direction of work, the most significant of the Commission's conclusions is that the existing separation of TV and Film studies is no longer tenable.

*Source: Len Masterman, *Teaching about Television* (Macmillan, London, 1980), pp. 1-20.

The Commission is generally agreed that we ought to think of all these areas (Film, TV, Radio, Music, the Press Advertising, etc.) in terms of media studies. All these various media are interrelated within society, in terms of structures of ownership and means of organisation. And if they were approached from the other end, in terms of their aesthetic systems, they would also be found to have much in common.

However, the Commission goes further than this. Not only is TV part of a wider area of study; it also ought to form the core of that study. Film, which has been pre-eminent so far, can no longer sustain that position, certainly within secondary education. TV is by almost every criterion (with the dubious exception of 'quality') more centrally important.[1]

2. FILM STUDIES

The Commission's advocacy of television as a more centrally important medium than film at least in part reflects a number of practical problems encountered by teachers of film during the last decade. Far from being the liberating, radicalising experience which they had in mind, many teachers discovered that the subject, through its institutionalisation, became, willy-nilly, an instrument of control. The Commission on CSE Film Studies at the York conference noted that: 'The problem of pupil alienation from the school situation is as serious for the teacher of Film as it is for any other subject. Indeed, the pupil brings to the Film class a history of attitudes and experiences which shape his expectations of the work to be engaged in.'[2]

Once film became a subject on the timetable, and formally examinable, the teacher did not simply face the problem of the pupil bringing into the film class alienating attitudes and expectations *from outside.* When files needed to be kept up to date, marks given, mock examinations set; when the examination was used as a threat, and assessment — in spite of the teacher's better judgement — became a prime instrument of control; when the teacher found that he had to judge as well as teach his pupils, discriminate between them, grade, order and rank them on grounds which he knew had little validity and which said nothing of the ways in which he valued them as individuals; and when the teacher finally realised that the compulsion for using these mechanisms of control arose from his knowledge that it was *he* who was being assessed by his pupils' results, his subject had already become reified, inert and instrumental before his very eyes.

It was not simply accommodation to the constraints of the examination system which caused problems for film teachers however. My own experience of teaching film to low-stream disenchanted secondary school pupils revealed that the medium itself was more remote from any of them than I had ever imagined — not one of them went to the cinema more than a couple of times each year, for example, and their experience of films was gained almost exclusively through watching television. Conventional approaches to the study of film cut no ice. There was no interest in genre, while Ford and even Hitchcock were as remote from them as Shelley and Keats. Discussion, when it occurred, was at a low, generally uninterested level, though it often raised unexpectedly important issues. From the teaching point of view, there were a surprising number of additional obstacles. No foreign films could ever be used since no one in the group could read quickly enough to catch even the simplest of subtitles as they flashed by; extracts inevitably provoked disappointed reactions, while features raised *too many* issues and complexities, caused timetabling problems and left no time for discussion immediately after viewing.

Apart from my own pedagogic inadequacies, many of the difficulties encountered with this group could be directly attributed to a rigidly streamed school organisation. At the age of eleven, on their first day in their new school, most of the group had been publicly placed in the lowest 'F' stream. It was a day they could all vividly remember. They responded to this calculated insult to their spirit by making life impossible for most teachers with whom they had come into contact ever since. Nevertheless the logic of my experience led me to the conclusion that film might be a less immediate, relevant and appropriate medium for classroom study than television. It was, as we have seen, a conclusion also reached by many other teachers who have recognised that it is time to redress the balance, to respond more sensitively to the direct viewing experiences of pupils and to acknowledge the greater significance and potency of the television medium.

3. MEDIA STUDIES

The study of television, where it finds a place at all in schools at the moment, is characterised by its heterogeneity and *ad-hocery*. The most common solution has undoubtedly been to treat television as a component part, lasting perhaps a half or one term, of a media studies course, an approach advocated as we have seen by the BFI/SEFT national conference on media education. There are, however, major conceptual and pedagogic difficulties involved in the notion of media studies. What insights or understandings would a one- or two-year course (the time-span of most media studies courses) give pupils in each of the media mentioned by the conference ('Film, TV, Radio, Music, the Press, Advertising, etc.' One wonders about the additional media suggested by that 'etc.' Books, perhaps? Telephones? Photographs? Cars?)? What would a half-term component in television or music look like? Could it be anything but superficial? And if so, is it worth doing at all? What would give coherence to the course's constituent units? A particular mode of enquiry? The examination of important cross-media concepts? Or what? And what would be the subject-matter under scrutiny — which of the many aspects of each of the media? What would be the status of this content? Would its acquisition be a desirable end in itself or a means of understanding general principles? Is there an essential body of knowledge or information? If so, what is it? And embracing all of these questions: what would constitute student learning? The acquisition of particular unnamed abilities, attitudes, information, techniques, methodologies or what? These are basic questions to which teachers will need to have answers before they can begin to set up coherent courses in media studies. They are questions which when raised at all have been answered with a resounding silence. As a result media studies courses invariably run the risk of being superficial and fragmented rag-bags, covering arbitrary issues, oriented towards content rather than process, asking different questions of different media and developing no consistent line of enquiry.

The difficulties of developing a coherent and organic framework which would comprehend each and all of the mass media are only too evident. Why then the compulsion to crowd them under the same umbrella? There are a number of reasons. Richard Collins has argued[3] the folly of regarding television and radio as discrete media, and there is obvious sense in this. Simply in terms of their

organisational structures — particularly since the advent of commercial radio and the evolution of the Independent Television
Authority to the Independent Broadcasting Authority — they
ought to be considered together under the heading of broadcasting. But, the argument continues, the broadcasting institutions
hold so many functions, attitudes and practices in common with
newspapers and magazines — they may even cover the same events
— that there is a kind of perversity about ignoring these connections and inter-relationships. Indeed, it is the establishment of
valid cross-media generalisations which can give to media studies
its worthwhileness and academic respectability. There is a further
important argument, put forward by Graham Murdock, Douglas
Lowndes and others for considering the mass media together: they
are *industries* which are connected with each other, and linked to a
vast range of service and consumer industries through their
structures of ownership and control. EMI, for example, which has
a substantial shareholding in Thames Television, is the country's
largest record manufacturer and owns approximately one-quarter
of the nation's cinemas as well as live theatres and restaurants
(including the Golden Egg restaurant chain). The Rank Organisation, with a substantial shareholding in Southern Television,
controls the country's largest cinema chain and owns Butlin's
holiday camps, large numbers of bingo and dance halls, hotels and
a group of radio, television and hi-fi manufacturers (Bush, Murphy
and Dansette). The International Publishing Corporation (owners
of the *Daily Mirror, Sunday Mirror* and *Sunday People*) is part of
a giant multinational combine Reed International, which has
interests in bathroom and sanitary ware (it owns Twyford's), wall-
papers, paints, do-it-yourself products, fabrics, building products
and publishing.[4] And so one could go on. The mass media are not
isolated phenomena but significant links in a vast capitalist chain.

The study of mass-media *products*, which is what generally
takes place in any educational study of the media, if it is to be of
any value at all, cannot be done in isolation. There are *industrial*,
professional and *organisational* constraints upon what appears in
newspapers, magazines or on the television screen. The *values* of
mass-media products are not likely to be very much at variance
with the values of capitalism and consumerism, and the pattern of
values and constraints (and of the individual communicator's
ability to break free from them) is likely to hang together in a
coherent way throughout all of the mass media.

There are then plausible arguments for the collective study of the media; but how strong are such arguments? To take Collins' first: the institutional and functional connections between the media ought not to blind us to the fundamental *distinctions* which exist between them. There is much that relates to the study of television to which radio and newspapers are an irrelevance, and vice versa, and I have seen no evidence in visiting schools that cross-media work within a media studies framework has illuminated either the specificity of a particular medium, or generated cross-media generalisations in a way that the study of an individual medium could not have done equally well. To argue for the detailed study of a particular medium is not to argue against the value of cross-media comparisons. Indeed such comparisons are inevitable. In studying television news, as we shall see, one continually needs to move outwards from the details of a particular news trans-mission to the interrogation of particular stories, journalistic practices or sources of bias as they exist in other media. 'Interrogation' is the key word, however; students examine the particular questions in mind, questions which have already been raised by the study of television news. Such questioning either pinpoints media specificities (where differences arise) or draws attention to general principles (where there are congruencies). It is this very *sharpness of focus* which is so often missing when pupils attempt to study news coverage across the media in a generalised way. Quite simply there is too much ground to cover, too much information, and no agreed methodological tools for processing it. Since the field must be delimited each teacher will do it in his own largely arbitrary way. As a result the content and procedures of media studies vary widely from school to school, syllabuses tend to be information-laden rather than question-orientated, and the ultimate outcome is to obscure cross-media principles rather than illuminate them.

All of the arguments in favour of studying the media collectively stem from *a priori* commitment to uncover for students either the institutional bases or the structures of ownership and control of the media. I have a great deal of sympathy with these commitments but there are great difficulties in urging their centrality to the study of media *in schools*. The major problem lies in the distinct differences which are likely to exist between what is considered important and interesting by the teacher, and what is of interest to his pupils. Like most articulate people who don't possess much of it, teachers and lecturers tend to be fascinated and even preoccupied with questions of power and control. It is not, by and large, a pre-occupation which is likely to be shared by many of their pupils. And even assuming that pupils are able to see its significance there is a genuine difficulty in relating questions of organisational structures or patterns of control to the direct experience of the pupil. Pupils buy records of course; they watch television, read magazines and some of them go to the pictures. Connections can be made and investigations can even be undertaken of who owns local newspapers, cinemas, bingo halls and the like, but the fact remains that media *products*, because they are immediate, concrete and involving are more intrinsically interesting to most pupils than media structures which are necessarily covert and abstract. If media control or the 'consciousness industry' are to become pre-dominant concerns in media studies then proponents of this view will need to work hard to find ways of embedding their concerns within concrete experiences which are familiar, interesting and comprehensible to their pupils. There is no evidence that they have yet found ways of doing this.[5]

In this context, it is necessary to draw attention to an analogous movement which has been taking place within film studies — the movement towards the study of *Film as Industry*[6] in which the financing and distribution of films, and such notions as film 'property' are explored. Notwithstanding the doubts and diffi-culties articulately expressed by some teachers,[7] setting the study of films firmly within the context of their industrial production has been an undoubted step forward, bringing home

> very forcibly to the students the economic and commercial basis of the film industry and throwing light on aspects such as the collaborative industrial nature of film, constraints on film directors, the reasons for the existence of certain types of film and the complexities and limitations of the systems of distri-bution and exhibition in this country.[8]

The promise of the *Film as Industry* unit has undoubtedly pro-vided some of the impetus towards a conception of media studies in which industrial constraints and structures of ownership would play a central part. It is worth stressing therefore that this study was confined to a *single* medium, and that even within this context teachers were clearly worried by the sheer volume of information which needed to be processed by pupils and by the difficulties of 'keeping the students away from content' during the discussion of films (it is ironic that one of the prime advantages of using visual material, its concreteness, should here be seen as obstructive). Finally it ought to be said that the *Film as Industry* unit was designed for and studied by 'examinable' pupils, many of them sixth formers. One can, to say the least, foresee difficulties in working out an approach to the study of the industrial bases of more than one of the mass media which might be appropriate for mixed-ability or low-stream groups.

This is not to denigrate the importance of this area of study, but to suggest that it can be most appropriately handled in the class-room if it is examined — as it is with *Film as Industry* — within the framework of a particular medium. Even within this circumscribed orbit however pedagogic procedures are by no means clear, and access to simple information by no means easy. What the television teacher can do is to work outwards from the concrete television images themselves towards a recognition of and feeling for — if not always a precise understanding of — the institutional and industrial contexts within which they are manufactured. This process begins with a reading of the total communication of the television image and an exploration of the values implicit within it, and ends with speculation upon four questions. Who is producing the images? For whose consumption? For what possible purposes? and What alternative images are thereby excluded? The teacher and his pupils must tread with care. Glib answers — the kind of crude determinism which equates commercialism with cynical audience manipulation for example — are easy; accurate ones more elusive and complex. We still know alarmingly little about the ways in which the major communication institutions operate; our know-ledge of the sociology of the communicating professions is scant; and as laymen we are still very largely in the dark about the precise nature of the process which ends with one version of reality upon the screen rather than others.[9]

4. THE CASE FOR TELEVISION STUDIES

So far I have tried to draw attention to two observable trends in media education. First of all an increasing awareness by teachers of the problems associated with the use of film material in the classroom, an awareness which has led to a growing feeling that television might be a more appropriate and important medium for study. The second trend concerned an observable movement towards the umbrella subject of media studies in which the study of television would play an important part. I have attempted to draw attention to the epistemological fuzziness surrounding media studies, to point to some of its deficiencies in existing classroom practice and to look at some of the problems raised by one version of the subject in which the study of the media as consciousness industries would provide the containing framework. It now remains to ask whether the medium of television itself can offer to the teacher a framework for disciplined study.

The need for a sound theoretical base capable of standing close scrutiny is paramount. At the moment the study of television in schools lacks not only intellectual coherence but even very much in the way of simple mechanical coordination. There are exceptions,[10] but, whether television is taught independently or within the context of the mass media, the tendency appears overwhelmingly to be for teachers to go very much their own way, guided principally by their own tastes and judgements and by a generalised desire to encourage discrimination and visual literacy. The proliferation of Mode III examinations, while bringing tremendous advantages in its encouragement of teacher independence and initiative, has tended to contribute to the current chaotic heterogeneity. As a result television courses at the moment are largely uninfluenced by one another, and good practice remains isolated within individual schools. The lack of course coordination, together with the familiar difficulty for overworked teachers of making space for themselves in which they can seriously reflect upon their own practice, has been responsible for television being taught in something of an intellectual vacuum. Yet there is evidence that some teachers are moving away from 'discriminatory' television teaching towards new approaches and that if only the right questions could be posed it might be possible to find a surprising amount of agreement about what might constitute the way ahead. The purpose of the rest of this chapter is to pose these questions and to suggest answers which might illuminate the way in which television teaching might develop in schools within the next decade.

To what extent can the study of television be constituted as a viable intellectual discipline? Before we can answer this question we must ask another: what is it that constitutes any discipline? Most fundamentally a discipline is characterised by *an agreed field of study or enquiry*, and is further defined by an *intellectual framework which delimits the questions to be asked*. Information is elicited from the field through a *distinctive mode of enquiry* and the purposes of this enquiry must be '*important*' or '*serious*' in ways which need no elaborate justification. Jerome Bruner has also argued that at the core of any discipline lie *concepts* and *principles* 'as *simple* as they are *powerful*' which 'may be taught to anybody at any age in some form'.[11] Can these considerations lead us to a more disciplined study of television? It is to this question which we must now turn.

a. The Field of Study

The primary object of study in television studies is observable and circumscribed; it is the continual flow of information which is communicated to us by television. What are the characteristics of this body of information? Most importantly the study of television is based upon the premiss that televisual information is *non-transparent*. As Nell Keddie has pointed out[12] this is also true of film studies, but the need to emphasise and demonstrate non-transparency is even more urgent in television since it is an apparently less synthetic medium than film with an apparently closer relationship to 'real' events. A 'window on the world' view of the medium would make the study of television impossible; one would not be studying it but other things — news, sport or light entertainment. The case for the study of television rests upon the significance and potency of a mediating process which exists independently of the existence of the event being televised.

Televisual communication is also characterised by its great diversity — it serves the functions of the newspaper, theatre, cinema, sports arena and music hall rolled into one. This apparent hindrance to its disciplined study (it is difficult to imagine any but the woolliest of conceptual structures being able to comprehend such diverse functions) again forces attention upon a major generic function of television which is to provide a field for the embodiment and revelation of beliefs, values and attitudes. This it must inevitably do. In practice one can say much more — that in every country in which it operates *television has an ideological function*, as James Halloran has succinctly pointed out:

Generally throughout Europe television serves the nation state, whatever the politics of the state ... On the one side there are the broadcasters with their professional ideologies, occupational routines, and self-protecting mythologies, who have been socialised into a profession within given socio-economic systems. These professionals select, process and present the message. On the other side, there are individuals who make up the non-participating audiences and who receive the messages in relative isolation. It is seen by many as an elitist, literary set-up where a small group of educated, articulate people who more or less share the same codes of the dominant culture — encode messages for consumption by others who have different codes ... generally the receiver will not be in a position to recognise all the professional rules and practices.[13]

Stuart Hood has drawn the connection between television's ideological function and the carefully fostered illusion of transparency: 'Since one of the principal functions of television is to convey the dominant ideology of society, the impression of immediacy or lack of intervention is important. What appears to be immediate is less likely to be questioned.'[14]

Roland Barthes' notion of myth — 'depoliticised speech' — takes the logic of the argument a stage further. When constructed meanings operate under the guise of 'givens', when ideological dimensions are suppressed, and speech depoliticised, then 'Nature seems to spontaneously produce the represented scene'.[15] Myth transforms ideological representations into natural ones. The study of television necessarily becomes the study of myths through the suppression of ideological functions and mediating processes. *Television education is therefore a demythologising process which will reveal the selective practices by which images reach the television screen, emphasise the constructed nature of the representations projected, and make explicit their suppressed ideological function.* Such an education will also necessarily be concerned with alternative realities — those constructions implicitly rejected, suppressed or filtered out by the images which appear on the screen.[16]

If this theoretical formulation seems remote from the kinds of activities which are normally considered to be within the capabilities of a mixed-ability comprehensive school class, it is because the sphere of ideology is one which pupils will approach as the final stage of a three-level process of analysis. The teacher's first task is to encourage his pupils to generate from images *descriptions* of what they see at a *denotative* level. This, it is suggested, may be achieved by increasing awareness of the multiplicity of ways in which television images communicate their meanings. Secondly he may encourage pupil *interpretation* by drawing attention to the *connotative* levels of meaning in cultural images and objects. What does each denotative quality *suggest*? What associations do that colour, that shape, that size, that material have? Discussion, at first free-flowing and open-ended, will gradually become less so as definite patterns and clusters of associations become evident and the groups move into interpretation at the *third* level, that of *ideology*, 'the final connotation of the totality of connotations of the sign' as Umberto Eco has described it. What does this programme *say* through its complex of signs and symbols? What values are embodied here, and what does it tell us of the society in which it finds a place? Who is producing this programme, for what audience and with what purpose?

To recapitulate: in television studies the field of investigation is constituted by the flow of information communicated to us by the medium. In spite of the apparent transparency, neutrality and diversity of function of this information it is both mediated and ideological. Mediation and ideology are themselves inextricably intertwined. Mediation is an ideological process, whilst ideology becomes 'visible' the moment that mediation processes are pinned down. The nature of that mediation and ideology can be partly revealed by a three-step process of analysis in which television information is examined at the levels of its denotative and connotative meanings before revealing itself as an ideological construct. For a fuller understanding of the constructed nature of the television image, however, further interrogation is necessary both of the images themselves and of the contexts within which they are embedded. Attention will need to be drawn to such diverse containing frameworks as the contextualising remarks of announcers, comperes and presenters; articles relating to television programmes in the press or in *Radio Times* and *TV Times*; the visual codings and conventions of the medium; and the routine professional practices of those who work within it.

Of all of the questions that can be asked of the television image it is those which reveal it as a mediated and ideological construct which provide the most significant structures within television studies' conceptual framework. Many other questions can, and often will, be asked by the student of the television image; for example,

What other programmes are like this one? What connections can be made between this programme and others featuring the same star/production team/writer? What insights does this programme give us into the problems and people it depicts? How does this programme compare with the novel or play it derives from? Do I like this programme? Does the programme/film/play/documentary have any kind of organic unity? Is it of greater or less value than comparable programmes?

These questions simultaneously open out further perspectives and delimit additional areas of enquiry. They are questions of *secondary significance* however since they are most properly applied only to part of the total output of television and not to all of it.

This is perhaps an appropriate point to stress that the discussion of questions ought in itself to play a significant role in television education. How many questions is it possible to ask of a television picture? What are the differences between these questions? Can they be categorised, or arranged into a hierarchy? These and other methodological problems ought not simply to be the concern of the teacher, but should be thought through and understood by pupils as well, for it is they who will ultimately be confronting the primary source material and who will need to be aware of the wide variety of tools at their disposal for making sense of it.[17]

b. The Mode of Enquiry

Some indication has already been given of the kind of enquiry in which television studies will engage. What will be the process of this enquiry? The task of the student of television is to *observe* and *describe* the images he sees, and *interpret* them at their connotative and ideological levels. This will involve the *analysis* of the codings, conventions and mediating processes which shape `television images. As I have stressed, however, this mode of enquiry cannot reveal mediating frameworks which exist outside of the medium itself; it cannot directly disclose those images which have been excluded from the screen, and it cannot inform us directly of the many constraints and influences operating upon the form of a particular communication, though in both areas legitimate inferences can often be made on the basis of the images themselves. Our mode of enquiry will need to incorporate a sensitivity to its own limitations, and an awareness that these less accessible strands will need to be woven into any coherent understanding of television images. Hence the importance attached to simulations in which pupils themselves become mediators and the acts of selection which make the television image a 'preferred' one can be replicated in the classroom.

c. Core Concepts and Principles

Teachers of the mass media will find it a useful exercise to try to formulate the 'simple' and 'powerful' concepts which lie at the heart of their work. The difficulties of achieving this *across* the media have already been touched upon. Central to the study of television there seem to me to be a number of core concepts: total communication, connotation, mediation and ideology; and a number of subsidiary ones such as genre, iconography and coding. Most of these — the concepts if not necessarily the words — seem to me to be capable of being passed on to the youngest of pupils in intellectually respectable versions via a spiral curriculum of the kind suggested by Bruner. The brief for television education in primary and early secondary education must be to find ways of introducing and deepening these concepts through the use of material appropriate to different age ranges.

d. The Importance of Television Studies

One of the most persistent arguments which the television teacher will meet from colleagues and parents is this: 'I find your work very interesting, most stimulating, etc., but do you *really* think it's important? I mean a lot of the material you're handling is pretty trivial stuff; and kids watch too much of it anyway without our needing to bring it into the classroom. Surely there are more important things for them to be doing in school.' According to Murdock and Phelps' survey[18] this view is still widely prevalent in schools, let alone amongst parents: 80 per cent of grammar schools and 42 per cent of the comprehensive schools surveyed felt that the study of the mass media had little or no legitimate claim to classroom attention. This whole question then is neither remote nor academic, but one that the television teacher will meet every day in the course of his work. In the last resort, any answer to the question 'Why is the study of television important?' must be a personal rather than a definitive one; in offering my own answer I do so in the recognition that the individual teacher will wish to add arguments of his own, and delete those with which he cannot agree.

The study of television is important because the medium itself is important. The Bullock Report is simply the latest of a number of sources to draw attention to the fact that most pupils spend far more time watching television than they do in the classroom.[19] To teach about television is to value this important and concrete part of pupils' experience and to assume its prime importance in real pupil learning. It is to attack a countervailing tendency in education to distrust the experience and judgement of the pupil, a process which whittles away the significance of his opinions, his dignity and ultimately his identity. One of the most damning indictments of schooling is that it can instil a conviction in pupils that neither they nor their experience are of any importance. A belief that one is not worthy of anything better is of course a precondition for the passive acceptance of slum houses, boring repetitive jobs and social and political subservience. Television studies assumes the prime importance of the experience of the learner, attempts to raise his consciousness by demythologising this experience; encourages him to posit alternatives; demonstrates the importance and strength of group experience; and continually fringes out from what is concrete and 'known' to a consideration of the wide range of social, aesthetic, industrial, political and philosophic issues raised by particular programmes.

Television is a major source of most people's information about the world. Because we live in a socially segregated society with total institutions for deviants, and socially segregated housing and schooling areas the medium is often our *only* source of information about a wide range of social problems and deviancies. Hartmann and Husband[20] have drawn attention to the importance of the frames of reference within which such issues are presented by television, and which need very careful scrutiny before any understanding of the issues involved can be reached. The study of television is vital not simply because it is such a pervasive and influential medium, but, as we have seen, because of its apparent transparency and naturalness. Knowledge of the mediated and constructed nature of the television message, and of the ways in which pictures are used selectively ought to be part of the common stock of every person's knowledge in a world where communication at all levels is both increasingly visual and industrialised. Television education is therefore part of an education for responsible citizenship. The case for its serious study seems to me to be very strong — even unanswerable; the fact that the medium continues to be ignored by vast numbers of schools in spite of a whole string of recommendations from official reports over the last twenty years is indeed an indictment of the conservatism and inflexibility of many educational establishments and of their inability to respond to developments and trends of major significance within society.

e. 'Appreciation' and 'Discrimination'

Apart from colleagues, headmasters, advisers and parents who believe there is little educational value in what he is doing, the television teacher will undoubtedly come into contact with many supporters and well-wishers who will need no convincing of the importance of his work. They will see it as an admirable attempt to foster 'discrimination' in pupils, and such colleagues, he may find, will occasionally refer to his work as 'television appreciation'. The appropriateness of the aim of fostering discrimination in media work has come under a good deal of critical scrutiny in recent years but its influence upon teachers and the general public remains so widely pervasive that it may be helpful to examine the concept in some detail, and to clarify some of the issues surrounding its use.

The birth of the whole discrimination argument in media education lay in a profound distrust of the media themselves. Traditionally ignored by the educational system, the mass media were drawn to the attention of teachers when they came to be identified as aspects of cultural decline, seducers of the innocent, and creeping diseases whose baleful influence clearly needed to be actively fought by the teacher and counterbalanced by doses of 'inoculative' education. The Spens Report on Secondary Education in 1938, for example, spoke of 'The hoarding, the cinema and ... the public press ... subtly corrupting the taste and habit of a rising generation', and advocated speech training as a way of combating 'the infectious accent of Hollywood' and of abolishing class barriers.[21] Twenty-one years later, the Crowther Report on the education of fifteen- to eighteen-year-olds suggested that

> Because they [the mass media] are so powerful they need to be
> treated with the discrimination that only education can give.
> There is ... a duty on those who are charged with the respon-
> sibility for education to see that teenagers ... are not suddenly
> exposed to the full force of the 'mass-media' without some
> counterbalancing assistance.[22]

The classic, and almost certainly the most influential argument
of the case for inoculative education was put by F.R. Leavis and
Denys Thompson in *Culture and Environment*, first published in
the 1930s but still widely influential amongst English readers in the
1950s and 1960s:

> those who in school are offered (perhaps) the beginnings of
> education in taste are exposed, out of school, to the competing
> exploitation of the cheapest emotional responses; films, news-
> papers, publicity in all its forms, commercially-catered fiction —
> all offer satisfaction at the lowest level, and inculcate the
> choosing of the most immediate pleasures, got with the least
> effort ... We cannot, as we might in a healthy state of culture,
> leave the citizen to be formed unconsciously by his environ-
> ment; if anything like a worthy idea of satisfactory living is to be
> saved he must be trained to discriminate and to resist.[23]

The importance and impact of Leavis and Thompson's little
book for the educationalist lay not only in its moralistic stance but
in the practical examples from advertisements, newspapers and
journals which crowded its pages. *Culture and Environment* was
essentially a handbook for teachers with an immediately practical
application, and for all its antipathy to the media it was instrumental in bringing media texts out from the cold and into the classroom. It was a movement which was to be irreversible, opening the
way in the 1960s for the classroom use of a wide range of materials
derived from books which cast a much more informed and sympathetic eye upon popular culture — Richard Hoggart's *The Uses
of Literacy* (1958 in its paperback edition), Vance Packard's *The
Hidden Persuaders* (1960) and Whannel and Hall's *The Popular
Arts* (1964).

The movement towards the increasing availability and use of popular texts was paralleled by an intellectual and emotional movement away from discrimination *against* the mass media towards discrimination *within* them. The strength and pervasiveness of this movement can be gauged from the fact that in 1960 it provided the theme for a national conference held by the National Union of Teachers on *Popular Culture and Personal Responsibility*. Old attitudes however continued to co-exist uneasily alongside the new. Denys Thompson could still write in his introduction to *Discrimination and Popular Culture*, a book arising directly out of the 1960 conference, and whose contents typify the stances and attitudes of the new movement, that 'The aim of schools is to provide children with standards against which the offerings of the mass media will appear cut down to size.'[24]

By now however this was coming to be seen as an unproductively elitist stance by many teachers and other voices were beginning to articulate more clearly what was to become the conventional wisdom for the remainder of the decade. In Hall and Whannel's words: 'In terms of actual quality ... the struggle between what is good and worthwhile and what is shoddy and debased is not a struggle against the modern forms of communication, but a conflict within these media.'[25]

One way of interpreting this was to assert the existence of a kind of high culture within the mass media, and there is no doubt that this approach informed a good deal of mass-media teaching in the 1960s. Discrimination came to mean a preference for foreign films and 'classics of the cinema' over the kinds of films shown at the local Odeon (a preference heavily underscored in Hall and Whannel's work for example);[26] for the *Guardian* rather than the *Mirror*, for *Panorama* rather than *Opportunity Knocks*; in short a preference for the rather high-brow, 'serious' media tastes of teachers rather than the popular media offerings most avidly consumed by their pupils.

This movement had received its official imprimatur with the publication of the Newsom Report in 1963. In words directly echoing Crowther, the report spoke of the need for schools to provide a 'counterbalancing assistance' to the mass media, and, in a passage well known to all film teachers, of the necessity of discrimination:

We need to train children to look critically and discriminate between what is good and bad in what they see. They must learn to realize that many makers of films and of television programmes present false or distorted views of people, relationships, and experience in general, besides producing much trivial and worthless stuff made according to stock patterns.

By presenting examples of films selected for the integrity of their treatment of human values, and the craftsmanship with which they were made, alongside others of mixed or poor quality, we can not only build up a way of evaluating but also lead the pupils to an understanding of film as a unique and potentially valuable art form in its own right as capable of communicating depth of experience as any other art form.[27]

It has often been remarked that Newsom was of immense importance in encouraging the serious study of film in colleges and schools since 1963. Newsom's influence upon the serious study of television has been less rarely scrutinised. It is worth observing in the above quotation that while film *and* television are condemned for presenting 'false or distorted views', television mysteriously disappears when examples of integrity and craftsmanship are mentioned. The report, notice, recommends the *way* in which film studies might develop — as the study of an *art form* comparable with literature, music and painting. Such an approach clearly has its limitations when applied to television, for though the medium might be said to have produced original works of aesthetic merit, it serves many other diverse functions. Newsom then provided the impetus for the establishment of 'high culture' courses in film at the expense of a medium clearly a more potent influence upon pupils, and a more integral part of their experience. It initiated a trend from which schools and colleges have scarcely yet begun to recover. Paradoxically the effect of Newsom was to *arrest* the development of the study of television by linking film and television together and encouraging teachers to think of them both in aesthetic terms, by failing to acknowledge the diverse functions of television and by offering no guidelines to teachers on how television might be studied in order to foster discrimination.[28] When teachers began to glimpse some of the pitfalls awaiting them on this particular route it is little wonder that they became reluctant to take the journey.

Richard Hoggart's attempt to move beyond this position and to interpret discrimination within the media rather more sympathetically clearly illustrates the potency of the concept and the peculiar grip it contrived to hold even upon those educators who could recognise the class basis of the current formulations. Writing in the *Observer* in 1961 he observed the tendency to carry

> ... into new and confused areas of cultural activity, the old, comfortable grading by height of brow ... reinforced by an implied social or educational grading ... 'Mass culture' is that enjoyed by the 80 per cent who have not been to a grammar school ... The crucial distinctions today are not those between the *News of the World* and *The Observer*, between the Third Programme and the Light Programme ... between the Top Ten and a celebrity concert ... The distinctions we should be making are those between the *News of the World* and the *Sunday Pictorial*, between 'skiffle' and the Top Ten; and, for 'highbrows', between *The Observer* and the *Sunday Times*. This is to make distinctions ... which require an active discrimination, not the application of a fixed 'brow' or educational scale ... Our job is to separate the Processed from the Living at all levels ... Processed culture has its eye always on the audience, the consumers, the customers. Living culture has its eye on the subject, the material. It expects the same attention to the subject from the members of its audience. Processed culture asks: 'What will they take? Will this get most of them?' Living culture asks 'What is the truth of this experience and how can I capture it?'[29]

What Hoggart is arguing here is that old forms of discrimination did not really constitute active discrimination at all. They were rigid preformulated class judgements requiring 'the application of a fixed "brow" or educational scale.' Active discrimination on the other hand is classless and involves separating the Processed from the Living in each thing of its own kind. Hoggart's attempt to raise the concept of discrimination, Phoenix-like from its own ashes is based upon the assumption that class connotations have accreted around the word, and simply need to be hacked from it like limpets from a rock in order for the word to become serviceable again. It seems much more likely however that class consensi are incorporated within the word's denotative meaning, and are ultimately inseparable from it. To see why this is the case it is necessary to turn to a detailed consideration of the concept of discrimination itself.

Attention needs to be drawn at the outset to three important features of the word 'discrimination'. Most obviously — but almost crucially — it is, as Raymond Williams has recently pointed out, 'a split word with a positive sense for good and informed judgement but also a strong negative sense of unreasonable *exclusion* or unfair treatment of some outside groups'.[30] Indeed one meaning of the word still widely employed refers *only* to the process of treating certain groups unfairly.

Secondly, the word elevates and generalises specific personal responses and preferences to the status of evident social facts. An example: on radio, film critic Alexander Walker discussing the making of a controversial film on the sex life of Christ says that controversies rarely surround films of any significance. He can think of only two exceptions: *Last Tango in Paris* and *A Clockwork Orange*.

The extensive nature of the 'hidden' exclusions is worth noting here, particularly for those who have followed Walker's public battles with Ken Russell. But it is the confidence, authority and glibness of judgement to which I really want to draw attention. And to its *ordinariness*. This kind of statement is the stock-in-trade of critics of all descriptions. There are no qualifications of the 'It-seems-to-me' or 'In-my-view' variety; the personal judgement is presented as straightforward fact, so that the listener might be forgiven for believing that film criticism had established well-defined and widely agreed criteria of evaluation. That the reverse is true ought to guarantee a degree of tentativeness in judgement which is conspicuously absent from the pronouncements of critics, and not a few media teachers.

Thirdly, 'this form of social development of personal responses to the point where they could be represented as standards of judgement'[31] was dependent on the social authority and confidence of the class making the response and indeed upon the existence of a social consensus of particular evaluations. The odd thing about 'discrimination' is that it is still widely used, yet it is blood brother to words such as 'taste', 'cultivation' and 'sensibility' which have been made virtually obsolete by their clear class overtones and by the fragmentation of the evaluative consensus which legitimised them. Discriminatory approaches in mass-media teaching — even Hoggart's — assume the existence and validity of a bourgeois hegemony. In the classroom the authority which the teacher requires to make his preferences into judgements is provided by his social class and his education. He it is who decides what counts as discrimination and this remains true whether the struggle is between 'the shoddy and the worthwhile' of Whannel and Hall or 'the Processed and the Living' of Hoggart.

Those elements of exclusion and rejection which tend to be hidden in much of the talking and writing about discrimination *are its very cornerstones in practice.* And what is excluded and rejected, what is being discriminated against, are *inevitably* those aspects of popular culture which are valued and have a potent influence among large numbers of pupils. If this were not so — if the 'shoddy and debased' or 'the Processed' had no hold upon pupils — then discriminatory approaches would be unnecessary. Discriminatory teaching is premissed by the assumption that genuine differences are likely to exist between the teacher's view of what is Living and Processed, and the pupil's. (Again, if this were not so discriminatory teaching would be unnecessary.) These differences carry unequal weight in the classroom however. By the sleight of hand outlined above teacher views becomes discriminatory judgements, while pupil preferences, lacking either authority or an acceptable language code, remain at the low-level status of preferences.

Teaching discrimination therefore involves attacking the personal preferences of many pupils. It is a practice as socially divisive and individually destructive as attacks upon (i.e. attempts to 'improve') a pupil's language. A working-class pupil who has been taught discrimination has almost certainly also been taught that his own judgement is unreliable, and no basis for the development of aesthetic sensitivity. Taught to distrust or even despise the television programmes and magazines habitually watched or read at home, the danger is that he may come finally to despise his parents, friends and indeed himself. Fortunately I have seen no evidence to suggest that discrimination cuts very much ice with large numbers of comprehensive school pupils who obstinately persist in asserting the validity of their own tastes.

In addition to all this it needs to be said that there are particular problems associated with applying the notion of discrimination to the study of television. It is clearly an inappropriate tool for handling a good deal of television material: there seems little point in trying to discriminate between televised news bulletins, weather forecasts, football matches, race meetings, quiz programmes or chat shows. And even when it might seem to make sense — with plays or comedy series for example — how does one begin to do it?

Little consensus exists on what constitutes 'good' and 'bad' television, and attempts to erect and defend generally agreed criteria for judgement have been singularly unsuccessful.[32] Finally, any criteria which were widely agreed would have no universal validity but simply be part of that society's dominant ideology.[33]

It has been necessary to outline the historical development, and some of the theoretical problems and practical difficulties of teaching 'discrimination', for in spite of the recent development of alternative semiological approaches to media studies the concept continues to have a powerful hold upon the minds of educators.[34] Even commentators as sympathetic to the media and sensitive to the needs of pupils as Murdock and Phelps could say in 1973 that:

> In even the simplest, most mechanical production there may be something worth salvaging, and it is with this elementary act of salvage that any attempts to encourage appreciation and discrimination must begin. There will of course be a sizeable gap between the tastes and expriences of the pupils and those of the teachers. This is inevitable, given the differences in social class background, age and training. Nevertheless if teachers are prepared to understand their own experience of popular culture and to take seriously the judgments and discriminations of their pupils, then a constructive dialogue can begin.[35]

To see media education in terms of a somewhat desperate salvaging operation is hardly far removed from the old inoculation theories which Murdock and Phelps profess to deplore; nor is it likely to generate in teachers the high degree of commitment and energy necessary to establish the serious study of the media within the school curriculum. It is worth drawing attention too to a familiar theme in our analysis of discrimination — the way in which Murdock and Phelps manage to slide over the implications of exclusion and rejection inherent within a discriminatory approach. The final sentences of the quotation ironically suggest a final argument against the value of teaching discrimination. For the barriers to classroom dialogue which do exist within media studies are not only a result of the gap between teacher and pupil tastes and experiences, but grow inevitably out of the element of rejection of pupil tastes *and* the teacher's view of his task as salvage operation implicit in most discriminatory approaches. The writers are glimpsing what every practising teacher knows: that the objective of arriving at value judgements closes up rather than opens out discussion; that it is too *easy* to obtain evaluative responses from pupils, and thereafter too difficult to move beyond them; that as soon as a programme is evaluated as bad (or Processed) or good (or Authentic) then the impetus for further investigation disappears and is likely to be seen by pupils as an unnecessary 'pulling to pieces'; that evaluative responses force students to make individual stands and take personal positions, a more threatening procedure and ultimately one less productive of dialogue than say a systematic group exploration; that one of the keys to unlocking responses is to move students towards making statements which seem to them to have some validity, *irrespective* of their own personal feelings and tastes. If judgement can be suspended and mass-media material simply examined — *seen* more clearly — so that a wider and more complex range of meanings and values can become apparent, then discussion can flow and the necessity for discrimination, an irrelevance to the process of understanding, withers away.

The movement advocated here from appreciation to investigation is underpinned by a shift away from an elitist definition of *culture* — 'the best that has been thought and written in the world' — to a view of culture which is *descriptive* of the values manifest in the arts and institutions of a society and the behaviour of its groups and individuals. The gain is intellectual as well as obviously social and political. For under the first definition of culture very little can be said about a wide range of television programmes; they are simply 'trivial', 'processed' and unworthy of serious reflection. Yet such programmes all need elucidation, all need to be read as cultural texts, iconic in character, which can be decoded to reveal large numbers of meanings. The codings themselves will reveal and embody the ideology and professional practices of the broadcasting institutions, demonstrate the constructed and mediated nature of the 'normal' world of the programmes, and invite a comparison with other possible, but suppressed codings. It is with cultural criticism in this sense that the study of television should be concerned.

NOTES

1. Report of the British Film Institute/Society for Education in Film and

Television Conference on *Film and Television Studies in Secondary Education*, York University, 1976, pp. 39-40 (available from the British Film Institute).

2. Ibid., p. 29.

3. At the York conference cited above.

4. See G. Murdock and P. Golding, 'Communications: the continuing crisis', *New Society*, 25 April 1974, for a more detailed study of patterns of ownership and control.

5. My own classroom experience of the excellent *Viewpoint* series (Thames), for example, was that the programme dealing specifically with the business side of the media (Programme 8: *Show Business*) was one of the least popular with pupils.

6. See *Screen Education*, no. 16 (Autumn 1975).

7. R. Exton and H. Hillier, 'Film as industry in the ILEA 6th form film study course', *Screen Education*, no. 16 (Autumn 1975).

8. I. Gilmour and M. Walker, 'Film as industry in the G.C.E. mode III O level in film studies', *Screen Education*, no. 16 (Autumn 1975).

9. More light has been thrown on these matters by M. Alvarado and E. Buscombe, *Hazell: the Making of a TV Series*, (BFI/Latimer, 1978). If anything, the conclusions to be drawn from this study should make the reader even more circumspect in drawing his own conclusions. Alvarado and Buscombe, after covering every aspect of the production of the Hazell series, can say that 'in the process of production ... They [the production team] were trying to produce a show which they thought was entertaining, and then hoping that the audience would like it too. Doubtless there are people producing television programmes which they believe to be rubbish, but who do it because they can make a lot of money. As a general rule we did not think that this was the case on *Hazell*... A model of popular television which sees it either as cynical manipulation or a straightforward identity of tastes between producers and audience (though there must be cases of both) would be, based on our experience of Hazell, an over-simplification' (pp. 250-1).

10. The ILEA for example is making an outstanding attempt not only to co-ordinate but to develop television work in schools, whilst in Lincolnshire co-operation between the local authority and two local colleges of education has resulted in the setting up of television facilities which are widely used by local schools.

11. J. Bruner, *The Process of Education* (Harvard, 1960) pp. 12-13.

12. N. Keddie, 'What are the criteria for relevance?', *Screen Education*, no. 15 (Summer 1975) p. 4.

13. J.D. Halloran, 'Understanding television', *Screen Education*, no. 14 (Spring 1975).

14. S. Hood, 'Visual literacy examined' in B. Luckham (ed.), *Audio-Visual Literacy* (Proceedings of Sixth Symposium on Broadcasting Policy) University of Manchester, 1975.

15. R. Barthes, *The Rhetoric of the Image*, Working Papers in Contemporary Cultural Studies, Spring 1971, Birmingham University.

16. The precise nature of the media's ideological function has been the subject of much debate. Some writers — following Marx's, 'the ideas of the ruling class are in every epoch the ruling ideas' — identify the dominant ideology as the pattern of ideas and beliefs of the dominant class, a position which leads to a view of media products as monolithic expressions of ruling-class values. But as Sylvia Harvey has observed, 'The notion of a single ruling class ideology organising and uniting the organs of mass communication ignores both the presence of divisions within the ruling class and the extent to which the ideology of free speech does open up a space for progressive journalists and media practitioners' (*May 1968 and Film Culture*, BFI 1978). More recent Marxist thinking has therefore suggested a more complex view of ideology as a process through which ruling-class ideas become transmuted into 'natural' representations and common-sense notions. This development has been clarified by

Barthes' concept of Myth, but owes most to a resurgence of interest in the work of Gramsci whose concept of *hegemony* moved beyond notions of imposition of ruling-class ideas to an understanding of how a dominant class's definitions of reality come *by consent* to constitute the lived reality of a subordinate class and to define the limits of common-sense for that class and for society as a whole. Common-sense is, as Geoffrey Nowell-Smith has suggested, 'the way a subordinate class in society lives its subordination'. This view of ideology involves an obvious paradox. For common-sense is, in its own terms, by definition, un-ideological, apolitical. The process of ideology, therefore, works most crucially in the very area where its existence is most strenuously denied. It is to be understood, in Stuart Hall's words, 'not as what is hidden and concealed but precisely as what is most open, apparent, manifest ... the most obvious and "transparent" forms of consciousness which operate in our everyday experience and ordinary language: common-sense'.

17. See. N. Postman and C. Weingartner, *Teaching as a Subversive Activity* (Penguin, 1971) for a detailed discussion on the importance of questions in the school curriculum.

18. G. Murdock and G. Phelps, *Mass Media and the Secondary School* (Macmillan, 1973) Chapter 5.

19. *A Language for Life* (The Bullock Report) (HMSO, 1975) Chapter 2, Para. 5. The *difference* between viewing and classroom hours may surprise even television teachers. Bullock gives the average figure of 25 hours viewing per week for pupils between the ages of 5 and 14. This gives an annual total of 1300 viewing hours. Assuming that pupils between 5 and 14 are in the classroom for 4 1/2 hours each day (rounding down to discount time spent in assemblies, sports, etc.) and for 40 weeks each year, this gives an annual total of 900 hours spent in the classroom. *Children between 5 and 14 therefore on average spend 44 per cent more time watching television than they do in the classroom.*

20. P. Hartmann and C. Husband, 'The mass-media and racial conflict' in S. Cohen and J. Young, *The Manufacture of News*, (Constable, 1973).

21. *Report on Secondary Education* (Spens Report) (HMSO, 1938) pp. 222-3.

22. *15-18* (The Crowther Report) (HMSO, 1959) vol. I, para. 65-6.

23. F.R. Leavis and D. Thompson, *Culture and Environment* (Chatto and Windus, 1948) pp. 3-5.

24. D. Thompson, 'Introduction' to D. Thompson (ed.), *Discrimination and Popular Culture* (Penguin, 1964) p. 20.

25. S. Hall and P. Whannel, *The Popular Arts* (Hutchinson, 1964) p. 15.

26. Ironically in *The Popular Arts*, popular films (i.e. British and American films), invariably described as having major flaws, are generally seen as works to be discriminated against. Cinematic art resides not in the popular cinema at all but in foreign language films. The book is littered with sentences such as 'No one has to be defended against de Sica, Bergman or Antonioni' or '... we can understand the claims of Renoir, Bunuel, Kurosawa and Antonioni to this area of "high culture"'. And following a brief analysis of the films of John Ford we read that 'He is essentially a poet/craftsman rather than an intellectual, and he does not bring to the cinema the cultural equipment of a Bergman or a Bunuel. It is partly this which prevents him from being a major director' (p. 109).

27. *Half Our Future* (The Newsom Report): *A Report of the Central Advisory Council for Education (England)* (HMSO, 1963) paras. 475-6.

28. Newsom cannot be held solely responsible for this paradox. As I have suggested the report simply reflects the most progressive thinking about media in the early 1960s. Hall and Whannel's enormously influential *The Popular Arts*, for example, simply treats television as a crude and inferior form of cinema. See their analysis of *Z Cars* (esp. p. 127), the only popular series to receive even a qualified endorsement.

29. R. Hoggart in the *Observer*, 14 May 1961, reprinted as 'Culture — dead and

alive' in *Speaking to Each Other*, vol. One: *About Society* (Chatto and Windus, 1970) pp. 131-3.

30. R. Williams, *Keywords* (Fontana, 1976) p. 75.

31. Ibid.

32. See P. Abrams, *Radio and Television* in D. Thompson *Discrimination and Popular Culture* for a reminder and dramatisation of the difficulties involved in arriving at discriminatory criteria within broadcasting.

33. For 'each class has its own political and artistic criteria' (Mao Tse Tung).

34. For two recent examples see R. Cathcart, *Education through Time Machines, Dr. Who and Star Trek* in B. Luckham *Audio-visual Literacy*; and M.L. Scarborough, *The Educational Value of Non-Educational Television* (Independent Broadcasting Authority Research Report, 1973) p. 2.

35. G. Murdock and G. Phelps, *Mass Media*, p. 148.

SECTION 5

INFORMATION, DISSEMINATION AND INNOVATION

INTRODUCTION

One of the issues that runs through the contributions in this section is the balance between different aspects of communication research. For example, in his survey of issues in information science (which appears for the first time in this volume) Wilson stresses the importance of using both qualitative and quantitative methods in studying the collection of data. He is also at pains to demystify the term 'information science' by referring to its origins in (special) librarianship. The vast growth of technical and scientific data that occurred after World War Two and the lesser and later growth of social research, each posed the problem of effective retrieval of information. Wilson demonstrates the diversity and dynamism of research into information science, covering as it does the organisation, transfer, retrieval and utilization of data. Nevertheless, he is also conscious of its deficiencies, particularly in regard to how little is known about how information is used to improve performance in industry, commerce and elsewhere and thus how better to organize the availability of information.

That the concern with various behavioural aspects of scientific and technical communication and with the flow of information is not new is shown by Menzel's article written some 20 years ago. Menzel drew attention to a number of important points: the argument for examining systems of specific information and the publics that consume them (in contrast to the traditional bias of communications research towards mass media and mass publics); the desirability of taking a systematic view of the scientific communication in any discipline; the various channels by which messages are effectively transmitted; and the role of informal and unplanned communication in the transmission of scientific information. In addition, he emphasized the variety of things that science information systems are called upon to provide: not only and not always speed and comprehensiveness, but also the means by which to attract the notice of a scientist to relevant information not belonging to a field he sees as his own.

Several of these points can be applied to Hounsell's survey of the supply and demand for data in the field of education. As well as the sheer amount of material relevant to education, Hounsell refers to the variations in the direction and degree of demand for information by different sub-groups within education, and to the fact that some sub-groups are much better catered for than others, both in terms of signposting mechanisms and the wealth of information beyond the signposts. In Hounsell's view, we should be cautious about making global statements about educational information because each of the sub-groups seems to have its own concerns: 'a successful model of communication for one group may be quite inappropriate for another'.

Something of Hounsell's caution is exemplified by what Stenhouse has to say about 'the Teacher as a focus for research', though he states his case in a rather polemical way. Beginning with the premise that what he calls 'the variability of educational situations' is grossly underestimated, Stenhouse argues that experimental research based on sampling cannot tell teachers how to act. Though, according to Stenhouse, it is widely assumed in faculties of education that research is scientific and is concerned with general laws, he asserts that good teachers are not dependent on researchers: they do not need to be told what to do. Perhaps as a consequence, the idea of the 'teacher-as-researcher' has found some support in universities in opposition to what Stenhouse refers to as the 'stranglehold of the psycho-statistical type of research'.

A parallel to these opposites can be discerned in Hargreaves's analysis of 'the Rhetoric of School-Centred Innovation'. Hargreaves contrasts the centralizing tendency of curriculum change with school-centred innovation. He notes that whereas academics treat the former with a degree of suspicion, the latter is perceived by them much less critically: indeed, in his view it is regarded as the patron of 'teacher autonomy', which itself is seen as a cure for educational malaise. Hargreaves argues for an equally critical approach to be taken to school-centred innovation. In part, this circumspection is based on an alleged dearth of empirically based accounts of particular schemes. In part, it is based on there having been little attempt to define what is meant by 'participation' or 'consultation'. In addition, Hargreaves asks to what extent are terms associated with teacher autonomy (e.g. 'accountability') in reality central in origin? Several of the issues raised by Hargreaves such as those concerning appropriate methods of research and matters of inequality, have been encountered in previous contributions. For example, he believes that conclusions about decision making based on survey research generally and the questionnaire in particular, may be invalid or inaccurate. Finally, Hargreaves asks how far democracy is attainable within the school when many teachers have no access to many decisions taken in centres outside the school and less access to educational theory than do head-teachers?

5.1 Trends and Issues in Information Science — a General Survey

TOM WILSON

A. THE EMERGENCE OF 'INFORMATION SCIENCE' AS A FIELD OF RESEARCH

The average person probably has little awareness of the terms information science and information research. They are related to the activities of a particular professional group (or, given the propensity to schism, particular groups); literature on the subject is found in specialized journals and rarely in the popular press; and it is written, at times, in a professional jargon that deters readers.

Things may become clearer, however, if the word 'librarianship' is used. The word is appropriate because information science has developed out of librarianship and many of its research concerns are held in common with library research. The Institute of Information Scientists in the UK has approximately 2,000 members and half of these are also members of the Library Association. In 1985 a conference of all professional bodies in the fields of information science, librarianship, archives management, and records management was held: an event which indicates the essential unity of the issues and problems faced by the different groups.

The branch of librarianship out of which information science has developed is generally known as 'special librarianship'. This term covers the activities of those working in specialized libraries and information units in business, industry, scientific research, government and local government. Its origins lie in the growth of industrial research activity during and following the First World War. Aslib, originally the Association of Special Libraries and Information Bureaux, was founded in 1924 and an American organization concerned with similar areas of work, the American Documentation Institute (now the American Society for Information Science) was founded in 1937.

Special librarianship and 'documentation' received a boost during and after the Second World War, partly as a result of the regeneration of industry, partly out of a need to deal with vast quantities of industrial research and development documentation found in Germany, and partly as a result of the development of a new industry based on nuclear energy. That development resulted in such an increase in published reports and papers that a major new journal of summaries, *Nuclear Science Abstracts*, was established by the US Atomic Energy Agency (USAEA) to disseminate information about information.

Fresh impetus to the generation of scientific and technical information was given by the launch of the first Russian sputnik in 1957. The effect in the USA in particular was galvanic, leading to an upsurge in research activity and publication.

In both the nuclear energy field and in space technology research one feature caused problems for librarians in government and industry. This was the emergence of a relatively new form of publication, the research report. This form was not unknown in industry where internal research reports had always been produced by those firms with research and development departments. The new feature was the wider publication of such material. Sometimes the 'publication' was limited; for example, the United Kingdom Atomic Energy Authority restricted some reports to contractors in the industry. Both the UKAEA and the USAEA, however, maintained depository collections in major public libraries.

The main problem in handling the vastly increased output of scientific and technical information was how to identify the subject content for effective retrieval of the material from storage. What in libraries had been known as 'cataloguing and classification' became known as 'information storage and retrieval' and a new field of information research arrived. It continues to thrive.

More recently, during the Johnson administration in the USA (1963-1969), there was a great upsurge of social research associated with many aspects of social welfare and other issues. Much of this took the form of evaluation research on social programmes in the cities and, while not equal in scale to the volume of scientific information, the consequent growth of the literature was considerable and the semi-published report made its appearance in the social sciences. Both developments and related events in the United Kingdom and in the agencies of the United Nations resulted in an interest in research into similar problems of information use and information storage and retrieval as in science and technology.

Today, however, the systems[1] that are created and used to control and disseminate information in industry, in government and in education make use of yet another force for change — the computer. This is not the place for a complete account of the role of the computer in information science. The aim here is simply to draw attention to its impact and to that of 'information technology' — a term which embraces computers, telecommunication systems, new means of storing information such as compact discs, and of communicating information such as teletext and viewdata systems.

Since the Second World War, therefore, there has been a series of continuing pressures on libraries and information systems as a result of the developments noted above. The field of information science has evolved as a consequence of these pressures and research in the field aims to help in adapting systems to the pressures.

B. THE PHENOMENA STUDIED — WHAT IS 'INFORMATION'?

'Information' is such a widely used word, such a commonsensical word, that it may seem surprising that it has given 'information scientists' so much trouble over the years. The problem stems from seeking to discriminate among related words such as 'data', or 'knowledge' or even 'wisdom'! In dictionary definitions these terms are associated as these extracts from the Random House Dictionary show:

1. Knowledge communicated or received concerning a particular fact or circumstance; news ...
6. (In communication theory) an indication of the number of possible choices of messages ...
7. Computer Technol. any data that can be coded for processing by a computer or similar device.

The same dictionary suggests data, facts, intelligence, advice as synonyms for information.

The definition used in this paper, then, will be that 'information' is an abstract noun, signifying some single fact or datum, or set of facts or data, which may be organized or not. Sometimes the abstract noun is used to signify concrete things which may be said to 'carry' information, such as books, journals, tape recordings, and visual media such as video recordings, maps, photographs, etc.

Some writers in information science, however, have not been satisfied to treat 'information' as a noun but have tried to define it as a *process* — the process whereby facts and data are integrated into existing knowledge or transformed into organized bodies of knowledge. This seems to do violence to the language. The processes whereby data and facts are transformed into knowledge are the processes of perception, cognition and understanding. They are almost entirely mysterious to us, having resisted the most serious scientific investigation. Indeed, consciousness itself is not yet clearly understood. To use the term 'information' to signify some cloudy set of terms in an attempt to give more solidity to the nature of information science hardly seems helpful.

Other writers have carefully defined what *they* mean by 'information' in carrying out their research. The most popular definitions of this kind relate information to decision-making in a form such as, 'Information is that which removes uncertainty'. Clearly, this is a *formal* definition because we all know that in the real world outside the experiment or the simulation we frequently receive communications of facts, data, news, or whatever which leave us more confused than ever. Under the formal definition these communications contain *no* information — party political broadcasts, perhaps.

C. INFORMATION SCIENCE AND ITS CHANGING SCOPE

What constitutes 'information science' is as much of a problem as the nature of information — naturally, since one depends upon the other. The definition used here is based on that given above:

> Information science is the study of the generation, organization, transfer, and utilization of information. It is concerned with the nature of information in general, with the channels or 'carriers' of information, and with the information user. It is concerned with all aspects of the design and evaluation of information systems and services, from public libraries to computer-based information retrieval systems.

As noted earlier, information science emerged originally out of the pressures placed on libraries and information services by the explosion of scientific and technical information. That bias exists to this day. Although research in information retrieval may now be concerned with such things as how children ask questions in libraries (Wanting, 1984) or how to devise a computer-based online catalogue for fiction (Pejtersen, 1984) there is a tendency for the literature to be very much concerned with scientific and technical information problems. This is partly a consequence of the dominance of scientific research over social science research in the scale of funding and in consequent publication. Some problems in scientific information have also been of continual interest, particularly those having to do with chemistry where chemical formulae and chemical structures lend themselves to highly structured methods of retrieval.

The emergence of social science from its original neglect in favour of scientific information can be dated in the USA to 1950 and the University of Chicago (1950) report on bibliographical services in the social sciences. This beginning, however, was not followed immediately by research into problems of access to information, or different patterns of information-seeking behaviour. Interest in bibliographical aspects, that is, in the compilation of bibliographies and other guides to the social science literature, continued, however (for example, Boehm, 1965; de Gazia, 1965).

In the UK the beginnings can be dated to the start of the INFROSS (Information Requirements of Social Scientists) project in 1967. In the course of the INFROSS project Maurice Line and his colleagues surveyed the information-seeking behaviour of (chiefly) academic social scientists, and carried out a number of subsidiary studies (Bath University, 1971; Line, 1971).

INFROSS was followed in 1971 by DISISS (Design of Information Systems for the Social Sciences) which was concerned chiefly with the growth of social science literature in a variety of fields, with the coverage of this literature by the abstracting and indexing services, and with implications for the planning of services (Bath University, 1980; Line 1981).

During the INFROSS/DISISS period there were two major developments in bibliographic services to social scientists: the ERIC service (Marron, 1968) which covered information resources for education and drew upon the large volume of research commissioned by the US Government, and the extension of the Institute for Scientific Information's citation indexing[2] into the social sciences (Garfield, 1972). In its early years the ERIC service attracted a good deal of comment, particularly on the quality of its indexing, and the entire service was subject to an intensive evaluation. The *Social Sciences Citation Index* built upon the strength of its predecessor in science, and both services were quick to take advantage of that other development of the period, the computer.

The terminology of the social sciences has always presented problems in information retrieval: not only does it use ordinary words in a technical fashion (for example, 'class') but some of its technical terms, like 'bureaucracy', have changed their meaning subtly in common usage. As a result, a search may result in a set of documents which includes a large number of items which deal with, say, bureaucracy, but not in the sense anticipated by the user. An additional difficulty is that adherents of different philosophical or ideological schools use the same term in different ways or with different associations. These issues were raised in connection with the ERIC service (Eller and Panek, 1968), were reviewed by Foskett (1963) and were the subject of research in relation to the sociology of education (Swift, Winn and Bramer, 1979).

Since 1967, therefore, there has been a growing awareness that the social sciences have information problems which are related to those in science and technology, in that they are the result of a similar 'information explosion'. The problems differ, however, because social scientific research differs from that in pure science. For example, controlled experiment is difficult, if not impossible, in social research. Directions of research may be more directly influenced by political considerations (witness Sir Keith Joseph's attempt to dispose of the Social Science Research Council). And society and its constituents are continually changing in character, whereas, generally, the phenomena studied by science are more stable in their structures — a molecule of hydrogen a century from now is likely to look very much the same as today's, while the nature of, say, the education system of the country could well be quite different. (See Brittain, 1979, for a review.)

Following the studies of the academic researcher in the social sciences, attention in the UK has focused upon the information problems of what might be called 'applied social sciences'. This era began with the study of local authority planning departments and planners in 1974 (White) and was followed by a major five-year project in the field of social services — Project INISS: Information Needs and Information Services in Local Authority Social Services Departments (Wilson & Streatfield, 1977; Wilson, Streatfield & Mullings, 1979; Streatfield & Wilson, 1980), and, simultaneously, by studies in education (Hounsell, *et al.* 1979). Subsequently, work was carried out in other local government departments (Grayson, 1978; Wilson, 1980a; Mullings, Francis & Wilson, 1980). In the USA over the same period the major project was probably URBANDOC (Sessions, 1971).

During the same period as the increase in interest in the social sciences took place there was a similar movement in relation to the citizen-at-large. In the 1930s there had been an interest in 'library surveys' culminating in an extensive review of the subject by McDiarmid (1940). At the end of the Second World War a major report on the public library user was carried out and reported on by Berelson (1949). In an attempt to provide a sound conceptual base for the study of the general information user the US Department of Health, Education and Welfare funded a study in Baltimore — Information Needs of Urban Residents (1973). This laid the ground for other studies in Syracuse (Gee, 1974), Seattle (Dervin *et al.*, 1976/77), Maryland's Eastern Shore (Eidleman, 1979), South Carolina (Barron and Curran, 1979), California (Palmour *et al.*, 1979) and New England (Chen and Hernon, 1982). There has been no investigation in the UK approaching the scale of these studies.

It is important to note that virtually none of the work carried out in the UK could have been done without the existence of the Office for Scientific and Technical Information and its successor the British Library Research and Development Department, which has the status of a research council for the field. Its resources have always been very restricted compared with other councils such as the SERC and the ESRC but there has been quite a high return on its investment in the shape of actual innovation, particularly in the adoption of computers for library tasks, as well as publication.

D. CHANGING RESEARCH PERSPECTIVES

Whether one is concerned with the information behaviour of scientists or with that of social scientists it is clear that in either case social research methods will be employed. In the period immediately after the Second World War, the model of social research employed by those researching the information behaviour of scientists was based on the then prevailing idea of quantitative research in social science, that is, the use of large-scale surveys intended to collect large amounts of data from which generalizations amounting to 'laws' similar to those in science could be derived. This is understandable: those who carried out the work were likely to be scientists themselves and they saw their task as very much concerned with the description of identifiable aspects of behaviour. The work (such as that reported in the proceedings of the Royal Society Scientific Information Conference (Royal Society, 1948)) was also restricted almost entirely to a consideration of the sources and channels of communication used. There was little or nothing on the use made of information in scientific research or on the individual patterns of behaviour in information seeking.

The result of this methodological limitation was that progress towards some theoretical understanding of the concept of 'information need'[3] was slow. This fact was recognized by virtually every commentator on the subject from Menzel (1960) onwards. Generally, reviewers of the field have expressed disappointment in the results. The disappointment can be attributed in part to poorly chosen methods but also to:

   — a failure to realize how expensive survey research is, if done properly;

   — a consequent failure to do it properly because of insufficient funding;

   — lack of adequate insight into user behaviour before devising research instruments;

   — inappropriate choice of self-completed questionnaires as the data-collection method with resulting low response rates when the proper preparation and follow-up procedures (Robin, 1965) are not used;

   — lack of adequate theoretical frameworks to guide research;

   — lack of interviewer training and interview performance assessment resulting in data of unknown quality; and

   — use of library or information system perspectives on information use which may not be held by the people under investigation. (Wilson, 1980b)

As long ago as 1965 William Paisley commented on the lack of case studies in the field in his review of the literature (Paisley, 1965). In other words, the need for a more qualitative approach, that is one which would recognize the subjectivity of information use and the need to generate hypotheses about behaviour rather than simply test other people's ideas about behaviour, was recognized early. Little was done in response to this call, however, and the early researchers in the field of information studies in the social sciences followed the path set out by the earlier researchers in science information studies. Thus, although the INFROSS team carried out a small number of interviews, its approach was that of large-scale, quantitative data-collection using a lengthy self-completed questionnaire.

In the 1970s, however, reflecting the increased awareness of the value of qualitative approaches in sociology, other researchers began to adopt more 'naturalistic', 'ethnographic', or phenomenological approaches.[4] Reports on some of these constituted part of a special issue of *Social Science Information Studies* in 1981. Lawrence Stenhouse discussed the use of case studies in a project concerned with library use and access in academic sixth-forms noting that: 'Researchers have turned to case-study in the face of the difficulties which have been encountered in attempting to apply a scientific paradigm of research to problems in which human behaviour, action or intention play a large part.' (Stenhouse, 1981: 221)

Harris, in the same symposium, reported on an 'illuminative evaluation' strategy (Harris, 1981). This was employed in an action research project designed to produce teaching materials for the education of information users. Harris drew upon the work of Parlett and Hamilton (1976) and commented that: '[Illuminative evaluation] provided a convincing argument against the classic social science research model ... It underlined the need to examine a wider range of contextual and environmental determinants of the success or otherwise of an education innovation.' (Harris, 1981: 251)

Earlier, in the same journal, Wilson and Streatfield had written on the use of structured observation in Project INISS and had noted that:

> ... all methods of investigation are ultimately based upon observation. Either the individual observes his own behaviour and his own perceptual states and reports upon them within

more or less artificially constrained frameworks (interview schedules, questionnaires, diary record sheets) or records of his
information-seeking behaviour are kept (e.g. book issue
records) from which deductions about the underlying needs are
made. (Wilson and Streatfield, 1981: 174)

Wilson also contributed to the qualitative methods symposium and
in his paper on Project INISS commented that: '. . . if anything is to
be learned from the work, it is that a more sensitive approach to
the collection of data and accounts will pay dividends in insights,
theory, and practical ideas for improvements in information
services'. (Wilson, 1981: 245)

In their concluding comments on the symposium the issue editors
noted: 'It would be mistaken in our view, to see qualitative
approaches as competing with quantitative ones. For many
purposes indeed it would be both appropriate and desirable to use
qualitative and quantitative approaches in combination so that
each can compensate for the weaknesses of the other.' (Hounsell
and Winn, 1981: 255)

This author heartily concurs in that view.

E. RELATIONS WITH OTHER FIELDS

The relationship between librarianship and information science has
been discussed earlier and, in terms of the field of practice to
which information science relates, this is probably the closest
association. Nor would one wish to draw an artificial distinction
between research and practice. However, it is possible to look at
the relationships between information science and other fields of
research.

We can begin by considering the definition quoted earlier and,
hence, by dividing the discussion into three parts: the generation of
information, the organization and handling of information, and the
transfer and utilization of information. In an essay such as this it
would be inappropriate to deal with the literature in detail but in
the paragraphs below one or two references are given for those
with specific interests.

In the case of the first of these there are strong links between
information science issues and related issues in the sociology of
knowledge, the sociology of science, and the sociology of various

professional fields. One area of considerable interest is that which links 'bibliometrics' to research 'performance'. Bibliometrics is the study of statistical regularities in various aspects of information generation and use. It has its origins in a study by Bradford (1948) which revealed the statistical distribution of periodicals borrowed from the Science Museum Library. The so-called 'Bradford's Law of Scattering'[5] was subsequently found to exist among citations to journals and with the advent of the *Science Citation Index* a great deal of work ensued on showing the universality of the 'law'. The idea has been misused (in this author's opinion) in seeking to show a relationship between the quality of a journal or of a particular scientist and the extent to which that journal or scientist is cited by others.

The second area, that of the organization and handling of information, is closely related to computer science. Although early work in information retrieval was closely associated with library classification and cataloguing, more recently it has become strongly identified with the use of computer systems. Thus, most library 'housekeeping' functions, such as book ordering, cataloguing, book issue, and journal ordering and receipt systems, are now computer-based. In addition, the retrieval of information from large files of computer records is now a commonplace and an event such as the International Online Meeting in London can attract thousands of visitors to its exhibition to see the latest offerings from companies providing such services (Williams, 1979). The actual retrieval mechanisms used in such systems are relatively crude, compared with the present state of knowledge and research in the field, but changes are taking place continually and as older computers are replaced and as novel computer architectures become more commercially viable the changes are likely to increase apace. Part of the information retrieval problem has close associations also with linguistics and computational linguistics. One continual problem has been the cost of 'indexing', that is, using human beings to select words and phrases to identify the subject content of documents. One solution has been so-called 'free-text searching', whereby the choice of words is made the responsibility of the searcher. The disadvantage here is that the words chosen by the searcher may not be a complete match for those used in the documents. One answer to this may be the development of more sophisticated computer systems based on the analysis of natural language (for a comprehensive survey of the indexing problem see Soergel, 1974).

As regards the transfer and utilization of information, the links with other fields are diverse. For example, early work in the field of public opinion which led to the idea of 'opinion leaders' in the community has been replicated in the study of communication networks in scientific research laboratories, leading to the analogous idea of 'gatekeepers' (Allen and Cohen, 1969). Project INISS also paid specific attention to the communication activities in organizations and drew on that literature, and related the study of information use to other aspects of the ordinary day-to-day work of people in organizations. In doing so the researchers acknowledged debts to such as Schutz (1946; 1970) and Berger and Luckmann (1966) for the relevance of the phenomenological viewpoint in studying the subjective aspects of the role of information in organizational life. The subject of the utilization of information is clearly closely related to that of the diffusion of innovations and technology transfer and a number of studies have dealt with this area (Robertson, 1973; Rothwell, 1975; Shuchman, 1980).

A special sub-set of problems relates to the economics of information. The emergence of this as a subject for research has had a great deal to do with the economic recession. Libraries and information systems have been called upon more and more to justify their activities in economic terms and the idea of 'cost/benefit' equations applied to information services gained some currency in the 1970s (Martyn and Flowerdew, 1983). The problem has proved virtually intractable, however. The chief problem lies in the nature of information: there is no standard measure of information according to which we can say that a person has become 'informed' to such-and-such a degree. What informs one, fails to inform another — what is news to one is old news to another. Researchers have also failed at times to distinguish between the 'exchange value' of information and its 'value-in-use'.[6] We may be able to evolve methods for determining exchange value, largely in terms of willingness to pay for information, but quantifying the value-in-use is likely to be a more difficult problem.

For a useful set of papers which demonstrates the links between information science and many other fields the reader is referred to a double issue of *Social Science Information Studies* volume 4, numbers 2 and 3, 1984, which reprinted the papers of the seminar on the psychological aspects of information searching.

5. CONCLUSION — FUTURE DIRECTIONS

It may be seen from this essay that information science is a very diverse, and very active, area of research. Whether it can be called a discipline is another matter, and whether it will have the resilience of the true disciplines of science is yet another matter. It may certainly be called a multi-disciplinary field and there is room for many different approaches to the problems with which it deals. Certain areas of research, however, may disappear into what might be called 'parent disciplines'. It seems that as workers in a particular area of research gain maturity and deeper understanding of their subject they draw more and more upon the theories and methods of these parents. When those in the parent discipline also become aware of interesting research issues in the field of information science, to which they can apply their own models, theories and methods, there is a tendency for the subject to be acknowledged as part of the parent discipline.

The increased interest of those in computer science in the problems of information retrieval is a case in point. When information scientists first began to be involved in this area the number of computer scientists who were working in the field was very small. Today the subject is a standard part of many computer science curricula.

As yet, however, there has been no great tendency for the social sciences to take over parts of information science. The economics of information is regarded as a research topic in economics but many other areas discussed above appear to hold little interest for those in the parent disciplines. There are exceptions to the rule, of course, but their solitary appearance in their fields proves rather than contradicts the rule.

In fact most of the areas to which social scientific knowledge, theories, models and methods have been applied remain interesting research areas. Little is known about how information is used to help in the performance of research, or innovation in industry, or the performance of work in business, or many other areas. How information from sources such as books, journals and library systems fits into the general information environment of an individual is still open to investigation. More remains to be done on the effectiveness of methods of disseminating information. The problem of effective storage and retrieval of information requires more work. The relationship of indexing and classification to

linguistics have been explored but answers which are useful in
practice await further understanding of human linguistic processes.
In other words, we are likely to see the field surviving and thriving
for some time to come.

NOTES

1. System: a general term signifying the set of related elements defined as
making up any whole. Thus, an information system may be thought of as comprising
such elements as the information resources, in the form of books and journals, the
technical means for acquiring and making such resources available for use — such as
the book-buying sub-system, and human resources in the form of specialist staff,
often divided into categories relating to different levels of service to different kinds of
user.
2. Citation indexing: a method for identifying documents which relies not upon
the use of subject terms but upon the fact of their citation by others in the scholarly
literature. Thus, knowing of a paper by Brown on, say, the politics of new religious
sects, one can find related papers by discovering who has cited Brown in later work,
or who has cited some of the same writers as cited by Brown. This principal is put
into practice in the Institute for Scientific Information's *Social Science Citation
Index*, and *Science Citation Index*.
3. Information need: a troublesome term in information science; dispute exists
as to the differences between 'needs', 'wants', and 'demands', with various
elaborations such as 'perceived need', 'expressed wants', etc. Used here the term is
taken to mean anything which motivates information-seeking behaviour, thereby
sidestepping the problems!
4. Naturalistic, etc.: used generally to describe social research methods which
rely upon a phenomenological approach, seeking to take account of the meaning of
acts as perceived by the actors themselves.
5. Bradford's Law: mathematical formulation of the observed phenomenon that
a small number of journals in any field accounts for a high proportion of all citations
in that field.
6. Exchange value, etc.: exchange value is simply the value of a product or
service in terms of 'units of exchange', i.e. money. 'Information' is very difficult to
value in this way because different individuals may find the same information more
or less useful. That is, the same information, whatever the price it is sold at, may have
different 'values in use' for different users.

REFERENCES

Allen, T.J. and Cohen, S.I. (1969) 'Information flow in research and development
    laboratories'. *Administrative Science Quarterly, 14*, 12-20.
Barron, D. and Curran, C. (1979) *Information need assessment of rural groups for
    library program development.* Columbia, SC: University of South Carolina.
Bath University Library (1971) *Information requirements of researchers in the social
    sciences.* 2 vols. Bath: University Library.
Bath University Library (1980) *Towards the improvement of social science
    information systems: overview of research carried out 1971-1975.* Bath:
    University Library.
Berelson, B. (1949) *The library's public.* New York: Columbia University.

Berger, P.L. and Luckman, T. (1966) *The social construction of reality.* London: Allen.

Boehm, E.H. (1965) *Blueprint for bibliography; a system for the social sciences and humanities.* Santa Barbara, Cal.: Clio press.

Bradford, S.C. (1948) *Documentation.* London: Crosby Lockwood.

Brittain, J.M. (1979) 'Information services and the structure of knowledge in the social sciences'. *International Social Science Journal 31*, 711-728.

Chen, C-C. and Hernon, P. (1982) *Information Seeking: assessing and anticipating user needs.* New York: Neal-Schuman.

de Grazia, A. (1965) 'The Universal Reference System'. *American Behavioral Scientists, 8* (8), 3-14.

Dervin, B. *et al.* (1976/77) *The development of strategies for dealing with the information needs of urban residents.* Seattle, WA: University of Washington, School of Communication.

Eidleman, M.L. (1979) *Information and referral services for residents of Maryland eastern shore (3 counties).* Baltimore, Md.: Maryland State Department of Education.

Eller, J.L. and Panek, R.L. (1968) 'Thesaurus development for a decentralized information network'. *American Documentation, 19,* 213-220.

Foskett, D.J. (1963) *Classification and indexing in the social sciences.* London: Butterworth.

Fry, B. (1972) *Evaluation study of ERIC products and services. Final report.* 4 vols. Bloomington: Indiana University.

Garfield, E. (1972) 'The new *Social Sciences Citation Index* (SSCI) will add a new dimension to research on man and society', *in*: Garfield, E. *Essays of an information scientist,* vol. 1. Philadelphia, Pa.: Institute for Scientific Information. p. 317-319.

Gee, G.M. (1974) *Urban information needs: a replication.* Syracuse, N.Y.: Syracuse University.

Grayson, L. (1978) *Library and information services for local government in Great Britain.* London: Library Association.

Harris, C. (1981) 'The Travelling Workshops experiment: an attempt at "illuminative evaluation"'. *Social Science Information Studies, 1,* 247-253.

Hounsell, D., Martin, E. and Needham, G. (1979) 'Information and the teacher'. *Education Libraries Bulletin, 22* (1), 1-26.

Hounsell, D. and Winn, V. (1981) 'Concluding remarks'. *Social Science Information Studies, 1,* 255-256.

Line, M.B. (1971) 'The information uses and needs of social scientists: an overview of INFROSS'. *Aslib Proceedings, 23,* 412-434.

Line, M.B. (1981) 'The structure of social science literature as shown by large-scale citation analysis'. *Social Science Information Studies, 1,* 67-87.

McDiarmid, E.W. (1940) *The library survey: problems and methods.* Chicago: American Library Association.

Marron, H. (1968) 'ERIC: a national network to disseminate educational information'. *Special Libraries, 59,* 775-782.

Martyn, J. and Flowerdew, A.D.J. (1983) *The economics of informtion.* London: British Library. (Library and information research report 17).

Menzel, H. (1960) *Review of studies in the flow of information among scientists.* 2 vols. New York: Columbia University.

Mullings, C., Francis, G.M. and Wilson, T.D. (1980) *A manual for the investigation of local government information needs.* London: British Library R & D Department.

Palmour, V.E., Rathbun, P.F., Brown, W.H., Dervin, B. and Dowd, P.M. (1979) *Information needs of Californians: summary report.* Rockville, MD: King Research.

422   TOM WILSON

Parlett, M. and Hamilton, D. (1976) 'Evaluation as illumination', *in*: Tawney, D. *ed. Curriculum evaluation today: trends and implications.* London: Macmillan.

Pejtersen, A.M. (1984) 'Design of a computer-aided user-system dialogue based on an analysis of users' search behaviour.' *Social Science Information Studies, 4,* 167-183.

Robertson, A. (1973) 'Information flow and industrial innovation'. *Aslib Proceedings, 25,* 130-139.

Rothwell, R. (1975) 'Patterns of information flow during the innovation process'. *Aslib Proceedings, 27,* 217-226.

Royal Society (1948) *Royal Society Scientific Information Conference, London, 1946. Report and papers submitted.* London: Royal Society.

Schutz, A. (1946) 'The well-informed citizen: an essay on the social distribution of knowledge'. *Social Research, 13,* 463-478.

Schutz, A. (1970) *On phenomenology and social relations: selected writings, edited and with an introduction by Helmut R. Wagner.* Chicago: University of Chicago Press.

Sessions, V.S. (1971) *URBANDOC/ a bibliographic information system.* 3 vols. New York: City University.

Shuchman, H.L. (1980) *Information transfer in engineering.* Glastonbury, CT: The Futures Group.

Soergel, D. (1974) *Indexing languages and thesauri: construction and maintenance.* Los Angeles: Melville.

Stenhouse, L. (1981) 'Using case study in library research'. *Social Science Information Studies, 1,* 221-230.

Streatfield, D.R. and Wilson, T.D. (1980) *The vital link: information in social services departments.* Sheffield: Community Care and the Joint Unit for Social Services Research.

Swift, D.F., Winn, V.A. and Bramer, D.A. (1979) 'A sociological approach to the design of information systems'. *Journal of the American Society for Information Science, 30,* 215-223.

University of Chicago. *Graduate library school and division of social science.* (1950) 'Bibliographical services in the social sciences'. *Library Quarterly, 20,* 79-100.

Wanting, B. (1984) 'How do children ask questions in children's libraries? Concepts of visual and auditory perception and language expression.' *Social Science Information Studies, 4,* 217-234.

White, B. (1974) *Information for planning.* Edinburgh: University of Edinburgh, Department of Urban Design and Regional Planning.

Williams, M.E. (1979) ed *Computer-readable data bases: a directory and data sourcebook.* Washington, DC: American Society for Information Science.

Wilson, T.D. (1980a) *Current awareness services and their value for local government.* Paper for the 40th FID Congress, Copenhagen, August 18th-21st.

Wilson, T.D. (1980b) 'On information science and the social sciences'. *Social Science Information Studies, 1,* 5-12.

Wilson, T.D. (1981) 'A case study in qualitative research?'. *Social Science Information Studies, 1,* 241-246.

Wilson, T.D. and Streatfield, D.R. (1977) 'Information needs in local authority social services departments: an interim report on Project INISS'. *Journal of Documentation, 33,* 277-293.

Wilson, T.D. and Streatfield, D.R. (1977) 'Information needs in local authority social services departments: an interim report on Project INISS', *Journal of* 173-184.

Wilson, T.D., Streatfield, D.R. and Mullings, C. (1979) 'Information needs in local authority social services departments: a second report on Project INISS'. *Journal of Documentation, 35,* 120-136.

5.2 Scientific Communication: Five Sociological Themes

HERBERT MENZEL*

The recent upsurge of interest in the behavioral aspects of scientific and technical communication and information flow has two distinct sources, a theoretical one in the development of communication research, and a practical one in the concerns of policy makers in scientific organizations and information services.

For some time past, the attention of sociologists and social psychologists studying communication processes, once focused on so-called mass phenomena and mass publics, has turned to the interplay of communication processes with more and more definitely delineated and mapped aspects of social structure. One aspect of this shift in interest has been in the increasing attention paid by behavioral scientists to the systems supplying information of a specialized sort, and to the publics which are consumers of this specialized information. The scientific and applied professions have been most prominent among the publics so studied.

At the same time those concerned with the planning of science information policy have become increasingly interested in so-called 'user studies' as possible sources of guidance. For a decade or two, as the mushrooming of the scientific enterprise has led to a multifold increase in the supply of scientific information as well as in the demand for such information on the part of scientists and technologists, the adequacy of the science information system whose task it is to link this supply and this demand has become a matter of increasing concern. A multitude of astonishing new services has been introduced into the system, alleviating some of the concerns, but also generating new questions of optimal allocation of resources and even giving rise to some additional strains in the information system itself. Concerns have led to attempts at planning and these have, after some lag, more recently led to demands

*Source: *American Psychologist*, 21 (1966), 999-1004 (reprinted by permission of the American Psychological Association and the author).

in some quarters that the information needs of science be ascertained as a basis for wise planning. While some have asked that the scientist users of scientific information be studied in order to ascertain these needs, others have countered that these needs can better be estimated by those who are experts in information handling. Both proponents and critics of the so-called 'user study' approach have often confused it with opinion polling — that is, with quizzing scientists on what should be done (see Menzel, 1959a, 1964; Shaw, 1959).

Actually, studies of the information-gathering behavior and experiences of scientists have been going on, in one form or another, for at least 20 years (reviewed in Paisley, 1965). Behavioral scientists have taken some part in this work for about 10 years. Many of the studies have been quite primitive in the techniques of data gathering, simplistic in the conceptualization of variables and research goals, poor in comparability, and questionable in generalizability. But although many of the shortcomings remain, sounder and more sophisticated approaches have increasingly been used, with an especially gratifying concentration in the last 3 years or so (Menzel, 1966c). Outstanding among these most recent accomplishments is the Project on Scientific Information Exchange in Psychology of the American Psychological Association (1963, 1965), which has refined and innovated research techniques and has used them in a battery of studies giving comprehensive coverage to the communication situation in a discipline. It has drawn together the results in a process model which has suggested several policy changes and has aided in the choice between them. Recent highlights from this work are reported in other articles in this issue of the *American Psychologist.*

Enough of this work has now accumulated to make it possible to discern certain themes which emerge with increasing insistence as the sophistication of the studies advances. A discussion of five of these interrelated themes will constitute the bulk of this paper. The selection of these particular themes was, no doubt, influenced by the author's sociological bias, but it is believed that they warrant special attention in the interest of both practical and theoretical advances in the field of science communication research.

ACTS OF SCIENTIFIC COMMUNICATION CONSTITUTE A SYSTEM

The first of these themes is that of the desirability of taking a systematic view of the scientific communication in any discipline. It is necessary to look upon any one arrangement, institution, facility, or policy for scientific and professional communication as a component of the total system of scientific communication for a profession, a system which includes *all* the provisions, *all* the publications, *all* the facilities, *all* the occasions and arrangements, and *all* the customs in the discipline that determine how scientific messages are transmitted.[1]

The systemic view, however, means more than comprehensiveness with regard to the channels and mechanisms encompassed. Thus, for example, it also seems useful to conceive of the flow of scientific information as a set of interaction processes in a social system. The information-receiving actions of any one individual often involve several of his roles (as researcher, teacher, consultant, editorial referee, etc.) and approaches to several different channels, including individuals standing in diverse relationships to him and serving now as sources, now as relays, of information. The scientists who generate and use the information in a given discipline can therefore be usefully looked upon as interconnected publics.

Furthermore, it is necessary to be comprehensive with regard to the varied functions served by the science information system. And finally, it is necessary to be comprehensive in the delineation of transactions of scientific information, for these frequently involve much more than a single encounter between a scientist and some one communication channel.

The systemic view is urged upon us by a number of considerations. One cannot obtain a true picture of what the functions of the science communication system are, how often the need for each function arises, and how well each is performed, unless one considers all the channels through which scientific information travels. Conversely, one cannot obtain a true picture of the significance of any particular channel or arrangement unless one considers all the information functions that it may perform. Changes and innovations introduced in any one component of the system will have their consequences on the utilization and efficacy of other components. (This is made very clear in APA, 1965, pp. 127-140.) Numerous transactions of scientific information within a public of scientists may have to be considered before aggregate regularities and patterns are revealed behind what appears to be accidental and idiosyncratic in the individual case (Menzel, 1959b). And finally, even the effective transmission of a single message to an individual scientist may involve a multitude of contacts with diverse channels extending over a period of time — a topic to which we now turn.

SEVERAL CHANNELS MAY ACT SYNERGISTICALLY TO BRING ABOUT THE EFFECTIVE TRANSMISSION OF A MESSAGE

Any given transaction between a scientist as a receiver of information and the channel that brings him that information usually has a history behind it and a future ahead of it that may be very relevant to the evaluation of the success of that transaction and to the prognosis of whether this kind of transaction will happen again with similar results.

Often one channel of communication calls attention to a message to be found in another; sometimes a third channel is required to locate the precise document in which the message is contained; frequently one or more persons serve as relays between the source of a message and its ultimate consumer; and contacts at each intervening step may be initiated now by the receiver, now by the bringer of the message. The events which thus interplay are often distributed over a period of time. The possible relevance of a message to a man's work may not become apparent at the time it is first received, but only when that same message is repeated, sometimes more than once, or when it is put together with other information yet to be received, or when changes occur and needs come up in the course of the scientist's own future work.

In fact, not only an individual scientist, but an entire scientific community may for years turn its back on some already published and significant piece of work, until it is 'brought home' by repetition, appearance in new media, rediscovery in new contexts, or other supplementary messages. Information must often be publicized repeatedly or through diverse channels before it will enter the stream of communications which will lead it to its ultimate user; and from the point of view of the consumer of information, it is frequently necessary to be exposed to the information repeatedly before it will make an impact (Menzel, 1958, pp. 14-

17, 32-49, 92-124). Much of this crucial multiple exposure is brought about in informal ways, largely through contacts between individual scientists. This phenomenon will be discussed in the next section.

INFORMAL AND UNPLANNED COMMUNICATION PLAYS A CRUCIAL ROLE IN THE SCIENCE INFORMATION SYSTEM

There is by now a fair amount of documentation (Ackoff, and Halbert, 1958; APA, 1965; Herner, 1954; Menzel, 1959b; Orr, Coyl, and Leeds, 1964; Pelz, 1956; Price, 1963; Rosenbloom, McLaughlin, and Wolek, 1965) for the great role played by informal, unplanned, person-to-person communication in the experiences of scientific investigators, often in ways that affect their work quite vitally. This comes as no surprise to communications researchers familiar with the 'multistep flow of communications' that prevails in so-called mass communications. (For a recent summary, see Lazarsfeld and Menzel, 1963.) However, the situation in the sciences differs from 'mass communication' in fundamental ways. The mass communication audience is typically apathetic, while the scientific audience is highly motivated; the familiar multistep flow serves to diffuse messages already contained in the mass media, while informal transmission of messages among scientists often antecedes their appearance in print; in mass communication, interpersonal links play their role primarily in persuasion, while in the sciences they seem to be crucial even in mere cognitive transmission. (For an example of persuasive communication in an applied profession, see Coleman, Katz and Menzel, 1966.) For these reasons, the importance of interpersonal communication in the sciences cannot simply be explained by the same factors as in mass communication, but will have to be accounted for through the specific characteristics of the scientific public. (For one attempt to do this, see Menzel, 1966b.)

While informal communication in the sciences is largely unplanned, and sometimes appears accidental, there is actually a good bit of regularity to it. Certain individuals, for example, tend to be the most frequent carriers of information from one place to another, the recipients of correspondence, the hosts of visiting scientists, the visitors to other institutions — largely due to the positions or obligations that researchers assume in addition to their primary activity as researchers. It is the people who serve as editors of journals, who serve on grant-application review committees, who go to summer laboratories, and so on, that play the role of 'the scientific troubadour', as it has been called.

There is also some regularity in the kinds of occasions, places, and times at which these information exchanges take place: at summer laboratories, in the corridors of scientific meetings, during and after colloquia and conferences. There is some regularity as to the patterns of initiative on the part of the conveyor and of the recipient of information through which unplanned communication comes about: seeking one kind of information and obtaining another; informing a colleague of current work and being rewarded with a relevant item of information; information brought up spontaneously by a colleague with whom one is together for another purpose; being sought out deliberately by a colleague who has information to convey; and so on (Menzel, 1959b).

And finally, there is some regularity as to the content of the information that seems preferentially to flow through these kinds of channels rather than through the more regular and systematized mechanisms of the printed word and the attendant bibliographic control devices. For example, there is a certain level of know-how information about the use and setting up of scientific apparatus that seems to go by preference through the word-of-mouth channels, perhaps because this kind of information is regarded as unworthy of being handled in detail in the printed word, and does not find a ready place under the subject terms of indexing procedures. Information that helps interpret results and information that helps a person become acquainted with a new field also seem to make their way differentially, often through the personal channels (APA, 1965, Report No. 11; Menzel, 1959b; Rosenbloom, McLaughlin, and Wolek, 1965).

The regularities inherent in the apparently accidental and unplanned ways of communicating hold out the hope of planned improvements in the system. On the one hand, as more is learned of the kinds of information that seem to go through these kinds of communication-switching devices, needs for better and more effective sources on the part of the formal devices become clear. On the other hand, as it is realized that some kinds of information will continue to be carried primarily through interpersonal interchanges, formal devices for making these informal interchanges more effective may be developed — planned mechanisms to make the so-called lucky accidents happen more often. These mechanisms may range from directories and newsletters that tell scientists who is doing what to the scheduling of working hours and the location of new institutes in such a way as to facilitate visits.

SCIENTISTS CONSTITUTE PUBLICS

The populations which are served by the science information systems — scientific researchers, practitioners in various disciplines and professions — can be usefully looked upon as publics, and described under the same categories that one uses when describing the more familiar publics of the mass media. These publics, can, for example, be described in terms of size, in terms of turnover, and in terms of the interaction that exists within them. They can also be described in terms of their interests in a range of topics, in terms of the fidelity with which they attend to given channels and in terms of the norms that they have created with regard to exposure to various channels.

Yet, while the scientific publics share certain characteristics with the mass publics, in certain other respects they are very different from the public of the newspaper, of the TV program, or the neighborhood public library. Number one, the scientists have a very high motivation to obtain the information that is channeled in their direction through the system that is designed to serve them. They go out of their way to reach out for this information. Second, they want this information to help in very specific activities — activities that form very essential parts of their professional roles and therefore of their lives. Third, because of both of these facts, they have very well-developed and very well-structured behavior patterns with regard to professional communication. In more concrete language, these professions have, in the course of their development, worked out a rich set of customs, habits, traditions, mechanisms, tricks, and devices as to how one goes about obtaining information, what one does by way of screening and listening for information, and what one need not listen or attend to. Planners of information policies must take into account this body of behavior patterns, of traditions, customs, and learned behavior. The members of these specialized publics have developed communication institutions and learned ways of interacting with them and with one another to a much higher degree than is true, for example, for the public of a newspaper. Furthermore, scientists themselves look upon the communications services and systems as instruments, and take an interest in their improvement as technologies.

Of course, the several scientific publics also differ from one another in many of these aspects (Menzel, 1966d). All of these aspects have implications for the wise planning of information services for these publics.

SCIENCE INFORMATION SYSTEMS SERVE MULTIPLE FUNCTIONS

The last theme to be taken up here is that it is rather important to draw qualitative distinctions between the several kinds of things that the science information systems are called upon to perform, especially in this current age of streamlining, of great technological strides, of great advances in logical systems. The reason is that these advances bring with them some risk that they may make some of these functions be served more efficiently and satisfactorily, while neglecting or even hampering others. Most of the great innovations have been instituted under the guiding themes of speed, efficiency, and comprehensiveness. The overriding aim has been to bring information to scientists promptly, to bring all the information that is relevant to the scientist's specific query, and to do so with a minimum of waste motion. The prototype of that activity is the exhaustive search. But this is only one of several types of services that are required of the science information system. To give but one example of another type, with characteristics almost the opposite of those of the exhaustive search, there is the requirement to call the scientist's attention to relevant developments in fields which he has not recognized as pertinent to his own work.

Can policies designed to satisfy some of these requirements really work to the detriment of others? If search and retrieval services and selected distribution arrangements were working optimally, they would bring to each scientist exactly that which he has asked for and nothing else. But, by that very fact they would eliminate browsing, and would thereby put an end to the occasions when a scientist's attention is called to information which he had not appreciated as relevant to his own interests. This is just one example of perhaps the crudest kind of optimizing one science information function to the detriment of others.

But what actually are all the various kinds of functions that these information systems must perform; how many of them is it worth distinguishing? Distinctions along a number of axes have been suggested. The most basic criterion of classification is probably that of the scope and permanence with which the information needed by a particular scientist can be described in advance.[2] Along this dimension one can distinguish the exhaustive search; the reference function (to give the scientist the single best answer to a specific question); the current awareness function (to keep the person abreast of developments in his predetermined area of attention); a function which consists of stimulating researchers from time to time to seek information outside of their predesigned areas of attention: and a function which consists of enabling a scientist to follow through on this stimulation by 'brushing up' or familiarizing himself with a well-defined field of inquiry which he had not previously included in his attention area. The two last-mentioned functions, it should be noted, transcend the informational requirements that each scientist can define for himself.

CONCLUSION

The themes enumerated above have implications for science information policy, but the translation of these implications into concrete steps requires that the themes be specified through a considerable amount of empirical research. As indicated in the opening paragraphs, much research on the use of information and information sources by scientists has been carried out, but until very recently the great variety and subtlety of potentially useful research questions and approaches was not realized. Discussions of 'methodology' in this field all too often are confined to a consideration of data-gathering techniques. Insufficient attention has been paid to the more fundamental questions of the conceptualization of units of observation, the choice of variables to be considered, the causal models to be employed, and the analytic designs to be used.[3]

432   HERBERT MENZEL

NOTES

1. For an excellent and thorough laying out of the information system and its components in biomedical research, see Orr, Abdian, Bourne, Coyl, Leeds, and Pings (1954).
2. For a fuller treatment, see Menzel (1964).
3. Some remarks on the conceptualization of units and on certain related methodological questions will be found in Menzel (1960) on the variety of analytic designs embodied in recent studies in Menzel (1966c) and on the feasibility of inferring science information needs from the past uses made of information services in Menzel (1966a).

REFERENCES

Ackoff, R.L., and Halbert, M.M. 'An operations research study of the scientific activity of chemists.' Cleveland: Case Institute of Technology, Operations Research Group, 1958. (Mimeo)
American Psychological Association, *Reports of the American Psychological Association's Project on Scientific Information Exchange in Psychology.* Vol. 1. Washington, D.C.: APA, 1963.
American Psychological Association. *Reports of the American Psychological Association's Project on Scientific Information Exchange in Psychology.* Vol. 2. Washington, D.C.: APA, 1965.
Coleman, J., Katz, E., and Menzel, H. *Medical Innovation — a diffusion study:* Indianapolis: Bobbs-Merrill, 1966.
Herner, S. 'Information-gathering habits of workers in pure and applied science.' *Industrial and Engineering Chemistry,* 1954, 46, 228-236.
Lazarsfeld, P.F. and Menzel, H. 'Mass media and personal influence.' In W. Schramm (Ed.), *The science of human communication,* New York: Basic Books, 1963. Pp 94-115.
Menzel. H. 'The flow of information among scientists — problems, opportunities, and research questions.' New York: Columbia University, Bureau of Applied Social Research, 1958. (Mimeo) (Available as Technical Report 144390 PB from the Clearinghouse, Department of Commerce, Springfield, Va.)
Menzel, H. 'Comment.' *College and Research Libraries,* 1959, 20, 419-420. (a)
Menzel, H. 'Planned and unplanned scientific communication.' In *Proceedings of the International Conference on Scientific Information.* Washington, D.C.: National Academy of Sciences, 1959. Pp. 199-243.(b)
Menzel, H. 'Review of studies in the flow of information among scientists.' New York: Columbia University. Bureau of Applied Social Research, 1960. 2 Vols. (Mimeo) (Available as Technical Report 156 941 PB from the Clearinghouse, Department of Commerce, Springfield, VA.)
Menzel, H. 'The information needs of current scientific research.' Library Quarterly, 1964, 34, 4-19.
Menzel, H. 'Can science information needs be ascertained empirically?' In L. Thayer (Ed.), *Communication: Concepts and perspectives (Proceedings of the Second International Symposium on Communication Theory and Research).* Washington, D.C.: Spartan Books, 1966. (a)
Menzel, H. 'Informal communication in science: Its advantages and its formal analogues.' In Dan Bergen (Ed.), *The foundations of access to knowledge.* Syracuse: Syracuse University Press, 1966, in press. (b)

SCIENTIFIC COMMUNICATION 433

Menzel, H. 'Information needs and uses in science and technology.' In C. Cuadra
(Ed.), *Annual review of information science and technology.* Vol. 1. New York:
Wiley. 1966. (c)
Menzel, H. 'Sociological perspectives on the information-gathering practices of the
scientific investigator and the medical practitioner.' In D. McCord (Ed.),
*Bibliotheca medica: Physician for tomorrow, dedication of the Countway
Library of Medicine.* Boston: Harvard Medical School, 1966. (d)
Orr, R.H., Abdian, G., Bourne, C.P., Coyle, E.D., Leeds, A.A., and Pings, V.M.
'The biomedical information complex viewed as a system.' *Federation
Proceedings*, 1964, 23, 1133-1145.
Orr, R.H., Coyl, E.B., and Leeds A.A. 'Trends in oral communication among
biomedical scientists.' *Federation Proceedings*, 1964, 23, 1146-54.
Paisley, W.J. 'The flow of (behavioral) science information — a review of the
research literature.' Stanford: Stanford University, Institute for Communication
Research, 1965. (Mimeo)
Pelz. R. C. 'Social factors related to performance in a research organization.'
Administrative Science Quarterly, 1956, 1, 310-325.
Price, D.J. de S. *Little science, big science*, New York: Columbia University Press,
1963.
Rosenbloom, R. S., McLaughlin, C.P., and Wolek, F.W. 'Technology transfer and
the flow of technical information in a large industrial corporation.' Boston:
Harvard University. Graduate School of Business Administration, 1965, 2 Vols.
(Mimeo)
Shaw, R. 'Review of "flow of information among scientists."' *College and Research
Libraries*, 1959, 20, 163-164.

5.3 The Supply and Demand for Information about Education

DAI HOUNSELL*

INTRODUCTION

Any attempt to survey the literature of education is fraught with formidable difficulties. Education can be variously defined as (i) 'the total processes developing human ability and behaviour'; (ii) a 'social process in which one achieves social competence and individual growth, carried on in a selected, controlled setting which can be institutionalised as a school or college'; and (iii) 'in the sense of theory of education or disciplines of education' (Page and Thomas, 1977). Most definitions also embody a distinction customarily made in Britain between education and training, with the latter defined as 'systematic practice in the performance of a skill' as in industrial training or teacher education (Page and Thomas, 1977), but this distinction has less to do with aims and purposes (which clearly have much in common) than with a history of separate organisation and development. Furthermore, whether education is a discipline in its own right is often challenged. Storer's argument that education is best regarded as a 'conjunctive domain' whose focus is 'a socially relevant whole rather than a natural cluster of abstract phenomena' (Storer, 1970, p. 123), reflects the uneasy status of a field of study which draws much of its strength from perspectives rooted in the so-called 'parent disciplines' of philosophy, history, sociology, psychology and, more recently, politics, economics and operational research. While this conceptual and methodological eclecticism alone would provide a daunting challenge for the documentalist, the diversity of professional and other interest-groups concerned (see below) adds a further dimension of complexity to an already tangled web.

For the purposes of this paper a working definition is adopted

*Source: in Brittain (ed.), *The Social Sciences: the Supply of and Demand for Documentation and Data* (1982).

which takes as its focus published literature concerne with the theory or practice of education and produced by or intended for those professionally* involved in the education and training services and/or those with a commitment to or an interest in educational issues, problems and practices. Circular though this definition is, it would be futile to attempt greater precision.

SUPPLY

Gauging the size of the literature provides an illustration of these problems. Statistics published annually in the *Library Association Record* give total numbers of education volumes published as 634 (in 1976), 539 (1977) and 536 (1978), but these figures are based on Dewey classes and exclude monographs on the teaching of specific subjects and relevant literature in the parent disciplines. The volume of journal articles can be gleaned from the coverage of the *British Education Index*, which has included references to approximately 3,000 articles annually since the early 1970s and draws on nearly 200 journals, chiefly of UK origin (Hounsell, Payne and Willett, 1978). These figures however mask a considerably larger corpus of documents. First, alongside commercially published monographs and nationally indexed articles is a large body of material in such forms as pamphlets, booklets, manuals and reports produced by educational and training institutions and organisations. Such documents often go unrecorded in the *British National Bibliography* and reliable statistics of them are difficult to come by. Second, the literature of the USA and of Commonwealth countries is extensively used in some quarters (particularly by educational researchers and teachers of education as a field of study, and much more strongly in some areas — e.g. educational psychology, economics of education — than in others). The coverage of the American *Current Index to Journals in Education* gives some indication of scale here: references to 22,866 articles were included in the 1978 volume (bringing the cumulative total since January 1969 to 186,217), and a total of 775 journals were being covered by May 1979 (Brandhorst, personal communication). Third, in looking at aspects of supply in education, the *kind* of documents produced is at least as important a factor as their

---

*Excluding technical, manual, secretarial and clerical staff.

ere is a richly varied mass of material which appears to have no common elements. My observation on the literature of higher education

> Specialist research monographs and sober institutional self-studies rub shoulders with works of opinion and polemic, heady accounts of curricular innovations, journalistic 'analyses' of student unrest, weighty reflections of former presidents, and a mass of conference proceedings, anthologies and readings. (Hounsell, 1977, p. 3425)

applies with equal facility to the literature of education as a whole. Similarly, convenient labels such as 'journal' or 'periodical' must be viewed with circumspection, since the terms are widely used in education to include such diverse publications as highly specialised research journals, the magazines of professional associations and trade union newspapers. Indeed, a ranking of periodicals contributing references to the *British Education Index* between 1973 and 1975 (Hounsell, Payne and Willett, 1978) showed that none of the first five items in the list (which together contributed almost one-fifth of all references) could be considered a scientific or scholarly journal when the usual criteria (such as refereeing by peers) are applied.

While the literature of education is abundant, diverse and diffuse, the level of availability in general terms is quite high. Several cooperative schemes have been established by the Librarians of Institutes and Schools of Education (LISE) to improve services to users in the geographical areas of England and Wales for which they are responsible (Humby, 1975); these include union catalogues of books and periodicals, cooperation in the storage of obsolescent books and the acquisition of overseas material, and union lists of stock on particular countries. And there have been similar cooperative efforts by the Annual Conference of Librarians in Scottish Colleges of Education. Foskett and Humby (1969) noted that 72% of requests made through the LISE scheme were satisfied.

This regional network is complemented by other national sources, the largest of which is the Department of Education and Science Library. This Library, which is open for reference and research enquiries, has a stock of 183,000 volumes and subscribes to 800 journals. Many other national organisations (the National

Foundation for Education Research, the National Union of Teachers and the National Institute of Adult Education are only three such examples) have their own library and information services, while there is a small number of more specialist libraries such as the Language Teaching Library of the Centre for Information on Language Teaching and the English Teaching Information Centre.

Not all kinds of material are widely available since some collections exclude specific categories of information, for example the DES collection does not include school textbooks, and documents such as curriculum materials, policy documents and progress reports on research are often difficult to trace. An interesting initiative has been the introduction of *CORE*, a new microfiche journal which publishes full-length versions of material such as conference proceedings and full-length research reports which may not be readily available elsewhere.

Cooperation and a readiness to link stock to bibliographical sources have helped to establish good inter-library loan services. For example, the Inter-Library Loans Service at Boston Spa has the entire collection of microfiche represented in the American *Resources in Education*, and has been willing to extend its holdings of journals to cover material appearing in the companion ERIC journal, the *Current Index to Journals in Education*, as comprehensively as possible. At the same time, a tradition of treating comparative education as one of the subjects studied in most teacher training courses has made a considerable contribution to the general availability of foreign-language material, further aided by the publication by LISE of union lists of stock on education in specific countries (see for example Andrews, 1979). This favourable picture should be qualified in two ways. Firstly, ease of availability is closely related to status and institutional affiliation; those working in academic institutions are likely to perceive the inter-library loans service as rapid, efficient and extensive, but others (such as schoolteachers) to whom use of these institutions' libraries has been extended, may find their access to inter-library loan facilities tightly constrained. Similarly, users of public libraries will in many cases be at a considerable disadvantage compared to those in academic institutions. Second, while the availability of foreign-language material is at least satisfactory, there has been no major effort to translate, summarise or synthesise this literature in any systematic way, and in those few instances which are the exception, the driving-force has tended to be the influence of a particular school of thought (e.g. French sociology of education) rather than an interest *per se* in the perspectives of other nations and cultures.

DEMAND

The potential market for educational information in the United Kingdom is large and varied. One detailed study (Hounsell, Payne and Willett, 1977) indicated that in excess of three-quarters of a million people are professionally employed in the education and training services. Breaking this figure down into the broad categories adopted by Mersel, Donohue and Morris (1966), by far the largest professional grouping is *teaching* (with over 700,000 staff employed) followed by *administration and ancillary services* (almost 50,000) and *research and scholarship* (4,000). Though often used, a tripartite categorisation of this kind serves to conceal differences both within and across categories. An example of the first kind is the administrative category, which embraces professional sub-groups as diverse as local education authority advisers, central government administrators, teachers centre wardens and educational correspondents. And an important across-category difference is that of employer or employing institution: as far as demand for documents is concerned, the university teacher seems likely to have more in common with the university-based researcher than with the schoolteacher, the adult education lecturer, the teacher in the Prison Education Service or the industrial training officer.

Differences in the kinds of demands made by these various sub-groups is in part a function of the diversity of the education and training services. While some questions (e.g. teaching method, models of course design) are manifestly of interest across a broad spectrum of groups, others tend to be viewed largely within the framework of specific parts of the system. On the one hand, differences in the age and ability levels of the students are inevitably one distinguishing factor in interest (clearly the educational concerns of the primary teacher are significantly different from those of the tutor of undergraduates); on the other, primary education, secondary education, higher education, adult education, further education and industrial training comprise more or less discrete organisational sub-systems each with its own characteristic rationales, procedures, etc. Subject affiliations are also a strong source of demand differences, since for many (if not most) teachers their subject or discipline is a more powerful reference-point than the kind of institution in which they are employed or the age or ability-level of the pupils or students for which they are responsible.

But if these differences make for variations in the *direction* of demand, perhaps the greatest single area of difference is in *intensity* of demand. It is generally accepted that the highest level of demand is from researchers and that here, as in the United States (see for example Nelson, 1972), the journal article is the chief medium of communication between researchers. Since, as we have seen, the number of educational journals in the English language alone is very high, monitoring through bibliographical sources is especially important for the researcher, and British sources include not only the *British Education Index* but three abstracting journals and over thirty current-awareness services (Hounsell, Payne and Willett, 1978), many of which have specialised interests and audiences which extend beyond the narrow confines of research. Brittain (1970, p. 120) has suggested that education 'is perhaps better covered by bibliographical tools and information services than any other social science', but the value of this wealth of information sources to those other than researchers is questionable, if not largely irrelevant. Indeed it can be argued that while the myriad assortment of documents which make up the primary literature generally represent responses to a host of different users' needs, the secondary literature is directed almost overwhelmingly towards an academic audience. And while the needs of researchers are well-known and are reasonably well catered for, the needs of teaching and administrative groups have been little researched and are often poorly understood.

Of those two groups, administrators are by far the most neglected. There is limited evidence from a recent study (Hounsell, Payne and Willett, 1979) that topics of interest change rapidly and that administrators have little time to look for information or to read it. The needs of teachers have been better documented (see for example Cane and Schroeder, 1970; *Information Requirements ...* 1971; Hounsell *et al.*, 1980) though the studies undertaken have tended to focus on research and development information rather than on subject-based curriculum and teaching materials. Cane and Schroeder concluded that:

Teachers felt that reading research was a small part of their professional life but they nevertheless attached importance to it. Some of those interviewed said that these writings were often incomprehensible, too long, phrased in tactless language, biased in their presentation or of limited applicability. While some were enthusiastic about research publications that spoke directly to the classroom teacher, many complained of inadequate reporting in the more popular journals. They believed that research findings ought to be disseminated through some system of regular comprehensive research summaries. (Cane and Schroeder, 1970, p. 60)

The Lancaster enquiry (Hounsell *et al.*, 1980) yielded similar findings. Four out of five of the teachers surveyed felt that a gulf existed between themselves and researchers, chiefly because of the tediousness of research reports, research jargon and poor dissemination of findings to schools. And while almost all of the teachers thought that being well-informed about educational research and development was important, there was a division of opinion on whether teachers were well-informed. The main obstacles to keeping up-to-date were a lack of time, both to read and to look for information, and a lack of advice. However one-third of the teachers had made a specific enquiry for information in the recent past, and more than half of the teachers had been influenced by research which they had read or heard about. There was also evidence that communication was by no means predominantly informal; books and reports (together with teaching colleagues) emerged as the most popular sources of information, and mainstream periodicals (such as the *Times Educational Supplement*) were widely read.

Two other findings are of interest here. The first of these is that information was more likely to be found useful if rooted in the experiences of individual teachers or specific schools. This provides an interesting contrast to the perspective of Allison (1974, p. 194), writing as a scholar-researcher, who criticises the educational literature for the very reason that 'personal experience seems to be the touchstone of truth'. The second is that there was a significant relationship between length of teaching experience and use of information: the more experienced teachers were more likely to have been influenced by research, to have made specific enquiries for information, to look for information beyond the immediate confines of the school, and to make greater use of periodicals and libraries.

SUPPLY AND DEMAND: CONCLUDING COMMENTS

It should be clear from the arguments presented in this paper that, in so far as educational documents are concerned, the scope for global observations on the relationship between supply and demand is strictly limited, principally because of the existence of a great variety of professional sub-groups, each of which would seem to have its own characteristic patterns of demand and use. And it follows that even where a satisfactory match between demand and supply can be identified — as in the case of researchers — the temptation to adopt this as a model which might be applied to other, less well matched groups of users should be resisted. A successful model of communication for one group may be quite inappropriate for another. It is not simply a question of differences in the kinds of documents demanded, but of their orientation, the relative weight assigned to theoretical rigour and practical reference and — most importantly — of the strength of demand. For it is difficult, certainly in the immediate future, to envisage a situation in which the pattern of commitments of administrators and teachers would change so significantly as to afford them anything approaching the researchers' opportunities to keep abreast of the literature. Nor, without a better understanding of the role of new information within their professional duties, do we even know whether becoming better 'informed' would have more than a negligible impact on their professional effectiveness.

It should also be recognised that any one measure to improve the supply-demand match may by itself make little headway. In our study of educational information and the teacher (Hounsell *et al.*, 1980) we concluded that a major improvement would come about only as a result of a strategic combination of measures which had regard to conceptions of the role of information within the teaching profession, user education in initial and in-service training, the establishment of a system or network of provision, the creation of appropriate information services, and dissemination strategies.

This is not to say that the situation is static, or that certain measures might not have some impact. Britain has been closely involved in the work of EUDISED (European Documentation and Information System for Education) (see for example Macgregor, 1975) which has resulted in a number of technical reports, a multi-lingual thesaurus, and registers of research in progress and experimental bulletins on periodical articles and audio-visual materials. There is also growing acknowledgement that research and development information seldom reaches practitioners who might learn most from it, and there have been recent initiatives by bodies such as the Schools Council, the National Foundation for Educational Research and the Social Science Research Council to examine or to improve dissemination.

These efforts undoubtedly need to be linked to an intensive study of the use of information by practitioners, using a more qualitative methodology than hitherto which also takes account of the context in which those being studied work and communicate with one another. The main stumbling-block here is the problem which besets information development in general; how is one to assess the potential impact of information, assuming that information could be presented in a form that the practitioners found both accessible and digestible? A valuable start could be made, even on a small scale, by experimenting with highly selective information services, perhaps based on extended summaries. The abstracting journal was designed above all for researchers: what is now needed is a new kind of bibliographical tool tailored to the very different requirements of teachers and administrators.

ACKNOWLEDGEMENTS

This paper draws on research studies sponsored by the Research and Development Department of the British Library and carried out in the Centre for Educational Research and Development, University of Lancaster.

REFERENCES

Allison, E.K. 'The evaluation of educational experience.' *Daedalus*, 103 (4), 188-195.
Andrews, J.S. (ed.), *Education in Germany: a union list of stock in institute and school of education libraries.* 3rd edn. Lancaster: Librarians of Institutes and Schools of Education, 1979.

Brandhorst, T. (Director, ERIC Processing and Reference Facility). Personal communication.

Brittain, J.M. *Information and its users.* Bath: Bath University Press/Oriel Press, 1970.

Cane, B. and Schroeder, C. *The teacher and research.* Windsor: NFER, 1970.

Core (Collected Original Resources in Education). Published three times a year by Carfax Publishing Company, Haddon House, Dorchester-on-Thames, Oxford OX9 8JZ.

Foskett, D.J. and Humby, M.J. United Kingdom 1: *EUDISED. European Documentation and Information System for Education. Vol. 11: National Reports.* Strasbourg: Council of Europe, Documentation Centre for Education in Europe, 1969, 77-96.

Hounsell, D. Publications, Higher Education. In: Knowles, A.S. (ed.). *The international encyclopedia of higher education.* San Francisco: Jossey-Bass, 1977, 3424-3434.

Hounsell, D., Payne, P. and Willett, I. *Personnel in education and training: a survey of the potential market for educational information services.* Lancaster: University of Lancaster, Centre for Educational Research and Development. BL R & D Report No. 5326, 1977.

Hounsell, D., Payne, P. and Willett, I. *Bibliographic services in education: a survey and analysis of secondary services in the United Kingdom.* University of Lancaster: University of Lancaster, Centre for Educational Research and Development. BL R & D Report No. 5447, 1978.

Hounsell, D., Martin, E., Needham, G. and Jones, H. *Educational information and the teacher.* London: The British Library, Research and Development Department. BL R & D Report No. 5505, 1980.

Hounsell, D., Payne, P. and Willett, I. *Experimental information services in education.* Final Report to The British Library Research and Development Department. Lancaster: University of Lancaster, Centre for Educational Research and Development, 1979.

Humby, M. *A guide to the literature of education. (Education Libraries Bulletin,* Supplement 1). 3rd edn. London: University of London, Institute of Education Library, 1975.

Information Requirements of College of Education Lecturers and Schoolteachers. (Investigation into Information Requirements of the Social Sciences, Research Report No. 3). Bath: Bath University Library, 1971.

Library Association Record. Book Prices. Vol. 79, no. 2, Feb. 1977, pp. 70-71; vol. 80, no. 2, Feb. 1978, p. 57; vol. 81, no. 2, Feb. 1979, p. 57.

Macgregor, A.N. Eudised — a progress report. *Education Libraries Bulletin,* 18 (1), 1975, 1-6.

Mersel, J., Donohue, J.C. and Morris, W.A. *Information transfer in educational research.* Sherman Oaks, Calif.: Informatics Inc., 1966.

Nelson, C.E. 'The communication system surrounding archival journals in educational research.' *Educational Researcher,* 1 (9), 1972, 13-16.

Page, G.T. and Thomas J.B. *International dictionary of education.* London: Kogan Page, 1977.

Storer, N.W. 'The organisation and differentiation of the scientific community: basic disciplines, applied research and conjunctive domains.' In: Dershimer, R.A. (ed.). *The educational research community: its communication and social structure.* Washington, DC: US Dept. of Health, Education and Welfare, Office of Education, Bureau of Research, 1970.

5.4 Artistry and Teaching: The Teacher as Focus of Research and Development

LAWRENCE STENHOUSE*

Experience tells me that if I am not to be misunderstood I must begin this chapter by offering you a brief sketch of my views on the relation of research to education action. These views are set out at a greater length in other works (Stenhouse 1979, 1980, 1983).

There is in England a strong doctrine that the study of education is fed by the contributory disciplines of history, philosophy, and sociology. I agree that these disciplines do contribute to our understanding of education. In my own personal experience I can say that in the curriculum project with which I am most closely associated, the Humanities Curriculum Project, my own contribution was substantially influenced by my knowledge of the history of elementary school readers (that is, text books), of the philosophical work of R S Peters, of the social psychology of groups, and of the sociology of knowledge. These disciplines, while they serve to stimulate educational imagination and to define the conditions of educational action, do not serve to guide such action. They provide for education — as rules of the game and traditions of play do for a sport — a context in which to plan intelligent action. But they do not tell us how to act.

The yearning towards a form of research which might guide educational action led educational researchers to look enviously at agricultural research. Here, in a tradition associated with Ronald Fisher, researchers had conducted field trials which utilized random sampling in block and pot designs in order to recommend to farmers those strains of seed and crop treatments which would maximize yield. Both random sampling — which legitimized the deployment of the statistics of probability to estimate error and sig-

*Source: David Hopkins and Martin Wideen (eds), *Alternative Perspectives on School Improvement* (Falmer Press, London, 1984), pp. 67-76.

nificance — and the measure of yield present problems in educational research. A number of classic papers, among which Campbell and Stanley's 'Experimental and Quasi-Experimental Designs for Research in Teaching' (1963) is prominent, have considered the robustness of various experimental designs and statistical procedures in terms of reliability and validity as sampling falls away from the desideratum of randomness. The doctrine of behavioural objectives allied to the development of criterion-referenced testing was developed to give a measure of educational yield.

Personally, I am satisfied that the application of this so-called 'psycho-statistical paradigm' (Fienberg 1977) in educational research provides no reliable guide to action (though it may contribute a little to theory). It has to assume, as agriculturalists assume in treating a crop in a field, consistency of treatment throughout the treatment group; but it is the teacher's job to work like a gardener rather than a farmer, differentiating the treatment of each subject and each learner as the gardener does each flower bed and each plant. The variability of educational situations is grossly underestimated: sampling procedure cannot be related to educational action except on a survey basis rather than an experimental basis. Further, behavioural objectives are quite inappropriate to education except in the case of skill learning. They are a monument to the philosophical naivete of a psychological tradition which simplifies intentionality and purpose to 'having a goal'. Purpose in education is about having an agenda.

Now, if I am right about this — and you will not readily persuade me that I am not — then the question arises: if experimental research based on sampling cannot tell us how to act in education, how are we as teachers to know what to do?

One answer to this question is that instructions shall be laid down for us in the form of curricula and specifications of teaching methods. I reject this. Education is learning in the context of a search for truth. Truth cannot be defined by the state even through democratic processes: close control of curricula and teaching methods in schools is to be likened to the totalitarian control of art. Reaching towards the truth through education is a matter of situational professional judgement; and professors of education or administrators cannot tell us what we should be doing. Prescriptions will vary according to cases. We do not need doctors if all they are going to give us is a treatment laid down by the state or suggested by their professor without bothering to examine us and make a diagnosis.

Educational action is concerned with varying according to case and to context the pursuit of truth through learning. In this subtle and complicated process, how is the teacher to conceive the problem: what shall I do? This riddle provides the context and occasion of my chapter.

The student who, during the course of ten years in school, meets two or three outstanding and congenial teachers has had a fortunate educational experience. Many are not so lucky.

The improvement of schooling hinges on increasing the numbers of outstanding teachers, on serving their needs, and on trying to ensure that their virtues are not frustrated by the system. The basic institutional framework of the educational enterprise — the neighbourhood elementary school and the comprehensive high school — are for the moment stably established or well on the way. Within these frameworks it is the outstanding teachers who transmute the process of instruction into the adventure of education. Others, it is true, may teach us; but it is *they* who teach us to delight in learning and to exult in the extension of powers that learning gives. [...]

Good teachers are necessarily autonomous in professional judgement. They do not need to be told what to do. They are not professionally the dependents of researchers or superintendents, of innovators or supervisors. This does not mean that they do not welcome access to ideas created by other people at other places or in other times. Nor do they reject advice, consultancy or support. But they do know that ideas and people are not of much real use until they are digested to the point where they are subject to the teacher's own judgement. In short, it is the task of all educationalists outside the classroom to serve the teachers; for only teachers are in the position to create good teaching.

Let me restate my case by saying that I am declaring teaching an art; and then elaborate on that. By an art I mean an exercise of skill expressive of meaning. The painter, the poet, the musician, the actor and the dancer all express meaning through skill. Some artists fly so high that we designate them geniuses, and that may be true of some teachers. But a claim as ambitious as that does not need to be made on behalf of the excellent teachers I have spoken of. It is enough that they have assiduously cultivated modest but worthwhile talents like those of the innumerable stonemasons who adorned the English parish churches or those sound repertory actors who exceed in number the jobs the theatre has to offer. In short I am not elevating teachers inordinately. Rather I am diagnosing the nature of their job in order to discern how performances may be improved. I am suggesting that just as dramatists, theatre school staff, producers, stage managers, front of house managers and even booking agencies need to understand to some degree the players' art, so curriculum developers, educational researchers, teacher educators, supervisors and administrators need to understand the art of the teacher.

Teaching is the art which expresses in a form accessible to learners an understanding of the nature of that which is to be learned. Thus, teaching music is about understanding the nature of music and having the skill to teach it true to one's understanding. Teaching tennis is about understanding the logic and psychology and techniques of the game and about expressing that understanding through skill in teaching. Similarly, the teaching of French expresses an understanding of the nature of language and culture and of that particular language and culture; the teaching of wrought ironwork, as a craft expresses the relationship of material to fitness for use and to concepts of beauty; and so forth. And one mainstream tradition of teaching is an expression of knowledge of a discipline or field of knowledge; it is always to 'teach' the epistemology of that discipline, the nature of its tenure on knowledge.

My own belief, as I have said, is that whether teaching is concerned with that knowledge we associate with the disciplines or with the arts or with practical skills, it should aspire to express a view of knowledge or of a field of activity. This epistemological desideratum might be expressed by saying that the teacher should aspire to give learners access to insight into the status of what they learn. The way towards this is that a view of knowledge comes to infuse the teacher's perception of subject matter and judgement of the performance of students, and that this view and its status becomes revealed, by teaching, to the student. Such a perception of knowledge develops and deepens throughout the career of a good teacher and it is the product of the teacher's personal construction or reconstruction of knowledge. It can be assisted by reading and instruction, but it is essentially a personal construction created from socially available resources and it cannot be imparted by others or to others in a straightforward manner.

Now, the construction of a personal perception of our world

from the knowledge and traditions that our culture makes available to us is a task that faces not only the teacher, but also the student; and teaching rests on both partners in the process being at different stages of the same enterprise. This is clear to us when we watch a great musician teaching a master class, but it tends to be obscured in schools in the ordinary classroom. The technical claptrap of learning systems and behavioural objectives is much to blame for this. Good learning is about making, not mere doing. It is about constructing a view of the world. It is not about showing that, although you have failed in that construction, you are capable of all the performances that would appear to make the construction possible. Education is for real: it is not about practice shots.

Let me sum up so far by an analogy (which is not to be pursued too far). The art of social comedy expresses a view of manners and morals as people live them: the art of education expresses a view of knowledge as people live it. The medium of one is theatrical entertainment; of the other, schooling. Both are at their highest when the audience or learner is brought to reflect consciously on the message he or she receives. This fulfilment depends not only upon the quality of the play or the curriculum, but also upon the art of the actor or teacher.

And now let me take a second step. All good art is an inquiry and an experiment. It is by virtue of being an artist that the teacher is a researcher. The point appears to be difficult to grasp because education faculties have been invaded by the idea that research is scientific and concerned with general laws. This notion persists even though our universities teach music and literature and history and art and lay an obligation on their staff in these fields to conduct research. Why then should research in education look only to science?

The artist is the researcher *par excellence*. So much so that prominent scientists are now arguing that, while routine consolidation in science can be achieved by following conventional scientific method, the big breakthroughs really show that science is an art. I am sceptical of that, but I am clear that all art rests upon research and the purpose of the artist's research is to improve the truth of his performance. Leonardo's sketchbooks, George Stubbs dissecting a horse in his studio, Nureyev working with a partner in a new ballet, Solti and the Chicago Symphony Orchestra tackling Beethoven, Derek Jacobi evolving his Hamlet, all are engaged in inquiry, in research and development of their own work. And this development, though it involves improvement of technique, is not for the sake of technique: it is for the sake of the expression of a truth in a performance which challenges criticism in those terms.

Thus, an elementary school teacher who wishes to improve his or her teaching of science will record teaching or invite a colleague in as an observer, and will, if possible, bring in an outsider to monitor the children's perceptions as a basis for 'triangulation'. From this the next aspiration is to drop the outsider and move towards open discourse between teacher and children about the teaching/learning process in the classroom and its 'meaning'. A crucial aspect of this meaning is the impression of science — always expressed in specific instances or episodes — that the children are acquiring. And this the teacher needs to criticize in the light of the philosophy of science. All teaching falsifies its subject as it shapes it into the form of teaching and learning: the art of pedagogy is to minimize the falsification of knowledge. It is the aspiration to do this, to shape understanding without distortion into pedagogic forms that is the challenge to develop one's art.

Now, if you say that most teachers are not like this, I shall reply that some are, and that it is the model of teaching that those teachers display to us that we need to disseminate. The way ahead is to disseminate the idea of teacher as artist with the implication that artists exercise autonomy of judgement founded upon research directed towards improvement in their art. The changes in school administration or curriculum or teaching arrangements which will be required are those which make it possible to implement that vision.

If I, as a teacher, absorb and accept the case I have just been putting, then it is clear to me that I am the focus of research and development. Who else could be? My problem then is how to get others to recognise it. That is not going to be easy. If teachers are at the bottom of the pile, there are bound to be lots of people who like it that way. So, though I can exercise my art in secret, or even in a small group of consenting adults, if I want the support of a movement, I need to make alliances and develop some political power.

Let me give you a short account of the kinds of support that have been developed round the teacher-as-researcher movement in Britain. There is an alliance between some universities or colleges of education and some teacher groups. What is required of the universities is that they break the stranglehold of the 'psycho-statistical and nomothetic paradigm' on educational research. The universities which have done this recognize forms of research alternative to the still dominant tradition of scientific positivism with its emphasis on experimental and survey procedures conducted on samples in field settings and giving rise to 'results'. Among these alternative forms are experimental or descriptive case studies which may be based upon the teacher's access either to the classroom as a laboratory or to the school or classroom as a setting for participant observation. In Britain standards for these research paradigms are now in process of being worked out at master's and doctoral levels, both through discussion at conferences and in the consultations between internal and external examiners.

This alliance with universities is important for the teachers because it gives access to a pattern of part-time study right up to the level of the doctorate which turns one towards one's professional work rather than away from it and offers a systematic training in the appropriate research skills as well as a grasp of the theoretical issues applicable to close-in, practitioner research. The tradition, once established at advanced levels, begins to influence patterns of in-service work.

Academic validation has drawn on alternative traditions which include the hermeneutic tradition and the neo-Marxist tradition from Germany, phenomenology and ethnomethodology. These theoretical currents are in harmony with reappraisals at present being conducted in the social science community whose interests lie outside education. This link is a source of validation and alliance. It turns the education faculty towards sociologists, anthropologists and historians as alternative allies to psychologists and philosophers. This shift of alliance has, of course, profound power implications in the academic community.

The academic endorsement of styles of research into schooling which are as accessible to practising school teachers as to university teachers and professional researchers can also, of course, create considerable hostility and fear among university faculties. In my view, this is misplaced. The universities can only thrive the more as a result of an extension of the boundaries of the research community. The shift is from lecturing on research results towards training researchers. There is room for both, of course, but the balance becomes different. The message is that the 'role' of universities is bound to be central in the development of a tradition that puts research at its heart.

Of course, teacher power expresses itself in unfamiliar ways within this tradition. The Schools Council for Curriculum and Examinations, the main funding agency for curriculum in Britain recently funded a conference of teachers on 'The Teacher as Researcher' (Nixon, 1981). The teachers who organized it did not invite anyone from a university. I guess we talk too much, and they wanted time to think over the issues in their own way. But they will need us; and we need them. In an age of accountability, educational research will be held accountable for its relevance to practice, and that relevance can only be validated by practitioners.

Enlightened administrators look benevolently on the teacher-researcher model of staff development, and one can gather support there. The idea has potential appeal for teacher unions, though that hasn't really been pressed home in Britain. One way or another there are the makings of a movement.

But what are the consequences to be expected of such a movement if it gathers momentum and power? May we expect teachers to demand schools fit for educational artist-researchers to live in? And what would those look like?

We can only guess. But I am suggesting that forms of schooling can best be seen as obsolescent when they constrict developments in teaching. I believe that the development of the teacher as artist means that some time in the future we are going to have to get rid of school principals. My own guess is that we shall need delegatory rather than legislative democracy. Committees will not decide what to do: artists grudge that use of time. They will delegate the power to decide to individuals for fixed periods and will hold them accountable. In the University in which I work professors who run departments or faculties are no different from those who teach or do research: their leadership role is more an award than an appointment. A capacity for intellectual leadership is appropriate, but the leadership role is not structured on the job. Perhaps we need such a concept in schools: persons appointed by their colleagues to a status which recognizes their distinctive capacity to contribute to the community of teachers.

A community of teachers whose attention is primarily focused on the art of teaching will require — as a company of actors does or as a university faculty does — an administrative support structure. It is important that the teacher who acts as president of the school faculty commands the highest salary in the institution, and below that the head of the administration has parity with the highest grade of teacher. It is vital that administrators service teaching, not lead it.

However, we shall not change teaching by creating a school organized on that model. The reform of school organization needs to be an adjustment to the development of teaching. It is the teacher who is the focus of research and development: only the teacher can change the teacher. You can reorganize schools yet teachers can still remain as they were. You can pull down the walls and make an open school; but open teaching remains an achievement of the teacher's art, and an achievement that is an expression of understanding.

What are the implications of all this for in-service development? My position is that in-service development must be the development of the teacher as artist. That means the development of understanding expressed in performance: understanding of the nature of knowledge expressed in the art form of teaching and learning. No skills unless they enhance understanding. What I am advocating is so radical that I may not be communicating it. Let me sharpen the message in the area of curriculum: I am saying that the purpose of any curriculum change, any curriculum research, any curriculum development is the enhancement of the art of teaching, of understanding expressed as performance. The idea that you want a change and the change is dependent on retraining teachers is a non-starter.

As a starting point teachers must want change, rather than others wanting to change them. That means that the option of professional development leading toward professional satisfaction of a kind that brings an enhancement of self must be made clear and open to teachers. Teachers have been taught that teaching is instrumental. When we say that teaching is an art, we are saying that the craft of teaching is inseparable from the understanding taught. In short, teaching is intrinsic.

Improving education is not about improving teaching as a delivery system. Crucial is the desire of the artist to improve his or her art. This art is what the experienced teacher brings to in-service development. Good in-service education recognizes and strengthens the power and primacy of the art. It offers curricula to teachers as music in-service offers Beethoven or Stravinsky to musicians: to further the art. In-service is linked to curriculum because art is about change and only develops in change. If the art of teaching could develop without change, then there would be no need for change in education. It is art's appetite for change that makes educational change necessary to the virtue of schooling.

The artist is the researcher whose inquiry expresses itself in performance of his or her art rather than (or as well as) in a research report. In an essentially practical art, like education, all the research and all the in-service education we offer should support that research towards performance on the part of the teacher. For there is in education no absolute and unperformed knowledge. In educational research and scholarship the ivory towers where the truth is neglected are so many theatres without players, galleries without pictures, music without musicians. Educational knowledge exists in, and is verified or falsified in, its performance.

REFERENCES

Campbell, D.T. and Stanley, J.C. (1963) 'Experimental and quasi-experimental designs for research on teaching' in Gage, N.L. (ed.) *Handbook of Research on Teaching* Chicago, Rand McNally.

Fienberg, S.E. (1977) 'The collection and analysis of ethnographic data in educational research' *Anthropology and Education Quarterly* 8(2) pp. 50-57.

Nixon, J. (ed.) (1981) *A Teacher's Guide to Action Research: Evaluation, Enquiry and Development in the Classroom* London, Grant McIntyre.

Stenhouse, L. (1979) 'Using research means doing research' in Dahl, H., Anders, L. and Rand, P. (eds) *Spotlight on Educational Research* Festchrift to Johannes Sandven. Oslo, Oslo University Press.

Stenhouse, L. (1980) 'Curriculum research and the art of the teacher' *curriculum* 1(1) pp. 40-44.

Stenhouse, L. (1983) *Authority, Education and Emancipation* London, Heinemann.

5.5 The Rhetoric of School-Centred Innovation

ANDY HARGREAVES*

INTRODUCTION

Two very different movements can be detected in contemporary patterns of curriculum development and change in England. On the face of it, they are worlds apart, diametrically opposed even. The first concerns the growing involvement of 'the Centre', of National Government and the Department of Education and Science (DES) in the direct control, administration and monitoring of the school curriculum. Because of wide media coverage of the host of official educational documents which have marked the state's long and sustained endeavour to exercise greater control over what is learned and by whom in schools — its attempt to bind schools more firmly in the service of society — this movement has become the best known one to the public at large and the most contentious among professional educators. With the publication of each Green Paper, Yellow Book and curriculum document, the teaching profession — raised on a tradition of school and class-room autonomy — has been voluble in its protests; and academics of different persuasions have registered their own dissatisfactions about the secret activities of the 'mandarins' of the DES,[1] about their attempt, with parliamentary government, to control the educational system by much closer regulation of the school curriculum and teacher practice than the broader and looser *licensed* autonomy that had been granted to teachers during the era of educational and economic expansion.[2] And they have shown themselves to be wary of the ideologically-loaded language in which HMI and DES documents have been couched.[3,4] Publicly, the centralizing tendency of curriculum change is the most visible and best-known one, and professionally it is certainly the most

*Source: *Journal Curriculum Studies*, vol. 14, no. 3 (1982), pp. 251-66.

contentious, occasioning the greatest amount of controversy and dissent.

Not so well known to those outside schooling, but making itself felt more pervasively in the everyday experience of teachers, is the decentralizing or localizing tendency towards innovation in curriculum provision and in-service training (these things tend to be linked) at the level of the school. This pattern is variously referred to as school-based curriculum development, school-focused curriculum development, school-based in-service education and training (INSET) and school-focused INSET. I shall refer to them all as school-centred innovation (SCI) for short, since it is their common localizing tendency rather than the fine distinctions which separate them that concerns me here. The proponents of SCI have claimed that it has had a staggering impact on the educational system over the last decade, far in excess of the amount of public recognition accorded it.[5,6] In part, the suggested strength and novelty of SCI has possibly been overrated by its advocates since the processes to which it refers had been going on unnoticed many years before the advent of the 'school-based'/'school-focused' label. However, the movement is not, as some have implied (for example Skilbeck[7]), simply a modest extension of a long-established trend, but has been shaped through definite, concerted and co-ordinated initiatives, that together far outweigh the previously disparate activities of thoughtful and enlightened teachers and heads in separate schools. That concerted effort can be seen in the very sizeable body of literature on SCI — in primers and readers for those new to the field,[8] as well as in well-known educational journals,[9] especially those which have published special issues on the subject.[10] In addition, conferences on different aspects of SCI are held year by year;[11] and various initiatives of some magnitude have been taken to generate, co-ordinate and evaluate large-scale programmes of school-centred work across the country.[12] To some, all this frenetic activity might seem an elaborate smoke-screen to disguise the more overtly and politically contentious efforts of the state to exercise central direction over the curriculum. While there is some truth in this, SCI has not been just talk and rhetoric. A good deal of real and consequential work has been going on within the schools themselves. This appears, in fact, to be one of those proverbial cases where there is no smoke without fire.

However, when one peers into the flames of SCI, what is most discomforting about it is the absence of that scepticism and watchfulness among academics and practitioners which so strongly characterizes the debate surrounding the centralizing tendency of curriculum change. In effect, SCI has been optimistically and zealously advanced as both guardian, if not modern patron, of teacher autonomy and professionalism and as a likely cure for much of the current educational malaise. This is not to deride the *principles* of SCI; principles which, in large part, accounted for its emergence. Against the backdrop of the failure of nationally based programmes of curriculum change, and the difficulties that teachers commonly experience when trying to apply the insights of university, college and LEA provided courses to the everyday demands of school life, SCI undoubtedly offers the very real hope that curriculum development and in-service training can be successfully related to the particular needs of each school for which it caters. And into the bargain, it almost certainly achieves these ends at considerably less expense than non-school-centred programmes.[13] More recently, in an educational system beleaguered by falling rolls and economic cuts, SCI has also been viewed as a way of compensating for the erosion of career opportunities by involving teachers in school decision-making processes. Thus, SCI has come to be regarded as a way of allowing innovation to 'take' at low cost while maintaining motivation and morale among teachers.[14] It is not in the least bit surprising, then, that so much hope, faith, time and energy should have been invested in it.

However, what gives cause for concern is the fact that hope, faith and optimism do not so much permeate the discussions and evaluations of SCI as consume them. In these discussions and commentaries, the virtues and successes of SCI appear to be legion; its drawbacks and failures few. In this article my argument is that such a heavy skewing of discussion away from sharp and constructively critical analysis of SCI, has created quite serious and widespread misunderstandings of the actuality of decision-making processes and their consequences at the level of the school. Given that strong wave of optimism, sometimes amounting to only mildly restrained self-congratulation on the part of those involved as leading participants in SCI, those misunderstandings may well be politically opposite ones, confirming an optimistic, democratic and 'sensibly' pragmatic ideology of SCI which serves to direct professional attention away from those things which other educational researchers have long held to be at the heart of the schooling process and which give it life — processes of conflict and struggle, power and constraint, domination and persuasion, the creation of consent and the suppression of opposition, and so forth. If a proper appraisal is to be made of SCI and the likelihood of its long-term success, then these other, less obviously appealing and benign aspects of formally democratic and collaborative decision-making processes must be subjected to the most rigorous scrutiny. So far, in the discussions of SCI, that task has hardly been begun.

TELLING IT LIKE IT OUGHT TO BE: ACCOUNTS OF SCI

When one surveys the SCI literature, what is most striking is the dearth of rigorous, critical and empirically-grounded accounts of particular schemes and projects. It is hard to find dispassionate studies of the actuality of decision-making processes, the particular forms that participation in decision-making takes and the effects that such participation has in the moment-by-moment process of deliberation. As Reid[15,16] reminds us, curriculum decision-making is a process of eminently *practical* deliberation made in an institutional context and within a formal distribution of power and experience between teachers and heads that places constraints on the sorts of decisions that are and can be made and on the kinds of accounts that teachers and heads tend to put forward to justify those decisions.[17] It is disappointing, then, that so little of the SCI literature gives any sense of the dynamics of the decision-making process and its effects on the perceptions, indeed on the motivation and morale, of those involved. Instead, what most writers in this field are concerned to do is either to persuade people of the importance of SCI, to outline the many possible forms it might take, or, somewhat anecdotally, to assert its success in particular cases. These kinds of accounts I shall call exhortatory, taxonomic and reflective.

Exhortatory Accounts

Exhortatory accounts seek to persuade people that SCI *should* take place.[18] Like most statements published during the early stages of educational movements, these accounts are at once intensely programmatic, issuing spirited moral and professional injunctions about the importance of school-centred work, and also rather vague, providing little guidance about the forms SCI might take, and the problems that might be encountered along the way.

After identifying the failure of centralized and non school-based forms of curriculum development and in-service training in the past, and outlining the challenge that a contracting school system presents to the educational imagination in the present, the authors of exhortatory accounts fervently recommend the participation and collaboration of teachers in SCI. But the way in which 'participation' is advocated does little to further people's understandings or expectations of the particular forms that participation might take. Thus, in answer to the question 'what kind of a context is best for promoting teacher development?', Eraut[19] includes 'participative decision-making and flexible policies' as one of the five defining characteristics of such a context, but never explains what these things mean. [...]

Terms like 'participation' and 'self-development' have barely any explanatory value at all. Their role in the SCI discourse is largely symbolic, their purpose being to arouse sympathy and support by locating SCI within the cherished tenets of social democratic thought and practice. Few could demur from the principle of participation advocated in this way, since all it seems to be doing is extolling virtue and pronouncing against sin.

Like primary school teachers who speak to each other as if they all know and agree what 'progressive education' means, then go away to operate widely different teaching styles in their own classrooms,[20] the enthusiastic proponents of 'participation' are almost certainly hiding more than they reveal. [...]

In a period of contraction, with all the problems that this presents for the internal management of schools, the need to be cautious about advancing overly simplistic internal solutions to large-scale problems that affect the educational system as a whole is especially great, since the collapse of these proposals may not only fail to *raise* motivation and morale, but might actually *depress* it still further. The recommendations of those who see SCI as a useful strategy for dealing with the effects of contraction should therefore be treated very warily. [...]

There does appear to be a danger that a bland advocacy of increased participation in school decision-making or, even further, a claim that such a trend is already well underway, might lead specialists in INSET and curriculum innovation to embrace dangerously simplistic panaceas. What is really required is close examination of the forms that participation takes when it is implemented in particular programmes of staff development and curriculum change. What needs to be adduced in particular is whether teacher participation leads them at present to being *in control* of the curriculum, or to their remaining *in service* to ends formulated by others. 'In service' or 'in control'? Paternalistic consultation or radical staff democracy? These are just some of the alternative meanings of teacher participation that need to be identified and examined in actual cases of educational change, for the consequences are likely to be very different in each case.

Taxonomic Accounts

Taxonomic accounts are also programmatic, but more elaborately so. In meticulous detail, they outline the many different kinds of SCI that might, in theory, be developed. The language in which such schemes are described is a hypothetical and conditional language of the possible. The authors of taxonomic accounts take it for granted that SCI *should* take place; their more precise purpose is to specify the different conceivable ways in which it *could* be organized, and their repetitive use of 'could', 'might' and 'may' reflects this nicely. A good example of the genre is Henderson and Perry's work on school-focused in-service education.[21] In it, they suggest that:

> Some needs *may* be met within the school, through staff conferences, curriculum development activities or personal study. Some *may* involve short-term visits to other schools, longer-term exchanges of staff between schools, or study groups involving two or more schools in a locality. ... Other types of need *may* be met by a consultancy approach; by the school inviting, say a local authority advisor, a training institution lecturer, or a teacher from elsewhere into the school to work with the whole staff, a small group of teachers, or an individual teacher ... One mode of consultancy operation *might* be the school-based course. An extension of this, when the same needs are being felt by a number of neighbouring schools, is a locally-based course or study group on a more conventional pattern, based in one of the schools concerned, a teachers' centre, or a local training institution. (My emphases).

Though writers such as Henderson and Perry draw a number of important fine conceptual distinctions within SCI (for example between school-based and school-focused work), the most powerful theme that pervades their accounts is that of the immensely, almost infinitely diverse forms that SCI *might* take.[...]

Undoubtedly these armchair exercises are very impressive undertakings. For all their taxonomic grandeur, though, their major effect is to draw attention away from the actual and patterned differences that can in practice be found between real, rather than hypothetical instances of SCI. Just as importantly, they lead to a neglect of those common difficulties and constraints that *all* SCI schemes are likely to face within the confines of the existing educational, economic and political situation. [...] Thus while the fascination for constructing elaborate taxonomies — the great strength of curriculum theory — has certainly given a sense of the diversity of SCI; it has, at the very same time precluded the careful description, explanation and evaluation of the nature and effects of teacher participation in different schemes. For the moment, what it has, in effect, done is to place the extremely important work of SCI outside the explanatory embrace of social science.

Reflective Accounts

In contrast to the speculative and hypothetical character of exhortatory and taxonomic accounts, reflective accounts do at least present reports on actual instances of SCI. However, instead of being presented as carefully constructed research-based analyses, reflective accounts normally take the form of journalistic recollections authored by leading participants in or instigators of the programmes that are being described. Though the reports are not always unreservedly flattering about the schemes concerned, criticism is rarely more than mild or sporadic. Any reservations that are expressed are usually rather brief and placed in parentheses. For the most part, the dominant interest is in providing an account of 'how it was done' as a contribution to the overall pool of professional experience of those involved in SCI in order to develop and enhance a tradition of 'good practice' in the area.[22]

While I would not wish to impugn the honesty and integrity of these story-tellers, the accuracy of their accounts is always bound to be open to a number of substantial doubts. Firstly, this is because of the mode of reporting: reflective accounts, rather like HMI reports, are presented as somewhat loose forms of description that do not allow the reader to check out the data on which that description is based, and therefore to assess its accuracy. The second problem concerns the status and interests of the reporter.

Because of their commitment to particular projects, the authors of reflective accounts have a strong stake in witnessing them reach a satisfactory conclusion and may therefore be unreceptive to evidence to the contrary. Furthermore, given their relatively senior position within the school or the project team, that evidence may simply be withheld from them — they are unlikely, for instance, to be fully cognizant of the perspectives and reactions of all their staff, especially those of their more junior colleagues, or of any teachers who nurture hidden reservations and resentments about the change.

It is not unreasonable, then, to ask for accounts that are more open to checking and scrutiny. There are many ways in which greater openness could be secured, but some might include giving examples of the kinds of data on which accounts are based, identifying the people whose perspectives have been elicited, noting what kind of interaction processes have been observed, indicating how accurately these have been documented, and so forth. Certainly, a wider range of accounts than those offered by leading and committed participants needs to be sampled. Only when these kind of precautionary measures have been taken, might it then be possible to determine whether any raconteur is an astutely observant participant, or an imaginatively unobservant one.

AN IDEOLOGY OF SCI

The overall outcome of the speculative outlines and retrospective views contained in exhortatory, taxonomic and reflective accounts, is an ideology of SCI which gives a distorted picture of the practice that occurs in many schools and of the consequences of that practice. That ideology emphasizes and encourages increased teacher *participation* in SCI, but does not assess the different forms that participation actually takes, nor the uses to which it tends to be put. In particular, it fails to acknowledge the resistance of many teachers, especially probationers, to the very idea of participation.[23,24] or to recognize the ways in which senior staff use a range of strategies in the decision-making process having the effect of frustrating the involvement and undercutting the contributions of other enthusiastic teachers within the school.[25,26] Secondly, the ideology of SCI stresses the value of *collaboration* between teachers, but neither examines the ways in which such collaboration is secured nor admits the presence and importance of conflict and struggle between different teachers, subject departments and so on, in the process of educational innovation.[27] Thirdly, the ideology celebrates the evolution of SCI as an instance of *grass-roots democracy*, which presents an important alternative and counterbalance to the encroachment of centrally generated curriculum initiatives (Eggleston,[6]) but, in so opposing these movements, fails to examine the extent to which the educational rhetoric and curriculum categories of 'standards', 'accountability' and so forth, employed in local discussions are themselves central in origin.[4] Attention has been focused so heavily on the centre's unsubtle attempts to storm the front gates of the citadel of teacher autonomy, that its quiet entry through the back door of SCI has been virtually undetected. Fourthly, the ideology posits a virtually infinite range of different possible kinds of SCI, according to the needs and demands of particular schools, but does not match this elusive *diversity* against any substantive study of existing practice. In other words, SCI writing does not *demonstrate* the presence of value-pluralism, it is simply predicated on the assumption of its existence.

Overall, then, the SCI literature encapsulates the highest ideals of liberal democracy as worthy and readily attainable goals in the management of schools. In effect, it promises no less than the realization of liberty (individual diversity), equality (participation and grass-roots democracy), and fraternity (collaboration).[28] Cast in these terms, it is not surprising therefore, that the ideology of SCI should have been imbued throughout with a widespread *optimism* about the necessity and impending success of the venture. In the light of the above observations, though, this seems less than fully warranted. However, more disconcerting still than the distortions created by the 'hard sell' approach of much of the SCI literature, is the fact that the rather limited amount of empirical research that is to be found in this area is a kind which tends, because of its methodological orientation, to reinforce rather than dispel the myths that programmatic and retrospective accounts have generated. This research will now be examined carefully in order to elucidate the exact ways in which it tends to confirm rather than challenge existing professional assumptions.

RESEARCH ON SCI

In the small amount of research that has been conducted on SCI, two strands are dominant. These are the traditions of survey research and 'tied' evaluation. Though the merits and demerits of each of these traditions are now reasonably well known, the appreciation of their limitations has not really penetrated into the SCI literature. For that reason, while the following points are hardly 'news' in the most general sense, they are worth reiterating in this particular context.

The Survey Tradition

A small number of studies of involvement in school decision-making have tried to discover staff perceptions of the decision-making process on the basis of questionnaires administered to a large sample of teachers. One of the largest surveys of this kind is Cohen and Harrison's study of decision-making in Australian schools.[29] Amongst other things, they were interested in who participates in making curriculum decisions. As part of their research, they carried out a national survey of the principal, three heads of departments and 10 teachers in each of 98 secondary schools. One of their findings — for them a lamentable one — was that only 24% of the sample considered that school objectives were written by the total staff. The researchers then claimed that this finding — an alleged indicator of low rates of teacher participation — was, as the others, 'generalizable to all Australian secondary schools because of the rigorous method of sampling' (a stratified random sample). This led them to bemoan the widespread absence of systems of participatory decision-making in Australian secondary schools.

In advancing strong claims for the generalizability of their findings about school decision-making, Cohen and Harrison are drawing sensibly on the traditional strength of survey research — its capacity to generate findings which are broadly applicable to a large number of people and institutions. But the crucial question which is begged in research which tries to get at people's perspectives on social life, via the survey method, is not the generalizability of the findings but their validity. Simply put, what people write 'in the cold' as a response to a brief item on a questionnaire, is often a poor document of their everyday working perspectives. If researchers want to examine the complexity of decision-making processes and people's perceptions of those processes, the questionnaire is therefore likely to prove a rather clumsy, inaccurate and imprecise tool. [...] The statement that objectives were written by 'the whole staff' may mean a host of different things — written simultaneously? Written by a working party chairman then co-ordinated with the statements of other working party chairmen? Written by the head-teacher after canvassing the views of individual members of staff? With or without their knowledge? Or what?

The overall consequence of such survey studies of teacher participation in curriculum decision-making is that unwarranted claims are made about allegedly generalized features of the decision-making process on the basis of what, given the methodology, are unavoidable simplifications and misunderstandings of the nature, process and meaning of participation. Such misunderstandings usually lead to shoring up rather than questioning of existing political and professional values and assumptions about school decision-making. This is not because of what *is* asserted, but more because of what is left out — because of certain possible meanings of participation and collaboration that are kept off the agenda.

A good illustration of this is the influential research of Rutter *et al.* on secondary schools and their effects.[30] In their survey of 12 secondary schools, Rutter and his colleagues found that one of the variables correlating with favourable pupil outcomes was the existence of a curriculum in the school that was group-planned rather than fragmented according to the interests and whims of individual teachers. 'Schools where most teachers planned jointly' they argue 'tended to have better attendance and less delinquency' (Rutter *et al.*, [30] p. 136). They acknowledge that 'group planning took many different forms', but emphasize that 'in the less successful schools, teachers were often left completely alone to plan what to teach with little guidance or supervision from their senior colleagues and little co-ordination with other teachers to ensure a coherent course from year to year'. The pattern of decision-making that was found to be most closely correlated with favourable outcomes was one where 'decisions were made at a senior level rather than in the staff room' but where teachers' own views were represented at the 'appropriate decision-making level' (Rutter *et al.*,[30]., p. 138). The conclusion the authors draw on the basis of these findings amounts to a vindication of democracy by consultation: 'The combination of decision-making by senior staff, after consideration of the views of the whole staff' they suggest 'may be a good one' (p. 138). In the light of 'findings' such as these, it is not difficult to see why many critics have discerned a 'tight ship' philosophy in Rutter's model of the good school. And yet the basis on which that model rests is exceedingly fragile. In effect, the most important distinctions — between different *kinds* of consultation — are not made in the study. It is a banal truism that most head-teachers and departmental heads consult their staff about curriculum decisions, at some level, in one form or another. What is more important to know is the particular forms that such consultation takes and which of those forms are more effective. All that Rutter and his team do, though, is to oppose a self-evidently virtuous model of order (group-planned curriculum, teachers' views taken into account) against an equally self-evidently unacceptable model of chaos (individually determined curriculum, teachers' views not represented). All the vital distinctions that separate 'ordered' schools from one another — and most British schools are of this kind — are glossed by unhelpfully vague phrases which refer to things like consultation at the 'appropriate decision-making level'. The most crucial and contentious questions concerning the *kinds* of consultation that are most effective are never asked. [...]

The Tied-evaluation Tradition

Much closer insights into the fine details of school decision-making have been provided by curriculum and INSET evaluators. The great merit of their work is that, in comparison to survey research, it certainly enriches our understanding of the dynamics of the curriculum decision-making process and of the perceptions of those who participate in that process. A strong sense is given of what actually happens during the long and tortuous process of deliberation, and in some of the very best accounts, as in much of the work produced by the Centre for Applied Research in Education (CARE) at the University of East Anglia, the authors have a commendable capacity to carry the reader along with the drama of innovation as it unfolds. Here, the power of human observation is sensitively put to work so as to bring alive the dynamics of decision-making among teachers. It is not without some justification that this tradition is often termed *illuminative* evaluation.[31]

However, the immense potential of first-hand observation, as a resource for explaining complex processes of social interaction in the schooling system, is never fully harnessed because of the use to which that observation is put — *evaluating* rather than *explaining* school-centred innovation. Of course, evaluation does not exist apart from explanation; indeed it is highly dependent on it. The. problem, though, is that the quality of the explanation in terms of its *accuracy*, its *scope*, and its possible *generalizability* to institutions beyond the ones being studied.[...] As with other SCI literature this writing is redolent with the irresistibly appealing symbols of participation, collaboration and grassroots democracy. If Henderson's prescriptions were acted upon, though (and in many places they are), it is difficult to see just how any generalized and rigorous explanations of SCI could be produced when the evaluation is explicitly consumer-serving, internal, informal and judgemental (Henderson and Perry,[21] p. 167). Why is this?

The most central and obvious point is that the very existence of evaluation and evaluators in a school has an immense impact on the process being evaluated. Often, this is precisely what is wanted since one clear purpose of evaluation is the improvement of existing practice. In one sense, there is nothing wrong with this: few people would wish to impede the process of bringing about change for the better in schools. But, it seems to me, it is not possible to have it both ways — to change the decision-making process under review even as it proceeds *and* to produce potentially generalizable explanations of the dynamics of that process as it would have unfolded had no evaluators been present. In this sense, the distillation of *experience* is a poor substitute for the generation and accumulation of rigorous *knowledge*. Of course, some evaluators might attempt to get round this problem by delaying the feedback of results to the schools concerned, but, even here, their very presence in the school as evaluators who are known as such is still likely to have a restricting effect on the sorts of knowledge and practices that teachers are prepared to disclose.

The very nature of evaluation, therefore, makes it almost impossible for its proponents to tell either the truth (the problem of accuracy) or the whole truth (the problems of scope and generalizability). School-centred evaluators tend to *tie* the analysis, findings and recommendations of the evaluation to a programme of change that can be practically carried out within the context of the school. This means that, while issues such as the time allowed for decision-making and the way in which working parties are composed receive full attention,[32] rather grander interpretations of the dynamics of school decision-making, the implications of which might extend beyond the problems of particular schools to things like the desirability of the very institution of headship (Weston,[25] p. 226), or the level of financing of the educational system,[25] tend to be ignored: these are just not 'practical' issues for any one school. The point is, though, that while such problems may be the least tractable ones, they could well be the most crucial. By keeping them off the agenda, the tradition of 'tied' evaluation may therefore be doing the cause of school-centred innovation a considerable disservice.

One particular strand of 'tied' evaluation, the 'theorizing practice' tradition, attempts to make a virtue out of this fundamental weakness, by pursuing a programme of action where 'the analysis of practice is followed by the application of relevant theory'.[33] This theory is not introduced from the outside, as it were, but is based on the already existing organizing categories of the practising teacher.[34] The aim, then, is to theorize teachers' existing craft knowledge for them (or, rather, with them) in order to help them cope better with their professional work.[35] The act of theorizing practice is therefore consciously related to the immediate practical needs of the classroom and, to that extent, is seen to be superior to the formal teaching of educational theory through the disciplines in a way that subsequently proves frustrating when teachers try to apply it to the classroom situation.

The fundamental drawbacks (and political attractiveness) of this eminently practical approach are not hard to see. It isolates the classroom from its wider determinants, whether these are in the authority structure of the school or in the economics of education, and treats existing practice more or less as a given, attempting only to identify and theorize its 'best' features. Alternative educational practices and the political and economic conditions that might be needed to establish them are therefore precluded from consideration. Furthermore, the use of teachers' present experience as the mainstay of the explanation of classroom practice, offers little hope of moving beyond the bounds of existing practice, of constructing collective and critical revisions of the nature of teaching. While teachers are left to innovate in this way by drawing on their experience alone, it is difficult to see how, in the absence of any dialogue with those who have undertaken rigorous observations of school life, that experience can be extended or transcended.

In the confines of the present schooling system, then, the truth of SCI is neither 'democratic' nor is it 'plain-tongued'. It is not 'democratic' because, in the present system, teachers have particular interests to defend, especially those that attach to their subject identities. The prospect of establishing truth through free, open and undistorted dialogue between researcher and researched,[36] therefore seems a remote one at present. Nor is the teacher necessarily the most likely party to breach the terms of the democratic bargain between researcher and researched. The researcher, while advocating plain-speaking at one level, also retains unequal access to the world of formal theory and its concepts at another, introducing these concepts into discussion in a way that leaves their origins and contentious nature unclear to teachers.[37] Moreover, the researchers may also exercise indirect control over the release of findings by drawing on their own privileged knowledge about tight publishing schedules and so on.[38]

[...] For these reasons, it is therefore somewhat regrettable that the very great capacity of first-hand observational research to get to the heart of the actuality of school decision-making has barely been exploited because of its containment within a widespread programme of 'applied' educational research and evaluation. This is not to deride the undeniable value of applied research in other respects, especially as a device for changing the particular schools under scrutiny; but it does cast doubt on its worth as a means of producing valid and potentially generalizable understandings of the everyday dynamics of SCI.

CONCLUSION

To sum up, it would appear that while great amounts of time, energy and resources, and not a little hope and optimism, have been invested in SCI, its success has by no means been demonstrated, nor is its future effectiveness in raising (or even maintaining) staff motivation and morale in any sense assured. In effect, although the heady rhetoric of SCI persists, promising everything from an effective method of managing innovation in schools, to the realization of staff democracy, fraternity and liberty, its practical success in actual instances of school change is, judging by the very limited amount of research available to date, precariously balanced on a knife-edge of uncertainty. For that reason, it is a matter of some urgency that SCI be subjected to a thorough, rigorous examination. Within that examination, it is of paramount importance that questions such as the following are not shuffled off the agenda. What, even in the terms which the SCI movement has itself set concerning the raising of staff motivation and morale, makes a successful or an unsuccessful scheme? What influence do head and deputy, for instance, exert in the moment-by-moment process of deliberation, and what implications do their interventions have for staff perceptions of the democratic process? More fundamentally, perhaps, is 'democracy' a realizable goal so long as heads retain final and long-standing responsibility for the decisions that are taken within schools? Can teachers reasonably be expected to participate in a democratic process of SCI when the majority are excluded from other important centres of decision-making — such as governors' meetings, contacts with HMIs and advisers and so on — that may run against the democratic grain? What effect does the relative exclusion of ordinary teachers from the wider governance of education, their restricted access to educational theory and other kinds of school practice, and the consequent overwhelming centrality of classroom practicalities to teachers, have on the kinds of *contributions* they make to staff discussion? What implications does the inequality of access between teachers and heads, to educational theory, experience of other schools, contact with educational politicians and administrators and familiarity with decision-making skills, for instance, have on the 'democratic' nature of SCI?[39]

These questions are perhaps uncomfortable ones to ask at a time when a number of heads and deputies are attempting to establish more open procedures of school management in a spirit of altruism and sincerity. But they are absolutely essential ones for academics and school practitioners to discuss, if the possible progeny of SCI — lower rather than higher staff motivation and morale — is not to be the next great irony of educational change.

The call for 'more research' then, is not just a matter of academic curiosity, but one of great educational importance. The everyday dynamics of the SCI process have as yet more or less eluded detailed academic study.[40] There are three groups of educational researchers who might, however, wish to turn their attention to such matters. The first, curriculum theorists, have to date, perhaps because of their generally greater preoccupation with taxonomy and evaluation, tended to shy away from this kind of endeavour. The second group — sociologists of the curriculum — have been equally remiss in carrying out empirical studies of curriculum decision-making. While they have produced a good deal of high-quality, imaginative and speculative theorizing about the curriculum, and how it is determined, few have chased up the implications of their work through empirical study. The third group, ethnographers of schooling — an assortment of sociological and psychological researchers of school processes — have certainly grasped the empirical nettle, but in doing so they have devoted most of their research attentions to teacher-pupil relations in the classroom at the expense of studying what Keddie calls the 'educationist context',[41] the context of teacher decision-making outside the classroom. However, if some of these imbalances in the research community can begin to be rectified, and the whole nature of SCI can be placed on the agenda of academic research and professional discussion, there may then be a growing awareness not only of the different forms SCI might take, along with their practical effects, but also of the context in which SCI takes place — a context of resource levels, authority structures and so on, that may be equally vital to the success or failure of the SCI enterprise.

NOTES

1. Lawton, D. *The Politics of the School Curriculum* (Routledge & Kegan Paul, London, 1980).

2. Dale, R. The politicisation of school deviance: reactions to William Tyndale. In Barton, L. and Meighan, R. (eds.), *Schools, Pupils and Deviance* (Nafferton Books, Driffield, 1979).

3. Donald, J. Green Paper: noise of crisis. *Screen Education*, 30 (1977).

4. Halpin, D. Exploring the secret garden. *Curriculum*, 1, 2 (1981).

5. Eggleston, J. *School-Based Curriculum Development* (OCED, Paris, 1979).

6. Eggleston, J. *School-Based Curriculum Development in Britain* (Routledge & Kegan Paul, London, 1980).

7. Skilbeck, M. 'School-based curriculum development and the task of in-service education.' In Adams, E. (ed.), *In-service Education and Teachers' Centres* (Pergamon Press, Oxford, 1976).

8. For example see Warwick, D. *School-Based In-service Education* (Oliver and Boyd, Edinburgh, 1975); Henderson, E., Note 41; Henderson, E. and Perry, W., Note 25; Eggleston, J. Note 6.

9. Foremost amongst these in the *British Journal of In-Service Education* but the *British Journal of Teacher Education* has also devoted many of its pages to various aspects of SCI and to school-based and school-focused INSET in particular.

10. See, for instance, *Curriculum*, 1, 1 (1980), and the *Cambridge Journal of Education*, 9, 2 and 3 (1979).

11. One of the best known of these was the *Priorities in In-Service Education* conference at La Sainte Union College of Higher Education, Southampton (1976).

12. Most notably the SITE project organized and co-ordinated by Bolam and Baker (Bolam, R., Note 26; Baker, K. The SITE project: an experiment in

approaches to INSET. *Cambridge Journal of Education*, 9, 2 and 3 [1979]), and the Open University IT/INSET project, organized by Ashton and Merritt (Note 44).

13. See Simmons, L.M. Staff development in schools. *Curriculum*, 1, 1 (1980), for a statement of this view.

14. For discussions of the role of SCI in a period of educational and economic recession see Lightfoot, M. The educational consequences of falling rolls. In Richards, C. (ed.), *Power and the Curriculum* (Nafferton Books, Driffield, 1978); Dennison, W.F. 'Falling rolls: teachers and shrinking schools.' *Durham and Newcastle Research Review*, IX (1979), p. 43; Hewitt, F.S. 'Teacher participation in planning and provision: the identification of pertinent factors.' *British Journal of In-Service Education*, 5, 1 (1978); Harlen, W.A. 'A stronger teacher role in curriculum development?' *Journal of Curriculum Studies*, 9, 1 (1977); Bradley, H. INSET now — taking stock. *Cambridge Journal of Education*, 9, 2 and 3 (1979); Sayer, J., Note 20; Hunter, C. and Heighway, P., Note 22.

15. Reid, W.A. *Thinking About the Curriculum* (London, Routledge & Kegan Paul, London, 1978).

16. Reid, W.A. 'Practical reasoning and curriculum theory: in search of a new paradigm.' *Curriculum Inquiry*, 9, 3 (1979).

17. For an interesting development of this view in relation to empirical data about teacher decision-making — see Walker, D.F. Curriculum development in an art project. In Reid, W.A. and Walker, D.F. (eds.), *Case Studies in Curriculum Change* (Routledge & Kegan Paul, London, 1975).

18. For examples of exhortatory accounts see Watkins, R. (ed.), *In-Service Training: Structure and Content* (Ward Lock Educational, London 1973); Warwick D. Note 8; Partington, G. School-focused INSET, *British Journal of In-Service Education*, 3, 1 (1976); Jones, J.A.G. 'An in-school approach to in-service training.' *Curriculum*, 1, 1 (1980); Golby, M. and Fish, M.A. School-focused INSET: clients and consultants.' *British Journal of In-Service Education*, 6, 2 (1980).

19. Eraut, M. 'Strategies for promoting teacher development.' *British Journal of In-service Education*, 4, 1 and 2 (1977), p. 11.

20. Sharp, R. and Green, A. *Education and Social Control* (Routledge & Kegan Paul, London, 1975).

21. Henderson, E. and Perry, W. *Change and Development in Schools: Case Studies in the Management of School-Focused In-Service Education* (McGraw-Hill, London, 1981), p. 14.

22. Examples of 'reflective' literature can be found in the collections edited by Eggleston, J., Note 6; Henderson, E. and Perry, W., Note 25; and articles by Broome, M. 'Professional self development through participation in curriculum development.' *Curriculum*, 1, 1 (1980); Carnie, J.M., Note 43; Simmons, L.M., Note 13; Keast, D.J. and Carr, V. 'School-based INSET — interim evaluation' *British Journal of In-Service Education*, 5, 3, (1978).

23. Bullock, A. 'Teacher participation in school decision-making.' *Cambridge Journal of Education*, 10, 1 (1980).

24. Richardson, D.A. 'Student-teacher attitudes towards decision-making in schools before and after taking up their first appointments.' *Educational Studies*, 7, 1 (1981).

25. Weston, P. *Negotiating the Curriculum* (NFER, Windsor, 1979).

26. Hargreaves, A. 'Contrastive rhetoric and extremist talk: teachers, hegemony and the educationist context.' In Barton, I., and Walker, S. (eds.), *Schools, Teachers and Teaching* (Falmer Press, Brighton, 1980).

27. Ball., S. *Beachside Comprehensive* (Cambridge University Press, Cambridge), Chapter 6.

28. Ideological features of this kind are by no means confined to SCI, but are common in educational discourse. For examples of their influence on writing about

middle school education, for instance, see Hargreaves, A. 'The ideology of the middle school.' In Hargreaves, A. and Tickle, L. (eds.), *Middle Schools: Origins, Ideology and Practice* (Harper and Row, London, 1980); and Nias, J. 'The ideal middle school: its public image.' In Hargreaves, A. and Tickle, L. (eds.), *Middle Schools: Origins, Ideology and Practice* (Harper and Row, London, 1980).

29. Cohen, D. and Harrison, M. 'Curriculum decision-making in Australian education: what decisions are made within schools? *Journal of Curriculum Studies*, 11, 3 (1979).

30. Rutter, M., Maughan, B., Mortimore, P. and Ouston, J. *Fifteen Thousand Hours: Secondary Schools and Their Effects on Children* (Open Books, London, 1979).

31. Parlett, M. and Hamilton, D. 'Evaluation as illumination.' In Tawney, D. (ed.), *Curriculum Evaluation Today* (Macmillan, London, 1976).

32. Abbs, P. 'Continuing curriculum change at Codsall School.' In Eggleston, J. (ed.), *School-based Curriculum Development in Britain* (Routledge & Kegan Paul, London, 1980).

33. Carnie, J.M. 'IT-INSET: a school-focused programme of initial training and in-service education,' *Curriculum*, 1, 1 (1980).

34. Ashton, P. and Merritt, J. 'INSET at a distance.' *Cambridge Journal of Education*, 9, 2 and 3 (1979).

35. Desforges, C. and MacNamara, D. 'Theory and practice: methodological procedures for the objectification of craft knowledge.' *British Journal of Teacher Education*, 5, 2 (1979).

36. Elliott, J. 'Methodology and ethics' (unpublished paper delivered to British Educational Research Association Conference, Cardiff, 1980).

37. Barton, L. and Lawn, M. 'Back inside the whale: a curriculum case study.' *Interchange*, 11, 4 (1981).

38. Jenkins, D. 'An adversary's account of SAFARI's ethics of case study.' In Richards, C. (ed.), *Power and the Curriculum* (Nafferton Books, Driffield, 1978).

39. I have touched on some of these matters in another empirical paper on the dynamics of staff decision-making (Hargreaves, A., Note 32).

40. Most existing studies of curriculum innovation in practice, tend to focus on the impact of national projects on school life (Shipman, M., Bolam, D. and Jenkins, D. *Inside a Curriculum Project* [Methuen, London, 1974]; Gleeson, D. 'Curriculum development and social change: towards a reappraisal of teacher action.' In Eggleston, J. [ed.], *Teacher Decision-Making in the Classroom* [Routledge & Kegan Paul, London, 1979]) or on the effects of innovation in the classroom (Smith, L. M. and Keith, P.M. *Anatomy of Educational Innovation* [Wiley, London, 1971]; and Gross, N.E., Giacquinta, J.B. and Bernstain, M. *Implementing Organizational Innovations: a Sociological Analysis of Planned Educational Change* [Harper and Row, London, 1971]), rather than on collective staff decision-making as such.

41. Keddie, N. 'Classroom knowledge.' In Young, M.F.D. (ed.), *Knowledge and Control* (Collier-Macmillan, London, 1971).

INDEX

abilities *see* skills
abstractness 254-5
academic *see* education
access function of computers 25
action/activity
  and access 36
  internalization of 242-3
  interveners 70
  learning 261
  television viewing 274-5; of
    documentaries 320-2
adminstrators, educational, and
  information 438, 439
adults
  literacy programmes 11
  television and 269, 297
advertisements 81
  audience-maximisation 66
  matrix 209, 212
  press 39
  semiology of 151
  television 34, 39, 267-8, 274
affectual effects 83, 87
Africa 7-8, 11, 13, 19-22
agenda-setting 63, 92-3, 97
aggression *see* violence
Aird Commission Report (Canada
  — 1928) 160-1
Allison, E.K. 440
alternatives, excluded 238
Althusser, L. 72, 73, 102
altruism 307
Alvarado, M. 398
analogy 147
Anderson, D.R. 275, 280, 298-9
Andrews, J.S. 437
'appreciation' of television 389-97
aptitude-treatment interaction (ATI)
  254
Arab countries *see* Middle East
arbitrariness 254-5
Arnott, J. 295
  on Prestel 369-73
art 202
artistry and teaching 404, 444-53
Asia 7-8, 11, 13, 19, 22, 189, 297
association 147
attention to television, children's

275-80, 297-300
  auditory 275-6
  form and content 276-7
  integrative model of 281-2
  salience and informativeness
    277-80
  salience, perceptual 270-1, 298
  visual 275
  see also comprehension *and under*
    television
audience, mass 18
  creation of 57, 58
  delivery of 66, 69
audio-visual *see* film; radio;
  television; visual
auditory attention of children 275-6
Australia 297, 463
autonomy of media institutions 69

Baker, T. 294
  on television case studies 317-36
Bandura, A. 231, 260, 309, 311
Barthes, R. 72, 133, 384, 399
Becker, L. 60, 93
behaviour
  categories of 234
  children's and effects of television
    304-9
  effects 83, 87
  modification 231, 236
  of scientists 429-30
Belgium 8, 28, 170
Berelson, B. 62, 82, 413
Berger, A.A. 55, 154, 418
  on semiology 132-55
bias 85, 97-9
bilingualism 9
biology teaching and computer
  models 294, 358-68
Blumler, J. 59, 60, 69, 82, 94
body language *see* non-verbal
books 20-1, 28
  numbers of 17-18
  semiology of 151
  see also reading
boustrophedon printing 220
Bouthilet, L. 310, 313
brainwashing *see* propaganda

473

Lang, K. and G.E. 82, 98
language 7-10, 29, 32
    acquisition of 259-60
    Canada 156, 157
    codes, television 268, 285-6
    development of 232
    instruction and 238-41
    internalization 258-9
    international 9, 10
    news agencies 19
    numbers in world 7-8
    physical resources and 44
    printing 9-10
    representational codes 271-4
    schematic display 217
    semiology and 134, 138-9
    teaching 9
    see also graphic; semiology;
        speech; writing
Latin script 9, 35, 202
Latin America 7-8, 13, 19
Lazar, J. 310, 313
Lazarsfeld, P. 59, 82, 427
learning 198-9, 226-50
    active 261
    by observation 259-60
    experience and 228-34, 246
    potential wasted 29
    see also education; information;
        knowledge; skills
legitimate power 88
letter formation and computers
    338-41
Lévi-Strauss, C. 72, 139, 146
liberal-pluralist and Marxist studies of
    media, distinction between 57-78
    passim
librarianship see information science
limitations of language 241
linear methods of configuration
    203-5, 210, 213, 216-17
linguistics see language
'link' languages 8, 29
list methods of configuration 203-5,
    208, 211, 214, 220, 222
literacy 11-12, 241
    media 266, 271
    see also illiteracy; reading; writing
local (little) media 15-17, 31
local educational administration see
    education, school-centred
long-term change, planned and
    unplanned 85, 94-6
Lorch, E.P. 280, 298-9

Lotka-Volterra equations 362-3
Luria, A.R. 258, 259
Lyman, P. 176-7

McArthur, General 98
McBride Commission: on means of
    communication 5-31
McCombs, M. 60, 92
McCron, R. 63, 97
MacDonald, Sir J.A. 158
McLaughlin, C.P. 427, 428
McLuhan, M. 158, 198, 199, 227,
    244, 268
McQuail, D. 53, 62, 93, 94
    on effects 80-107
magazines see press
Maier, N.R.F. 227-8
mail 13-14, 30
maps 219
Marcuse, H. 61, 62
marine satellites 25
market, medium as 38-9
Marx, K. and Marxism 71, 398-9
    and liberal-pluralist study of
        media, distinction between
        57-78 passim
    effects of television, views on
        100-1
mass communications 46-9
    history of 40-1
    increased 17-23
    see also communication; press;
        radio; television
Massey Commission Report (Canada
    — 1951) 164-6
Masterman, L. 295
    on education in media 374-400
mathematical notation 44
meanings
    messages and relationships 42-3
    semiology and 133-5, 138
means of communication 3, 5-31
    group and local 15-17
    mass media 17-23
    signs and words 5-7
    see also computers; language;
        press; radio; reading;
        satellites; semiology; speech;
        television writing
media see communication
media education studies 377-81
mediated experience, learning
    through 231-2
memory television 300